Early Cinema in Russia and its Cultural Reception

Poster advertising *Stenka Razin* [Sten'ka-Razin, 1908]

Early Cinema in Russia and its Cultural Reception

Yuri Tsivian
Translated by Alan Bodger
with a foreword by Tom Gunning

Edited by Richard Taylor

The University of Chicago Press
Chicago and London

First published in Russian in 1991 as *The History of Film Reception: Cinema in Russia, 1896–1930* by Zinātne Publishers, Riga, Latvia.

Revised English Language edition translated by Alan Bodger first published 1994 by Routledge, London and New York.

This edition published by arrangement with Routledge, 11 New Fetter Lane, London EC4P 4EE.

The University of Chicago Press, Chicago 60637
The University of Chicago Press, Ltd., London
© 1991, 1994 Yuri Tsivian
Translation © 1994 Routledge
All rights reserved. Originally published 1994
University of Chicago Press Edition 1998
Printed in the United States of America

03 02 01 00 99 98   6 5 4 3 2 1

Library of Congress Cataloging-in-Publication Data

Tsivian, Yuri.
    [Istoricheskaia retseptsiia kino. English]
    Early cinema in Russia and its cultural reception / Yuri Tsivian ; translated by Alan Bodger ; with a foreword by Tom Gunning ; edited by Richard Taylor.
        p.   cm.
    Originally published: London : New York : Routledge, 1994.
    Includes bibliographical references and index.
    ISBN 0-226-81426-2 (paperback : alk. paper).
    1. Motion pictures—Russia (Federation)—History.
2. Motion picture audiences—Russia (Federation)—History.   3. Motion pictures—Russia (Federation)—Appreciation.   I. Taylor, Richard, 1946–
II. Title.
PN1993.5.R9T7713   1998
791.43′0947—dc21   98–4704
                                                   CIP

♾ The paper used in this publication meets the minimum requirements of the American National Standard for Information Sciences—Permanence of Paper for Printed Library Materials, ANSI Z39.48-1992.

For Roman Timenchik

Contents

Illustrations

General editors' preface

Cinema has been the predominant popular art form of the first half of the twentieth century, at least in Europe and North America. Nowhere was this more apparent than in the former Soviet Union, where Lenin's remark that 'of all the arts for us cinema is the most important' became a cliché and where cinema attendances were until recently still among the highest in the world. In the age of mass politics Soviet cinema developed from a fragile but effective tool to gain support among the overwhelmingly illiterate peasant masses in the Civil War that followed the October 1917 Revolution, through a welter of experimentation, into a mass weapon of propaganda through entertainment that shaped the public image of the Soviet Union – both at home and abroad and for both élite and mass audiences – and latterly into an instrument to expose the weaknesses of the past and present in the twin processes of glasnost and perestroika. Now the national cinemas of the successor republics to the old USSR are encountering the same bewildering array of problems, from the trivial to the terminal, as all the other ex-Soviet institutions.

Cinema's central position in Russian and Soviet cultural history and its unique combination of mass medium, art form and entertainment industry have made it a continuing battlefield for conflicts of broader ideological and artistic significance, not only for Russia and the Soviet Union but also for the world outside. The debates that raged in the 1920s about the relative revolutionary merits of documentary as opposed to fiction film, of cinema as opposed to theatre or painting, or of the proper role of cinema in the forging of post-Revolutionary Soviet culture and the shaping of the new Soviet man, have their echoes in current discussions about the role of cinema vis-à-vis other art forms in effecting the cultural and psychological revolution in human consciousness necessitated by the processes of economic and political transformation of the former Soviet Union into modern democratic and industrial societies and states governed by the rule of law. Cinema's central position has also made it a vital instrument for scrutinising the blank pages of Russian and Soviet history and enabling the present generation to come to terms with its own past.

This series of books intends to examine Russian and Soviet films in the context of Russian and Soviet cinema, and Russian and Soviet cinema in the context of the political and cultural history of Russia, the Soviet Union and the world at large. Within that framework the series, drawing its authors from both East and West, aims to cover a wide variety of topics and to employ a broad range of methodological approaches and presentational formats. Inevitably this will involve ploughing once again over old ground in order to re-examine received opinions but it principally means increasing the breadth and depth of our knowledge, finding new answers to old questions and, above all, raising new questions for further enquiry and new areas for further research.

Yuri Tsivian's book fulfils several of these objectives and opens up two major fields of enquiry. On the one hand, it brings to our attention one of the great lost periods in cinema history, that of *pre*-Revolutionary Russia, against much of which *post*-Revolutionary Soviet cinema was enjoined to react. Tsivian draws out the distinctive characteristics of that cinema, from the specific meaning of close-ups to the insistence on *un*happy endings, from the ambiguous significance of the foyer to the pervading influence of Symbolism and its peculiar obsessions. On the other hand, as Tom Gunning points out in his foreword, Tsivian takes reception studies further than they have previously been taken by Western academics by expanding the context of reception to include the whole experience of film viewing in Russia at the turn of the century. This in turn raises new questions that can be applied back to reception studies of cinema in other countries. Tsivian's book is therefore a significant contribution to the study of cinema history as a whole.

The continuing aim of the series is to situate Russian and Soviet cinema in their proper historical and aesthetic context, both as a major cultural force in Russian history and Soviet politics and as a crucible for experimentation that is of central significance to the development of world cinema culture. Books in the series strive to combine the best of scholarship, past, present and future, with a style of writing that is accessible to a broad readership, whether that readership's primary interest lies in cinema or in Russian and Soviet political history.

Richard Taylor and Ian Christie

Acknowledgements

The title of this book – *Early Cinema in Russia and its Cultural Reception* – came about as a last-minute decision. The Russian original was entitled *The History of Film Reception: Cinema in Russia, 1896–1930*, and was about twice the length of the present volume, which covers a shorter time-span. This accounts for the shrinkage: rather than compress the whole silent period into 100,000 words, I followed Richard Taylor's suggestion and cut out the 1920s, on the assumption that the Soviet period must be more familiar to the Western reader. My story now ends in 1920 – the last year of private film production in Russia.

The change of the key word was prompted by a letter from Tom Gunning, to whom I had the nerve to send the English version of this book as soon as the manuscript was (or so I thought) ready to be shown to anyone. Together with other kind suggestions (which the reader will find integrated in the book), Tom Gunning observed that the term 'reception' as used by Western film scholars has a different shade of meaning from mine, which is based on the way reception is traditionally understood within Russian cultural studies. Because Gunning's letter defines this variance in approach as liberating rather than confusing, I decided to let the term 'reception' stay as it is, just specifying it as 'cultural'. I am profoundly indebted to Tom for this and other valuable suggestions.

I cannot list all those to whom I am indebted for the preparation of the Russian version of this book, but I must just mention the names of my co-authors on other works: Roman Timenchik, with whom I was privileged to work on an anthology of Russian articles and poetry on cinema from 1896 to 1917 and whose suggestions the reader will recognise *ex ungue leonem*; Mikhail Yampolsky, whose knowledge of Western film culture helped me better understand film culture in Russia; and Yuri Lotman, whose conversations – I would like to hope – have influenced my vision of cultural history.

With only one exception, the staff of the archive collections mentioned in the list of abbreviations readily assisted me in my searches. I should like to express my gratitude to the staff of what were then called the Central Film Museum in Moscow, the State Film Archive of the USSR [Gosfilmofond], and to the highly efficient and knowledgeable archivists at the Central State Archive of Literature and Art of the USSR.

For the English version, my gratitude goes to my translator Alan Bodger for his helpful suggestions, his excellent Russian and his patience with the neurotic author. Richard Taylor is to be thanked for all these things as well, and also for his clever guidance through the stages of bringing this book to fruition. Bruno and Zanete Ascuki, Zenta Auzina, Boris Avramets, Eileen Bowser, Stephen Bottomore, Ben Brewster, Paolo Cherchi Usai, Andrei Chernyshev, Marietta Chudakova, Haralds Elceris, Mikhail Gasparov, Julian Graffy, Miriam Hansen, Chris Horak, Naum Kleiman, Nat Klipper, Hiroshi Komatsu, Albin Konechny, Aleksander Lavrov, Georgi Levinton, Olga Matich, Lina Mikhelson, Viktoria Mylnikova, Natasha Nusinova, Aleksandr Ospovat, Irina Paperno, Tatyana Pavlova, Inga Perkone, Jayne Pilling, Kathy Porter, David Shepard, Svetlana Skovorodnikova, Yevgeni Toddes, Lyubov Zamyshlyayeva and Rashit Yangirov are among those who kindly helped me with different things at different stages.

And I am infinitely indebted to the Pordenone Silent Film Festival – its organisers as well as its regulars, of whose collective mind I am proud to feel myself a part.

Yuri Tsivian

Abbreviations

GAP   Arkhiv Glavnogo arkhitekturno-planirovochnogo upravleniya
           Rizhskogo gorispolkoma [Archive of the Architectural and
           Planning Department of the Riga Municipal Executive Committee]

GBL   Otdel rukopisei Gosudarstvennoi biblioteki imeni V. I. Lenina
           [Manuscript Department of the Lenin State Library] (Moscow)

GFF   Gosudarstvennyi fil'movyi fond SSSR (Gosfilmofond) [State Film
           Archive of the USSR] (Moscow)

GIK   Gosudarstvennyi institut kino [State Cinema Institute, 1930–4]

GPB   Gosudarstvennaya publichnaya biblioteka imeni M. E. Saltykov-
           Shchedrina [M. E. Saltykov-Shchedrin State Public Library]
           (St Petersburg)

IMLI   Otdel rukopisei Instituta mirovoi literatury imeni A. M. Gor'kogo
           [Manuscript Department of the A. M. Gor'kii Institute of World
           Literature] (Moscow)

IRLI   Otdel rukopisei Instituta russkoi literatury (Pushkinskii Dom)
           [Manuscript Department of the Institute of Russian Literature
           (Pushkin House)] (St Petersburg)

LGALI   Leningradskii gosudarstvennyi arkhiv literatury i iskusstva
           [Leningrad State Archive of Literature and Art] (St Petersburg)

LGITMIK   Leningradskii gosudarstvennyi institut teatra, muzyki i kino
           [Leningrad State Institute of Theatre, Music and Cinema]
           (St Petersburg)

MKhAT   Moskovskii khudozhestvennyi akademicheskii teatr [Moscow Art
           Theatre]

RKM   Rīgas kino muzejs [Riga Cinema Museum]

RLM   Muzei istorii literatury i iskusstva imeni Ya. Rainisa [J. Rainis
           Museum of the History of Literature and Art] (Riga)

TsGALI   Tsentral'nyi gosudarstvennyi arkhiv literatury i iskusstva [Central
           State Archive of Literature and Art] (Moscow)

TsGIAL   Tsentral'nyi gosudarstvennyi istoricheskii arkhiv Leningrada
           [Leningrad Central State Historical Archive]

TsMK   Tsentral'nyi muzei kino SSSR [Central Film Museum of the USSR]
           (Moscow)

VGIK   Vsesoyuznyi gosudarstvennyi institut kino [All-Union State
           Cinema Institute, since 1934] (Moscow)

Note on transliteration, translation and the Russian calendar

Transliteration from the Cyrillic to the Latin alphabet is a perennial problem for writers on Russian subjects. We have opted for a dual system: in the text we have transliterated in a way that will, we hope, render Russian names and terms more accessible to the non-specialist, while in the scholarly apparatus we have adhered to a more accurate system for the specialist. Accepted English spellings of Russian names have been used wherever possible and Russian names of Germanic origin have been returned to their roots.

The translation of film titles poses problems as Russian does not have either an indefinite or a definite article. We have preferred to insert an article: hence *The Battleship Potemkin*, *The Arsenal*, etc. The convention by which Soviet films are known by bald titles like *Earth*, *Mother*, *Strike* is itself arbitrary: consider, for example, how Chekhov's plays have become known in English as *The Seagull* and *The Cherry Orchard*, but *Three Sisters*.

Russia did not abandon the Julian calendar and replace it with the Gregorian until February 1918. Dates in the Russian calendar are therefore in the nineteenth century twelve days, and in the twentieth century until the change thirteen days, 'behind' those in countries that had adopted the Gregorian calendar earlier: hence the Revolution of 25 October 1917 [Old Style] took place on a date marked elsewhere as 7 November. Where appropriate, both dates are given in the text.

Foreword

Tom Gunning

In this modest-seeming volume Yuri Tsivian casts a probing beam of illumination into some of the most obscure areas of film history. And the terrain he lights up with his careful assembly and insightful reading of the records of early film viewing in Russia not only changes our sense of the history of this period but also, I believe, causes us to re-evaluate some of our most basic theoretical and historical assumptions about what a film is and how it affects its audiences. The territory Tsivian enters into here has remained basically uncharted for decades (at least in English). First, he is dealing with cinema's first two decades, a period which has only recently benefited from both thorough research and a theoretical perspective unclouded by narrow assumptions of organic evolution or simple narratives of progress.

In addition, Tsivian explores this previously ignored period in *Russia*. For most Western film historians Russian film has simply been equated with Soviet cinema, relegating the large number of films made in Russia before the October Revolution to the status of little-seen works against whose theatricality and decadence the masters of Soviet cinema revolted. However in the last decade our sense of the history of Russian films has been transformed, largely through the efforts of Tsivian, who (aided by the historical factor of glasnost and the heroic efforts of the Moscow film archives and a number of Western film enthusiasts) has brought to the West the riches of Russian silent film and such forgotten film artists as Yevgeni Bauer. But Tsivian has chronicled the production background and the stylistic evolution of Russian films before the Revolution in his previous book *Silent Witnesses: Russian Films 1908–1919*. With this new book he moves into another obscure aspect of film history – that of film reception, rather than production.

It is only recently that the concept of reception has been directly addressed in both theoretical and historical studies, first in literature and then in the other arts. Although often tacitly assumed, the contribution that a viewer, listener or reader of a work of art makes to the final impression which a work leaves in history has rarely formed the central subject of critical enquiry. A number of scholars have begun to prowl through research material in order to discover the factors that determined reception of films in American history including (among others), Janet Staiger's pioneering work *Interpreting Movies: Studies in the Historical Reception of American Cinema*, Roberta Pearsòn's and William Uricchio's research into the audiences for early film and their cultural backgrounds and assumptions, Barbara Klinger's work on the way the melodramas of Douglas Sirk were prepared for audiences by publicity and understood by contemporary reviewers, Steve Neal's probing of what genre terms actually meant to distributors and exhibitors during the sound era and, from a bold theoretical position, Miriam Hansen's investigation of the public sphere of American silent film, *Babel and Babylon: Spectatorship in American Silent Film*.[1]

But, if Tsivian shares a basic area of enquiry and a number of assumptions with these scholars, his discoveries and even methods may prove surprising to readers familiar with recent Western studies in film reception. To a large extent this is because the experience of filmgoing that he investigates takes on a different form from the dominant modes of film reception in the West. It is perhaps of more theoretical interest to note that Tsivian uses the investigation of reception to push our understanding of the film text beyond its traditional borders. And, since he explores not only the official sources utilised in the West (trade journal editorials and reviews and other forms of journalism) but also the works of poets and novelists, he uncovers a uniquely vivid picture of the discovery of cinema, one that will strike readers both with its unusual intensity and, perhaps, with an uncanny familiarity.

The first published reactions to motion pictures in the United States came primarily from journalists who saw the films in specially arranged press screenings or theatrical premières. These screenings took place in such respectable sites as the Edison laboratories in West Orange, in large vaudeville theatres such as Koster and Bial's Music Hall in New York City, or in smaller lecture halls, which frequently presented scientific marvels accompanied by explanatory lectures. These journalists were mainly anonymous or, if their names are known, they mean little to us today. In simple but effective prose they registered their approval of the latest technological invention and generally praised it for its life-like realism. For many journalists the invention of motion pictures was a source of national pride, since the machines that they first saw were either American inventions or direct offspring, so they believed, of the kinetoscope invented by Thomas Edison, the 'Wizard of Menlo Park', the peep-show device that had sparked interest in moving pictures.

But, if we turn to the canonical early account of projected films in Russia, the scene shifts sharply. The young writer who reviewed an exhibition of the Lumière *cinématographe* in 1896 at the Nizhny Novgorod Fair saw the films projected at Aumont's *café chantant* as one part of a programme of entertainment which cloaked, and perhaps augmented, Aumont's true enterprise – prostitution. The latest technological marvel came spiced with a foreign flavour – more precisely a piquant Parisian savour of easy French morals – and was associated less with scientific curiosity than with lascivious visual pleasure. The context in which the reviewer received these moving images certainly shaped his perception of them. Describing the Lumières' film *La Partie d'écarté*, he noted 'the cupidity of the players is betrayed by the trembling fingers and by the twitching of their facial muscles', expressive details that have either not been noticed or have been interpreted more innocently by most other viewers of this film. For the most part, however, it was the contrast between the Lumières' basically innocent views of daily life and their place of exhibition that struck the Russian journalist, who happened to be the emerging man of Russian letters Maxim Gorky. Instead of a workmanlike journalistic account celebrating the march of progress, Gorky's review recalls a literary essay filled with metaphors and dominated by suspicious dissatisfaction with both the films and the place where they were shown.

Already this simple contrast between American and Russian reactions to the earliest projections of motion pictures demonstrates essential points made by Yuri Tsivian in this pioneering and revelatory study. As a theoretical starting-point Tsivian posits the view that no film is completed until it has been received – viewed and pondered on – and that this reception not only completes the film but does so in a very specific way that bears the mark of the historical and social position of the viewer. A journalist in pre-Revolutionary Russia seated in a house of semi-ill repute sees a film very differently from an American newspaperman poised at the feet of Thomas Edison, let alone a contemporary film scholar crouched over a viewing table in a film archive or a student dozing in a university lecture screening room. Records of the reception of films will tell us, Tsivian proves, not only about the films themselves, but also about the assumptions and viewing protocols of the viewer who left the record, perhaps even revealing things of which the original writer was only dimly aware.

The writer on films filters his or her perception of the films through more than a subjective grid. As they participate in the passions and tacit assumptions of their age and nation (not to mention class and gender) they stain the image they present of the film with them. In addition, the immediate context of their viewing experience – the theatre, the musical accompaniment and the environment in which a film is projected – all may leave an imprint on viewers' impressions of the films they watch, as Gorky's awareness of being downstairs from a bordello certainly shaped his sense of *La Partie d'écarté*. Therefore, Tsivian opens up a whole new dimension of film history in this book. He not only captures the way the reception of films reflects a particular place and time, but he analyses film reception as a confluence of cultural forces. Theatre architecture, musical accompaniment, speed of projection, the condition of prints and a host of other contingencies usually dismissed as ephemera are all demonstrated to have shaped the unique experience of film in Russia during the first decades of the twentieth century.

This may be the most exciting aspect of this unique study, an analysis of all the elements of cinema that made a strong impression on Russia's first film viewers, from the snake-like hissing of the light source for certain early film projectors to the fascination exerted by the sudden falling of a shadow of a member of the audience on to the screen, obscuring momentarily the figures in a drama composed of light. As Tsivian proves, a truly detailed and historical picture of film reception makes the boundaries between the aesthetic and the contingent waver, as early spectators become entranced by all aspects of the new medium, often privileging accidents of technology over the intentions of artistry. These revelations of the range of cinematic experiences that viewers focused on during this early period call into question, I believe, previous theories of the pleasures of cinema as coming primarily from fantasies of visual mastery or narrative engagement. The richness of the accounts of early film viewing that Tsivian has uncovered must make us rethink the nature of the fascination that motion pictures exerted historically, and perhaps continue to exert today.

One might be tempted to question whether one of the major sources that Tsivian draws on – the descriptions literary writers have left of early cinema in poems, letters or memoirs – may have eccentrically determined this rather de-centred and impressionistic image of cinema reception. Tsivian does in fact indicate that, given the nature of written records of film viewing experiences, he cannot claim to provide an overview of the majority of Russian audiences, particularly the illiterate audiences of the provinces. His account of film reception necessarily focuses on the educated and urbane audiences of Moscow and St Petersburg. However, there is strong evidence that the effect of contingent elements like music or projection speed was widely and even officially recognised as shaping audience response to films generally.

Perhaps the clearest indication of this comes from the very specific regulations covering the showing of films portraying the Imperial Family. Such films, Tsivian reveals, had to be shown without musical accompaniment (for fear that music inappropriate to imperial dignity might undermine the spectacle), cranked by hand at a proper speed with the theatre manager present (to avoid the risible effects overcranking or undercranking might give to imperial deportment) and shown separately from any other films in the programme. This last point substantiates Tsivian's discovery that the eclectic programmes of short films that made up early film shows were often received in a way that blurred the barriers between one film and the next, so that unrelated films projected in close succession often gave birth to surreal 'phantom narratives' in which the action of one film carried over into the next. The protocols of imperial projection guarded against precisely the sort of creative reception Tsivian claims was rampant in turn-of-the-century Russia as a number of convergent factors were combined by viewers to create a truly unique film experience. Imperial authority had to be on guard against such semiotic infection and mandated an isolated controlled reception, rather than the carnivalesque semiotic blends that delighted Russia's first film audiences.

If we return to Gorky's description of the Lumière films, other contrasts between his reception of these moving images and the most familiar accounts of first films in the West assert themselves. Most Western journalists stressed the life-like quality of the new invention, its ability to extend the possibilities of photography into the portrayal of motion. But for Gorky this addition of motion to photography did not so much increase technology's ability to capture life as create an uncanny parallel universe resembling ours but with marked deficiencies: 'a life deprived of words and shorn of the living spectrum of colours – grey, soundless, bleak and dismal life'. For Gorky the cinematograph presented a phantom world, not life but 'its soundless spectre'. Gorky's description most certainly de-familiarises our dominant contemporary reception of these films, which are usually presented in film history books as bold steps in the progress of an art and industry, exemplars of realism and ancestors of the documentary film.

In fact, similar if less eloquent responses to the ghostly aspect of early film *can* be found in the West, but they appear less frequently than the optimistic and progressive claim that through this new technology man has in a sense triumphed over death. Although Gorky was not a Symbolist, he was aware that his highly metaphorical and fantastic description of the cinematograph resembled the prose of this literary movement current in Russia at the turn of the century. Tsivian in this volume reveals how much the Symbolist mentality shaped the reception of cinema in Russia, at least among the urban educated classes. The dimly flickering silent black-and-white images of motion pictures were experienced by many of the Symbolists not as the latest step in realism (whose temporary lack of sound and colour could be seen as preliminary stages in the pursuit of total cinema) but rather as phantasma-gorical moonlit visions which conveyed the Symbolist sense of a veiled and occult reality of which the visible world was merely a shadow. Fyodor Sologub, the Symbolist writer, found a perfect metaphor for the crepuscular dream-like existence experienced by these aestheticised pre-modernists when he wrote: 'We are but pale shadows like pictures in a cinema.'

By drawing on the impressions of early cinema left by literary figures as much as journalists, Tsivian uncovers both the Symbolists' role in Russian reception of cinema and those areas of the cinematic experience that the Symbolists could highlight uniquely. While the older generation of Sym-bolists like Dmitri Merezhkovsky and Zinaida Gippius viewed cinema with suspicion as a mechanical product of a modern culture for which they had little sympathy, the somewhat younger Symbolists Alexander Blok and Andrei Bely embraced the new medium precisely as an embodiment of a fascinating and frightening new world exemplified by urban life, speed and instability. For Blok the cinema formed an essential part of the 'city mystery' that obsessed him. Here again Tsivian's understanding of film reception as including the whole dynamics of what he calls the 'poetics of film per-formance' reveals what drew these major writers to the cinema. For Blok the new experience offered by the cinema as opposed to theatre lay partly in its casual nature, the aleatory aspect of a spectacle one simply 'dropped into' as part of the random trajectory of a city flâneur. These chance encounters with the cinema, like an erotic city pick-up, endowed it with a different energy from the traditional arts and served as an initiation into the new atmosphere of modernity.

If the Symbolists saw nearly everything as emblems of occult forces of transformation, the cinema appeared ripe as a source of metaphors. Symbolist writing constantly reflects the sense of being on the brink of some great catastrophe, moving towards a cataclysm of change. For Bely the sudden explosions and transformations of the trick film genre so popular in cinema's first decade presented a tangible image of the instability of existence, liable to explode suddenly in a puff of hand-coloured smoke and dissolve into nothingness. For Bely such film tricks portrayed visible reality as nothing more than 'a lady suffering from a cold, a lady who sneezes and explodes. And we, who hold on to her; who are we?' Bely and other Symbolists approached cinema as an unexpected prophecy, a preview of an apocalypse they all felt was imminent. They were right, of course, even if we now understand the transformation that shook their society as social and political rather than the metaphysical and occult *eschaton* that they awaited. The cinema served as a harbinger of technological change and, just as the Revolutionary Soviet society embraced it as a modern medium uniquely suited to convey the message of a new Marxist society, the Symbolists saw its pale illumination casting the shadows of the final twilight (a phantom world, as Gorky had first announced) which anticipated the world of the dead.

This complex image of a cinema received with ambivalence, announcing a future that was feared as much as desired, stands at the centre of the Russian reception of early cinema. If the cinema seemed to summon up a primal fear of a world of shades this was partly because pre-Revolutionary Russia was a dying society obsessed with imagining its own demise. But beyond this historical specificity the Symbolist reception of early cinema also brings to light an undertone evident in a number of early receptions of film. The very unfamiliarity of this uncanny reception reveals a dimension to the emergence of cinema ignored in most canonical histories. Since the receptions discussed by Tsivian are for the most part encounters with something very new, they approach a medium we now take for granted as novel and exotic.

As Tsivian puts it, 'going to the cinema in those years always had something of the same sense of adventure that flying has for us'. Not the least of the interests of these accounts of cinema's emergence is their de-familiarising effect on a contemporary reader as we encounter a novel experience of the uncanny power of cinema, generally occluded in Western film theory and history. Undoubtedly Russian intellectuals were peculiarly suited to speculate on this emissary of modern Western technology and mass culture from an ambiguous viewpoint. But they alert us to a motif that did appear, even if it was never dominant, in early Western receptions of cinema. Certain commentators on film's first appearance in the United States and Europe also recognised the strange ontology of this new medium, its phantom-like position between the present and the absent, displaying a trace rather than a full-bodied presence, as well as the hypnotic and trance-like fascination it exerted over viewers. This uncanny dimension of the film medium may still persist today to be explored both by certain avant-garde practices as well as popular genres such as the horror film (a genre frequently marked by a self-conscious invocation of the power of the film medium).

The film spectator from the period of the discovery of the cinema was, as Tsivian puts it, a 'medium-sensitive film viewer', one who went to see a film show in order to experience the new medium more than to see a specific film. In other words, the earliest period of film reception foregrounds the attraction of filmgoing itself often over the specific story or content of the films shown, which may serve as little more than pretexts for a trip to the cinema. Since this attitude inverts what we usually understand as the priorities of filmgoers for most historical periods, it allows us to explore reception from a different angle. It invites us to develop theses about other pleasures of filmgoing which may yet persist beneath the culturally dominant regimes of narrative and information. It encourages us to ask new questions about historical spectators and even to wonder if contemporary spectators are as 'medium-oblivious' as some academic theorists seem to assume.

One finds in Tsivian's book, then, not only a rich description of a type of historical spectator, the literate urban film viewer of pre-Revolutionary Russia, but also a new perspective on what sort of questions we can ask concerning historical film viewers and the range of issues and information relevant to such investigations. As reception studies have become part of film history, the concept of the film viewer has moved from a disembodied theoretical 'spectator-in-the-text', which was simply an epiphenomenon of the film itself (established, of course, by a contemporary film analyst), to a quest for the flesh-and-blood audience members who sat before the screens on tangible seats in actual theatres. This attempt to rediscover embodied and historical film viewers has led film historians to move beyond film analysis and begin sifting through sociological surveys of audiences, newspaper and trade reviews and other accounts for the traces of the film experiences which constitute the ground of a history of reception. While Tsivian's work is most certainly a contribution to this endeavour, the specific nature of his approach has yielded unique insights.

Instead of placing the accent on interpretation of plots that a survey of contemporaneous reviews inevitably entails, Tsivian's use of poetry and literature from the period of the emergence of cinema sketches an audience member who reacted as much to the temperature of the theatre, the social life enacted in the foyer, or the effect of a sudden break in the film, as to the film's plot. Rarely has our sense of the film viewer been so sensual and physical, so attuned to the actual environmental pressures of the film show. A film viewer who can evaluate non-aesthetic aspects of the film show – such as the scratches that the film print has acquired over many projections – and endow them with a new sort of meaning reveals the uniquely creative powers of film viewers who do not simply passively decode film texts but create new thresholds for aesthetic experience.

In his analysis of Bely's and Sologub's 1918 (unfilmed, but still stylistically revolutionary) film scripts, Tsivian shows these Symbolist filmgoers incorporating into their proposed films some of the accidents of film projection that drew their attention as spectators (such as scratches and breaks in the film), re-working them as conscious elements of film style. As Tsivian indicates, reception indeed completes a film, displaying a creative power that can be fed back into film production. But to understand this circuit fully one needs to explore film viewing as an active process sensitive not only to the purported meanings of the film texts but also to its accidents as well as its surrounding environment.

As the Russian Formalists demonstrated around the end of the period Tsivian covers, de-familiarising an experience takes on a critical and aesthetic function by intensifying our experience of something too often taken for granted. Tsivian not only surveys the historical reception of cinema in pre-Revolutionary Russia in this book, he de-familiarises our concept of both reception and the film text to take in horizons rarely sighted previously by film historians.

Introduction

CULTURAL RECEPTION

Ideally, the practice of film history presupposes that each fact be considered from a dual perspective: as it appears to the film historian today and as it was viewed by the spectator at the time. On the one hand, history reads texts; on the other, each text has its own history of readings. It is scarcely worth discussing the evolution of film discourse if we think of discourse as something restricted to the films themselves. It is not only things that change, but the measure of things. If we admit that films imply their viewers, we have also to admit that it is not only films but viewers too that are subject to evolutionary change. In this respect a study of film reception can be expected to provide a significant corrective to any merely factual history of film.

This book presents an attempt to historicise the notion of the viewer in Russia in the years between 1896 and 1920. Yet it is not about ordinary cinemagoers. In my attempt to reconstruct contemporary reception, I have had to rely upon written evidence, yet most Russian audiences could neither read nor write; no trace of their response survives. Nor was this response clear to contemporaries. In January 1916 *The Petrograd Cinema Journal* wrote about what they called in those days 'the reaction of the crowd': 'The cinemagoer is as silent and mute as the cinema itself . . . the cinema public, a new public brought into being by this new form of theatre, is enigmatic and incomprehensible.'[1] Even today, I know of no one in Russia who would be prepared to claim that they had the key to this enigma.

This book, then, is an attempt to reconstruct the response to cinema of the educated Russian public rather than to give a general overview of Russian spectatorship as a whole. Yet it is not just about the reception of films by cinema critics (although it does refer to contemporary film reviews). Nor is it a history of a 'viewer-in-the-text', an 'implied subject' believed to appear at the point where textual strategies converge.

What this book *is* about is what might be called *cultural reception*. I am interested in reflective rather than reactive response. By 'reflective' I mean a response that is active, creative, interventionist, or even aggressive. Let us take an example: two contemporary newspaper accounts of the Lumière brothers' 1896 programme. Compare the different ways their authors describe the monochromatic effect film images produced. A correspondent of *The New Review* [Novoe obozrenie] wrote that he was struck by the lack of the sun's warmth and of bright, living colours.[2] The Paris correspondent of *New Times* described what took place on the screen in the following words: 'The lighting is not quite natural; it's just like bright moonlight.'[3]

In the first example the visual text is revealed as deficient and is described in terms of 'absence': you see the sun and yet you feel no warmth; you see the light but perceive no colours. In the second the same absence of colour is described as a peculiarity rather than a deficiency; the monochrome 'black-and-whiteness' of the image was identified (or, rather, intentionally mis-identified) as a special quality of the world this image portrayed. Film images fascinated the writer because they turned day into night and the sun into the moon.

The distinction between the two examples may seem microscopic, yet it marks the boundary between two types of response: that pertaining to the psychology of sense perception and that involving cultural interpretation. The next logical step would be to describe the world of cinema as a world of eternal night; and indeed, that is what we find in Maxim Gorky's 1896 article on the same subject:

> If only you knew how strange it felt. There were no sounds and no colours. Everything – earth, trees, people, water, air – was portrayed in a grey monotone: in a grey sky there were grey rays of sunlight; in grey faces – grey eyes, and the leaves of the tree were grey like ashes . . . Silently the ash-grey foliage of the trees swayed in the wind and the grey silhouettes of the people glided silently along the grey ground, as if condemned to eternal silence and cruelly punished by being deprived of all life's colours.[4]

Thus, where one would expect a description of a deficient image, one finds a sophisticated description of a world 'made strange'. This is the way cultural reception works. At the input we have a simple moving image, at the output we get a 'reception text' that Gorky himself characterised as rich and complicated: 'The impression they created was so unusual, so complex and original! I shall try to convey the essence, but I doubt whether I shall be able to capture every nuance.'[5]

A remarkable analogy borrowed from a book written in 1924 by the Polish philosopher Karol Irzykowski helps to give an idea of the way cultures read technology. The analogy is Irzykowski's response to the question raised by the French theory of *photogénie*: 'What is the nature of cinema?' Such questions, Irzykowski argued, have no possible answer whatsoever: 'Cinema is a technical invention, but it is treated as if it were capable of being "solved" like a chess problem.'[6]

In culture there are phenomena that may be likened to the interpretation of blurs or smudges. According to the vision or imagination of the viewer, random plaster stains, damp marks or smudges of ink on a wall may be seen to resemble certain objects. By elongating them or adding bits to them one can get these marks to 'yield up' the hidden object, so that even someone without any artistic ability can sketch a tolerable representation of it. The history of language, for example, brings up more and more 'lexical smudges', which are then piously given meaning. Word precedes idea: in the beginning is the word, then comes the search for its meaning. Fictitious problems appear, which are, however, in one sense both valuable and fruitful.[7]

This astonishing remark was made at least one year before the ink-blot test invented by Rorschach was made known to the general public. The task of those who take up the study of cultural reception is quite similar to that of the Rorschach psychologist: to summarise and interpret the recurrent associations and fixed ideas that each culture reads into the 'moving smudges' of early cinema.

THE TROPES OF FILM RECEPTION

The manner in which viewers received the first films can be defined as a culturally conditioned response to cinema as a medium. Yet what does 'culturally conditioned' mean? Is there any way in which human responses are not culturally conditioned? Strictly speaking, any act of behaviour (including reactive ones such as shame or fear) can be described as being culturally determined. A less definitive approach, however, would be more instrumental. In 1908 the Symbolist poet Alexander Blok made the following remark in a letter to a friend after reading Bram Stoker's *Dracula*: 'I finished it in two nights feeling terribly frightened. And then I realised just how deep this [fear] went, quite apart from any literary convention, etc.'[8] This distinction between literary and non-literary, that is, between learned and instinctual responses, will help us towards a better understanding of the way in which viewers responded to the first films.

For example, we are used to believing that the feeling of fear reported by audiences at the Lumières' cinema shows was an instinctive reaction to the train that was about to leave the screen and burst into the auditorium. This may be true in the majority of cases. Nevertheless, in a number of contemporary accounts this filmic event was articulated in terms of previous literary experience. This is how Vladimir Stasov, a well-known art and music critic of the day, described, in an 1896 letter to his brother, the impression the Lumières' programme made on him: 'All of a sudden a whole railway train comes rushing out of the picture towards you; it gets bigger and bigger, and you think it's going to run you over, just like in *Anna Karenina* – it's incredible.'[9]

In many ways reception means acculturation, just as Stasov's response to Lumière was mediated through Tolstoy's novel. 'Real' fear acquired cultural framework and turned into 'literary' fear.

Take another example, that of mirrors and portraits. In the Russian cinema of the 1910s mirrors and portraits were often used to create 'mystical' or 'uncanny' effects.[10] Yet as an early metaphor for the medium, the motif of living mirrors and living portraits was a part of Russian film culture years before it was incorporated textually into Russian films.

Two sources can be cited to illustrate this point. One of them is a book of memoirs by Olga Vysotskaya, a Russian theatre actress of the 1910s. At that time, cinema in Russia venerated the cult of letters and writers well known to Russian culture as a whole. Beginning in 1909, film-makers were in the habit of hunting down famous writers, and a short film about 'writer so-and-so in his garden' would be a regular newsreel item. The following story from Vysotskaya's memoirs is about one such film:

> One evening at Meyerhold's place I met Alexei Tolstoi. 'Are you free now?', he asked, 'In a cinema off Ofitserskaya Street they are showing a picture about me. Let's go and see it.' On the screen Tolstoi was shown sitting on a bench, then taking out a cigarette and lighting it. 'You know – I don't know why – but I feel frightened', Alexei Nikolayevich said, and left the theatre. I stayed to watch the main film.[11]

A similar thing happened to Leonid Andreyev, another well-known writer of the time. After having seen his own face on the screen in 1909, Andreyev wrote an article in which he tried to analyse the peculiar feeling this experience evoked:

> Cinema kills the very idea of identity. Today my mental image of myself is still formed by what I am at this moment. Imagine what will happen when the cinematograph splits my self-image into what I was at eight years old, at eighteen, at twenty-five! ... What on earth will remain of my integrity if I am given free access to what I was at different stages of my life? ... It's frightening![12]

As these two stories seem to indicate, early film reception worked by putting new life into old literary clichés. Whatever its immediate cause, more often than not the first shock of seeing images in motion assumed the form of recognisable cultural patterns. We will call them the 'tropes of film reception'. These patterns (or tropes) formed a buffer zone between film and culture. Specifically, familiar faces on the screen would evoke the motif of doubles and duality with the traditional accessories of magic mirrors and haunted portraits. The kind of fear experienced by Andreyev and Tolstoy belonged to the same literary tradition as, for example, 'Saint Agnes of Intercession', an unfinished mystical story by Dante Gabriel Rossetti in which the hero recognises his own face in an ancient painting: 'I can recall my feeling at that moment as one of acute and exquisite fear.'[13]

It can be argued that some early pictures dating back to the trick period of film history had their own way of textualising such an initial response. From

1899 to 1908 at least eight films by Méliès alone were variations of the 'living portrait' plot.[14] There is a Pathé trick comedy preserved at the National Film Archive in London under the German title *Lebendige Spiegelbilder* [Living Mirror Images]: a character comes out into the street holding a large mirror. Each time a passer-by is reflected in it, the mirror brings the reflection to life and sends it back into the street to pursue its terrified owner. This trick film tells us as much about mirrors as about the cinema itself and the phenomenological fear embedded in its reception.

CINEMA AND SYMBOLIST SENSIBILITY

To study film reception, therefore, means to research the position accorded and the meaning ascribed to this or that feature of cinema within the dominant cultural pattern of the epoch.

The 1900s – a decade during which the majority of Russian audiences became familiar with cinema – were the years when Russian culture was dominated by the mentality of Symbolism, and one of the tasks of this book will be to show the specific ways in which cinema was absorbed by Russian Symbolist culture and made a part of its vocabulary.

In the summer of 1896 when the cinema was first shown in Russia, Maxim Gorky called the cinema, in his above quoted article about the Lumière performance, 'The Kingdom of Shadows':

> Three men are seated at a table, playing cards. Their faces are tense, their hands move swiftly. The cupidity of the players is betrayed by their trembling fingers and by the twitching of their facial muscles. They play . . . Suddenly, they break into laughter, and the waiter, who has stopped at their table with beer, laughs too. They laugh until their sides split but not a sound is heard. It seems as if these people have died and their shadows have been condemned to play cards in silence into eternity.[15]

This description is a literary allusion, not unlike that of Stasov, for whom the Lumières' train evoked Tolstoy's *Anna Karenina*. On the one hand, it is an accurate rendering of *La Partie d'écarté* [The Card-Game], shot by the Lumières in 1895. On the other hand, this film reminded Gorky of the 'game in Hell', an archetypal literary situation found in Russian folk tales and in Pushkin's 'Sketches for Faust', to which Gorky's description seems to refer. At a feast in Satan's palace Pushkin's Faust accuses Death of cheating, and Death answers:

> Be quiet, foolish youth!
> Think you can catch me out?
> We don't play for money here,
> But just to pass the eternity![16]

What was it that caused Gorky's mind to leap from Lumière to Pushkin? Early film reception works very much like the mechanism of 'de-familiarisation' [*ostranenie*] that Viktor Shklovsky, one of the key figures in the Russian Formalist school of literary criticism, believed was the basic principle of art. It is a complex game of similarities and dissimilarities, of the presence and absence of familiar features. The uncanny feeling that films somehow belonged to the world of the dead was prompted by mutually contradictory signals (or 'commands', to use a computer analogy) coming from the image. Some of them drew attention to the life-like quality of film, others rejected life: the presence of movement made the image look strikingly life-like, while the absence of sound and colour turned it into a haunted frame. Furthermore, the early spectator was aware of the fact that the fleeting moment on screen was in fact something that could be endlessly repeated, and this awareness helped to project the picture into eternity. A game on film turned into a game in the world of the dead.

The uncanny quality of the film medium, registered by Gorky in 1896, was a feeling shared by many. One can almost say that Russian writers treated cinema as a minor literary cliché. Just as the circus was a frequent metaphor for the human condition in turn-of-the-century culture (Pablo Picasso, Leonid Andreyev, Hermann Bang), so the cinema became a convenient metaphor for death, and the theme saw several variations. In 1907, for example, Mikhail Artsibashev published his novel *Sanin*, in which he tried to describe the everyday environment as seen through the eyes of a dying person:

> Semyonov heard sounds clearly, but it was as if he couldn't hear them, and as if figures moved noiselessly, like shadows in a cinematograph. Now and again familiar faces drifted into his field of vision, but it was as if they were strangers, striking no chord in his memory.
>
> By the bed next to his a man with a strangely shaven face was reading a newspaper aloud, but Semyonov was unable to understand why he was reading or to whom. . . . The lips moved, the teeth opened and closed, the round eyes turned, the sheet of paper rustled, the lamp burned evenly on the shelf, and what appeared to be large, sinister black flies soundlessly and incessantly circled around it.[17]

In 1911, in her novel *The Devil's Doll*, Zinaida Gippius (a major Symbolist writer) used this metaphor to renovate the traditional literary landscape of St Petersburg. As shown above, the black-and-white quality of the film image was powerfully evocative of the transformation of 'day into night' and of 'sunlight into moonlight'. For Zinaida Gippius, however, the colourless figures of the screen evoked the legendary 'White Nights' of Russia's northern capital and, by association, the phantoms that they were believed to conjure up. Hence the night scene in *The Devil's Doll*, set in a St Petersburg public park:

> It was already twelve o'clock. The garden stirred, not coming to life

exactly, but everything seemed to be in motion; the darkness thickened around the tables; on the stage grey shadows quivered, the grey dead of the cinematograph, their whispers cutting through the sound of the music.

'Look, isn't that a symbol of our modern, white nocturnal Petersburg life?' Ryzhkov, who had had far too much to drink, asked Zhulka.

She turned away, showing no interest.

'The cinema's boring. It's stupid . . . everywhere you look . . . you can't get away from it.'[18]

The 'symbolism' that the fictional Ryzhkov perceives in the cinema (and which his girlfriend ignores as a commonplace observation) was a part of a larger cultural pattern, the so-called 'myth of St Petersburg'. The city had been built on marshland at the arbitrary command of Peter the Great, and the myth, created in the nineteenth century by Pushkin, Gogol and Dostoyevsky, condemned it as an artificial and 'unorganic' city, haunted by phantoms and doomed to perish. In the early twentieth century the St Petersburg myth became a favourite point of reference for Russian Symbolist writers, to whom the ending of the world and the swamp-like instability of seemingly solid reality were of special interest as literary motifs. Cinema presented an easy way of modernising the myth; besides, one's first response to cinema was so much like reading Symbolist prose that in his 1896 article Maxim Gorky felt he ought to point it out:

This is not life but the shadow of life and this is not movement but the soundless shadow of movement.

I must explain, lest I be suspected of symbolism or madness. I was at Aumont's café and I was watching the Lumières' cinematograph – moving photographs.[19]

Twenty years later the idea of an internal identity between film reception and the reception of St Petersburg in Russian literature was explicitly formulated in an article by Fyodor Otsep (not yet a film director but an adolescent adherent of Russian élitist poetry):

[In cinema] we are dealing with a manifestation of delusion, a kind of hallucination. After Dostoyevsky's evocative descriptions, St Petersburg (now Petrograd) has become regarded as a devilish hallucination. Even Pushkin, as we can see from several of his remarks, felt the same about the city. Cinema is an entire, transparent land; it is a hallucination all the more mysterious in that it conceals within itself some idea or other that we have still not grasped.[20]

MECHANICAL VERSUS ORGANIC

In a 1914 short story by Zinaida Gippius the nihilist hero sells his soul to the Devil and finds himself, instead of in Hell, on a cinema screen:

> I walked about, I could move – but I was surrounded by a cinematograph: everything was black and grey, fast-moving. Agitated and voiceless. And I too was part of the cinematograph. I wasn't afraid, just bored.[21]

Soon the hero discovers that this grey and silent 'cinematic' version of Hades (which is worse than torment) is a punishment for those who do not believe in Hell: it is a Hell for nihilists, a visualised Nothing [*Nihil*]. A world without faith is like the world of the cinema: full of movement but devoid of life.

This passage brings us to an important category of film reception, one for which Russian film literature had a name: 'the fallacy of movement' [*lozh' dvizheniya*]. For Gippius (and her hero) 'rapid and agitated' movement betrayed the cinema even more than its 'grey and voiceless' image. This judgement was connected with Russian Bergsonianism. Henri Bergson (a French 'process philosopher', whose book *Creative Evolution*[22] was published in Russian translation in 1914 and was much discussed in Moscow and St Petersburg) used cinema as an example of false impression of continuity. According to Bergson, a temporal process cannot be depicted spatially. Films register movement by slicing it into regular discrete sections of space (frames), whereas, in reality, time is duration; it is experienced as continuous and cannot be measured.

Russian film literature seized on the idea. Theatre periodicals published simplified forms of Bergson's reasoning that argued the ontological superiority of stage over screen. The argument would run as follows:

> In cinema static moments are the basis of everything. Their swift succession creates movement and a kind of plastic picture. But this movement, this plasticity, this rhythm, is only a mirage, a delusion. . . . The magic force of living rhythm is unknown to cinema and it cannot be replaced by a cheap aesthetic substitute, by lavish décor, by expensive dresses, a superabundance of flowers, etc. Even genuine mountains, seas, streets, and walls are unable to conceal the absence of living rhythm. In theatre art all this can be conventionally conveyed by décor, by painted scenery, as long as the rhythm of the movement is genuine. In cinema it is the other way round: instead of décor there is real nature and buildings, but real rhythm is replaced by a kind of 'décor of rhythm'.[23]

Bergson's repudiation of cinema had yet another dimension connected with his intuitivism and his notion of *élan vital* [living momentum]. Unlike the spacialised 'public' time, measured by clocks and falsified in a series of film frames, time as duration can only be intuited. Discursive reason was believed to be too mechanical to grasp the living soul of time.

This distinction bore rich fruit in Russian film literature. Russian aesthetic thought in the age of Symbolism was still dominated by a fundamental axiom on the nature of art as formulated by the German Romantics: that art is a living organism. 'Living' and 'organic' were the two key words used to express the highest praise for a product of the creative imagination. To speak of a work of art as 'mechanical' would be unambiguously pejorative.

The idea of art and culture as organic forms (or as 'forms of life', which at that time appeared synonymous) was reinforced by the aesthetics of *art nouveau*, the most influential style in pre-First-World-War Russia. Fascinated by Darwin's excursions into the depth of the biological past, *art nouveau* artists created a biomorphic style that favoured organic forms and was itself based on patterns of natural growth.[24]

The machine was cast as the antithesis of life; being a machine, cinema was judged to be incompatible with art. Dmitri Merezhkovsky, the Symbolist writer and a founding member of a famous religious and philosophical discussion group, expressed a dictum that was much quoted at the time: the cinematograph is first and foremost a mechanical phenomenon and can never compete with the theatre as as organic phenomenon.[25]

Zinaida Gippius (Merezhkovsky's wife and collaborator) attempted a deeper phenomenological analysis of what present-day film theorists term 'the cinema apparatus':

> Try not going to the cinema for ten years . . . then go to see a film . . . What strikes you first? . . . You have grown too accustomed to the movement of life, and the filmic fallacy of movement, its blatant (in the sense of obvious) temporal 'pointillisme' [*punktual'nost'*] – the way moments of time are broken up to reveal the spaces between them – serves only to confuse the unpractised eye. We are frightened by them in the same way we are frightened by a mechanism that passes itself off as an organism – by an automaton, for example.
>
> An organic movement, of whatever kind, is linked with its rhythm, and, through it, with time. A mechanical movement arbitrarily violates this link and evokes a feeling of alarm in an organic being with a normal physiology. The fallacy of movement is not all: it is only the first thing you notice. Alarmingly agitated objects, animals, human figures and faces have only the *form* of life; they have no colour, that is *light*, since colour and light are indivisible: light always has a particular colour, or it doesn't exist at all. The chopped-up, jumpy movement of colourless figures is far more reminiscent of a dance of death than the flow of life. . . . Look at that grimacing, greyish face; those lips, black as earth with their soundless mouthings; that eye with its glassy sheen . . . When the muscles contract into a cadaverous smile, then, however much the trombones may ring out, a human being can not help but give a shiver.[26]

As this disturbing diagnosis indicates, cinema in Russia was brought into the Hoffmannesque universe of Romantic and post-Romantic literature. As subsequent chapters will argue, the 'organism myth' affected various aspects of early film culture including the choice of music, the interior décor of film theatres and even the form of narrative itself. The demise of this influence lies outside the chronological framework of this book. The First World War brought the *art nouveau* epoch to an end. The new age of machines and machine production would redefine the old paradigm. Art as organism was soon to become an outdated idea. The Bauhaus in the West and Constructivism in Russia would proclaim the machine an epitome for art. Viktor Shklovsky would assert that it took a motorist really to understand how art was 'made'. Dziga Vertov would invent his 'metrical montage' and announce the advent of the 'new electrical man'. The 'mechanical art' of cinema would see itself hailed as the dominant art of the twentieth century.

THE IMAGE OF THE TEXT

Cultural awareness was probably the key feature in Russian art at the turn of the century. Russian painters were unrivalled in the art of filigree stylisation; Russian theatres were famous for their parodies; Russian poetry (and not just poetry) identified itself closely with music. The gift of textual mimicry was held in high esteem.

Cinema too was part of this game. As early as 1897 several daily newspapers in Russia started to run columns under the title of 'The Cinematograph'. The contents had nothing to do with cinema, but were an indiscriminate medley of casual street scenes and fragments of overheard conversations: in short, everything that seemed not to fit into any other column. Such a column (previously known as a 'miscellany') was now legitimised by the very first, Lumière-inspired image of the cinematic text: the unrestricted flow of fragmentary, disconnected, outdoor scenes.

For all that was said and written criticising the 'mechanical nature of cinema', Russian writers were secretly in love with the technology they so loudly denounced. As Maximilian Voloshin (a leading Symbolist poet) wrote in 1910: 'The popularity of the cinema is primarily based on the fact that it is a machine; and the soul of the contemporary European, in its most naive aspects, is turned towards the machine.'[27]

Although spectators were not admitted to the projection box, it was common knowledge that films were recorded on a celluloid ribbon and kept in reels. As integral to film reception as the screw to the mental image of a steamship, the image of the ribbon agreed with the image of cinematic narrative as perceived as cumulative, episodic, perennially unwinding text. Cinematic narrative was perceived as a kind of Wagnerian 'endless melody', as something that corresponded textually to the endless celluloid strip on which it was recorded – the image pinpointed by Osip Mandelstam's sarcastic metaphor 'the metamorphic tapeworm',[28] or imprinted in the well-known name of a French fairground cinema of the 1890s, the 'Lentielectroplastichromomimocoliserpentograph',[29] the 'lenti-', 'plasti-' and 'serpento-' segments of which semantically reinforced the impression produced by the format of the word. Because films were purchased or rented in terms of footage, the length of a film would be indicated immediately after its title and announced proudly on the advertising posters. Defining the format of the narrative in metrical terms (as if one were selling lengths of dress material) seemed so funny that the habit became proverbial. *Cinema, or the Innocent Victim of Mad Passion and an Old Man's Bloodthirsty Love*, a stage spoof written by the playwright Boris Geyer and performed on the stage of the Petersburg satire theatre, The Distorting Mirror, in 1911, was announced as a 'powerfully dramatic drama 11,764 metres long in colourful colours, natural nature and dialogues.'[30] The notion of projection speed (as well as the vague idea that cinema was all about sprocket wheels and gears) reinforced the image of the cinematic text as a function of time and distance, a race against time. One theatre critic wrote of Yevgeni Bauer's *Silent Witnesses* [Nemye svideteli, 1914] that it moved 'no faster than four miles an hour'.[31] And this is the way another critic described how Yakov Protazanov's *Miss Mary* [Panna Meri, 1916] – a title that sounded to a Russian ear like the name of a racehorse – was projected in several Moscow film theatres:

> It is rumoured that *horse-racing* has recently been organised at the Ars, the Modern, the Artistic and at other cinema theatres, and has been attracting great crowds. *Miss Mary* started off in the first race at a speed of 200 metres a second, and galloped home confidently at the same pace. Her partner [Vladimir] Gaidarov, a man with a feeble constitution, had two refusals and came in half a lap behind.[32]

Although primarily this critical metaphor was aimed at the habit of projecting films without breaks between reels (a novelty for 1916), it also hyperbolises the endless loop as a cultural image of film.

OVERLAPPING IMAGES

As subsequent chapters will argue in more detail, reception works like a diffusing lens: whatever comes into its field 'goes out of focus' and comes to look like something else rather than itself. As soon as the image of cinematic discourse as a ceaselessly unfolding ribbon was settled in the collective mind of Russian audiences, we find it applied to things other than cinema, for example, literature. Here is what Osip Mandelstam wrote in his 1912 review of the Russian translation of Jack London's stories:

> What the cinematograph does best are so-called scenic pictures; London portrays the endless monotony of the northern landscape, daubed on like a painted panorama, and flickering like a living photograph that hypnotises the reader by its automatic readiness to show as many thousand metres as you please. London's 'artistic' device is continuity of action.[33]

The ways we perceive things intertwine and overlap. One can say that reception works by superimposing images one on another. We start by contrasting cinema to traditional narrative; then we come to discover cinema within literary discourse. Here we have to do with something similar to what Robert Schmutzler calls 'reciprocal osmosis' in turn-of-the-century culture.[34] One ought to think of it as an ensemble rather than as consisting of discrete art forms.

What follows is an example of how such an ensemble is constituted. In 1913 the general craze for cinema reached its peak in Russia; this was also the year when Russian Futurists intensified their onslaught on 'the public taste'. These events (purely coincidental as seen by an art historian) were treated by contemporaries as two aspects of a single phenomenon. On 1 January 1914, an influential conservative newspaper summarised the cultural life of the past year thus:

> What events can we call typical for the year that has just passed? . . . If we were to answer this question frankly it would emerge that what interested most people was Willy Ferrero [a seven-year-old American-born conductor touring in Europe], Max Linder and the Futurists: a *Wunderkind*, a clown, and a bunch of half-wits. . . . People chased after novelty for novelty's sake; the main mover was curiosity; the main attraction – the rapid succession of impressions. People looked as briefly and as quickly as possible, and chased on after tomorrow.[35]

The reception of two separate phenomena – cinema and Futurist poetry – overlapped and formed a single image of what the author of the above article called 'the increasingly feverish pulse of the big city'.

The immediate consequence of this was the process of mutual distillation. The image of the cinematic text was catalysed and distilled from what readers perceived as the vagaries of Futurist poetics; similarly, cinema contributed to the image of Futurist discourse. Ungrammatical, asyntactic, incoherent, spasmodic, senseless – these are only some of the features that Futurists and cinema were found to have in common. Here is one such statement (from the pen of Fyodor Otsep):

> The Futurists have neither wonder, nor belief in wonders. But if such things do not exist, then long live drunken visions, nightmares, delusions. . . . It is the same in the cinematograph: instead of ecstasy, there are hallucinations; instead of pathos, there are drunken daydreams. . . . It is as if the cinematograph and Futurism are converging.[36]

Intertextuality is not always the property of the text itself. Sometimes we find it only in post-textual images. One might say that reception provides a kind of refracting, diffusing medium which alone enables separate texts to be seen as convergent. This justifies the study of film reception as a step towards the history of film culture and the true history of film.

Part I

Chapter 1

Early cinema architecture and the evolution of the social composition of cinema

THE INNER SPACE OF CINEMA, 1904–8

As long as cinema remained an ambulant form of entertainment, no specific cinema architecture existed in Russia. Cinema shows were put on in rented premises, most frequently in seasonal theatres. Proprietors of mobile cinemas had hired circus marquees, market stalls, vacant storerooms, dockside warehouses, etc.[1] If any special premises did exist at that time, they were only small, light structures like fairground booths. Attempts were nevertheless made to adapt to specifically Russian conditions. Vast distances and bad roads made overland travel very difficult, and so, in 1906, a 'floating electrical theatre' that could house five hundred spectators was erected on a barge towed by a river steamer. It was called the Stenka Razin; its planned route was down the Volga river. It had coloured sails and its crew and ushers were supposed to be dressed as Razin's brigand gang. Since its projection machine was most probably equipped with oxygen lamps, it was extremely likely that it would eventually catch fire. Fortunately, it did so before the first spectator set foot on board.

The Stenka Razin was the last leviathan of the ambulant age. Already in 1903 property owners, who had previously been unwilling to provide premises for cinema, began to rent out conversions.[2] Gradually a kind of cinema hall with its own architectonics began to emerge. The interior of the early cinemas in the 1904–8 period differed greatly not only from that of buildings where public amusements had previously taken place but also from that of the cinemas that came later. This early type of auditorium did not last long; in 1908 it was pushed out from the centre of town to the fringes. Between 1904 and 1908 the cinema theatre, as a rule, consisted of a single room without a foyer or vestibule. If – as most frequently happened – the cinema was in a converted flat with the partition walls removed, the public came into the building by the main staircase and bought their tickets at a desk behind the door, just inside the auditorium. The following descriptions capture the atmosphere of those early auditoria. As early as 1919 the critic I. N. Ignatov was reminiscing with nostalgia:

In those days, when cinema was in its infancy, the electric theatres sought refuge in humble premises, where the spectators sometimes sat on wooden benches, where there were no decorations or any amenities for the public, but where you could enjoy so many lively and curious impressions.[3]

In his memoirs A. L. Pasternak also recalled those early days of cinema:

The door of the auditorium had been removed from its hinges, possibly as a safety precaution in case of fire, and replaced by a heavy plush curtain, which was tightly closed during the performance. It divided the darkened auditorium from the brightly lit landing. Two or three rows of plain bent-wood chairs were arranged in rows in the room. The Pathé projector, with its trade mark of the 'all-seeing and all-knowing' cockerel, stood in front of the audience, not at the back as in all later cinemas, and brought to mind our magic lantern. It was mounted on a sort of primitive stand, rather like a trestle. On the wall in front of the projector hung a screen: if not a sheet, as we had at home for the magic lantern, then something equally crude, which suddenly began to undulate during the performance.[4]

The Russian actor Alexander Werner described his childhood memories of the early cinema in Odessa:

It was a small, permanently stuffy room crowded with chairs. Down at the front stood some weird apparatus, which we lads found terribly fascinating, but which was jealously guarded by a mysterious man whom we called either 'the mechanic' or 'the technician'. He was both impresario, owner of the 'theatre of illusions' and ticket collector. He was the one who cranked the handle and the one who collected the money. On the wall hung a grubby bit of cloth, called the screen, and this was the focus of all our attention. The audience, which usually consisted of children and young people, were pretty unrestrained in their behaviour; they chewed seeds and munched apples, throwing the husks and cores on the floor, and sometimes at one another.[5]

Finally, a semi-autobiographical essay by the film journalist Vsevolod Chaikovsky gives us some idea of the average size of a Moscow cinema at about that time:

In September 1904 a cinema belonging to two sisters, Belinskaya and Genzel, opened on Tverskaya Street, at the corner of Bolshoi Gnezdnikovsky Lane. It was a small room, with only twenty-four seats and standing room at the back for another thirty. Those at the back used to chew seeds all the time and spit out the husks on the heads of the people in the seats. Old Belinskaya used to sit inside the room selling the tickets, while Genzel was the usherette, dealing vigorously with irrepressible small boys who were real pests and drove these two ladies to distraction.[6]

THE EARLY CINEMA AUDITORIUM AS AN OBJECT OF CULTURAL RECEPTION

The few descriptions cited above are enough to suggest that the atmosphere of the cinema auditorium was unique among the range of visual public entertainments existing at the beginning of the twentieth century. It was not, therefore, just the films that came into the focus of film reception; the milieu also played a part. Memoirists, who give us scrupulous and lively descriptions of the interior of cinema auditoria, telling us how the performances took place and how the audience behaved, do not, as a rule, remember the films themselves. This is not simply because the films were always changing, while the space they were being shown in stayed the same. It is also because at that time people who went to the cinema looked around them more keenly than they do today. Early patrons were fascinated not by films alone but rather by films *and* the environment, which, taken together, contributed to the as yet undifferentiated, overall impression of 'cinema'. Let us look now at two details that went to make up this impression: the illumination and the temperature of the auditorium.

In the early 1900s the source of light used in cinema projectors was not electricity but mainly ether-oxygen burners, or 'saturators'. For the cinema-goer of those years the spluttering of the lamps, the flickering, yellowish, unsteady beam of the projector, the faint but exciting smell of the ether were essential attributes of the show.[7] Another feature of ether–oxygen projectors (apart from the improved Lawson burners)[8] was that they overheated very quickly, and when this happened the temperature in the auditorium rose significantly. One Moscow cinema was even named 'The Hot Box' [Goryachaya budka], and no doubt the large Volcano cinema on Taganskaya Square held more than merely exotic associations for Muscovites. The situation looked all the more unreal since the audience were not supposed to take off their coats, although etiquette – quickly dictated by pressure from the rear rows – required the removal of headgear. At the beginning of the century it was not done to remain in a public place with one's coat on: this was allowed only in church. In winter (the season of cinema) some people dropped into the cinema just to get warm. The newspaper satirist Lolo [Munshtein] published a eulogy in verse to cinema, which had the following lines: 'We went to the pictures. My girlfriend whispered: "It's as lovely and warm as a Turkish bath!"'[9] And a casual passer-by, strolling on the streets of Vasilevsky Island in St Petersburg, could easily recognise a cinema from a distance: 'Chattering sparrows on telephone wires/Clouds of steam from the cinema doors . . . '[10]

However, the dominant feature, which immediately determined the nature of cinema reception in early twentieth-century culture, was the darkened auditorium. Although complete or partial darkness was familiar from magic lantern shows and some theatre performances, it was in cinema that it acquired the character of a dominant cultural symbol (in the Tadzhik language the first word for cinema was, in fact, the word for darkness, 'torikiston').[11] For a newcomer to cinema, the darkness of the auditorium, coupled with the silence of the characters on the screen and the black-and-white quality of the image, might stir an association with the depths of the ocean or a subterranean world. Several passages from Russian film literature could be cited to illustrate this point, but the best example can be found in an essay by Robert Musil: 'Mute as a fish and pale as an underground creature the film swims in the pool of the barely visible' ['Stumm wie ein Fisch und bleich wie Unterirdisches schwimmt der Film im Teich des Nursichtbaren'].[12] This metaphor provides a graphic example of the way in which an ordinary trope of film reception may grow into a (very German) phenomenological statement.

Thus, the darkness of the auditorium, which was believed to enhance the reception of the film and to make it easier for the viewer to be drawn into the world of the image, itself became an object of reception. In a way, this was a repetition of an effect experienced some twenty years earlier by European theatre audiences under the impact of Wagner's music dramas. As Richard Sieburth writes:

> Unlike the French theatres, which traditionally kept the houselights on during the entire performance (thus effectively maintaining the audience itself as part of the spectacle), Bayreuth plunged its public into a community of shared darkness. With all attention reverently directed at the illuminated stage, the entire aesthetic experience of drama thus took on the mystical quality of a religious event – the theatre as temple, the audience as anonymous officiants at a redemptive rite.[13]

In a similar manner, the sight of half-illuminated faces silently concentrated on the rectangle of light evoked images of occult circles, in particular the rituals of secret sects, which Andrei Bely's novel *The Silver Dove* had done so much to bring to the interest of the public. In 1910 Maximilian Voloshin wrote about cinema: 'In a small room with bare walls, reminding one of the prayer rooms of the flagellants, an ancient, ecstatic, purifying rite is enacted.'[14]

When in 1902 the well-known newspaper reporter N. G. Shebuyev visited the all-night shelter for vagrants at the Khitrov market in Moscow, he was not slow to compare it with the cinema:

> I held up a candle and illuminated the faces of my informants. It flickered over tramps and down-and-outs. Faces shone for a few moments in the light of the candle and then disappeared in the semi-gloom. It was living cinema.[15]

Shebuyev's comparison owes much to the stubborn reputation of cinema as the nadir, the underworld, the catacomb of culture. This motif was a variation on a theme that was central to film reception in Russia: cinema as a world beyond the grave. In the Introduction I have discussed the way in which early film reception contributed to Symbolist sensibility and how cinema became part of the mythology of St Petersburg. Later on these themes will be treated more fully in the passages describing certain features of Andrei Bely's script for a film based on his novel *Petersburg*.[16] Here it should be noted that 'beyond the grave' did not refer exclusively to what was happening on the screen. Reception works by diffusion rather than distinction: it blurs all boundaries. At times the entire edifice of the film theatre, and not just the auditorium, would be described as the house of the dead.

Here is an example. By coincidence, 1907 – the year the revolution of 1905 was finally crushed – was also the year of the big cinema-building boom in Russia. In the gloom of the moral depression that hung over the whole nation these new buildings looked like ominous fungi on the dead bodies of the cities. In an article of that year Alexander Koiransky, writing in emigration, described the scene:

> they [cinemas] grew like mushrooms at a time when one had to distract oneself at any cost, when nerves shattered by the upheavals of the revolution were unable to stand theatre or concerts . . . And they still have a forbidding air about them: tense (but not happy) faces in the strange, deathly light of the electric lamps; the gloomy auditorium; the sepulchral voices of the gramophones.[17]

Thirty years later, in the age of sound, the idea of cinema as an evocation of eternal night appeared again in Boris Poplavsky's novel *Home from the Clouds*, which describes the aimless wanderings of another émigré, this time a fugitive from the Bolshevik Revolution of 1917:

> I am free. I am completely free to turn right or left; to stay in the same place; to smoke; to go home and go to bed in the middle of the day; to go to the pictures in the daytime, and thereby to pass in an instant from day into night, into the subterranean realm of speaking shadows.[18]

THE 'LONG AUDITORIUM' PERIOD

> In 1908 a former contractor, one Abramovich, arrived from Siberia. He rebuilt the old house on Tverskaya Street (opposite Mamonovsky Lane), which used to belong to the Shilovsky family and where, long ago, Glinka introduced Muscovites to his new work, *Ruslan and Ludmilla*. But the drawing room was too small for a cinema auditorium, so Abramovich pulled down the internal walls and turned it into a hall big enough to hold three hundred people. It was thought of at the time as a large and splendid cinema.[19]

Conversions of this kind were typical for the end of the 1900s. At this time it became the custom to pull down the partition walls in former residential premises in order to form something like suites of rooms. This was when cinema auditoria took on the shape of a long gallery. The long, narrow hall was the most rational shape for a cinema. The effective area of the screen was increased by placing it further from the projector, which at that time was moved from the front rows to the back, and the angle of view for those sitting at the sides was not too far off the optimum. This kind of auditorium was not at all like a theatre, since in a theatre the acoustics did not allow the seats at the back to be situated too far from the stage, so in the 1908–15 period this elongated auditorium ('that long giraffe-necked hall')[20] became accepted as a distinctive feature of the new form of entertainment.

The 'long auditorium' period did not see out the decade; in the chronology of architecture it comes between the period of temporarily hired, improvised auditoria and the age of the luxury cinemas of the 1910s. The few cinemas which have avoided major reconstruction have preserved this archaic form untouched down to the present day; it coincides – unexpectedly – with the plan of the nave in Roman Catholic and Protestant churches.

'Corridor', 'tunnel', 'train compartment': the cinema of the 'long auditorium' period was too reminiscent of these functional spaces to enable the strict rationalism of the oblong interior to survive into the Empire period of cinema style, which dominated throughout the following decade, and at the end of which the evolution of the auditorium could be summarised thus: 'The building was at first narrow and elongated, it then started to become more square-shaped and is now well on the way to becoming completely square.'[21]

THE EVOLUTION OF NAMES

Before passing from the 'long auditorium' period to the 'rectangular period', we ought to pause to consider another metamorphosis that took place during those years, and which – it would appear – occurred for the same reasons that led to the evolution of architectural forms mentioned above. This was the wave of new names for cinema, which swept in at the turn of the 1900s and 1910s.

There are two aspects in the history of names that enable us to reconstruct the changing cultural context of what we now call 'cinema': names given to film theatres and names that were attached to the medium itself.

By 1902, the words 'cinematograph' and 'kinematograph', which had entered the language in 1886 and had been used interchangeably, had lost their equality, with the latter Greek-rooted form coming to be regarded as the more 'cultured' of the two. An article in *New Times* wrote of 'the kinematograph, which the illiterate often call the "cinematograph"'.[22] Over the next few years both words came to be regarded as old-fashioned: 'It is high time to replace that clumsy word "kinematograph"', wrote the newspaper *Russian Freedom* [Russkaya volya] on 19 January 1917 – very much in the spirit of that year of revolution.

In the 1900s two abbreviations of these words were borrowed from French and German: *cinéma* and *kinema* respectively; they were, however, still felt to be unsatisfactory. At that time a kind of lexical ambivalence arose around cinema, which lasted right up to the beginning of the 1920s. On the one hand there was a shortage of suitable terms, and on the other a number of regional variants: in the south of Russia, for example, the word 'illusion' [*illyuzion*] was used.[23] This situation led to an outburst of inventiveness on the part of amateur lexicographers. From the beginning of the 1910s articles on cinema in the Russian press would often begin with suggestions for new names. Cinema seemed to attract the would-be arbiters of cultural fashion; in the 1910s they produced an abundance of neologisms. The word 'kinema', which was treated in Russia as a masculine noun despite ending in a feminine 'a', offended the ear and was replaced by the more Russian-sounding 'kinemo'. This form spread, partly owing to a well-known article by Leonid Andreyev (1911) in which the author prefaced the word with the polemical-sounding epithet 'Great' [*Velikii*].[24] From then on, according to the press, 'Thanks to Leonid Andreyev, all new terms which the modern age uses to describe the cultural role of cinema in our everyday life, are invariably accompanied by the epithet "Great".'[25] In St Petersburg, owing to the twin processes of haplology and popular etymology, Andreyev's expression, 'The Great Cinema' [*Velikii Kinemo*], was changed to 'The Great Silent One' [*Velikii Nemoi*], a form which for some time became the term in general use.

At the same time the search for diminutive forms of 'kinematograph' also continued among bisyllabic words. This was dictated by an attempt to domesticate the new form of entertainment, and also by the growing stratification of cinema genres. The internal motivation behind this process is revealed, for example, in the following observations by a German writer in 1913:

> We must draw a distinction between the 'Kinematograph' and the 'Kino'. Kinematograph the father resembles a respectable, cultured scholar, who has made a real contribution to learning . . . But what a difference there is between him and his offspring, 'Kino'! How little the son resembles his serious father! He keeps bad company and falls under the influence of the uneducated.[26]

In that same year the Russian critic Peter Boborykin, writing from Germany, where – in his words – 'the "Kinematograph" is no longer even called "Kinema", but has been further shortened to *Kino*', suggested that Russians should 'adopt the latter form as the simplest'.[27] Although the term 'kino' was already to be found in Russian, it became the generally accepted word for cinema only in the 1920s. At the beginning of the 1910s it competed – without much success – with *kintop*, from the German *Kintopp*. *Kintop* had first been suggested by Alexander Koiransky in 1907: 'I like this word: "kintop". It is shorter and sounds better than the Parisian "cinémo-chromo-phono-méga-scopo-graph". *Kintop* – that's a splendid name! I recommend it to you!'[28] The German-derived *kintop* was eventually shortened to a

Japanese-sounding neuter noun ending in 'o', as we see in a 1916 poem: 'V mertsan'i prizrachnom kinto . . . / Gde nas ne vysledit nikto'. [In the ghostly cinema hall . . . / where no one will find us at all].[29] In 1917 the artist Alexander Benois made a curious but unsuccessful attempt to introduce into Russian a term which, although formed on the pattern of reduplicating French nursery words, did not actually exist in French and was most probably the product of his own linguistic imagination: 'I have', he wrote, 'a criminal weakness for the cinematograph, or – as one says now – "the cinema", or – even more simply – the *kiki*.'[30]

Among the diminutive names that actually were in colloquial use in Russia during the 1910s, we may mention *kinemusha*, *kinemoshka*, and a word that is still sometimes used today, *kinoshka*, which is the closest Russian ever came to the American 'movies'.

Russia's entry into the First World War and the ensuing nationalism brought dissatisfaction with loan words, and the search for new terms turned into a drive for Russification. The writer and critic Alexander Amfiteatrov proposed *dvigopis*, a calque of the word 'cinematograph' [moving de-piction], which was introduced by the Moscow journal *Pegasus* in 1916–17. In Petrograd Sergei Gorodetsky suggested the word *zhiznopis* [life depiction],[31] possibly derived from the American film company trade marks 'Biograph' or 'Vitagraph', the second of which was well known in Russia. The term *svetotvorchestvo* [light creation], invented by Nikolai and Valentin Turkin, was probably also a translation of the American 'photo-play', or the German *Lichtspiel*.

As the above examples show, the evolution of the term indicates a move away from the original, scientific-sounding Greek form of the word towards domesticated forms like *kiki*, or cultivated forms like *svetotvorchestvo*.

A similar process took place with the names given to cinema theatres. Initially the proprietors of cinema theatres named them after the particular models of projector they had installed. In the early 1900s cinemas in Moscow were called the Bioscope, the Thaumatograph, the Pathégraph, etc., and in St Petersburg there were also the Messter Theatre and the Edison Theatre. Early exhibitors went out of their way to accentuate the technical aspect of the new form of entertainment, making up words like 'Electrobiograph', 'Prima-vivograph', just as, in other European countries, names like 'Velograph', 'Cosmograph', 'Cineograph', etc. appeared.[32]

However, at the turn of the 1900s and 1910s, cinema proprietors carefully began to avoid these technical terms. If we compare lists of cinemas active during the middle and end of the 1900s with similar lists for the beginning of the 1910s, we shall see that the earlier lexicon of scientific-sounding names was giving way to names evocative of luminescence, or splendour. A typical example: in 1910 the owner of the first permanent cinema in Riga, the Synchrophone, informed the city's building department of his intention to change its name to the Northern Lights. Other cinema names typical for the

1910s were: the Palace of Mirrors, the Universal, the Renaissance, the Niagara, the Equator, the Alabaster, the Lyre, the Mirage, the Helius, the Ideal, and even the Zeppelin.

RECEPTION SHIFT

The wave of new names attached to film theatres was a part of a more general process, which may be called a 'reception shift', that took place towards the end of the 1900s: cinema was changing its cultural identity. This change corresponded with another major shift going on around the same time, one that, on the surface, looked like a mere renewal of repertoire: dramatically constructed stories gradually replaced 'trick films' and newsreels. In fact, as demonstrated by Tom Gunning and André Gaudreault, this was more than a change of fashion: films were changing their mode of address.[33] The early 'fairground' cinema had been centred on provoking the type of response that, to use Gunning's term, pertained to an 'aesthetic of astonishment'.[34] Displaying the apparatus of cinema (or, to paraphrase Russian Formalist idiom, 'baring the technology') was a part of this exhibitionist stratagem. Speaking of film reception, this can be called a 'sciolistic', or pseudo-scientific, period in its history: technology was on display in theatre windows, the projector occupied the centre of the auditorium, quasi-scientific terms featured in advertising posters and cinema was still called the 'cinematograph'.

Obviously, this type of response ceased to work as soon as cinema passed out of the sphere of 'the new' and entered the sphere of 'the familiar'. Now cinema was expected to behave according to domestic rules. In terms of response, astonishment was giving way to narrative involvement. Tricks were being replaced by tamer 'real stories'. In terms of exhibition, the reception shift of the late 1900s meant adaptation to traditional forms of culture. Primarily, this was a declaration of war on technology. The technical apparatus, proudly displayed in the previous decade, was pushed behind the scenes. Prejudice against 'the mechanical' (which comes from the nineteenth century and which we still experience each time 'high technology' – be it video, laser discs, or digital images, etc. – threatens to replace the 'familiar' cinema) made cultural organisms resistant to an outright penetration of this sort. Exhibitors had to conform: wherever possible, the new and the astonishing was replaced by the familiar and the respectable.

True, it seems never to have worked as it ought to have done. Some observers (like Zinaida Gippius and Igor Grabar) persisted in their disdain for cinema, claiming that it was a fatal cancer on the body of culture; others saw it as heralding the dawn of the new 'machine age'. But, one way or another, 'the mechanical', as opposed to 'the organic', remained one of the principal axes of film reception well into the 1910s.

Besides, the 'glamorous' names that came to replace the technical ones betrayed the somewhat *nouveau riche* nature of cinema's new cultural identity.

The reception shift that cinema underwent before the 1910s made it run from one extreme to another. New names also meant a new style in the interior architecture of cinema theatres. The functional architecture of the 'long auditorium' (dominant in the sciolistic period) gave way to a hall fashioned after an opera theatre. In the new period the drive was to forget, suppress or force technological references out of the framework of film reception.

THE CITY CENTRE LUXURY CINEMAS: THE BEGINNING OF THE 'RECTANGULAR' PERIOD

Some observers see the end of the 1910s as the period when the early auditorium began to exhibit signs of architectural exuberance:

> Converted shop premises no longer satisfied either the cinema proprietors or the public, so people who rented cinemas had to enlarge them – as their profits increased – by knocking down main walls, by replacing benches with bent-wood chairs or some other more expensive seating, and by putting up heavy, expensive tapestries instead of plain calico curtains.[35]

Indeed, although the luxury cinema really became established only in the mid-1910s, modest signs of the future style were already to be seen by 1907. As Boris Dushen, a veteran film technician, recalled in his memoirs: 'several cinemas "suddenly" opened on Nevsky Avenue, all at the same time; some were even fitted out with "luxury-style" interiors.'[36] The actor N. I. Orlov, a friend of F. A. Vasilyeva, the daughter of a gold merchant from Omsk, described this event in detail:

> On one of her trips abroad, F. Vasilyeva saw a film being shot on a street in Paris. She was curious, and asked the actors, cameramen and director to explain what was going on. The Frenchmen were flattered by the attention of this rich Russian lady and invited her to visit the Pathé brothers' studios ... she entered into negotiations with them and managed to acquire, on very favourable terms, Pathé's screening rights for the whole of Russia. She could screen all Pathé's pictures in Petersburg free, but all the income from screenings in other Russian towns (less the administrative and postal costs) had to be remitted to Paris. The business took off straight away and expanded rapidly. Cinemas opened one after another in Petersburg. These were all exact copies of Parisian cinemas, with orchestras, cafés, foyers, beautiful young barmaids and usherettes. The first cinema, called Just like Paris [Kak v Parizhe], was situated in a cosy, detached house in a courtyard off Nevsky Avenue. Outside there were two huge coloured posters of Paris; in summer the entrance was decorated with flowers and in winter with Christmas trees. A deep-pile carpet led the public into an elegant foyer. After twelve o'clock there were performances of 'Parisian genre' films (of pornographic pictures, to be frank). These were put on free-of-charge for

very select members of the city authorities (the chief of police, court officers and other officials, all with very smart and respectable ladies). A second cinema, Just like Nice [Kak v Nitse], was opened on the other side of the street, on the corner of Nevsky and Liteiny Avenues. In this one there were two auditoria. On the ground floor they showed very serious, documentary pictures. I remember one about how silk was produced; there was also one about submarines . . . On the first floor there were feature films. The décor was quite magnificent: gilt furniture, huge gilt-framed mirrors, marvellous carpets, silk material on the walls and door curtains to match. Of course, not everyone could afford to go to this kind of cinema; tickets cost from a rouble upwards, and (as Vasilyeva herself used to say) they were really just places where the well-off could meet one another, where they could arrange their rendezvous.[37]

This kind of secondary specialisation of the city-centre cinema houses in the 1910s soon aroused disquiet. In Germany Emilie Altenloh and Karl Lange argued that the auditorium should not be fully darkened. Rudolf Harms cited the advertisement of one Mannheim cinema which ran: 'Visit us. Ours is the darkest cinema in town'.[38] M. Swartz considers that because of the darkened auditorium it was predominantly men who went to the cinema in America.[39]

Things were rather more decorously arranged in Russia. The programme of the above-mentioned Just like Paris bore the motto: '"Lead the field, create the ideal cinema!" That's our goal.' In the same cinema the publicity for Le Bargy's and Calmettes' film L'Assassinat du Duc de Guise [The Assassination of the Duc de Guise, 1908] was accompanied by the assurance: 'All the tableaux are strictly decent'.

Dating needs affected the architecture of Russian city-centre cinemas through the provision of special boxes, which could be booked (fully or in part) for the season, or rented for the day or the performance. Telephones were a sign of 'loge de luxe' status, and they were installed in the luxury boxes at the Empire and the Just like Paris in Petersburg.[40] T. Vechorka recorded the psychology of the habitué of the 'loge de luxe' in this poem written in 1916:

Enchanted by the cinema, I recall it like a dream:
In the shadowy 'loge de luxe', feeling like a queen.
His coat still on, he's waiting there,
Clutching a crumpled rose.
And in the dark I feel his lips
Caressing my scented hair.
So secret and so urgent, the touch of silky furs.
So wicked and so wilful, my smiling, sinful gaze.
Shadows flicker on the screen,
The violinist plays.
The morning cares just drift away –
A cosy, rose-pink haze.[41]

'CENTRE AND PERIPHERY' IN THE SOCIAL TOPOGRAPHY OF CINEMA

By the beginning of the First World War, according to one eyewitness, 'the old, improvised, barn-like cinema theatres had almost disappeared from the centres of the two capitals. In their place there rose up huge cinema palaces, which were specially built for the screen and as carefully designed as if they could actually anticipate the public's taste in such matters.'[42]

The distinction between the city-centre cinemas and those in the outer city areas also became a regulator of the repertoire. As early as 1907 the theatre critic Lyubov Gurevich drew attention to the difference between cinemas 'intended for the intelligent classes', and 'the whole net of small cinemas serving the general public, which were scattered throughout the streets and alleys of the outer city districts'. According to Gurevich, the latter were 'particularly interesting as far as their selection of pictures was concerned'. They showed sentimental melodramas and, generally speaking, 'anything with a touching or moving content'.[43] At the beginning of 1909 another observer, a reviewer for the newspaper *Life* writing under the pen-name *Flanyor* [Flâneur], provided a more detailed picture of the specific repertoires of the central and outer city cinemas. Audiences outside the centre preferred 'predominantly realistic films, whether dramatic or comic; they didn't like anything to do with fairy tales, witches, magical transformations, etc.'. Newsreels, on the other hand, were widely shown. The cinema owners of the Zamoskvoretsky district, for example, just south of the river Moskva, 'earned masses of money by showing pictures of the Moscow floods. Every viewer was flattered by seeing pictures of his own daily life (no matter how dull) on the screen.'[44] The same author reported the details of the repertoires of the central Moscow luxury cinemas: 'If it's a drama, then it's got to be a particularly bloody one. If it's a comic picture, it's caricatured to the nth degree. The public enjoys the depiction of horrors, catastrophes, and of course anything even remotely to do with sex.'[45]

Neya Zorkaya has pointed out that passage in Maria Beketova's memoirs where she describes Alexander Blok's strolls around Petersburg:

> Alexander Alexandrovich didn't like smart luxury cinemas with their well-scrubbed clientèle. He couldn't stand places like the Parisiana or the Soleil for the same reasons that he hated Nevsky and Morskoi Avenues: they were full of that same class of well-fed bourgeois, gilded youth, prosperous engineers and aristocrats whom he detested and whom he called the 'dregs of society' . . . He loved to get to some out-of-the-way place in the Petersburg district or English Avenue (not far from his flat), where the audience consisted of all sorts of people who were far from being either smart or well-fed – most of them were naively impressionable – and where he could surrender himself to the cinema with his own form of childish curiosity and delight.[46]

Such behaviour should certainly not be thought eccentric: among Russian intellectuals of the 1910s it was a matter of good taste to prefer the outer city districts to the centre. It was the reverse of snobbery: for Blok, going to films or attending circus wrestling meant getting oneself involved with what he believed to be the 'real Russia'. Sharing the 'naive' unmediated reactions of working-class audiences to the equally unsophisticated stories they saw on the screen was Blok's way of establishing contact with 'the people'.

There was also movement in the opposite direction. The real, flesh and blood audiences of the outer city cinemas (as opposed to the idealised 'folk audiences' beloved of democratically minded intellectuals) were also attracted to the luxury film theatres of the city centre. We can reconstruct the social stratification of the internal space of the central theatres by studying the differentially priced seating layout (see 31–3): it is clear that the less well-off public did visit them. Most probably, the inhabitants of the outer city districts used to go to their local cinemas during the week, whereas the luxury theatres of Nevsky Avenue in St Petersburg, or Arbat Street in Moscow, served more for their Sunday evening entertainment. Shortly after 1917, when most social barriers collapsed, the central theatres were flooded by working-class cinemagoers. Ignatov observed this 'class mingling' in 1919:

It was easier to observe these groups when they took themselves to different establishments – the one to the fringes of town, the other to explore the enticing prospects of the centre – than when they come together and mingle in one establishment. This mingling has become particularly noticeable lately, and there can hardly be a single cinema where the 'outer city' people do not heavily outnumber the 'central' group.[47]

Still, for all the relativity of this division in terms of attendance, the opposition of periphery to centre was an important component of reception. This may be confirmed by considering the experience of the provinces; provincial cinemas were always situated in the centre of town. A 1914 article in a Moscow cinema magazine described a typical provincial scene:

On the main square, right opposite the town hall, a garland of fairy lights shines out around the façade of the Magic electric theatre. A dozen or so steps away, on the other side of the street, nestles the Express 'theatre of illusions'. Around the corner of the next block we glimpse the suffused light from two large lanterns: this is the third cinema, the Empire. And finally, at the very end of the main street, where the bazaar begins, there is the Giant, in its own bright pool of light. This is a common sight in any small provincial town. For a population of twenty-five or thirty thousand there are at least four electric theatres, which for some reason or other are all grouped close together on the one main street.[48]

Nevertheless, the opposition of centre and periphery, which was initially a feature of the two capital cities, was not long in appearing in the provincial cinemas of Russia, even in places which hardly deserved to be called towns. There only needed to be two cinemas – usually named after famous metropolitan theatres – for one of them to be regarded by the inhabitants as 'central', and the other as 'outer'. Count Sergei Volkonsky, who in 1917 lived for a while in the Cossack village of Uryupino, later recalled:

> When I asked my landlord (the village sexton) which cinema (or 'illusion', as it was called there) was the better, the Artistic or the Modern, he replied that they were both good, but that there was no comparison between the kind of people they attracted: 'You just ought to see the people who go to the Artistic! It's all bowler hats and feather boas, bowler hats and feather boas . . .'[49]

THE CONCEPT OF THE CITY-CENTRE LUXURY CINEMA

The new generation cinema theatres unexpectedly acquired some rudimentary features whose sole function was to stress the fact that they were genetically related to the auditorium of the stage theatre. The transition from the long to the square auditorium could be explained as a rational adaptation to circumstances: the limited power of the projector beam made it impossible to lengthen the space indefinitely, and therefore to increase the size of the auditorium it had to be widened. This was what ultimately brought cinema proprietors to the optimal, egg-shaped, layout of the auditorium.[50] But the introduction of a curtain and something bearing a distant resemblance to a theatre stage was certainly part of a décor policy that was dictated by the reception shift discussed above. As Yevgeni Maurin observed in his guidebook for cinema organisers:

> Strictly speaking, of course, the curtain is not necessary for the cinema itself; it is there for the viewer, who instinctively associates the beginning of a theatrical performance with the raising of the curtain dividing him from the stage. The curtain conveys a feeling of completeness, of wholeness: when lowered, it intrigues, and teases the imagination. So, as a concession to the psychology of the average viewer and all his habits, the curtain – we repeat – is essential, and this must never be forgotten.[51]

It is characteristic that this dictum was based on the 'psychology of the average viewer' of 1916. It was only after the reception shift that the 'feeling of completeness, of wholeness' became part of the viewer's psychology. Previously there had been no need to delineate any kind of wholeness because films were shown in an unbroken, continuous sequence. Besides, the viewer of the earlier 'fairground period' responded to the technological nakedness of the performance. Most certainly, early viewers would have objected to the presence of a curtain. Contemporary reports and later reminiscences record that there was usually at least one curious spectator who, once the show was over, approached the projector or the screen in order to examine it. For him the screen was part of the 'technical marvel', no less (if no more) intriguing than the projector itself: 'Is it transparent?' 'Is there someone hidden behind it?' The usual reaction of this incredulous spectator was to touch the screen with his fingers. Once the 'fairground period' was over, the naked screen seemed to start getting on people's nerves. In 1913 the *The Cinema Courier* [Kino-Kuryer] grudgingly mentioned 'that . . . framed, white screen, which becomes an ugly white eyesore as soon as the auditorium is fully illuminated'.[52] Possibly, the 'aesthetics of involvement' that came to replace the 'aesthetics of astonishment' were somewhat undermined by the flat surface that preceded and followed the three-dimensional 'images of life'. Be that as it may, the naked screen came to be regarded as something almost indecent, something that needed to be covered up by a curtain. The curtain came as a part of the general drive of the 1910s to drape the entire cinematic apparatus, to give it new 'cultured' names, to hide away the projector, to kill the flicker, to suppress any suggestion of technology. This was a process of readjusting film reception to more habitual cultural forms.

The same process of cultural mimicry was responsible for the appearance under the screen of a rudimentary projecting stage. On rare occasions divertissements were performed on it (although divertissements were not a characteristic feature of Russian cinema history), but usually this stage remained empty. In 1917 the poet and artist Pavel Nilus, who had decided to come out in favour of the democratisation of cinema, launched a particularly strong attack on this accessory:

> The stage on which the screen stands, and the action within its frame, remind one of the theatre, but the stage is only a residual feature, which has got to wither away; the cinema stage will be replaced by a flat, white, modern wall. A cinema with a stage is much like a car designed to look – quite needlessly – like a horse-drawn carriage; and we can see that this shape is now being replaced by other, more appropriate, designs.[53]

However, in urging that cinemas should be rebuilt in the Constructivist spirit of the future, Nilus had apparently forgotten that a 'flat white wall' in place of a screen had been a universal attribute of the earlier, improvised cinemas of the sciolistic period; this demonstrates just how firmly the concept of 'cinema' had fused in the mind of the recipient with the concept of the luxury interior.

Although the central cinemas of the 1910s took the theatre as their architectural model, it is not surprising that they surpassed it in richness of décor. 'Excess' is the key word for cinema architecture of the 1910s. With all the 'archaisms' typical of film palaces, architectural and technical devices were sometimes used in order to imply that this was the style of the future.

Contemporaries, for example, recalled the starry heavens, which, as in a planetarium, appeared on the ceiling in several cinemas when the lights went down. According to V. Puce, the main cinema in Riga, the Palladium, had one of these ceilings.[54] The Parisiana, the most comfortable cinema on Nevsky Avenue, with an auditorium more than thirty-five feet long, had a vast ceiling which could be automatically opened out down the middle (presumably like a double drawbridge). A cinema like this is shown in Bertolucci's film *La luna* (Italy, 1979) and in Ettore Scola's *Splendor* (Italy/USA, 1989).

The peculiar mixture of elements referring both to the past and the future made Russian picture palaces look like a late version of architectural *art nouveau*. It was a style that could also be seen in the architecture of international exhibitions.

What was the fate of these luxury film palaces after October 1917? In the archives of Goskino [State Film Committee] a mandate is preserved authorising the remaking of the Amur cinema into a pan-Anarchist club.[55] An idea of what happened to this cinema can be gleaned from a small detail found in a 1927 poem by Ilya Selvinsky (written long after the Anarchist party was officially disbanded) where the author describes an Anarchist band sallying forth:

The honey-cake troika, daubed in red.
Pell-mell down the pavement, bells a-tinkle.
The lads with breeches from cinema curtains.
A blue fox fur round the driver's neck.[56]

It must, however, be admitted that the city-centre luxury cinema served the public in ways whose passing can only be regretted. In 1913 the programmes of the Première Theatre on Nevsky Avenue contained the following announcement: 'Would members of the public wishing to have the programme delivered, kindly leave their addresses at the cinema box office.' Some cinemas, for example, the Comic, also on Nevsky Avenue, stated in their programmes: 'We can give performances in your home. Special rates available.'

THE SOCIAL TOPOLOGY OF THE AUDITORIUM

In the 1910s there was a joke about how to tell the expensive areas in the cinema from the inexpensive and the very cheap seats: pick your way through the button-holes, and wade through the discarded programme area until you hear seed-husks crunching under your feet.[57] The social stratification of the auditorium, which today is imperceptible – except possibly in segregation by age-group – was so clear in those days that for many it was itself a sight worth seeing. It is characteristic that Fyodor Sologub, in his poem 'In the Cinema' (1915), described this scene without even so much as mentioning the film:

Down in the long, giraffe-necked hall
A sudden break annoys the fans.
Seat threes call out and bang and shout.
Seat twos just laugh at all the fuss.
While seat ones sit and quietly wait.[58]

Apparently naive and simplistic, this poem is remarkable. It was one of Sologub's experiments in introducing to Russian literature short cameo-like oriental forms (borrowed from Persian and Japanese poetry). Like Japanese 'haiku', the poem contains a covert, unstated metaphor. The 'seat threes', 'seat twos' and 'seat ones' recall the social stratification of the railway train with its first-class, second-class and third-class carriages – a traditional theme of Russian literature of the late nineteenth to early twentieth century (and also of Victorian art in England). To be more specific, the allusion must have been to Alexander Blok's famous lines, where the social stratification of the travelling public is conveyed by the colour coding then used in Russia:

Another line of carriages
Clangs and clatters along;
The yellows and blues are silent;
In the greens there are tears and song.[59]

In terms of film reception, Sologub's poem is based on a pivotal trope of early film literature: cinema as a runaway train with a 'chaos of tangled panoramas'[60] sliding past its windows; film as a celluloid railway rushing its story to the predetermined end; cinema and Lumière's train; and, finally, the cinema auditorium as a place where different social groups might provisionally co-exist, or – to use a later term invented by Michel Foucault – a kind of 'heterotopia', a space for everyone. For, as Lynne Kirby writes in her research on trains in early films:

Both the train and the cinema are heterotopic siblings of the railway station, where the condensation of urban life, as well as the juxtaposition of all social types entering and leaving, give the station an eclectic and undefinable character with respect to class and sex.[61]

And still, eclectic as it was, this microcosm of urban life was organised according to its own social rules.

The first cinemas (1904–6) made do with just two price ranges. In Rosenwald's Thaumatograph, for example, which seated sixty viewers, 'the expensive seats were in the first row, right in front of the screen. Behind them there was standing room which cost fifteen kopecks.'[62] As the auditorium expanded, the standing area disappeared, and a price differential was applied to the seats. In small theatres the front rows were considered the best; in the 'long auditorium' period, preferences changed. According to Maurin:

from the back seats of a very long auditorium the image on the screen will seem blurred (due to the distance the projector beam has to travel), and consequently the most expensive seats will be those in the middle, with the ones nearer the front and the back getting progressively cheaper.[63]

In the 1910s a campaign against cinema was launched by eye specialists. Several newspapers, quoting qualified opticians, spread the story that cinema would cause 'cinematophthalmia', a disease that would ruin the eysight of a whole generation of viewers and possibly induce blindness among regular cinemagoers.[64] It takes a specialist to confirm or deny the medical basis for this assumption; as to the wave of public apprehension it caused, it looks like another case of 'technophobia', an inevitable stage in the history of reception of technical inventions.[65]

The cinema owners' reaction (which was just as arbitrary as the rumour of 'cinema blindness') was to assert that the viewer's sight was only affected if he or she sat in the first few rows; further back, in the more expensive seats, there was really no problem.

It was about this time that the system whereby the seats became more expensive the further they were from the screen (which still survives today) was established. Those who could afford to pay more made do with the back seats, which, perhaps, did not contradict the 'proxemic' instinct of the better-off, more reserved viewer, who sought refuge in anonymity and kept his internal distance from the events on the screen.

Although the above assumption may be true with regard to the psychology of the urban middle classes, it certainly was not confirmed by the behaviour of a section of the public who were quite prosperous but not burdened with middle-class inhibitions or intellectual habits: the merchant class. Ya. A. Zhdanov, who for many years toured the cinemas of Russia with a group of 'film-reciters' [kinodeklamatory], recalled that merchants behaved in the cinema just as if they were at home: 'they used to bring their own food in with them, and something to drink too. Whole families would occupy the front rows, and it was utterly impossible to persuade them that they could see better from further back.'[66]

The topography of seat prices became extremely complex in the luxury-cinema period. To the horizontal scale was added a vertical scale for the two-tiered auditoria. Since cinema at that time took theatre for its model, the upper tier (in the shape of a small amphitheatre with a raked gallery) corresponded to the traditional theatre gallery (the 'gods') with seats at very reasonable prices. Even today cinemagoers feel that there is something slightly inferior about the balcony, although it gives, in fact, a very good view of the screen. So that the 'select' public would not have to mix with the 'common people', the gallery and the stalls were sometimes provided with separate exits, their own foyer and vestibule. This allowed for the creation of two isolated viewing areas for the one screen. But, even in the stalls, the seat prices were widely differentiated. The general area, from the second to the fourth sections, was called 'the chairs' [stul'ya] with prices varying – according to a 1914 list – from 35 to 75 kopecks. The front area was called 'the armchairs' [kresla], and seats there cost a rouble. A box for four at the Artistic (on Nevsky Avenue) cost 4 roubles; a ticket for a single seat in a box cost one rouble. In the Tivoli (also on Nevsky Avenue) a box could be taken for just two or three people.

The reason why boxes were so expensive was their erotically loaded seclusion; this cultural connotation (confirmed by what often really happened in cinema boxes of the 1910s) was inherited from the nineteenth-century theatre ('a mysterious beauty in the box'). This is what some filmgoers alluded to when they wondered with feigned surprise why the prices should be so high when the view of the screen was so poor.[67] And poor it was indeed: boxes were usually situated along the sides and sometimes quite close to the screen, which made the screen image look almost anamorphic. The poet Mikhail Kuzmin, after he went to see *Das Kabinett des Doktor Caligari* [The Cabinet of Dr Caligari, 1919], made the following note in his diary: 'We were ushered into a box upstairs; everything was distorted, but the film looked even better from this "El Greco" perspective.'[68]

In the larger cinemas (like the Saturn in Petersburg), which had two or three auditoria with a different programme in each, it was cheaper to buy one ticket for all the auditoria than for each one separately. Unused tickets for the three auditoria were valid for seven days.

All cinemas offered children and students a fifty per cent reduction.

THE IMAGE OF THE CINEMA PUBLIC

The acute sociological insight that characterised the Russian press at the beginning of the twentieth century does not help us to form a clear picture of the Russian cinemagoing public. Emilie Altenloh's book *Towards a Sociology of Cinema: the Cinema Business and the Social Strata of Cinema-Goers*,[69] published in Germany in 1914, was immediately noted and sympathetically reviewed in the periodical *Cine-Phono*,[70] but did not lead to any comparable analysis in Russian writing on cinema. As Ignatov found himself forced to admit: 'The cinemagoing public is as obscure and incomprehensible as the history of the Midianites, and is extremely diverse.'[71] The 'diversity' of the audience was one of the key concepts in writings on film. As early as 1907 it had become standard practice to present a breakdown of the audience by social class, followed by the all-embracing 'everybody'. 'The cinema has its own special public, those who love its crowded auditoria' – wrote Alexander Koiransky in 1907 – 'but it's not just the regulars, everyone – absolutely everyone – goes to the cinema.'[72] At the very beginning of 1912 A. Serafimovich laid emphasis on the key word:

If you look into the auditorium the composition of the audience will amaze you. Everyone is there – students and policemen, writers and prostitutes, officers and girl students, all kinds of bearded and bespectacled intellectuals, workers, shop assistants, tradesmen, society ladies, dressmakers, civil servants – in a word: everyone.[73]

Cinema at the beginning of the century, unlike both theatre, which attracted a 'better' public, and places of 'popular' entertainment, was valued for the way it appealed to a broad social spectrum. But vertical cross-sections of the cinemagoing public were not supported by any statistics and, generally speaking, rarely pretended to be scientific. We ought to see such statements only as very broad social generalisations. Essayists writing about cinema at that time were enamoured of the image of the cinema audience as a microcosm of Russian urban society as a whole, and frequently saw the cinema auditorium as anticipating the social changes they hoped for. K. and O. Kovalsky, for instance, who were literary essayists of leftist persuasions, clearly alluded in that same year of 1912 to the role played by cinema – in their opinion – as a prototype for the harmonious society of the future:

You can come across just about everybody in the foyer: the elderly editor of a solid progressive paper, a lady of society, a university tutor, a nanny with the children of a respectable family, a schoolboy, a merchant from the provinces, a typesetter, a street urchin, an officer cadet, a prostitute. It is only on the neutral and undemanding territory of the cinema that the most varied levels of society can meet, all delighting together in the vision of a storm-tossed ocean or laughing at the escapades of Glupyshkin and Max Linder. An invisible exchange of heartfelt emotions takes place and all social and economic inequalities are forgotten.[74]

It was also suggested that cinema preserved the mood of unity that had prevailed in Russian society at the time of the 1905 revolution.[75] But chronologically (and genetically), it was an article on cinema by Andrei Bely in 1907 that set the tone.[76] This article was part of the continuing polemical debate between the Moscow and Petersburg groups of Symbolist poets and was levelled at the St Petersburg Symbolists' idea of the Utopian society of the future. According to the Petersburg poets, the basis for this society lay in Russian *sobornost* (an untranslatable archaism suggesting something between togetherness and ecumenicity), and they held that this spirit was attainable through the 'mystical' theatre. In his article the Moscow Symbolist Bely used the image of the cinema public as an example of true and authentic unity: a down-to-earth *sobornost*, as opposed to what he thought to be the stilted theories of the Petersburg Symbolists:[77]

The cinema is a club. People come together here to undergo a moral experience, to travel to America, to learn about tobacco farming and the stupidity of policemen, to sigh over the *midinette* who has to sell her body.

Absolutely everyone comes here to meet their friends: aristocrats and democrats, soldiers, students, workers, schoolgirls, poets and prostitutes.[78]

It was Bely's article that set the tone for treating cinema as a kind of 'Utopia next door'. This tone, as well as the formula he used in order to substantiate his idea ('everyone and everything: this person and that; this thing and that'), was taken up, with very few changes, in article after article.

CINEMA AND THE PROSTITUTE

Let us take a closer look at these passages portraying cinema audiences. The collective, or, more precisely, the enumerative, image of the cinemagoing public, while varying from author to author, never omits to mention the prostitute; usually she brings up the rear in the social groups represented. In his poem 'A Living Photograph' [Zhivaya fotografiya] Georgi Chulkov concludes a picture in verse of the social structure of the cinema audience with a 'close-up' of this figure:

Just look at the people bewitched by the scene:
The lad from the shop with his mouth open wide,
The corsetted lady fit to explode,
The sullen tart staring, moist-eyed, at the screen.[79]

What lay behind this recurrent metonym: the prostitute in the cinema? In 1913 an article by S. Lyubosh appeared in *The Cinematograph Herald* where these ladies' love of cinema was explained by the severity of the Petersburg winter:

After sauntering professionally for hours up and down the Nevsky or some other street it is so nice to be able to snatch a sandwich or a cake at Kvissisan's and to sit in the warmth of a cinema and follow the extraordinarily moving story of an elegant Parisian *cocotte* or some jilted baroness.[80]

However, the circumstances of everyday life are hardly sufficient to explain the persistence of that repetitive image. It seems that the image stands for the cinema public as a whole rather than for just a part of it. The figure of the prostitute, by comparison with the other members of the audience, seems to express a higher collectivity; she represents, as it were, the image of the whole audience in the same way as this image stands for society as a whole. The semantics of the word 'everyone', which is central to the formula we are examining, fits equally the image of the audience and the image of the prostitute. This is why in some texts the list of characters is reduced to this metonymic minimum. Thus Alexander Kugel, describing a cinema performance in 1913, used only a single reference: 'Beside me sat a young person with – I thought – slightly rouged cheeks. Probably some "priestess of love". Her eyes were moist. She had brought her purifying sacrifice to the altar of cinema.'[81]

The image of the prostitute seems to be as immanently connected with film reception as that of Lumière's train. As far as cinema in Russia is concerned, the figure of the 'priestess of love with moist eyes' is a part of its myth of origin. The point is that the way film was received in Russian culture differed somewhat from the way it was received in the country where it was invented. The Lumières' first performances were set up as scientific demonstrations, but in Russia the public was introduced to cinema in rather disreputable circumstances. It is well known that the first large-scale acquaintance with cinema took place at Charles Aumont's *café-chantant* on tour at the Nizhny Novgorod All-Russian Exhibition in 1896. Aumont's *Théâtre-concert Parisien* was reputed to be a brothel. From the very beginning, cinema and prostitution were perceived, both by visitors to the café and by visitors to the first cinema performances, as being closely related. Russian literature was amazingly quick to pick up this perception. Two weeks after visiting the cinema performance at the Nizhny Novgorod Exhibition on 30 June or 1 July 1896, and after two reports in the local and Odessa press, Maxim Gorky published his short story 'Revenge' in no. 185 of the *Nizhny Novgorod Newsletter* on 7 July. The story featured the Lumières' film, *Baby's Breakfast*, and was based on two seemingly unconnected events, which occurred at about the same time and place. Two days after Gorky had seen the Lumières' film at the exhibition, Lily d'Artaud, one of the 'chorus girls' at the café, tried to commit suicide. From an article Gorky wrote before the Lily d'Artaud incident, and which appeared in the *Nizhny Novgorod Newsletter* on 4 July, we learn that Aumont's 'show-girls' were supposed to go in to the auditorium and watch the films together with the guests of the establishment. In this article Gorky touched on what was to be the basis of his story 'Revenge' – the contrast between what was shown on the screen and the fate of those 'victims of social mores' among the girls of the *café-chantant*:

> A young married couple and their bouncing baby are having breakfast. They are both so happy and the baby is so amusing; it creates a lovely, warm, impression. But isn't this picture of domestic bliss out of place at Aumont's? Another picture: happy, laughing, working girls are streaming out of the factory gates and into the street. This is also out of place. What is the point in reminding the people here that there can be such a thing as a decent, hard-working life? The very best it can do is to cause a stab of pain in the heart of a woman who sells her kisses for money. That's all.[82]

It may be noted in passing that the journal *The New Word*, which posed these rhetorical questions in its provincial press section without mentioning Gorky's name, offered its own explanation of why Aumont needed the cinema: 'without it many respected guests at the exhibition might have found it distinctly awkward to pay a visit to Aumont's.'[83]

In 'Revenge' Gorky – as if re-establishing the missing connection between the showing of the film and the suicide of Lily d'Artaud – chose as his theme the spiritual drama of the prostitute who takes a new look at her life as a result of the impression the Lumières' picture made on her:

> 'I liked one picture in particular. It's about a young couple, a husband and wife ... they're so, well, healthy and attractive, you know ... They're having breakfast and feeding the baby – such a sweet little thing! He's eating and pulling faces ... Oh, it's so lovely! You can't take your eyes off the picture, it's so full of meaning ... In this place, you know, well ... it really makes you think.' She stopped, lost for words, and drummed her fingers impatiently on the table. He noticed that her eyes had become somehow deeper, and clearer ... It aroused his curiosity.
>
> 'Why do you like this picture in particular?', he asked. 'It's family life!', she exclaimed, 'I am a woman, you know!'[84]

Metonymic in relation to the social composition of the audience, the image of the prostitute cinemagoer was not immune to a metaphorical reading. In 1917 one of the contributors to *The Cinema Journal* devoted a whole article to prostitution as a metaphor not just for the cinema audience but for cinema as an art form:

> The spectator goes to the cinema with the same cynicism with which he goes to a prostitute. He knows that what he is about to see is just a pantomime, a comedy, nothing more than that. He knows that the prostitute's caresses are no more than the studied gestures of a puppet; but still he goes to her, and he goes to her because he has to have this pantomime.[85]

The cheap luxury, the emotional repetitiveness, the sense of entering a perverse and criminal world, of being totally immersed in the life of the city, and finally the egalitarianism of the street – these are the qualities that turned the cinema and the brothel into another pair of 'heterotopic siblings'.

As one reads in Miriam Hansen's recent book on spectatorship in American silent film, cinema as prostitution appears among the international tropes of film reception (particularly prominent in early German discourse on cinema). This metaphorical association, according to Hansen, was a by-product of the rapid enlargement of the public sphere brought about by the new medium: 'The cinema, as an art form that thrives at intimate commerce with the urban masses, promising happiness to everyone but faithful to no one, could only be troped as a prostitute.'[86]

Indeed, cinema was often seen as an enormous machine reworking the private into the public. A student song rhymed 'Pathé' and 'décolleté'. This is what Alexander Kugel wrote in 1913: 'There is something naked, something shamelessly physiological in the mere fact that cinema removes walls and shows "life as it is" in its minute details: in bedrooms, in drawing rooms.'[87] This dictum shows that cinema would not have been forgiven even if all its films had been strictly decent, and all the prostitutes kept away from its audiences. It was not so much films or audiences as the very nature of cinematic discourse that predicated intrusion, immodesty and the violation of privacy.

'GOING TO THE PICTURES': THE EVERYDAY BEHAVIOUR OF THE CINEMAGOER

A key factor in the reception of early cinema was that it could offer a casual, i.e. impromptu, experience. Researchers have already discussed why Alexander Blok, from 1904 onwards, preferred the cinema: it was because one could go at a moment's notice and select one's film at random.[88] Freedom from the usual ritual associated with visits to the theatre (evenings only, the bother of getting tickets, dressing up, the burden of socialising during the intervals) very soon became a recognised feature of the poetics of the cinema performance. The actor Konstantin Varlamov, joining those praising cinema as 'the most democratic form of entertainment',[89] put it like this: 'If, for instance, I am invited to the theatre, I think, "Can I really be bothered? I've got to dress up, put on a dinner jacket, collar and tie, studs and cuff-links. I'd rather go to the cinema, just as I am."'[90] The cinema proprietors took advantage of this and the programmes – even of large cinemas equipped with cloakrooms – noted that 'Ladies are most respectfully requested to remove their hats; outer garments need not be removed'.[91] Another important feature of the early stylistics of cinema performance was the rule which allowed 'the public to come into the theatre at any time during the performance and to sit there as long as they liked'.[92] This system did not last long in Russia – only until the programme ceased to consist of several separate short pictures. In Germany the tradition of the open performance lasted longer, and even in the mid-1920s one commentator, comparing the earliest cinemas with the changes that had taken place by his day, observed: 'Only one custom has survived in cinema till today: everyone can come and go at any time, whether in the middle of the performance, at the beginning or at the end.'[93] In America and Britain continuous performances lasted until well after the Second World War.

Continuous performance, however, had considerable importance for the way cinema was perceived. First, it gave the act of cinemagoing an aura of improvisation, of adventure, of illicit and abrupt departure from daily routine. In his diary Blok comments, 'I was on my way to visit someone but ended up at the cinema.' One could probably find many similar remarks in other diaries of the time. Second, the early viewer found himself in a specific situation vis-à-vis the object perceived. In the situation familiar to us, when the beginning of the film is synchronous with our appearance in the auditorium, we experience the film as an 'object for us'. A psychological dependence is established between the text and its recipient. The film imperceptibly becomes the regulator of the viewer's behaviour, compelling him to appear at the beginning and to leave at the end. The behaviour of the text and the behaviour of the recipient are mutually conditioned.

The casual continuous programme did not assume that the object and subject of perception were mutually determined. In the first place, unfixed entry into the auditorium redefined the concepts of the beginning and the end of the film. Nowadays coming late to a performance means that we get an incomplete impression of the film; just as leaving before the end of a performance lays the blame for incompleteness on the film itself. For visitors to the early cinema the situation was quite different: 'You didn't have to rush to catch the beginning of the film; the beginning was wherever you happened to come in.'[94] In other words film performance was perceived as continuous self-propelled action. It was to be received, by definition, in fragmentary fashion and in doses determined by the recipient himself. It can be said that, although the full extent of the film was the same for the audience as a whole, each viewer set his own beginning and end.

The American author Stanley Cavell, on the basis of his own experience as a cinemagoer, describes the difference between the two modes of performance as follows:

> When moviegoing was casual and we entered at no matter what point in the proceedings (during the news or short subject or somewhere in the feature – enjoying the recognition, later, of the return of the exact moment at which one entered, and from then on feeling free to decide when to leave, or whether to see the familiar part through again), we took our fantasies and companions and anonymity inside and left with them intact. Now that there is an audience, a claim is made upon my privacy; so it matters to me that our responses to the film are not really shared.[95]

Furthermore, casual entry into the auditorium led to a minimum of interdependence between the film and the viewer. For anyone dropping casually into the cinema the film became one of those events one comes across by chance. The film appeared as 'text in itself' rather than as 'text for me', and its impromptu nature and autarchy placed it among the ranks of natural phenomena. For the Russian observer in the early twentieth century it was, first and foremost, the spontaneously developing element of the modern city. The Symbolist imagination welcomed the cinema exactly for this role as Andrei Bely's article 'The City' [Gorod][96] or Maximilian Voloshin's 'Thoughts on the Theatre'[97] clearly show. Entering a cinema in the age of Symbolism, one comes into contact not with the film and not even with cinema but with the city, condensed into cinematographic text. For Blok this contact was in the nature of a game in which the choice of film, the choice of cinema and even the actual decision whether or not to go to the cinema, was not made by the individual but dictated by the dominating spontaneity of city life. A well-known passage in a letter to E.P. Ivanov in 1904 refers to this level of reception:

Yesterday I set off for your place. I suddenly saw that cinema on Liteinaya Street. I went in and watched the moving pictures for about an hour. I sensed a kind of symbolism in it all, but nevertheless I resolved to overcome all the obstacles lying in wait for me on my way to Nikolayevskaya Street. This is no joke. There is a kind of city mystery here . . . hidden ambushes . . . The thing to do is to trick yourself into slipping past them. Oh, the city. . . .[98]

In Paris, where the culture of 'flânerie' was brought to a fine art, Jacques Vache in 1919 taught André Breton the proper way to go to the cinema. In order to achieve the maximum intensity of impression one should go into a cinema 'whatever they are showing, at any point in the performance, and dash off to another one at the first sign of boredom . . . and so on *ad infinitum*'.[99] Breton mastered this technique and was staggered by the effect of arbitrarily clashing images and actions. Richard Abel suggests that this was how Breton first experienced what he later called 'the surreal'.[100]

By the beginning of the 1910s the poetics of the Russian cinema performance had begun to undergo a transformation – a development not unnoticed by the cinema press. Gradually, beginning with the city-centre cinemas, the mode of performance changed. In Russia, as everywhere else in Europe, the style of the performance came to reflect the nature of the repertoire. The fashion for full-length pictures did not of itself threaten casual entry to the cinema; programmes not only gave the contents of multi-reel films but also indicated what occurred in each reel. Things were more difficult with screen adaptations of best-selling novels. In these cases the linearity of reception was more firmly grounded in the audience's expectations; the public had the right to demand a sequential repetition of the literary experience.

A key event in this process was the screen version of Henryk Sienkiewicz's novel *Quo Vadis?* (dir. Enrico Guazzoni, Italy, 1912). The lavish scale of this production affected the distribution procedure and the style in which it was presented. In Berlin the Cines company opened a special cinema for the première of *Quo Vadis?* – Georges Sadoul claims that it was managed by the writer Hanns Ewers.[101] There is an article by a writer who was present at the première. In it the author noted with surprise that the invitation ticket stated the time the film was to start and also requested that the audience should 'appear in evening dress [*Gesellschaftstoilette*]'.[102] The advance publicity put out by Russian cinemas showing *Quo Vadis?* noted the length of the performance (two-and-a-half hours with intervals between the parts), but did not say at what time it was due to start. Tension emerged between the custom of impromptu visits to the cinema and the tendency of the new repertoire to impose more rigid habits on the public. An open letter to film-makers from a group of cinema proprietors complained that pictures were becoming 'unnaturally long': 'People who turn up after the performance has started are frequently obliged to wait an unusually long time for it to end; this is extremely tiring and naturally tends to put them off the cinema'.[103]

An attempt to smooth out this problem by creating something like a 'sliding timetable' of performances was made by the Petersburg Saturn cinema on Nevsky Avenue, which ran three adjacent auditoria. Here the publicity announcing *Quo Vadis?* carried a special announcement: 'In order to spare the public the inconvenience of waiting, the picture will be shown in its entirety in two auditoria simultaneously.'[104]

The psychological climate surrounding 'going to the cinema' also changed. In 1912 Arkadi Bukhov attempted to portray the coarseness of the cinema public in an article in verse:

Fragments flying on the screen,
Glass and plates in smithereens.
In the darkness belly laughter,
High-pitched squeals and frenzied screams.[105]

But just three years later, in 1915, the same author finds signs of a new code of behaviour among the cinema public.

The kind of cinemagoer who chews seeds and guffaws at dramatic moments is already dying out. You now get the same sort of people who flock to the theatre. The public is now evolving its own tastes, even beginning to have its favourite actors and actresses . . . The public, which at first only dropped in to the cinema in passing and was attracted by the announcement on the posters that you did not have to take off your galoshes and outer garments, is now beginning to see serial pictures and going two or even three evenings to see the same story over and over again . . . [106]

Or, as one reviewer summed it up, 'people no longer say they "drop in" to the cinema; they "go to" the cinema, or "visit" the cinema, as they would the theatre.'[107]

Meanwhile, although the situation had actually changed, with cinema now occupying its own legitimate slot in the timetable of everyday life, this had little effect on the style of 'going to the cinema'. As before, the basic feature remained a carefully preserved spontaneity. It became evident during the 1910s that freedom from the 'cloakroom routine' was itself ritualistic in character. Ignatov drew attention to this in 1919:

the public, given mankind's inherent mental conservatism, is still con-vinced that going to the cinema is not a time-consuming business, that there are no fixed times for the start of the performance, and that the film begins whenever it happens to come in. It hasn't been like that for some time, but nevertheless the public still continues to maintain that for busy people cinema has the inestimable advantage over theatre that it does not oblige one to turn up at any definite time and that it allows the audience, not the author, or the director, or the theatre administration, to fix the start of the performance.[108]

Observers inclined to self-analysis have detected an element of hypocrisy in the psychology of the cinemagoer. The same Ignatov singled out among the cinema public a large group of 'embarrassed' spectators: 'They are embarrassed and ashamed of being in the cinema; they laugh at the tragic sufferings of the screen heroes and at their own visits to such seductive places.'[109] Although some reviewers were inclined to attribute this ambiguity to the specifics of the national culture, non-Russian sources attest to its universal nature. Erwin Panofsky remarked on it in the 1930s:

> Small wonder that the 'better classes', when they slowly began to venture into these early picture theaters, did so, not by way of seeking normal and possibly serious entertainment, but with that characteristic sensation of self-conscious condescension with which we may plunge, in gay company, into the folkloristic depths of Coney Island or a European kermis.[110]

N. Lopatin's response clothed a similar observation in the form of a newspaper aphorism: 'We love cinema so much and yet we try so hard to convince ourselves that we despise this cheap and vulgar form of entertainment'.[111]

The ostentatiously informal ritual that going to the cinema remained helped to reconcile this ambiguity. What were its indications? Contemporary observers singled out the following characteristics as typical of cinemagoers' behaviour: spontaneity, group behaviour, vacillation, a feigned lack of sophistication and a system of false motivation.

A studiously observed spontaneity reduced the danger of being suspected of 'cinemania'. In 1916 a reviewer, noting the difference between theatre and cinema crowds, underlined the conventions attaching to both:

> do not imagine that it is the circumstances of everyday life that cause the psychological difference between them. You very rarely just 'pop in' to the theatre or simply put your coat on and go. It's only young men and their girlfriends who do that. Usually you make lengthy preparations, perhaps several days ahead; you fix on a day, choose the play, see who's acting in it etc., but you often set off for the cinema without any previous desire or inclination, just at a moment's notice: 'Come on everyone, let's go to the cinema!'[112]

Going to the cinema in a group contributed to an atmosphere of collective responsibility and meant that the act itself involved no private preferences:

> And so the party sets out, often still not knowing which cinema they are going to. Carried along in the crowd they go past one brightly lit entrance, with its vividly coloured posters, past another, hesitate, pass on and finally turn off somewhere into a crowded foyer, just as they are, in fur hats and galoshes . . . [113]

This also illustrates the element of vacillation. We see the feigned lack of sophistication (which turns into its opposite) in the behaviour 'of those people who so despise the cinema yet who suddenly turn out to be mines of precise information about where the pictures are more interesting, or where the projector is not so jerky'.[114]

Addiction to the cinema could be concealed by a system of false motivation, by referring to the force of circumstances, as Pavel Tavrichanin related:

> The writer of these lines, on meeting acquaintances in the foyer, has often heard the following kind of semi-justification: 'Well, you know, we just dropped in by chance . . . Maria Ivanovna and I were sitting at home and just popped out for a breath of fresh air. We got a bit tired and she felt like a drink . . . Sometimes it's amusing, but mostly it's rubbish'.[115]

Going to the cinema could sometimes be explained away by the curiosity of an amateur sociologist: 'Come on, let's go! . . . Of course the pictures aren't interesting, but it's always curious to observe how fascinated the public is by trivialities!'[116] Or the pretext might be an interest in films as symptoms of the decadence of contemporary civilisation. We catch a glimpse of this theme in the course of the polemic between Kornei Chukovsky and Vladimir Rozanov in 1910. Chukovsky's well-known philippic against the cinema in his lecture *Nat Pinkerton and Contemporary Literature*[117] drew the following remark by Rozanov:

> How childish! You go to the cinema, you see that all the benches are full and you shout like Jeremiah: 'My people have perished, Jerusalem has perished . . .' Well, you were in the cinema and judging by your lecture you must have seen nearly the whole performance. So stop posing and pretending, and admit that you didn't go there just to get material for your lecture. It's more likely that the subject suggested itself to you later on. While you were sitting there looking at the pictures you probably thought: 'H'm, there's a whole literature here; I can make a lecture out of this!' But until this occurred to you you were probably enjoying the entertainment – not a lot, perhaps, but that's why you had gone there: to be entertained.[118]

This, briefly, was the psychological climate that determined the particular way the Russian audience received cinema in the first two decades of the twentieth century. It found its most precise formulation in L. Dobychin's novel, *The Town of N*, where the psychology of the family trip to the cinema is expressed in the words of a child narrator:

> We loved those dramas with their picturesque lakes; where the poor girl would leave her baby at the rich man's door. We loved those comic pictures too. 'How silly!', we would say from time to time . . . contentedly.[119]

In his book *Screening Out the Past*, Lary May tells us that American cinema proprietors boosted the prestige of their establishments by inviting to their premières representatives of the best families: the Roosevelts, Carnegies,

Vanderbilts, etc.[120] Russian cinema journals evidently had the same aim with their social columns: 'His Imperial Highness Grand Duke Dmitri Pavlovich, at present residing in Kiev, visited the Shantser cinema-theatre on 20th August and saw the whole performance.'[121] Writing about the exiled King Manuel of Portugal's enthusiasm for cinema, *The Cinematograph Herald* observed: 'The royal couple never miss a new film. The ex-King good-naturedly queues up at the box-office and buys two tickets for the cheap seats, just like any other member of the public.'[122]

In the early years of the century there formed in the mind of the cinemagoer an image of cinema as a space where the available and the forbidden commingled, where you could find yourself in the 'cheap seats' sitting next to the ex-King of Portugal. In other words the space of the cinema acquired characteristics that linked it to the fictional world depicted on the screen. The foyer was the focal point for these characteristics.

THE EVOLUTION OF THE FOYER

The film theatre foyer may seem an unimportant or peripheral detail of film history; the first auditoria had only a non-soundproof curtain or a door to separate them from the outside world. As the foyer developed, however, it became an important part of the viewers' experience of cinema, and extremely important for those who are interested in the history of film culture rather than just the history of films. The point is that the world of the foyer was mimetic of the world on the screen, and, as sometimes happens with the periphery in art, it would exaggerate the features it absorbed.

In Moscow the first foyer appeared quite early – at the end of 1904 at Rosenwald's cinema, in Solodovnikov's Arcade. The proprietor intended this cinema to attract the public by presenting a symbiosis of the arts; its posters proclaimed it to be a 'Cinema-Theatre and Exhibition of Post-Cards, Water Colours and Pictures.'[123] As well as the exhibition in the foyer Rosenwald displayed a 'curiosity', the armless artist Signor Bartoggi. Essentially such a foyer was an offshoot of the aesthetics of the fairground – as was for several years the seasonal alliance between the Salamonsky circus and the Circus cinema in Riga. In the period 1908 to 1913, the atmosphere of an ordinary 'non-luxury' foyer – a common waiting room – bore the imprint of the same sentimental idyll that observers found appealing in the repertoire of these cinemas, which consisted in the main of French – more rarely English – melodramas with happy endings:

> Along the walls there are rows of rather inoffensive automatic machines: a doll dancing on a five-kopek coin, a dwarf offering a bar of chocolate, a singing nightingale, a fortune-teller . . . The thin fingers of a dress-maker, or of a governess with her five-year-old charge, put a coin into the slot and a crowd of spectators gathers around. An urchin with shiny black boots and

darting eyes clumps up and down with a tray of sweets. The scene in this unpretentious foyer has an uncontrived domesticity, or reminds one of the saloon on a steamboat, where everyone feels closer and more at ease than, for example, in the theatre.[124]

The increase in film footage made exhibitors redefine their earlier conception of the performance: the length of the latter was now determined by the length of the 'feature film', and audiences had to get used to the novel idea that the performance began at a specific time. Cinema owners also had to face up to the need to provide somewhere for people to wait before they could be allowed into the auditorium. This chain of events led to changes in the architectural space of cinema, and by the mid-1910s the foyer had become an important part of the film theatre. A comfortable foyer now had to have tropical plants, preferably palms. Even in 1907 Koiransky had noted that bay trees had begun to appear in cinema foyers,[125] and in 1913 the programme of the Saturn in Petersburg announced the introduction of a whole winter garden in the cinema, with daily concerts by a string orchestra.

Let me take a brief 'flash-forward' into the 1920s before discussing this 'mimetic' aspect of the 'luxury foyer'. There was a clear tendency in the cinema architecture of the 1920s to return to the proto-Constructivist simplicity of the sciolistic period of pre-1908. 'Laying bare' the technology was central to both the first and the last periods of silent film culture (albeit for completely different reasons).

It is not surprising that among Constructivist artists at the end of the 1920s voices were heard demanding the abolition of the foyer. In 1928 the architect N. Ledovsky published in the journal *Cinema* a design for 'the cinema of the future' (which he wanted to consist of ten small auditoria) with the following commentary:

> The foyer is redundant and must die. Logical organisation and economic considerations – economy of both time and space – demand it. The consumer is tired of waiting for the beginning of the performance, no matter how successfully this waiting time may be reduced.[126]

A week later the same journal published a reply, 'What should an ideal cinema be like?', signed by Mikhail Boitler, the owner of one of the best cinemas in Moscow – Sergei Eisenstein used to go there every day at the beginning of the 1920s. Boitler ridiculed Ledovsky's crude utopia:

> 'The foyer' – Ledovsky lectures – 'exists for waiting; waiting is unpleasant and useless; abolish waiting and the foyer will disappear.' But Ledovsky doesn't know how to abolish the waiting. He thinks that you can do it by partitioning off several small auditoria where you can let the public in after ten minutes. There will be about ten such small auditoria . . . Professor Ledovsky's ideal is to have a very old and basic cinema hall with a pianist – ten orchestras are out of the question – with one projector and no

cloakroom, no toilets and no heated exit. That's what he wants us to accept as 'the ideal, the way ahead'; but, whatever fantasies he may have from his reminiscences of the pioneering days of cinema, all his constructs collapse at the slightest contact with everyday reality.[127]

What was so important about the 'luxurious' foyer of the mid-1910s? This was a time when a process began that can be defined as the externalisation of cinema styles. As early as the end of 1913 a Petersburg newspaper reporter observed:

There is a new technique of acting (specific gestures and specific facial expressions) developed in cinema and unconsciously adopted by cinemagoers. This new style not only penetrates everyday life but also makes its influence felt in the theatre.[128]

The externalisation of art was a part of the general tendency of the age. This is what Alister Mackintosh writes about *art nouveau* culture: 'One of the central issues of modern art has been the erosion of the idea that art is something separate from life. Art now takes place in the streets as well as the art gallery, and the first manifestation of this idea was the advertisement.'[129]

A similar process in film culture was enhanced by a public passion for publicity postcards picturing film stars (the cult of stars was launched in Russia by Asta Nielsen's films). Through these postcards films came to influence the world of fashion (especially millinery and hairstyles), body language, etc. The externalisation of cinema style gave rise to an emerging subculture of 'cinephiles'. In 1916 Emmanuel Beskin observed with surprise that people

form something like a foyer or a club outside the cinema. They stroll up and down, joking and flirting, listening to what the people coming out are saying and so on. The bright lights illuminate the crowd; the smart commissionaire and the 'vulgar extravagant décor' lure them in.[130]

The arrival of the 'luxury foyer' was opportune. Its musical winter gardens presented a most natural place for the *cinephiles* to get together. Thanks to them, the exoticism of the cinema interior was not just a commonplace of the style of the era but rather a commonplace of the dominant style of cinema. The space of the foyer was least of all thought of as a fact of actual topography, as a part of Riga, Petersburg or Moscow. The foyer was an extraterritorial space, and this was underlined not only by the details of the décor. *The Journal of Journals* wrote – not without malice – of 'grave ushers with southern profiles' slowly crossing the vestibule.[131] Where does this figure come from? Lida Borelli, Pina Menicelli, Francesca Bertini, who all released the essence of the *femme fatale* into the cinema, brought to the style of screen behaviour the static pose, which was used to denote any emotion, whether of indecision or passion. No less expressive was the acting style of the influential Danish cinema; in Asta Nielsen's acting the critical moments of the action were stressed by freezing the body in space – something which Barry Salt calls 'an occasional well-placed "thinks" look towards the camera.'[132] This style of screen behaviour was adopted not only by cinema ushers but also – and indeed mainly – by the cinemagoers themselves, and this must have turned the foyer into something like a catalogue of the mimic and gesticulatory features of this style. A reviewer for *The Moscow Gazette* in March 1917 gave the following description of what took place at the door of the auditorium:

> A tall, Anglicised gentleman with an arrogant smooth-shaven face, his slender form draped in a faultlessly cut mess jacket, negligently proffers his ticket. An Italian orchestra plays in the spacious foyer . . . Ladies and gentlemen predominate; their movements are theatrical, they strike affected poses, their expressions are artificially animated and their glances mannered as they cast deliberately slowly around the room or stare haughtily at the public. There is a crowd of slim and clean-shaven young men with unctuous physiognomies striking uncertain poses as if following some studied example. The attire, both male and female, is fashionable, and it is as though its wearers adapt their movements to it. In the figures and faces of almost all of these people, from the effete young men of androgynous appearance to high school girls with provocative eyes, from merchants imitating foreign capitalists to semi-intellectuals affecting English style, one can detect a kind of common pattern. One can feel something second-hand, something borrowed and unnatural.[133]

The world of the cinema foyer, being free of narrative obligations (unlike the world of the screen), was the ideal space for modelling cinema style in its purest form. The 'theatricalisation' of life in the manner of cinema was such a fascinating business that – according to some sources – there existed a whole section of the public that 'took their curiosity no further than the foyer'.[134] Besides, this Wildean game (Russian dandies worshipped Wilde) was not always 'theatre for oneself'. Specialists in cinema architecture insisted that a real foyer ought to be visible from the street: 'When it's cold or wet outside, the foyer, bathed in light with soft furniture and decorative plants, creates for the passer-by an impression of inviting cosiness.'[135] The Aquarium cinema on Nevsky Avenue was – of course! – furnished with windows like these, floodlit and decorated with tropical trees. 'The illuminated window as stage, the street as theatre and the passers-by as audience – this is the scene of big-city night life,'[136] writes Wolfgang Schivelbusch in his study on the industrialisation of light in the nineteenth century. For the habitué of the cinema foyer that rectangle of light giving on to the dark nocturnal street was even more alluring than the two-dimensional screen – for here the actor was the habitué himself. This was the space where life came to imitate art.

The relationship between the two foci of cinema style (the central one of the screen and the reflected one of the foyer) brings us back to the more general question of the interrelationship between the concepts of centre and periphery. A letter from Boris Pasternak to Sergei Bobrov, written in 1913, discusses this opposition of the 'core' of drama (in the broadest sense) to its surrounding 'plasma'. Theatre – according to the writer – is called upon to express the core, and cinema the peripheral plasma:

> You will understand me if I call actuality – and the actuality of the city – the preferred stage of lyric precisely in the sense I was talking about. Because the city as stage enters into a competitive and tragic relationship with the auditorium of Word and Language that is all around us . . . Cinema must leave to one side the core of drama and lyric – it distorts their meaning; so much is clear to me already, I'll explain why below – . . . but only cinema is able to reflect and record the system surrounding the core: its origins, its vagueness, its aura. And we have just seen that this husk of the grain is the central drama of the wider stage. Consequently, cinema can grasp what is paramount here because it has access to what is secondary; and this last thing is that first thing. Fortunately cinema distorts the core of drama because it is called upon to express what is true in it: the surrounding plasma. Let it photograph not the tale, but the mood of tales.[137]

Pasternak is evidently referring here to the all-embracing quality of synecdoche in the poetics of cinema: spoken words reflected in silent intertitle; the whole conveyed in a fragment; cause invoked by consequence. But a paradoxical assertion of the primary nature of the aureola and not of the core itself can also be applied to cinema as an object of study, in which the use of couplets such as 'centre and periphery', 'screen and foyer', 'film and reception' should not imply that there is a difference of value between the two terms in each couplet, with the first necessarily being more important than the second.

Chapter 2

Projection technique as a factor in aesthetic perception

THE IMAGE OF THE PROJECTIONIST

The previous chapter dealt mainly with the physiology of cinema life without going into the question of how the viewer understood the technological parameters of the performance. Meanwhile, the machinery of film projection gave rise to several persistent ideas which – with greater or lesser clarity – were shared by everyone who saw a cinema performance. The natural focal point for these ideas was the figure of the projectionist, an image that embodied the basic oxymoron of cinema as a whole: the mundaneness of the arcane.

The prime mythologising factor here was the fact that the figure of the projectionist was invisible. Except in the very earliest cinema halls, where the projectionist stood in the middle of the audience, the projector was always situated behind the back row. Besides, as early as 1908 cinema fire regulations stipulated that the projector had to be housed in a small metal-lined room, the so-called 'box' where the projectionist also sat. The viewer could only assume that there was someone behind him operating the whole show. This faceless figure left much room for fantasy.

In the modern study of film reception there is a special sector called 'apparatus theory'. According to this theory, the apparatus (a concept that includes such spatial arrangements as the placing of the projector, the darkening of the auditorium, the position of the spectators in relation to the projectionist and the screen, etc.) 'refers to the general conditions and relations of cinematic reception, the technologically changing yet ideologically constant parameters of the institution'.[1] Some writers working within the framework of apparatus theory insist on the analogy of the auditorium with Plato's cave, an idea suggested by the beam of light that emanates from behind the spectator's head and throws shadows on the wall in front of him.[2]

Leaving aside the issue of whether or not this parallel helps to account for the way we perceive films, I ought to observe that the image of Plato's cave belongs among the earliest tropes of film reception. In Russia, Plato's cave was the closest analogy one could find to illustrate the fundamentals of the Symbolist poetic doctrine. In 1894 Konstantin Balmont relocated Plato's parable in the dark world beneath the sea, a favourite *art nouveau* setting. His sonnet 'Underwater Plants', which was not just a poem but rather a meta-Symbolist statement, tells of the loneliness of seaweeds that dream of the world above the sea with its light, its struggles and its flowers that one can actually smell. The sonnet ends with these lines:

No path leads to the land of light and struggle,
All around is cold and silent water.
– Now and again a shark glides by.

No ray of light, no sound, no greeting.
The choppy seas above send down
Only corpses and the wrecks of ships.[3]

In 1904 Valeri Bryusov coined a fresher version of the parable, furnished with tokens of modernity – the telephone and the diving suit:

We 'decadents', practitioners of the new art, are all somehow divorced from everyday reality, from what people like to call the real truth of life. We go through life cut off from our surroundings (and this, of course, is one of our weakest sides) as if we were walking under water in a diving bell, preserving a telephone link only with those outside our surroundings, on the surface, where the sun shines.[4]

The cinema with its bulky apparatus (darkness, beam, screen) came opportunely to further update this Platonic idea. The Symbolist paradox concerning the true reality of art and the mere seemingness of actual life took 'cinematic' shape in the following point made by Fyodor Sologub:

Compared with them [artistic images] we are but pale shadows, like pictures in a cinema. We are but multiple duplicate copies of someone's original, just like those many images of women, played once and for all by the unique Asta Nielsen, that flash across countless screens.[5]

The reflected space of 'shadows on the wall' suggests the idea that there exists another, 'true', space. The layout of the auditorium pointed back to the source of the beam of light, and at the apex of this imaginary cone was the projectionist. It was this that made it seem as if the projectionist was carrying out the function of an intermediary between this world and the next, an impression which was conveyed in Alexander Kranzfeld's metaphor for the projectionist as the 'high priest of cinema'.[6]

Where does this figure come from? In his pioneering studies on the symbolism of telephones and trams in Russian poetry of the 'Silver Age', Roman Timenchik traced various aspects that 'cultural biographies' of 'modern' objects have in common. One of these common features is that the existential metaphorism that informed technical items of modernity would lead to a mediating figure being singled out.[7] The eighteenth century with its clockwork idea of the world gave birth to the image of the Supreme Clock-Maker; improved city lighting brought about Gogol's demonic figure of the Lamp-Lighter; the telephone operator (that 'incorporeal deity') provided transcendental connections with the other world; likewise, the Tram-Driver and Film Projectionist were fictionalised as masters of human destiny. Indeed, the train was perceived as a machine with a once-and-for-all predetermined trajectory of movement, much in the same manner as the cinematograph was read as a machine with an unchangeable programme: while film characters were still rejoicing on the screen, their death was already there, lurking at the core of the reel, though known only to the projectionist. Hence an image of the projectionist first drawn by Kornei Chukovsky in 1907: that of a spotty lad possessing the combined power of a Dr Faustus and a Joshua.[8]

The early cinema projectionist did not always remain invisible: 'Sometimes the box became so intolerably hot that the projectionist used to go out and sit for a while in the auditorium.'[9] At those moments the sense of the projectionist as something of a demonic figure – one film reviewer in the 1910s chose the pseudonym 'Demon Strator' – contrasted amusingly with his workaday appearance. Unlike the chauffeur, aviator or cameraman of the time, the projectionist did not wear leather breeches and did not in any way 'dress up' for his job. The image of the projectionist entered another plane, and the archetype of Plato's cave gave way to another genre of literary discourse: the theme of the transience of the artist and the grandeur of the images he evokes. This theme typically appeared in poems about cinema, where the narrators were screen characters: beautiful women or their gallant beaux, who depended entirely on the imbecile projectionist to grant them the gift of life as and when he chose: 'And the sleepy projectionist commands me to life.'[10] Or he could deprive them of life, too:

The projectionist with his purple nose
Plunges all in dark and sleep.
He doesn't even stop to ask
How many lives he's snuffing out.[11]

This image of the projectionist was reinforced by the danger of fire. Nitrate-based film burned with an intense flame which was very difficult to extinguish. Contemporaries likened it to the way celluloid dolls burned – ping-pong balls today burn the same way. The reader may recall that cinema fire regulations stipulated that the projector had to be housed in a small metal-lined room, the 'box', where the projectionist also sat. One cannot understand the atmosphere that prevailed in cinemas in those early days unless one takes into account several dreadful fires believed to have occurred due to projector malfunction, and that their consequences were well known to every visitor to the cinema.[12] As Yevgeni Maurin relates: 'The slightest hiccup in the running of the projector, any abrupt break in the performance, any sudden brightening of the screen, and a suppressed murmur runs around the hall; people begin to glance back nervously towards the projection box window.'[13]

In 1911 the magazine *Our Week* described one such incident:

> There was a great commotion recently at Mityayev's electric theatre: it is only by sheer luck that it did not end in disaster. A Mr A and his wife were sitting near the back of the cinema. Behind them sat an engineer who had had too much to drink. The engineer started to take liberties with Mrs A. He began to touch her hat, her arm, and so on. The husband (who happened to be an army officer) noticed this offensive behaviour, leapt up, hit the engineer in the face, and pulled his sword from its scabbard. Luckily a man sitting nearby managed to restrain Mr A. Hearing the shouting, everyone imagined that fire had broken out and made a mad rush for the exit. There was a crush; several women fainted, many tried to fight their way out on to the street. The worst hurt were the children: one little girl was so badly crushed that she began to cough up blood.[14]

Going to the cinema in those years always had about it something of the same sense of adventure that flying has for us today. The one who was exposed to the greatest danger was of course the projectionist, which meant that he could be seen as something of a romantic and chivalric figure. 'O projectionist, behind your mask!' exclaimed the writer Yuri Krichevsky, referring to the front of the projection box.[15] Safety regulations demanded that the window in it had a metal shutter that could be closed like a visor in case of danger.

PROJECTION SPEED

In the 1910s both cinema cameras and projectors were driven mainly by hand, which meant that the speed at which a film was run depended on the cameraman and the projectionist. When camera speed and projection speed coincided, the film ran normally and there were no objections from the audience. But, as Kevin Brownlow and Barry Salt have reminded us, although the two speeds were meant to coincide, this did not occur often.[16] Projectionists had no reservations about exploiting to the full the potential for improvisation offered by the difference between the two speeds. Dmitri Kirsanov, a film director particularly noted for his feeling for slow rhythm,[17] recalled the way films were shown in his home town of Yurevo (now Tartu):

> I well remember the impressions of my first visits to the cinema. It was a long time ago, when the cinematograph first appeared, and since the Kinematograph, where I used to go, was in a provincial town where lethargy was a rule of life, I saw most of the films at a kind of slowed-down

pace. It was just like watching a modern slow-motion film. Consequently, the thing that most appealed to me in the cinema was the slow and unnatural movements of the actors. I used to think, of course, that the ability to move like that was a special artistic gift, and I tried – without success – to imitate the inimitable movements of cinema. [18]

It was, of course, rare for the whole film to be shown in slow motion. Usually the projectionists, who were thoroughly familiar with the films and the audience's reactions to the various scenes, altered the projection speed to match the shots: they speeded it up though the *longueurs* and slowed it down for the sentimental scenes. The most constant correlation was that between projection speed and genre: chases and comedies were speeded up in projection. In one of his essays G. K. Chesterton expressed his dissatisfaction with this practice:

> In order that a man riding on horse should look as if he were riding hard, it is first necessary that he should look like a man riding on a horse. It is not even an impossibly rapid ride, if he only looks like a Catherine wheel seen through a fog. It is not an impression of swiftness; because it is not an impression of anything. [19]

In his monograph on Abel Gance, Kevin Brownlow mentions that some projectionists used to synchronise the film with the accompanying musical score, following the conductor's baton rather than watching the screen. There do not appear to be any complaints about this practice in the 1910s, but for rapid editing it could be disastrous. Sergei Eisenstein recalled that Edmund Meisel, who wrote the score for *The Battleship Potemkin* (1926),

> ruined a public showing of *Potemkin* in London, in the autumn of 1929, by having the film projected slightly more slowly than normal, without my agreement, for the sake of the music. This destroyed all the dynamics of the rhythmic relationships to such a degree that for the first time in *Potemkin*'s whole existence the effect of the 'lions jumping up' caused laughter. [20]

The considerations which most of all affected the choice of projection speed were those of the 'picture turnover' factor. A reviewer for *The Theatre Paper*, complaining of the lifelessness of plastic representation inherent – in his opinion – in the 'mechanistic' nature of screen movement, did not hesitate to include the projectionist in his criticism:

> Moved by some alien, heteronomous will, the screen heroes only parody what is enacted in front of the lens of the studio camera. They walk as no one in real life ever walks; they gesture like puppets, and at the last performance they acquire the magic ability to move and act with great speed and a truly amazing and fabulous alacrity. [21]

The last remark reveals the author to have been a regular cinemagoer. In the 1910s the *cognoscenti* avoided the late performances for fear of falling victim to the projectionist who was in a hurry to get off home. *Cine-Phono*, with the gravity befitting a specialist journal, explained what happened in such cases:

> If the film is made to run at – let us say – double speed, with thirty-two instead of sixteen frames a second, then all the movements on the screen will seem twice as fast as in real life. For example, the steps of a man walking normally will look like rapid jumps: walking turns into running; every calm fluent gesture is turned into a jerky, convulsive twitch.[22]

Even if viewers somehow managed to come to terms with the arbitrary behaviour of the projectionist, the last performances could turn out to be disastrous for particular styles of acting. While the Mack Sennet kind of comedy could not exist without speeded-up movement, the statuesque plasticity of the Russian actor needed to be projected if not in slow motion exactly then certainly not at an accelerated speed. I have already mentioned (in another context) the Italian 'diva' style of acting, which constructed a trajectory of movement as a progression from one significant pose to another. The Russian cinema of the 1910s – not uninfluenced by the theories of dramatic timing associated with the Moscow Art Theatre – raised this style of acting to the level of a conscious aesthetic programme. As Kevin Brownlow observed, Russian cinema seems to have only two speeds: 'slow' and 'stop'.

This 'stretched' style, recognised as a unique attribute of Russian cinema, was also accompanied by attempts to give it a theoretical basis. At one time it was energetically sponsored by the journals *The Projector* and *Pegasus*. The former wrote:

> It may sound paradoxical for the art of cinema (which got its name from the Greek word for movement) but the style of our best cinema actors amounts to moving as slowly as possible. The art of the screen relies on mime in just the same way as theatre relies on words. On the stage, actors try to speak distinctly, clearly, and without undue haste; on the screen it is even more essential to mime clearly and distinctly, and hence as slowly as possible. Every one of our best actors has his or her own style of mime: Mosjoukine has his steely hypnotic stare; Gzovskaya – her tender, end-lessly varied facial lyricism; Maximov's mime is tense and nervous, while Polonsky's is full of refinement and grace. But all of them subordinate their acting – with an unusual economy of gesture – to a rhythm that rises and falls particularly *slowly*.[23]

We can easily imagine how frequently cinema actors used to complain about projectionists. In fact in 1914 this conflict was the subject of an open letter from Ivan Mosjoukine to *The Theatre Paper*, in which the actor vigorously brushed aside all accusations that he had got the rhythm of a particular role quite wrong, and laid the blame for this entirely on the projectionist:

When the film is being shot the camera is run at a precisely set speed. It reproduces movements on the screen which correspond exactly to the actor's movements in front of the camera. If the same speed is used when the film is being projected the audience will see living people with fluent, slow movements . . . The gentlemen who own our cinemas recognise no such laws. Apart from those few 'first-class' cinemas which do take an interest in artistic considerations, what most of them do, when the programme is a long one and has to be shown three times a night (which cannot be done using the normal, prescribed tempo), is to order the 'lad in the box' to 'speed it up'. The poor actors, through no fault of their own, jump and twitch like cardboard clowns and the audience, not initiated into the secrets of the projection box, dismisses them as untalented and inexperienced. I cannot tell you what it feels like when you see your own normal movements transformed into a wild dance at the whim of this mere boy. You feel as if you were being slandered on all sides without having any way of proving your innocence.[24]

The acting fraternity and the projection room staff were constantly at loggerheads; their hostility was traditional. The film director Nikolai Shpikovsky, not without a certain fondness, described how, in the 1920s, the great stage actor Ivan Moskvin, a tyro in the cinema, successfully took on the air of an old hand at the game:

They say that at a working run-through of *The Station Master* [Kollezhskii registrator, 1925], Moskvin stated that the reason for his poor acting in one part of the picture was that the projectionist was cranking the handle too fast. This is quite superb – and touching. If the Moskvin of the theatre strikes us as an exclusively unique and fresh actor on the screen, then this is only because it turns out that he loves cinema and cares about the handle of the projector![25]

But there was also a feedback between the projection box and the audience. If the film was going too fast the audience used to shout 'Don't rush the picture!' [Ne goni kartinu!]. If the film was going too slowly they would call out 'Turn it, Mickey!' [Mishka, verti!]. In the 1910s all projectionists were called 'Mishka' (just as all Moscow cabmen were called 'Vanka'), and the phrase 'Turn it, Mickey!' came from the immensely popular 1911 satirical show *The Cinematograph*, staged in the Distorting Mirror Theatre [Krivoe zerkalo] in Petersburg. 'Don't rush the picture!' still exists as a Russian conversational idiom, though with no reference to films, which are no longer manually operated.

Early projectionists were particularly fond of playing with speed in those cases when the slow tempo was expected to be an integral part of the event. Speeding up funerals and official ceremonies became notorious long before the idea occurred to René Clair. In 1915 the journal *Pegasus* fulminated at

what by then seemed to be an established practice: 'solemn funeral proces-
sions are turned into crazy gallops through the streets; individuals do not
gesture, they twitch; hands flail about in the air – goodness only knows what's
going on.'[26]

Traditionally, the kinesics of social life in Russia presumed an inverse
relationship between the importance of an event and the speed with which it
unfolded: as the importance of an event or a person increased, the action
slowed down. The rule affected theatrical *mise-en-scène*, diplomatic protocol
and, to a certain extent, the kinesics of everyday behaviour. Russians
generally judged American films to be 'too hectic' [*suetlivyi*], and a standard
epithet for a foreigner was 'fidgety' [*vertlyavyi*].

Old textbooks for theatre actors stressed that a Russian noble of the Middle
Ages (a boyar) ought to be portrayed as being fat and slow – long before
such an image became a standard caricature of a boyar. It was tacitly assumed
that events officially appoved of as 'historical' unfolded at such a slow tempo
that the jerky medium of film was unable to record them correctly. Recommendations were sounded restricting the 'cinematisation' of historical events
that formed part of the educational curriculum in Russian schools.[27] In the
'Conclusion of the Standing Commission of the National Lecture Committee
on Questions Relating to the Use of Film in Schools and Public Lecture
Halls', dated 11 November 1915, one point stood out: 'for technical reasons
the movements of the actors in cinematic images are accelerated and
therefore sometimes comical. This is quite out of place in the presentation
of historical events'.[28]

A year beforehand N. A. Savvin, an active educationalist, raised the alarm
in *The Education Herald*:

> In *Princess Tarakanova* [Knyazhna Tarakanova, 1910] the messengers
> give such hilariously exaggerated bows to the Empress that you cannot help
> wanting to burst out laughing . . . In the last part of *Nero* [Nerone
> e Agrippina, Italy, 1914] the actor playing the Emperor sprints around
> the vast hall. Napoleon's mincing little walk . . . [in the film *The Year
> 1812* [1812 god], Russia, 1912], Petronius in *Quo Vadis?* [Italy, 1912] with
> his ungainly movements . . . All this bears absolutely no resemblance to
> real life![29]

The magazine *Life and the Lawcourts*, hearing of a forthcoming series of
films based on the Old Testament, also expressed its concern: 'the script of
the history of the Jewish people, which ran on the "screen" of the whole
world for six thousand years, testifies that the "Great" Max Linder did not
appear in it.'[30]

According to censorship rules, newsreels involving the Imperial Family
had to be projected at a specified speed, and the owner of the film theatre had
to be present in the projection box while the film was being shown.[31]
Although I know of no record of any particular case, this requirement

indicates that some projectionists with 'progressive' views may have speeded up their machines in order to poke fun at the Tsar.

TEMPUS REVERSUS

Some early projectors could also be run backwards. The aesthetic possibilities this presented were recognised in Lumière's time. His 1896 repertoire included *La Démolition d'un mur* [The Demolition of a Wall] shown backwards. In February 1897 an American newspaper reported another novelty of this sort:

> In one of the cinematographic views to be shown the machine will be run backwards. The scene selected for this curious experiment is the one representing the crossing of the Saône River by the mounted French dragoons. After the troopers reach the other side of the stream the picture machine will be reversed and the men and horses will immediately start backward across the river, the scene closing with the horses backing up the steep bank down which they had plunged but a few moments before.[32]

A year later a Russian reviewer recorded his impressions of a similar event:

> In order to amuse the audience they sometimes show some lively pictures in the right order, and then run them backwards, from the end to the beginning. First you see a man dining in a restaurant. He has some roast chicken on his plate. He cuts off a piece, puts it in his mouth on a fork and eats it. Then he cuts off another piece and eats that, and so on, until it's all gone. Then all of a sudden everything goes topsy-turvy: he puts an empty fork into his mouth and takes it out with a piece of chicken on it. He lowers the fork and the chicken slides off and lands on the plate. The man again puts an empty fork into his mouth and takes it out with another piece of chicken on it, and so on and so on. And after a while there's a whole chicken back on his plate again.[33]

Besides being an unfailing joke, the reversed projection stunt fitted surprisingly well into the mainstream of cognitive experiments at the turn of the century. Projectors equipped with reversible controls provided, one might say, an optical refutation of the second law of thermodynamics, according to which all natural processes flowed in one direction only and could not be reversed. As the physicist and philosopher Ernst Mach (who chose to doubt the reality of such basic concepts of classical physics as space, time and movement) put it, 'cinematography opens up the possibility of changing the scale and direction of time to suit ourselves.'[34] And Rudolf Harms, in his book *The Philosophy of Film*, argued that this endowed film 'with great versatility and flexibility, which turn it into a free soaring frolic with an actuality otherwise strictly bound by the laws of space and time.'[35] Pictures of people jumping into water were among favourite subjects for reversals.[36]

We come across shots of reversed jumps from a tower in the Lumières' *Les Bains de Diane à Milan* [The Baths of Diana in Milan, 1896],[37] most probably the first film made with reverse-projection attraction in mind, and in self-referential films of the 1920s like Buster Keaton's *The Cameraman* [USA, 1929] and Dziga Vertov's *The Man with the Movie Camera* [Chelovek s kinoapparatom, 1929].

At first, the reversal was done during the projection, so any film could be turned into a comedy. In the days of trick comedies cameramen began to shoot reverse motion in camera, and reverse motion almost became a genre of its own, sometimes added to chase films (horses driven backwards enjoyed great popularity), sometimes serving as the basis for the whole film. Boris Likhachev's notes mention the film *Back, Back* [Nazad, nazad].[38] This early (Pathé or Gaumont?) film is described twice in Russian periodicals: in the journal *The Spectator* in 1905, and in the above-mentioned article by Alexander Koiransky in *Our Monday Paper*. Koiransky's response was of a philosophical order – he was impressed not so much by the sight of a burning cigar filmed backwards as by the reversal of the cause and effect relationship in general:

> Effect begins to precede cause, and human logic flies out of the window. A cigar butt leaps from the pavement into the mouth of a man in a top hat. The man steps back and lets out a cloud of smoke. Meanwhile the cigar gets bigger and becomes covered with ash. The man goes back step by step. The cigar gets bigger and bigger. Finally he blows on a match; it flares up. He raises it to the cigar; it immediately goes out, and the man puts it away, safe and sound, in his cigar case. Thus, before the eyes of the audience, the wonder of the cinematograph compels the irreversible river of Time to flow backwards.[39]

Reversed projection as a cognitive metaphor was specially productive in the popularisation of the theory of relativity. In 1925 R. Tun called the cinematograph 'a device for demonstrating negative time', adding – with some regret – that there were as yet no devices for registering negative space:

> A careful examination of certain processes, shown in reverse order, will perhaps still have some fruitful significance in the field of the theory of knowledge. Later, with the help of this kind of demonstration, it may be possible to give a person of average education some understanding of some of the latest theories which today are still very difficult to understand, for example, the theory of relativity.[40]

Indeed, the theory of relativity, in addition to being expressed mathematically, called urgently for the creation of a 'graphic language' capable of conveying its meaning in spatial or sensational terms. As early as 1911 the Russian theoretical physicist N. A. Umov, in an address to the Second Mendeleyevan Congress, proposed the cinematograph as a non-mathematical model of the Einsteinian universe. In his paper Umov asserted that it was impossible for the contemporary scientific mind to visualise new scientific models:

Number remains, as before, the legislator of nature but, since it cannot be visually represented, it has disappeared from the field of a philosophy that assumes that the world can only be depicted by mechanical models. The new discovery supplies quite a number of images for the way the world is structured, but they break up its former familiar architecture and can only be reconciled in a new style whose familiar lines go way beyond the boundaries not only of the old external world but also of the basic forms of our thinking.[41]

The scientist further proposed that the new should not be explained by reference to the old but with the help of the new itself: the cinematograph with its ability to vary the way the film passes through the projector:

Let us assume that we have a film on which we have images of people in different poses, clocks with hands showing different times, various phases of a movement about to be performed. But, as long as the film stands still, there is neither movement, nor time, nor action. This is in keeping with a system which moves with the speed of light. When the film starts the pictures on the screen change at a particular speed, and you, who are watching it and not moving, get an impression of life and of action. People move about, suffer, the drama is enacted, the clock moves on. For you, the tempo of the action, the working of the clock, the speed of people's movements, and thus the speed of their decisions, depend on the speed at which the film moves, but the people in the film notice no changes; they cannot tell whether things are going faster or more slowly. Let us say, the cinematograph shows you a drama unfolding extremely slowly. You are surprised at the insipidness of the characters' emotions; but they are insipid only to you; to the characters they are as strong as ours are to us. The phenomena of the world are just like the images of the cinematograph. Don't you see that the idea of time as something absolute disappears, as does the idea that natural phenomena have an absolute tempo? On the earth, which moves at a fixed speed, natural phenomena are a film running at that same speed; for another planet they would be another film at a different speed . . . If we slow down the movement of the film, beginning with the speed that matches the tempo of phenomena on earth, we shall gradually be approaching the tempo of phenomena in bodies whose movement is closer to the speed of light. When the film stops, it has reached the speed of light. If we now begin to run the film in the opposite direction, the phenomena we shall see will match the speed of a body moving faster than the speed of light; the cinematograph shows how phenomena would behave in a world moving faster than the speed of light. You have seen pictures clearly showing a horse running forwards, yet going away from you. In such a world everything goes backwards: old men get younger; corpses come back to life; effects precede causes; reconciliations come before quarrels. The last act of a man's life is to return to the womb of his mother, i.e. death in reverse.[42]

We should note that the last example led Umov into the field of biological processes. He was not alone in this flight of fancy. After the film *Back, Back*, periodicals – with varying degrees of taste – were not slow to take up the theme of reversed biographical time:

> solemn people carefully take the corpse out of its coffin, undress it, wash it, lay it on a bed and begin to cry bitterly over it. Then, in excruciating agony, life returns to the body. And it begins to live again right before our eyes, getting younger and younger . . . All the thoughts and actions that he had and did during his life flood back into him just like the smoke of the man with the cigar.[43]

And here is another reconstruction of a 'reversed text of life', this time in verse, with a minor theme derived from the Lumières' film *The Demolition of a Wall*, and with another theme anticipating a text-book sequence from Vertov's *The Cine-Eye* [Kinoglaz, 1924]:

> Run it backwards if you like . . .
> Dresses appear before cutting,
> Bread is baked into dough.
> Stones from a fallen ruin
> Rise up again in their place.
> The corpse bids farewell to his coffin.
> The baby creeps back, ungrateful,
> Into his mother's womb.[44]

Life's course is reversed: from the coffin to the womb. In the 1910s it was not only at the level of popular journalism that this theme crept into Russian literature. It also featured in Velimir Khlebnikov's play *The World Reversed* [Mirskontsa, 1912]. Its five episodes represent five stages in the rejuvenation of the hero and his wife. He runs away from his own funeral and the play finishes with a silent scene in his pram – a kind of self-liquidation of a dramatic theme which went back to a pre-linguistic stage. 'To float from death to infancy', wrote Khlebnikov in another extract, linking this current of life with Stenka Razin's voyage *up* the Volga, that is – from its mouth to its source.[45]

In Ignatov's manuscripts we come across another typical theme in this cycle:

> In the early years of cinema a motor car might run over someone who would immediately jump up and chase after the offender. Such scenes delighted the audience and they would greet every accident of this sort with 'Homeric' or 'uncontrollable' laughter.[46]

In one such film, shown in Russia under the title *The Drunkard's Cure* [Istselenie p'yanitsy. Original title and date unknown], legs cut off by a car are instantly stuck back on again; in Vladimir Mayakovsky's 1916 Futurist poem 'War and the World' [Voina i mir], which the poet himself used to call 'cinematic',[47] a similar reverse mutilation scene appears as an anti-war hyperbole:

From the burial mounds
they rise.
Once buried bones
grow flesh.
Did severed legs ever
seek their owners?
Did cut-off heads ever
call their names?
Now look!
A scalp leaps back on its skull;
two legs run up
alive beneath him again![48]

In any event, for an observer at the time this relationship was indisputable.[49]

As discussed in the Introduction, the 'public image' of the cinematic text was influenced by the 'public image' of the Moscow Futurists. Being the two major attractions of the year in 1913, cinema and Futurism were bound to be presented as a single phenomenon. Whatever absurdity the critics discovered in films was immediately labelled 'Futuristic'; conversely, Mayakovsky's poems were criticised for being as illiterate as cinema intertitles.

Similarly, in the 1910s the showing of a film in reverse, from the end to the beginning, was identified as 'Futuristic'. Thus the author of the notes entitled 'Lenten Themes' in *Cine-Phono* described how in Moscow

a company of young people, who were clearly unable to survive for a week without the cinematograph, rented a separate room in a restaurant and invited in a pianist and a projectionist with all his equipment . . . Someone there had the bright idea of running one of the comedy films backwards. It turned out to be incredibly funny: dead people came to life, the hero first drowned then hurled himself out of the water, and so on . . . Those people were just born Futurists, they were longing for the appearance of what our *old* Futurists call 'the world reversed' [Mirskontsa].[50]

The week in question 'without the cinematograph' was due to the ban on public entertainments during Lent. If we contrast the scene described with the scriptural content of the festival of Lent we can see clearly the sacrilegious nature of the 'young people's' behaviour, and also the kind of mental associations that the technological possibilities of the cinematograph held for people in the 1910s.

Fantasies generated by the reverse motion cinema often reached the area of historical time. Mikhail Yampolsky, in a profound article, 'Cinema's Language of the Stars',[51] showed how Flammarion's philosophical dialogue 'Lumen' served as the inspiration for the idea of the 'cosmic cinematograph', which made its appearance in the twentieth century. By reversing the direction control mechanism, one could transform the end of the world into the creation, and vice versa. This is the maximum time-span across which the metaphorical potential of the reversed film script could be sustained. Its opposite would be the instantaneous, but crucial historical event, whose very irreversibility would seem to call for the use of the device of reversed projection.

Predictably, for anyone living in Russia there was one moment in time above all others that begged to be rewound and replayed: that of the Revolution of 1917. Russian history consists of periods of stagnation alternating with vertiginous leaps into the dark. Those who have experienced one of these leaps know the thrill of being part of accelerated history, and literary or cinematic discourse on this theme frequently conveys a powerful feeling of irreversibility. In his film *October* [Oktyabr', 1927] Eisenstein used *tempus reversus* as a kind of apophasis, or proof through opposition, in order to drive home this sense of the irreversibility of a moment in history:

> the picture begins with semi-symbolic shots of the overthrowing of autocracy, represented by the toppling of the statue of Alexander III, which stood beside the Cathedral of Christ the Saviour . . . the collapse of the statue was also shot in reverse motion: the throne with the armless and legless torso flew back on to the pedestal. Arms, legs, sceptre and orb flew up to join it. The indestructible figure of Alexander III once again sat in state, staring vacantly into space. This scene was shot for the episode of Kornilov's attack on Petrograd in the autumn of 1917, and represented the dreams of all those reactionaries who hoped that the general's success would lead to the restoration of the monarchy . . . Visually, the scene was a great success . . . Reversed motion is always highly entertaining, and I have recalled somewhere how frequently and how richly this device was used in the first old comic films.[52]

The music accompanying the reversed photography in this film consisted of the score for the original scene played backwards.[53]

By way of commentary on this episode from *October*, perhaps I might mention three other examples, each of which illustrates, in its own way, this 'apophasic' use of *tempus reversus*. The first has been cited (in a different context) by Jay Leyda, and comes from the memoirs of Sir Bernard Pares, who was attached to General Baluyev's headquarters during the First World War. There was a stock of films at the general's headquarters (war newsreels, apparently, and some pictures on military and patriotic themes), which had not aroused much interest among the lower ranks and had hardly ever been shown. It was a difficult time for Baluyev; a commission had just visited his headquarters to investigate his military failures and allegations of incompetence. Sir Bernard Pares recalled:

> when they had gone his staff felt they ought to do something to cheer [Baluyev] up, so they proposed a cinema show in the little garden. There we sat in the dark among the fruit trees, and the show began. The corporal who was operating was nervous, and the picture came on with great jolts upside down. A nervous voice came through the darkness: 'Your Excellency, I beg leave to stop this picture; it's coming on upside down,' and from the front bench of the spectators came Baluyev's gruff reply: 'I command you to continue upside down.' He then suggested that the whole thing should be done backwards.[54]

Two other texts that specifically explore the application of the reversed-time metaphor to actual historical events are Sergei Yablonsky's 'The Cinematograph', and Arkadi Averchenko's 'The Secret of the Great Cinema' [Fokus velikogo kino]. It should be noted that both articles were written after revolutions. The first appeared in *The Russian Word* on 6 December 1906, and the second at the beginning of the 1920s. Yablonsky's article begins with the description of a film about a goose that comes back to life: a diner takes the morsels from his mouth, they grow together on his plate, acquire feathers and, lo and behold, the goose is alive again! The cook carries it into the yard and begins to run away from the triumphant bird. Then comes the parallel:

> I think that our whole life is nothing but cinematograph, and that the maestro giving the performance has run the whole thing in reverse. First he showed us a very vivid and interesting picture entitled *The Revolutionary Movement*, then he suddenly pressed a few knobs, pulled some levers, moved a few things around, said, 'eins, zwei, drei', and off went the picture at double speed – only in reverse order: exactly the opposite of what happened a year ago, then what happened a month later, and so on and so on – all strictly in reversed order. The very first picture, which showed the petty bourgeoisie creeping out of their burrows and becoming citizens, now becomes the last, and shows exactly the opposite process: citizens turning into petty bourgeoisie and hiding away in their bourgeois burrows ... Silence was; and silence is. Peace was; and peace has descended again. Everything is back in its original order; that's exactly what happens when you run a film starting at the end ... Take a look at the papers – those that are left, naturally! They've all calmed down now, and it makes us feel more relaxed too. Don't even bother to see what's going on in the assembly! What assembly, anyway? Assemblies belong to the past! All this would be well and good if this idyllic tranquillity were not already being disturbed by a new noise; it's still a long way off, but it's extremely alarming: it's the sound of a Japanese military band ...

'Reverse the film!' I scream.

But the Japanese military band gets louder and louder, and more and more threatening, and it tells me that this is the start of the Japanese cinematograph show, a show which is so badly made that there is absolutely no way it can be put into reverse motion.[55]

Arkadi Averchenko, the author of the second story on the same theme, was driven by opposite emotions. Unlike Yablonsky, Averchenko was no democrat, and his nostalgia was for times of social peace rather than upheaval. His book of short stories, *A Dozen Knives in the Back of the Revolution*, was written in 1921 in Paris where Averchenko lived as an émigré. It was the first major anti-communist book of prose, singled out by Lenin as extremely talented and extremely hostile. One of his stories, 'The Secret of the Great Cinema', takes advantage of the trope of reverse projection. It opens with a description of a picture already mentioned, *Back, Back*:

> The sea appears, and some cliffs . . . One of the cliffs is absolutely sheer, about seventy feet high . . . Suddenly the sea beneath the cliff foams up, a head shoots out of the water and a man soars up seventy feet into the air, like a gigantic bouncing ball, and stands on the edge of the cliff – quite dry. He crosses himself in reverse order: first his fingers touch his left shoulder, then his right shoulder, then his chest, and, finally, his forehead.[56]

There follows a detailed description of the well-known reversed episodes of the cigar being smoked and the chicken being devoured. Averchenko then wonders what would happen if one could do the same with recent historical events:

> Oh, if only life were as passive as a ribbon of film! If only you could make it run backwards just by pulling a lever . . .
>
> I've got this sheet of paper in front of me, evenly covered with the lines I've just written. Suddenly my pen goes into reverse, scrabbling it all up and leaving nothing but a blank sheet. I put on my hat, pick up my cane, and back out on to the street . . .
>
> The film whirrs away, spinning backwards.
>
> Now it's September, the year before last. I am sitting in a railway carriage; the train lurches off backwards and rushes towards Petrograd.
>
> Marvellous things are going on there: traders are packing up their stalls and leaving the Nevsky Prospect; peasant women selling herrings, gherkins, and apples; non-combatant soldiers selling cigarettes – they're all disappearing . . . Bolshevik decrees are flying off the walls of the buildings like scales, and the walls are neat and tidy again. Look, there's Alexander Kerensky's car charging up at full speed – backwards! Has he returned?
>
> Turn it, Mishka – faster!
>
> He's just driven into the Winter Palace. Look, the film is still flashing past; Lenin and Trotsky are coming backwards out of Kshesinskaya's villa;

they're driving backwards to the station; they sit in the unsealed carriage; it's sealed up straight away and off they all go to Germany – backwards.

Now here's a pretty sight! It's Kerensky rushing backwards out of the Winter Palace (not before time); he jumps up on a table and pompously harangues the workers: 'Comrades! Kill me with your bare hands if I ever desert you! I'm with you to the death!'

He's lying, the scoundrel! It's very handy sometimes to be able to reverse the film!

The February Revolution flashes past too. It's funny to see machine-gun bullets flying out of people lying in the street and zipping straight back into the muzzles of the guns; dead people are jumping up and running backwards, gesticulating wildly.

Faster, Mishka – run it faster!

Rasputin dashes out of the Tsar's palace and goes off home to Tyumen. The film is in reverse, you see!

The cost of living gets cheaper and cheaper . . . There's piles of bread, and meat, and all kinds of food in the markets.

But now the terrible war is melting away like snow on a white-hot sheet of iron. Corpses get up out of the ground and are quietly carried back to their units. Mobilisation turns swiftly into demobilisation. Now there's Kaiser Wilhelm standing on a balcony in front of his people, but his terrible words declaring war – the words of a blood-sucking spider – do not come out of his mouth but disappear into it and he swallows them up; his lips just pluck them out of the air. Oh, if only they would choke you! . . .

Come on Mishka, run it faster, lad!

The Fourth, Third, Second and First Dumas flash past in succession, and now we see on the screen the vivid, horrible, details of the 1905 pogroms.

But it doesn't seem so frightening, somehow. Thugs wrench their knives out of dead bodies; the bodies stir, stand up, and run away. Feathers fly tidily back into Jewish quilts, and everything is as it was before. . .

Stop, Mishka! Don't show us any more! We don't want to see ourselves as we were fifteen years ago – we were little more than boys. Oh, what hopes we had! How we loved – and how we were loved![57]

1 The Splendid-Palace cinema in Riga
(*a*) The plan combined various geometrical elements: the circle, the ellipse and the polyhedron
(*b*) The plan for the entrance
(*c*) The entrance itself
(*d*) The plan for the screen and stage area
(*e*) The screen and stage area
(*f*) The 'Versailles effect' in the foyer

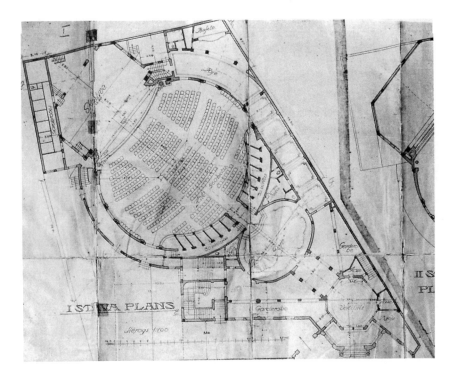

(a)

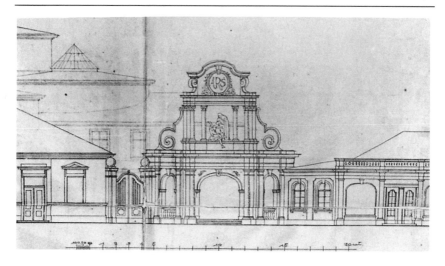

(b)

(c)

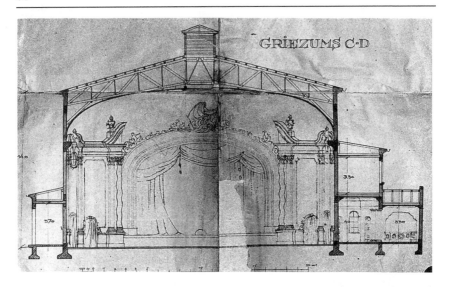

(d)

(e)

(f)

2 The Vulcan cinema in Moscow: several houses knocked into one auditoruim

3 The long auditorium
   (*a*) Plan for the Grand cinema in Riga
   (*b*) The Théâtre Soleil in St Petersburg was reminiscent of a corridor

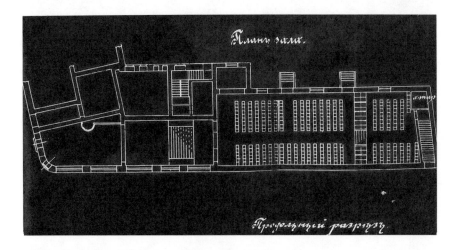

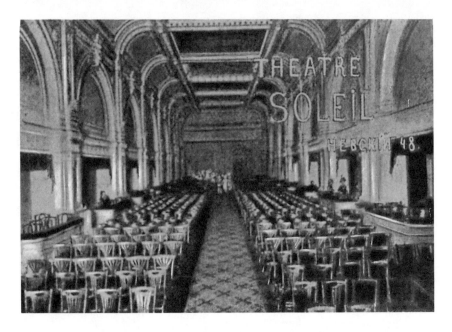

4 This advertisement for the Just Like Paris cinema in St Petersburg used *art nouveau* calligraphy reminiscent of Church Slavonic script

72

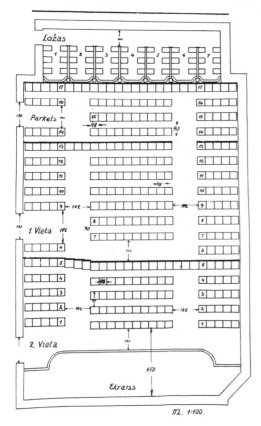

5 The rectangular period of cinema architecture: the AT in Riga
(a) Plan for the façade
(b) Plan for the auditorium
(c) The courtyard

6 The rectangular period of cinema architecture: the Shantser in Kiev
(*a*) The auditorium

(*b*) The upper foyer

7 The foyer of the Marble Palace

№ 439. Обозрѣніе кинематогр., скетингъ-ринковъ, увес. и Спорта. Апр. 1913 г.

БОЛЬШОЙ ТЕАТРЪ

„САТУРНЪ"

Невскій пр. 67, прот. Надеждинской. Тел. 99-97 и 199-33.

3 зрительныхъ зала. 3 большія программы.

Только въ „САТУРНѢ" при трехъ разныхъ программахъ можно видѣть **всѣ новѣйшія избранныя** картины кинематографа.

Программы мѣняются въ каждомъ залѣ **2 раза** въ недѣлю по **понедѣльникамъ и пятницамъ**.

Обширное фойе. Зимній садъ.

2 входа съ Невскаго просп.

Въ саду ежедневные концерты струннаго оркестра.

Первоклассный чайный и фруктовый буфетъ.

Театръ открытъ въ будніе дни съ 3 часовъ и по праздникамъ съ часу дня.

Окончаніе сеансовъ не позже 11 1/2 ч. вечера.

За храненіе верхняго платья 10 коп.

— *Снимать верхнее платье необязательно.* —

---

8 Advertisement for the Saturn in St Petersburg, 1913, offering 'three auditoria, three great programmes', a spacious foyer and a winter garden featuring a string orchestra and 'first-class tea and fruit buffet' – and patrons can keep their coats on!

Chapter 3

The acoustics of cinema performance

FILM MUSIC

Music is pivotal to the study of film reception. Apart from the 'mood music' that was occasionally performed on the set, a practice introduced into Russia by Yevgeni Bauer, music for the silents was part of film exhibition rather than of film production. Music played in auditoria enhanced reception, and film accompanists received reviews that now form a separate historical source for reception studies. Music was both object, factor and instrument of film reception.

This chapter examines four aspects of early film music in Russia: music and cinema audiences, music and film, the place of music in the auditorium, and contemporary discussions of what type of music was best suited to cinema.

With Russian films, the question arises as to how far film music was actually controlled by the exhibitors. The first Russian film was made in 1908 – a year of great cultural aspirations in international film-making. The 'cultured' style introduced by the French company Film d'Art brought with it the idea of having special scores written by well-known composers. The distributors of *L'Assassinat du Duc de Guise* (1908) offered a score by Camille Saint-Saëns together with the print. Consequently, Drankov's *Stenka Razin* (1908) had an overture composed by Mikhail Ippolitov-Ivanov (a disciple of Rimsky-Korsakov). Nevertheless, it was the cinema proprietor who was in charge of the musical side of the business, and ultimately it was all in the hands of the accompanist. In Russia no specially composed score had a chance of surviving beyond the opening week at a first-run theatre. A dialogue that took place in 1914 between the writer Alexander Kuprin and the film director Vladimir Gardin illustrates this point. As Gardin was trying to lure Kuprin into selling performance rights to his story *The Garnet Bracelet* [Granatovy braslet] the author put forward an argument which revealed him to be a hardened cinemagoer:

'In the Ars', said Gardin, 'they've got a fine orchestra. We want the scene where Princess Vera lays a rose by the head of the dead Zheltkov to be accompanied by Beethoven's Second Sonata, as in your story.'

'But everywhere else it will just be something going tumpety-tumpety, won't it?' answered Kuprin.[1]

By 'something going tumpety-tumpety' Kuprin meant the piano accompaniment common in the Russian cinema at that time. What kind of music was it and how was it received? Most frequently, film music would be bluntly described as bad. The following verdict was passed in 1914 by Leonid Sabaneyev, the musical critic known for his refined judgement:

> The art of accompanying films on the piano, which has come about due to the way cinema has expanded lately, may be described briefly as the art of confidently playing whatever comes into one's head, without the slightest twinge of artistic conscience or the least regard for logic or good taste.[2]

At the same time, Sabaneyev, as well as three or four other regular contributors to the discussion, was obviously intrigued by what was then considered the 'enigma' of film music. One of two main topics was why bad music for films was better than no music at all (I will return to this later in the chapter). The other was why and how the practice of playing music for films generated new musical forms.

According to the German philosopher Ernst Bloch, writing in 1913, film music contributed to the legitimisation of neglected forms of musical activity:

> One knows that the harmonium has to be played tremolo when the son of the house has shot himself or the city of Messina is swallowed up in the earthquake. One has also learnt to distinguish fast and slow, light and dark, but the essential thing is the way the worthy village schoolteacher, after the trials and tribulations of the day, fantasises on the piano. This has been raised to a real art form.[3]

The most astonishing thing was that, by virtue of catering for film shows, the 'tum-de-tum' music assimilated some formal characteristics of the film show itself. It was the purest case of textual mimicry. Instantly changing intertitles, moods and events challenged the accompanist to keep in step. In the article quoted above, Sabaneyev described this new musical syntax as follows:

> The need for the music to follow the changing moods of the picture quickly and closely is frequently expressed in the 'spontaneous' transition from one kind of music to another, sometimes even without any attempt to use all the musical resources with which such transitions are usually – if only for decency's sake – accompanied.[4]

In his recent study of a 1912 score for an American film Martin Marks gave an average rate of one transition each three quarters of a minute. Citing a phrase used at the period, he called this type of accompaniment 'continuous music continuously changing'.[5] One might assume that life was somewhat easier for Russian accompanists, given a much slower cutting rate in Russian films of the 1910s (the average shot length of Yevgeni Bauer's *Silent Witnesses* (1914) is 50 seconds at projection speed 20 fps). But again, Russian production constituted a minor part of films shown in Russia at that time, which means that the musicians did not in fact have too much time to relax.

By the mid-1910s the specific art of film music developed into a recognisable genre. One might cite an episode mentioned by Konstantin Stanislavsky in a letter dated 3 July 1915. During their summer vacation, actors from the Moscow Art Theatre used to get together in the evenings to perform comic sketches and parodies. At one of these parties Yevgeni Vakhtangov (Stanislavsky's favourite disciple) 'mimicked the accompaniment to a film where the projector wasn't working properly. It was hilarious'.[6] Thus, by 1915 the genre of film music was well enough established to enable Vakhtangov to invoke the irregular pace of a broken projector by means of musical parody alone.

MUSIC REVIEWS

While in the West film music was used as early as 1895 for the first runs of the Cinématographe Lumière[7] and for Edison's Kinetophone shows,[8] it did not become an established practice in Russia until the late 1900s.[9] On 17 January 1909 a police decree was issued banning music in cinemas.[10] The ban, which was withdrawn soon after it had been announced, can hardly be explained otherwise than by the authorities' intention to extort bribes from exhibitors, since by that time music was already felt to be an essential accompaniment to films. Alexander Anoshchenko (a film journalist and accompanist of the 1910s) recalled that in 1909 the audience would demand their money back if the pianist failed to turn up – or at least those did who stayed to watch the whole unaccompanied programme.[11]

Initially the repertoire of film accompanists was rather basic: '"Can you play marches, waltzes and ballads?" asked the cinema owner, engaging a new accompanist.'[12] If we add polkas, it will give us an idea of the minimal thesaurus of an average film musician. The following description (1912) shows how these musical themes were applied:

> and the young lady also knows what to play for a newsreel. For the unveiling of a statue in Milan, with important gentlemen in side-whiskers and top hats passing in the ceremonial procession, she plays a march . . . For some peculiar winter sport in Norway – a polka. For a scenic picture – sardine fishing in Sicily, for example – she switches to a waltz. When Durashkin ['Dopey' – André Deed's Russian screen name] jumps off the fifth floor into his aunt's bowl of soup, or when the pig lands on Max Linder's top hat, again from the fifth floor – she reverts to a polka.[13]

In the 1910s music became more and more necessary, but not just any kind of music: it had to be appropriate. In 1915 a reviewer for a Rostov-on-Don journal wrote: 'Quite often you overhear people deciding which cinema to go to depending on which accompanist is playing.'[14] Anoshchenko, who was himself one of the best accompanists in Moscow, reported the same thing:

> I knew several cultured film lovers who used to go to the Continental rather than the Modern, which was nearer, purely and simply because [Nikolai] Kruchinin was the accompanist there. His improvisations used to harmonise perfectly with the dramatic action and significantly enhanced its emotional content.[15]

In 1911 cinema magazines started mentioning film music. There were no special film music columns, but reviews of film music would sometimes form an important part of film reviews. Music played in cinema foyers was reviewed under a separate heading. I quote two passages on film music from 1911 reviews in order to convey the air of concern that contemporary audiences felt about this aspect of film art. A review of *Princess Tarakanova* [Knyazhna Tarakanova, 1911] praised the skill of the unnamed accompanist:

> I would go as far as to say that in this case it was the music that created the main atmosphere. The performance spoke for itself: excerpts and entire arias from the work of our Russian composers blended so smoothly with folk songs, scene after scene, that the result was absolutely enchanting.[16]

Occasionally, a reviewer would even claim that the music saved a bad film, as in the case of an anonymous Smolensk pianist who happened to illustrate *Oedipus Rex* [Oedipe-Roi, France, 1908], a Film d'Art picture with the famous French theatre actor Jean Mounet-Sully in the lead. In his review the critic (also anonymous) made a significant distinction between 'melodramatic' and 'impartial' styles of accompaniment:

> I particularly remember the way *Oedipus* was produced. The melodramatic style of acting, which was not at all in keeping with the classical mode, was not too conspicuous, thanks – one can confidently say – to the accompaniment: the tunes were well chosen and the pianist performed them well. Oedipus kept lifting his arms up to heaven and shaking his head tragically, adopting statuesque poses and indicating his intention to make a step without actually making it – all this looked like pure melodrama. And – who would have thought it? – it was the music that saved the thing. The pianist both complemented and highlighted the action – but he didn't really do that either; because if he had chosen to emphasise Oedipus' every gesture (which would have been essential in real melodrama) the music would have been as false, as melodramatic, as the action on the screen. But the pianist, with extraordinary sensibility, selected just the right motifs, and supplied music that corresponded to the plot and not to the style of acting. The result was that the music 'drowned' the acting and allowed the plot to take centre stage. *Oedipus* came to life.[17]

FILM IN THE ABSENCE OF MUSIC

Contemporary reviews may be misleading. The ones cited above point towards the importance of good accompaniment for making films work better. We should not conclude, though, that bad music could easily spoil a good film. Indeed, a sensitive observer like Sabaneyev was inclined to think that what really spoiled a film was music that was too good for it. He felt that very good music was liable to overshadow the film and usurp its position as the main source of artistic impression. On these grounds he defended the use of commonplace music as film accompaniment:

> The focus of attention is on the picture, not the music; this can easily be proved by the simple fact that the most musically horrendous illustration frequently provokes no strong reaction from a musically sensitive viewer deeply engrossed in the picture. But on the occasions when my attention wandered from the screen, and I found myself listening to the music, I was horrified; at times it sounded like nothing on earth![18]

In other words, music played for silent films was not subject to aesthetic discrimination because it was perceived as a norm. As we do not usually notice norms except when they are violated, it may be useful to look into the ways films were received in those rather anomalous cases when the music was interrupted or was not provided.

The only place films were always shown without music (shown 'cold', as Kevin Brownlow aptly put it) were studio previews. As Brownlow remarked, 'a film that survived the ordeal of a projection-room press screening and also received good reviews certainly deserved the praise it received'.[19] From time to time a film journalist would confess to an uneasy feeling at these screenings. As one of them commented in a 1913 essay, without the help of music not even a 'scenic picture' like *Vistas of Italy* was able to transport the audience to the land of green valleys: 'No. Fantasy fails to take wing; instead of journeying to Italy, we remained in the stifling viewing room'.[20] The absence of music could also be experienced as an ominous silence, as witness Yuri Tynyanov's description from the 1920s:

> As soon as the music stops, a strained silence descends. Even when the projector is running quietly there is a humming noise that gets in the way of seeing – and this isn't simply because we have become accustomed to having music in the cinema. If you deprive cinema of music, it becomes empty; it becomes an incomplete, inadequate art. Without music it becomes a positive torment to have to sit and look at those gaping, cavernous, talking mouths. Look carefully at the movements on the screen: see how heavily the horses seem to gallop in that yawning void.[21]

Even a quick comparative overview of analogous descriptions shows that watching films without music was an experience that bore upon the cultural mythology of reception examined in previous chapters. One would expect observers to stress 'the silence' that enveloped the audience on such occasions. Instead, in such cases we are more likely to find references to 'the yawning void' so aptly described by Tynyanov. It is as if the space of the auditorium became 'reactualised' (or 'made strange', to use a Formalist term again). Apart from 'the emptiness', 'the darkness' of this space is rediscovered when the music fails. Erwin Panofsky's account registers this uncanny sensation:

> we also recall the weird and spectral feeling overtaking us when this pianist left his post for a few minutes and the film was allowed to run by itself, the darkness haunted by the monotonous rattle of the machinery.[22]

Finally, Rudolf Harms placed the absent music within a mental landscape reminiscent of a Gothic novel or a Symbolist drama:

> The viewer is immediately gripped by a terrible, frightening emptiness, a kind of naked, cold, alien, limitless void, which has no connection with the external world – with us. An unbridgeable abyss yawns between us and the film. It is as if hundreds of us are locked up in one room, and we are sitting there for hours, silently, just looking at one another. It's terrifying![23]

The final remark – 'it's terrifying!' (a familiar refrain in film literature from the earliest days of cinema) – invokes the fear of the medium (and, more generally, the fear of technology) which accompanied the new art form. This may be regarded as one of the basic impulses for adding music to films. Theodor Adorno has compared instrumental accompaniment in the silent cinema to a child singing in the dark to ward off fear.[24] Music made the 'cold' medium inhabitable. In this regard music was as much about the film as about the 'barely visible' space in which, as Robert Musil had it, the film was swimming. Music helped to bridge the gap, to fill the void, between 'me' and the film. Performed here, in the auditorium, it was in constant interaction with what was taking place on the screen (interaction in the broad sense, including the absence of direct correspondence). Film music formed 'the space between': a geometrically unlocalisable semantic space felt to belong both to the world of the film and the world of the auditorium.

THE BLIND ACCOMPANIST

Thus, to use the words of a modern researcher, 'musical accompaniment gave the audience a sense of collective presence, . . . maintained a sense of continuity between the space/time of the theatre and the illusionist world on the screen'.[25] This mediating function was personified in the figure of the accompanist, who was always in view of the audience. References to the accompanist in Russian writings on cinema recalled in tone the ironical demonology we are familiar with in connection with the image of the projectionist.

Andrey Bely described the 'sound of a beaten up piano over which crouched some musical no-hoper, or a woman with toothache (usually a spinster)'.[26] The poet Georgi Chulkov wrote of a 'bald old man with wise eyes and a thin smile, playing a waltz on the piano'.[27] For Vsevolod Chaikovsky it was 'a sleepy old woman, almost nodding off over her own improvisations'.[28]

Some eyewitness sources recalled accompanists who used to keep their eyes glued to the screen,[29] but they also remembered some who played 'blind', without glancing up even once. It would be natural to assume that the latter were no different from the former, but that they had just come to know the programme off by heart. This, however, would be jumping to conclusions. Two styles predominated in the silent cinema: one adapted itself to the picture (this was the dominant style of the 1910s); the other, which was more archaic, was one in which the pianist paid no attention to the film at all. The historian should not dismiss this style of playing as 'hackwork', even though it often resulted in 'a cake-walk being played for a funeral, and a funeral march for a wedding.'[30] For many people an autonomous musical sequence, an 'ethereal' acoustic background against which the 'fateful' events of the film drama unfolded, was a tangible aesthetic asset. For some this very impassivity quite possibly reawakened what they had learned in school about the function of the chorus in classical Greek tragedy; for others it would evoke the detached fatalism of Chekhovian 'mood' drama as, for example, emulated in an amateurish poetic exercise by the screenwriter Oleg Leonidov:

> The aloof piano tinkled,
> The enchanted screen beguiled.
> There, in an azure farness,
> Truth, caprice and falseness
> All were intertwined.[31]

The 'aloof' accompaniment, understood as an aesthetic fact, compels us to believe in the authenticity of the evidence, which – despite the reliability of the several sources that mention it – seems at first sight improbable. Boris Dushen recalls:

> For some reason it seemed to be quite firmly believed that *blind* musicians, who 'bashed out' the accompaniment on out-of-tune pianos, made the best accompanists. And indeed, for many years they did virtually monopolise all film accompaniment.[32]

This point was also made by the theoretician of film accompaniment, Anatoli Goldobin, in 1912. As his book explains, the change of reels and films was signalled to the blind piano player by a bell sounded from the projection box.[33]

What substance was there to the legendary predominance of the blind accompanist? The legend itself may have had its roots in 'cinematophthalmia' (a widespread fear of blindness caused by excessive cinemagoing); it may have derived from the epic image of the blind singer/musician (Homer, Ukrainian kobza-players), or have reflected a practice encouraged by this tradition. But although there is a whiff of mythology about the legend as relayed by Dushen, we ought not to be too sceptical. It might have been the case, for example, that cinema managers preferred to employ blind musicians because they did not charge much for their services. The fact that they were invited to work as accompanists, or the extent of the practice, is not in itself as important as the fact that contemporaries found it easy to believe it was possible to accompany a picture one could not actually see. At first glance the blind accompanist ought to stand as the extreme expression of the independence and non-convergence of the two planes of a film show – the acoustic and the visual. But, when I expressed this view at an academic conference recently, it was observed that unsighted musicians were not totally isolated from what was taking place on the screen. Blind people have particularly sensitive hearing, and they were therefore able to respond to emotional feedback coming from the audience (any musician can, in fact, do this, but only a blind musician would have to rely on such acoustic feedback as his or her sole source of information about the events taking place on the screen). How closely the accompaniment matched the plot would depend very much on how the audience experienced the film and reacted to it.[34] If this assumption is correct, this kind of accompaniment might have suited the film better than specially commissioned music – since 'blind music' was born anew with each audience. It was, as it were, a musical expression of the process of reception itself, which – as we know – changes not only from film to film but from audience to audience. The question whether music in the silent cinema belonged to the atmosphere of the auditorium or to the plot of the film is thus put in a new light. Every accompanist, whether he played 'from the screen' or reacted to the emotional vibrations given off by the audience, was on 'this side' of the screen, i.e. was a member of the audience. He did more than just illustrate screen events, being also the agent of the audience's collective sensibility. Sabaneyev called this triple relationship 'psychological resonance' – a felicitous choice of words: 'Music must be played down and only fill the acoustic void by resonating psychologically to the moods of the screen.'[35]

'MECHANISM' VERSUS 'ORGANISM'

The question of film music was promptly integrated into the ongoing discourse on the 'nature of the cinematograph'. Thus, it was effectively inscribed into the basic trope of film reception in Russia: cinema as a mechanical parvenu that had come to supplant the organic principle of the authentic arts. Why did cinema need music? 'Like the "bourgeois gentil-homme" it has to conceal all traces of its "bourgeois" [viz. 'mechanical'] origin'[36] – responds one perceptive observer, echoing Dmitri Merezhkovsky's words on the incompatibility of cinema and theatre as mechanism and organism discussed in the Introduction to this book.[37] One should not dismiss similar statements as mere rhetoric. While such things as opposition between 'mechanism' and 'organism' cannot account for the 'hard' facts of tangible film history, they are crucial for the history of film culture. The 'mechanistic' factor was more than idle talk – it was a reality of reception, and as such it was also a factor in film history.

As contemporary reports attest, the decade between 1905 and 1915, which was a period of rapid evolution in the form of the cinema performance, also saw great changes in film accompaniment. A historical survey of cinema music published in 1914 noted that while early films were accompanied only by a 'scratchy gramophone', 'live' music had come to oust 'mechanical' music in the auditorium, and the gramophone was now relegated to providing entertainment during the intervals.[38] According to Vsevolod Chaikovsky, the 'sleepy lady at the piano' did not appear until 1905.[39] He also noted the novelty of the mandolin quartet who were engaged to play at the Great Parisian Theatre on the Arbat in 1906. A term 'interval music' [antraktnaya muzyka] was coined, which first meant the music played during reel changes. Later, when exhibitors, forced by the increase in film footage, introduced double-projector equipment and institutionalised 'waiting for the show', 'interval music' came to mean music played in the foyer.

> As interval music developed it was provided not just by gramophones, but by orchestrions as well, and even – the height of chic – by string trios. The popularity of the orchestrion – an instrument of the barrel organ family – with its little pipes, bells, and electric lights flashing on and off in time to the music, lasted quite some time.[40]

This is how the 1914 observer described what happened next:

> But eventually even orchestrions ceased to satisfy the demands and spirit of the age. With a few exceptions they were driven out of the electric theatres. They had come under heavy fire from the ranks of instrumentalists. Students at the conservatoires, former regimental bandsmen, balalaika players – all began to form their own trios, and even small orchestras; and the trios, in their turn, began to move from the foyers into the auditoria as accompaniment to the films.[41]

These changes conform to the general restyling of the cinema environment during the years of reception shift. It was presumed that the technical side of cinema should be made as unobtrusive as possible. The changed shape of the auditorium, the curtain in front of the screen, the semblance of a stage, the new style in names, the banishment of mechanical intruments – the gramophone and the orchestrion – first from the auditorium, and then from the foyer: all this manifested an urge to suppress the image of 'the machine' that had fascinated cinemagoers of the earlier period. Now that cinema claimed to embody cultural values, no mechanical process could have a part in it.

The expulsion of 'mechanical' features from the collective mental image of 'cinema' was reflected in debates on the future of cinema music that took place in the film journals of the mid-1910s. Anoshchenko and Sabaneyev put forward the idea that the accompanist would eventually be replaced by complicated music machines with changeable programmes that would synchronise sound and image. Their arguments constantly ran up against the same objection: that the cinematograph was already too much of a 'mechanism' for it to be accompanied by mechanical music. Their opponents argued that it was not so much live music itself as the living presence of the humble accompanist (the 'spinster with toothache') that was needed to tip the balance in favour of the organic principle:

> To have [live] music accompanying pictures is cinema renouncing itself, attempting to forget its mechanical nature and to become organic. All these grand pianos, uprights and harmoniums that stand next to the screen in electric theatres – they all cry out with one voice: 'It [the cinematograph] does not want to be dead, it does not want to be a ghost.' Of course we need the sound of the piano in the cinematograph! Even inept, imperfect, boringly amateurish and musically jejune – perhaps even illiterate – but always far more alive than the most dynamic picture on the screen . . . Music will always serve to conceal the mechanical nature of the cinematograph.[42]

IMPROVISATION VERSUS SPECIALLY WRITTEN MUSIC

By 1911 (in many ways an important year in the history of Russian film music) three different styles of accompaniment began to take shape, each having its own party of supporters and its star performers. I. Khudyakov wrote: 'A moving picture can be illustrated in three ways: by "ready made" music, by music specially composed for the occasion, or by improvisation.'[43] The three styles of accompaniment varied in the extent to which they had been specifically composed for a particular film.

Improvisation was the middle way between so-called 'compilation' (ready-made musical fragments loosely attached to action) and special music. In Russia at the turn of the century the very word 'improvisation' had an exciting ring; it invoked the lost paradise of *commedia dell' arte* and eighteenth-century musical evenings in aristocratic salons. Konstantin Argamakov, a popular musician and improvisator of the 1910s, who never actually played for films, gave concerts at which he would compose music to themes prompted by the audience. There were famous improvisators in the cinema world as well. I. Khudyakov, for example, whose classification I cited above, was unanimously recognised in Moscow as an incomparable cinema improvisator. As another well-known film musician of the 1910s, Alexander Anoshchenko, recalled:

> When he appeared by the screen the piano accompaniment to the picture made such a powerful impression that it became accepted by the more intelligent members of the public as an art in itself. Extremely well-read musically and possessing a good musical memory, Khudyakov compiled an elegant musical and dramatic selection of themes, which he drew upon for his improvisations illustrating the development of a film's dramatic action.[44]

The thousand themes mentioned in Khudyakov's film illustration handbook give a good idea of his musical erudition as a practising accompanist.[45] However, in spite of Khudyakov's unchallenged competence in the field, his ideas on improvising for cinema met with objections. Improvisation as a method was criticised for a number of disadvantages. First, the technique was not suited to orchestras. The champions of improvisation did not, however, see this as an inconvenience. Khudyakov put the point as follows: 'Only the individual can create: collective creativity is impossible. Therefore the illustration of film by means of ensembles (orchestras, trios, accompanied voices) is a nonsense.'[46] Second, although improvisation was commonly believed to require some very special skills, in its everyday cinematic application it would often result in the famous 'tumpety-tumpety' effect. Third, as opponents of improvisational accompaniment used to point out, in practice the boundaries between improvisation and compilation were blurred (it should be added that it concerns terminology as well: the word 'improvisation' was sometimes used as a generic term for any non-orchestral film music). In an article written in 1915, Sabaneyev denied that cinema music was a legitimate form of improvisation at all:

> I know some people who warmly welcomed the art of illustrative musical accompaniment, and who assumed that this was a reincarnation of the forgotten art of 'improvisation' that flourished in the age of classicism. But this form of improvisation was genuinely artistic, whereas what we have in cinema today is tasteless vamping to film, slick (and not so slick) plagiarism, the art of distorting great works of art. The two are not in the least comparable.[47]

Surprisingly, Alexander Scriabin, who would be the last person one would suspect of being interested in film music, had something to say about the topic, at least in informal conversation. After his death, his close friend and constant companion, Leonid Sabaneyev, published a book of memoirs in which he reproduced a conversation that took place after one of their improvisation sessions at the composer's home. Scriabin's second wife Tatyana was also present:

Scriabin . . . did not recognise improvisation as an art.

'Of course, I could earn money at it,' he joked, 'I reckon I would make a good cinema improvisator. You know, I have a relative who plays the piano in a cinema on the Arbat – his name is Scriabin as well.'

'I shouldn't think they would pay you much, Sasha,' teased his wife, 'That relative of yours improvises a lot better than you do . . . You haven't really got a gift for it.'

'I just don't happen to think that there's any real merit in improvisation or in the ability to improvise,' replied Scriabin. 'Every form of creativity rests on planning and thought, and there can be no planning or thought where improvisation is concerned.'

But despite what he said, his works did ultimately spring from a genius for improvisation.[48]

Usually, those who rejected improvisation were also advocates of music specially written (or pre-programmed) for each specific film. It takes a musicologist to venture into the history of scores composed for silents. Instead, I will cite more radical ideas that were sounded in favour of refining music machines rather than using the services of composers.

It was Sabaneyev again who kept insisting on a clear-cut, one-to-one relationship between acoustic and visual sequences:

Just as there should be nothing accidental in this mechanical art, so there should be nothing accidental on the musical side either. It should be carefully arranged and strictly timed to coincide with specific moments in the drama; it should also be written down. I think it is just as mechanical as the drama itself. The reproduction of this musical composition should not be left to a single individual with his accidental moods, but should be played by an accompanying instrument that is as mechanical as the cinema itself. Instruments that record sounds and performances already exist – there are all kinds of pianolas and miniolas. Once a film has been shot, once it has recorded all the peripeteia of a drama, it should be 'mechanically' combined with the pianola ribbon and both these ribbons should then travel the world together.[49]

That is how it seemed to a musicologist who had no experience of accompanying films. Although this passage sounds like a manifesto rather than a practical recommendation (mechanical music never became widely used in Russian cinemas), this form of accompaniment was quite feasible even in the 1910s. Sabaneyev's doctrine was put into practice by the Moscow cinema accompanist Alexander Anoshchenko in a test that, in its own way, predates avant-garde experiments with mechanical music: instead of punching a programme-tape by playing a tune on a 'master-piano' with a perforating mechanism attached, Anoshchenko punched the tape by hand, an idea roughly similar to that of 'drawing' music straight on to an optical soundtrack:

Once I demonstrated a waltz for Khudyakov that I had composed specially for the phonola or the pianola. The phonola and pianola are mechanisms attached to the keyboard of a grand piano, and a roll of paper ribbon with a perfectly recorded piece of piano music is fed into it. These ribbons could also be made straight from a score without having to be pre-recorded. A couple of levers allowed one to control the mechanism by changing tempo and loudness. The melody flowed in unison, an octave higher than the quiet background, which was formed by many rapidly moving, abrupt sounds, and within this pattern of sound the chords followed one another in smooth succession. Khudyakov, himself a sophisticated musician, liked my composition. He also observed that a human musician could not play it by hand on a piano. I explained my idea of using instruments like this to improve film illustration. Although we had a lot in common as far as our general aesthetic tastes were concerned, on this issue our views differed quite sharply. I dreamed of a musical film drama, constructed in synthesis, with music recorded on ribbon for the automatic piano. Even a pianist with only rudimentary qualifications would be able to 'conduct' the instrument and co-ordinate it with the film. In the majority of cinemas this would facilitate both the task of the accompanist and the lot of the audience, who would experience an artistic illustration via the actual sounds of the piano. Khudyakov was quite opposed to this idea, since he subscribed to the aesthetic principles of John Ruskin and William Morris, who did not accept that works of art could be produced by machines. Accordingly, Khudyakov held that a cinema picture was merely the shadow of an art that only came to life artistically thanks to the creativity of the musician accompanying the picture. Khudyakov was a great artist of improvisation.[50]

As to Khudyakov himself, he formulated his position in a way we are already familiar with:

Film illustration demands a creativity that only a human being possesses. If you try to use mechanical music for this purpose – however good it may be, however well it may coincide with the feel of the picture or adapt itself to the changes of mood within the picture – it will never replace the live illustrator. A machine can never create or replace the human soul, and any artificiality will always produce a most jarring effect.[51]

FILM FOR MUSIC

Music specially written for film is the most fully researched aspect of the problem of 'music and film'. Less well researched is the mirror image of this process: when a silent film is shot with a certain piece of music in mind or, as occurred in the history of Russian film culture, when a film script is designed as a straightforward illustration to music.

Starting from 1908, Russian cinema became more orientated towards music. Inspired by the example of *L'Assassinat du Duc de Guise*, with a score composed by Saint-Saëns, Drankov commissioned Ippolitov-Ivanov to write a score for *Stenka Razin*.[52] The music was written with one peculiarity of Russian audiences in mind: Ippolitov-Ivanov did not write a completely new musical score but used the folk song that was associated with the film's story. The song established a 'common ground' of shared experience between the audience and the film. As a publicity hand-out for the film emphasised,

> As legend has it, the song that we all know and love, 'Mother Volga' [Vniz po matushke po Volge], was composed by Stenka Razin's comrades. That was two centuries ago, and now it is a folk song closely associated with the name of the Volga pirate. Every Russian knows the tune: it is sung at concerts, in polite society and in the poorest peasant families.[53]

According to Jay Leyda (a reliable source, as he is the only film historian who was able to discuss this with Drankov himself), the audience picked up the tune and sang it throughout the entire film.[54] In this respect *Stenka Razin* looked less like *L'Assassinat du Duc de Guise* than like those films in the early history of Italian cinema that screened popular operas (*Il Trovatore*, *Rigoletto* and *Manon Lescaut*) and were called '*opere sincronizzate*' (synchronised operas) because they allowed the Italian spectators to join in famous arias.[55]

After 1913 a major part of Russian salon melodramas were loosely based on motifs from '*romansy*' (romantic ballads). It was not intended that the audience should join in, but the piano player was certainly supposed to know the tune. From time to time the tune would be 'cued' by a close-up of the score lying on a piano in someone's room.[56] However, the commonest way to cue the motif was a literary rather than a musical one: by the title of the film. The film star Ivan Perestiani described the usual way a ballad would be chosen for screen adaptation:

> They said that the studio owner Dmitri Kharitonov kept Zimmermann's sheet music catalogue on his desk with the names of popular ballads ticked off, and that he insisted that his directors made pictures to match the names.[57]

In a manuscript dating from 1919 I. N. Ignatov explained the technique:

> You took two or three verses and composed a story corresponding to their mood. At the key moment, when the action was approaching its dénouement, the words of the ballad were displayed in an explanatory panel [i.e. an intertitle] and the film would end. The ballad would begin with the words 'Driver, don't flog the horses', and that would also be the name of the film. An elderly man has fallen in love with a young girl; he thinks she also loves him, that he has rediscovered his youth, that life is wonderful – all caresses and love. But then he overhears a conversation between the

young girl and his son and realises that all his hopes are dashed. Alone, he makes his way home, and the driver of the troika whips up the horses: 'Driver, don't flog the horses. I'm not hurrying anywhere now. I've no one to love any more.'[58]

This was a viewer's description of Yevgeni Bauer's film *Driver, Don't Flog the Horses* [Yamshchik, ne goni loshadei, 1916] and it is interesting to compare it with how the picture was remembered by someone who made his film début in it, Ivan Perestiani:

> As frequently happens (more frequently than it ought to, in fact) my first appearance on film was in the concluding sequences of a picture. I played a man who, rather late in life, had become infatuated with a young girl and was undergoing all the sufferings of autumnal love. The intertitle read:
>   'I've nowhere to hurry to now,
>   I've no one to love any more.'
> So, I had to walk – with a heavy heart – down a very long corridor, go into a sort of lobby adjoining the corridor and sit down at a grand piano where *she* had only just been playing. On the way, I had to pause at a window lit by the rays of the setting sun.[59]

One can easily imagine the power that was generated by the 'psychological resonance'[60] between the familiar music and the way in which its theme had been given new motivation.[61] The 'mood cueing' technique worked so well because the familiar song was reinforced by an unfamiliar story inscribed into it. It is quite possible that some of the idiosyncrasies of Russian film style (certain static pauses, for example) will some day be explained by the music that was supposed to be played with these films – especially because the 'moods' themselves were often induced into actors by 'mood music' played on the set.

There were also other methods of 'addressing' the potential accompanist from the screen: intertitles and what we might call 'diegetic music' (as far as the term can be applied to silent cinema). The biggest Russian box-office success, *Still, Sadness, Still . . .* [Molchi, grust', molchi . . ., 1918], made for Kharitonov by the director Peter Chardynin, used both. The same intertitle bearing the phrase 'Still, sadness, still . . .' (the first line of a popular ballad) was repeated four times at different stages of the story – both as a literary leitmotif and as a prompt for the accompanist. For a trio or orchestra, a striking instrumental arrangement was prompted by Vera Kholodnaya playing it on the guitar as a poor street singer, or on the piano when she became a courtesan. When he was abandoned by Vera, the lonely clown Lorio (Peter Chardynin) played the tune on the violin.

It is interesting to note that ten years later, when Chardynin's film had long been forgotten by the public, the tune lived on in the repertoire of a Moscow accompanist who would play it at the slightest opportunity. A satirist writing for *Kino* was indignant: 'On the screen my eyes were watching a Red Army parade, but all I heard from the piano was 'Still, Sadness, Still'.[62]

Apart from 'ballad films' (i.e. films that were more concerned with musical 'moods' rather than the music itself) there were also films whose appeal, according to the popular press of the day, lay specifically in their 'musical' origin. As *The Exchange Gazette* wrote in 1915:

> In Moscow they have just finished shooting a very interesting picture; it is called *Fairy Tale of the World* [Skazka mira], and it is dedicated to the memory of Scriabin. For the first time an attempt has been made to convey the spirit of some of the deceased composer's works.[63]

The Fairy Tale of the World (1915) was about an imaginary composer and, according to the publicity, it demonstrated 'the workings of his creative process' – this alone must have presented an unimaginative accompanist with some serious problems.

More radical attempts to discover the cinema equivalent of a musical production remained unrealised. In the 1910s V. E. Cheshikhin and the leader of a symphonic choir, V. A. Bulychev,[64] both wrote film scripts: the former based his on Beethoven's Pastoral Symphony, while the latter followed Schumann's oratorio, *Paradise and the Peri*.[65] We can get a glimpse of what these scripts were like from Anoshchenko, who had the idea of making a film based on Berlioz's music that would be played by a symphony orchestra specially engaged for the purpose. The orchestra and Berlioz were to be the primary element of the spectacle, while the film itself was subordinated to the music and formed a sort of 'visual accompaniment' to it. This is how Anoshchenko outlined the script in 1914:

> In his day Berlioz was a musical revolutionary; the musician in him was inseparable from the romantically inclined dramatist. The flight of fancy of a Victor Hugo, the delicate artistry of the poet Alfred de Musset, the vivid colours of a Delacroix were all uniquely combined in Berlioz's works. After listening to his symphonic poem, and having been moved by the dramatic quality of the plot, I suddenly saw visual images begin to come alive in the work. I was helped by my experience in feeling for the music in silent film drama and saw emerge a film poem in synthesis with Berlioz's symphony. The plot, briefly, runs as follows. A poor artist is in love with a girl who deceives him with a rich man. Drugged with hashish, he is haunted by her image, both at a ball, among strangers, and out in the countryside. In his sleep he is tormented by an orgy of repulsive monsters all resembling her seducer. The image of his sweetheart is announced by the appearance of a musical 'idée fixe' as the symphonic form develops. The artist imagines that he kills his sweetheart together with her seducer. The artist is taken to the scaffold, accompanied by the sympathetic clamour of the crowd. He hears the note of a clarinet as he thinks about his

sweetheart for the very last time. The guillotine falls – and the musical poem ends with a violent crash from the whole orchestra and the rolling of kettledrums.[66]

A COMPILER'S GLOSSARY AND THE THEMATIC RANGE OF EARLY CINEMA

In practice, the majority of film musicians chose the third of Khudyakov's variations: an accompaniment consisting of bits and pieces of ready-made music. As we know, certain musical forms had become firmly associated with particular genres of film: the romantic ballad with drama; the polka or the cake-walk with comedy; the waltz or nocturne with scenic pictures; the march with military sequences. 'If we add the funeral march,' Khudyakov's article acidly suggested, 'then the repertoire will be quite broad enough for any purpose. It is a bit like a style book for writing love letters, only it covers virtually all eventualities.'[67]

Anoshchenko's memoirs give some idea of the technique used to connect up music and image. This is how he described his first shot at film accompaniment (around 1909), when he was determined to give an inspired improvisation:

> I sat down at the piano; it was against the side wall, right under the screen. Although I could improvise pretty easily, I didn't feel all that sure of myself . . . When a dramatic film came up, I discovered that this was far more difficult to illustrate . . . After marking time for a bit with a few modulated passages, I abandoned my good, but unrealistic, intentions, and went over to a sad waltz. The left hand represented the hero; the right hand the heroine, and the melody either went up or down according to the action. That was all I had managed to learn half-way through an unseen short-length drama.[68]

However unpretentious this method might have been, compilation had its champions among film reviewers. Their main argument was that compilation facilitated score writing, and a compiled score opened the road for instrumental ensembles (the most widespread form in the early years being the violin and piano duo, which expanded to a small orchestra by the end of the 1910s), while the improvisator was fated to remain a solitary figure.

Another argument was that 'ready-made' music gave the accompaniment an unlimited variety of choice. As if to contest the commonly held view that the average film piano accompanist had only a very limited musical vocabulary, in 1912 the accompanists Anatoli Goldobin and Boris Azancheyev published their manual *Accompanying Cinematograph Pictures on the Piano* (see note 33), which listed 'all the usual themes' met with in the contemporary cinematograph, and suggested suitable musical accompaniments.[69] This book's importance for the film historian is self-evident. As well as telling us the repertoire that film illustrators used (or more correctly, could draw upon), it gives us a good idea of the subjects, emotions and themes which the accompanist thought deserved special musical treatment. This list of musical themes is also a rich source of information on the way the cinematograph was received at the beginning of the 1910s; it presents a cross-section of film reception in 1912. Although the cinematic 'phenomena' that the authors enumerate are mediated through their own musical preferences and the stock of tunes available – the authors would hardly have made special mention of 'Lithuanians' if Lithuanian folk songs had not been to hand – this is precisely what gives the list its value for the historian of film reception: for the world of the screen (something we may also call the aggregate diegesis of the films shown in the 1910s) reached the viewer 'prepackaged' in the accompanist's chosen musical compilation. The list is remarkable for its fullness and inclusiveness, not in the sense that it reflects cinema's entire thematic range at that time but rather the opposite: we get the feeling that the list is exhaustive yet at the same time we do not lose sight of its lacunae. Its fullness is a fullness from within, while its lacunae give it a definite shape. Reception is never encyclopaedic: its configuration consists of 'blind' spots and improbably magnified details. Goldobin's and Azancheyev's glossary reflects that quality.

The full glossary of cinematographic themes contained in the manual are listed below. The musical recommendations, which are of more specialised interest, have been omitted.

Internal Phenomena

Anger, animation, arrogance, bravery, carelessness, complaint, concern, contempt, courage, daydreams, decisiveness, desire, dreams, enjoyment, enmity, ecstasy, fear, fright, happiness, horror, inspiration, joy, laughter, love, loneliness, longing, madness, melancholia, modesty, oaths, passion, peace, persistence, prayer, pride, reflection, remembrance, remorse, repentance, reproach, revenge, sadness, satisfaction, sickness, sleep, suffering, tears, thoughtfulness, weeping, woe.

External Phenomena

Abuse, Africa, ambush, America, Arabs, Armenians, ascent, Austria, autumn, balalaika, ballet, barrel organ, battle, bell, Bible, bird, blind people, Bohemia, Bulgaria, butterfly, Caucasus, cemetery, ceremony, childhood, chiming clocks, China, church, clock, comedy, conflagration, conflict, cradle song, Creoles, Croatians, cry, cuckoo, cursing, dances [see below], dawn, death, Denmark, departure, desert, devil, Dnieper, drunkenness, dusk, east, echo, Egypt, epic, execution, fairytale, farewell, feast, Finland, flies, flight, flowers, flute, folk songs, forced labour, forest, fountain, France, funeral, Germany,

Greece, guitar, Gypsies, harp, Holland, horse, humming, Hungary, hunting, hymn, idyll, India, Indians, inspection, Ireland, Italy, Japan, Jews, jokes, Kirghiz, legend, letter, lion, Lithuanians, Little Russia, locomotive, magic, mandolin, march, mill, monastery, Montenegro, moon, Moravia, mosquitoes, murmuring, Naples, negroes, night, nightingale, Norway, noise, old style, panpipes, parrot, pastorale, patrol, pearl, Persia, pipe, plot, prison, procession, pursuit, raspberry, raven, revolt, ruin, Romania, savages, scenery, sea, Serbia, serenade, shadowing, shepherd, shooting, shot, Siam, signal, skylark, smithy, snow, sorcery, Spain, spinning wheel, spring, steppe, storm, stream, struggle, students, summer, sunset, swan, Tatars, temple, thunderstorm, toast, tram, tundra, Turkey, violet, violin, vision, Volga, waltz, war, waterfall, waves, wedding, winter, wizard, zither.

Dances

Aeronet, alikaz, apache, arcadienne, bal-bourré, barynya, berlinka, bi-ba-bo, cake-walk, dibolette, gavotte, gallop, geisha, grossvater, gopak, jiganette, kamarinskaya, karama, kazachok, kikapu, ki-king, kitayanka, kraket, krakowiak, krestyanochka, krizol, kokhanochka, lablador, lawn-tennis, lezginka, liket, matchisch, matchischinette, mazurochka, mélange, minuet, mirmiton, negrelle, negrityanochka, New Yorkaise, oy-ra!, pas-de-gras, pas-de-quatre, pas-de-patineur, vampire, varshavyanka, vengerka, waltz, yermak.

Was this range of musical topics ever used in practice? There is no way of knowing. As was well realised at the time, film music is at its best when it least draws attention to itself. What were noticed were any major incongruities. The most straightforward case was where the music ran so counter to the content of the picture that it gave the screen action a comic twist. Observers were keen collectors of such amusing incidents and passed them on to magazines and newspapers; we can mention a few examples in chronological order.

Arkadi Averchenko, writing for *Satirikon* in 1908, observed: 'The dimwitted pianist belted out a merry gallop while the railwayman's daughter was dying under the murderer's knife, and played a funeral march while a crowd was chasing a boy who had stolen a goose.'[70]

'When there was a fire, a train disaster or an aeroplane crash the melancholy, sweet little thing with freckles at the piano would tinkle out a cake-walk', observed the writer Yefim Zozulya in 1912.[71]

Konstantin Argamakov, who wrote several works on musical improvisation, reported that he happened to have seen scenes from Pushkin's *Eugene Onegin* (1911) in a provincial cinema, and that Tatyana's letter scene had been illustrated by the popular waltz 'In the Hills of Manchuria' [Na sopkakh Manchzhurii].[72]

The critic A. Stavritsky mentioned other examples in 1923:

They were showing the funeral of a much-loved Red Army commander, a man from an ordinary working-class family and a leading trade-union member, and the piano was bashing out 'Little Pippin' [Yablochko]! ... The picture also showed an emergency session of the Central Committee of the clandestine pre-Revolutionary Bolshevik party, while the pianist rattled off 'Beauties of the Cabaret'![73]

Not all such incongruities were accidental. The censor banned any musical accompaniment to newsreels about the Imperial Family, which suggests that some accompanists had allowed themselves a few imprudent experiments in illustrating films of this genre. Another musical joke (in the 1900s) was described as follows: 'I remember how delighted Russian viewers were at seeing a carnival in Nice shown to the tune of the old Russian folk dance 'Down the Kazanka River' [Vdol' da po rechke, vdol' da po Kazanke], hammered out by a spirited accompanist on an untuned piano.'[74] As this incident seems to show, the public of the 1900s had a soft spot for bravura performances on the part of the accompanist.

MUSIC AND COLOUR

Some writers on cinema held to the view that incidental music was more suitable than specially composed scores. To demonstrate the difference between specially written music and compilation they used the analogy of film colouring. Silent films could be coloured either by using one tint per shot ('toning' or 'tinting') or by using one of the techniques that gave film frames a look loosely similar to modern colour images, such as hand or stencil colouring, Kinemacolour, Kodachrome, etc.[75] Specially composed scores 'hand-colour' images by imposing strong musical interpretation on action, which – as far as one can judge by the review of Mounet-Sully's *Oedipus-Rex* cited earlier in this chapter – was not always considered the right way to do it. Compiled music, on the other hand, did not interfere with the image by highlighting separate gestures, but rather added an even emotional 'hue' to the scene as a whole. This is what Anoshchenko has to say about the way he accompanied an 'uneventful scenic picture' in 1909:

I did no more than provide a general musical 'colouring', as one used to give a light blue tint to a photograph of a moonlit landscape. Although the piano was out of tune the music harmonised quite satisfactorily with the picture.[76]

Writing as an apostle of the idea of absolute musical control ('synthesis') over images, Anoshchenko, who (as Stravinsky was to do in 1917) was 'programming' music for pianolas and wrote a script based on a symphony by Berlioz, elaborated the metaphor of monochrome colouring as a first stage to the cinematic *Gesamtkunstwerk*, an idea that anticipated some of

Eisenstein's theories. In a paper presented at a discussion on 'Film and Music' held at the editorial offices of the journal *The Cinematheatre and Life* in 1913 we find the following assertion:

> Compilative illustration is a primitive method of satisfying the demand for a synthesis of music and cinema which is analogous to the tinting or toning of different parts of a picture in different colours. Compilative illustration can catch the general mood of a scene, but the most important thing is left out: i.e. the expression of dramatic periods, especially in the interplay of differentiated characters with identical significance to the plot. Both piano and symphonic music for the screen must deploy a 'stereoscopic' quality and colour in order to express the characters' emotional dynamics.[77]

As this passage indicates, by becoming more and more image-specific, film music was returning to the melodramatic technique of investing action with emotion by adding emphasis to gestures and ascribing certain motifs to certain characters – something Sergei Eisenstein and Sergei Prokofiev did for *Ivan the Terrible* [Ivan Grozny] in the 1940s.

RHYTHM

Rhythmic versus 'dramatic' accompaniment, the latter being understood as 'illustration of action and feelings',[78] constituted yet another dimension of the debate on cinema music. Pavel Muratov wrote: 'In the cinematograph music has a dual illustrative character: on the one hand, emotional (the more vulgar aspect), and on the other, rhythmic (the more interesting aspect).'[79]

Several observers explained the effectiveness of rhythmic illustration directly by referring to the very nature of 'moving photographs', to the quality that Elie Faure must have had in mind when he asserted (in 1920) that 'the interpenetration, the crossing and the association of movements and cadences already gives us the impression that even the most mediocre films unfold in musical space.'[80] By 'musical space' Faure meant the film medium itself, not its musical accompaniment. A similar idea occured to Vladimir Stasov (Russia's major authority on music) when he saw Lumière's *Le Baignade en mer* [Sea Bathing] in 1896:

> It was like a new kind of music: it wasn't Mendelssohn's 'Meeresstille', it wasn't anybody's music; it came straight out of what took place on that stretch of beach all day and every day – people bathing in the sea. What could be more unimportant, more ordinary, more prosaic? Naked bodies dashing into the water to cool off – nothing particularly interesting, significant or beautiful. But no! Out of all this ordinariness something interesting, and important, and beautiful is made, something you can not express in words.[81]

'Music underlines the eminently rhythmic nature of the cinematograph,' wrote Muratov in the 1920s, as an explanation of how and why film music works.[82] The rhythmic contours of 'real music' and the internal musicality of 'all this ordinariness' created a kind of audio-visual counterpoint. Music changes the way we perceive films. The 'silent musicality' of movement within the frame finds in the music of the accompanist a 'unique rhythmic ornament' (Alexander Anoshchenko) – if not a direct equivalent – that re-accentuates movement and makes film's rhythmic articulation more complex.[83]

The impact was reciprocal. Unlike concert improvisators, the film accompanist could not simply follow the natural, immanent, development of the musical form. One way or another, music in cinema had to come to terms with the confused reality of the screen and the changing moods of the auditorium. The internal pulse of cinematic movement – as well as the neurotic tempo of changing shots, intertitles and subjects – was observed to have infected the accompaniment. Something like a musical counterpart (or a 'musical image') of the cinematic text was born.

Musical illustration became as fragmentary, unbalanced and erratic as the kind of art it was called upon to illustrate. It was easy to see this as a degeneration of musical form, yet some perceptive observers were beginning to discover an aesthetic system behind all these anomalies. This is how Alexander Anoshchenko, the most militant philosopher among early film musicians, presented the new style in a speech made in 1913:

> The improvisator at the piano . . . has to be untrammelled by the 'laws' of music in the abstract and has to base his method on *exceptions to these laws*. Extended and abbreviated musical phrases and sentences; displaced metres; constantly changing melody steps and dissonant chords in contrapuntal movement; decisive harmonic modulations; the use of sound effects and timbres of new instruments; voice resonators, and much else besides – all these allow him to intensify the impression of the action on the screen.[84]

It may seem even stranger that among the enthusiasts of 'cinema style' music there were people of refined European taste, and discriminating adherents of aesthetic conservatism such as Pavel Muratov:

> Listen carefully to a skilful cinema accompanist. Not in the least bit embarrassed, he weaves his improbable mosaic from Chopin, from Verdi's or Tchaikovsky's operas, from music-hall ballads and café dances, picking them up, breaking off in mid-passage, switching from one to another – but always at the right moment, not in the sense of emotional correspondence to the action, but in a deeper and more important rhythmic sense. And sometimes even a musically fastidious viewer will overlook this grotesque confusion, since he is carried along by the rhythm of the entire spectacle without actually hearing the details or noticing the separate musical 'pieces' of the mosaic, and is responding only to the rhythm of its overall sonic pattern.[85]

The author draws the following conclusion: 'Cinema accompaniment has taught us how to be captivated by the music of the jazz band, the music of sounds that are scattered out and threaded on rhythms like beads.'[86] Although a music historian might dispute this parallel, it is still precious as a testimony that comes to us from the heart of the 1920s, the time of cinema and the age of jazz. Be it as it may, in 1929 (one of the very last years of silent film) a musical composition was written which proves that silent film did indeed have an influence on 'pure music'. It was Darius Milhaud's orchestral suite 'Newsreel' (1929) – a piece that was written for a non-existent film. As the Russian conductor Gennady Rozhdestvensky noted on the dust jacket of a record released by the Soviet recording organisation Melodia in 1984, 'This is music for an imaginary newsreel. Fast changes of musical sequences and thoroughly pre-meditated alteration of tempos and timbres create the sonic equivalent of shifting film shots.'

SOUND EFFECTS

The fashion for accompanying films with sound effects arrived in Russia about 1906: 'In their newspaper advertisements cinema theatres gave wide coverage to their sound effects, while the names of the films were often printed in smaller type.'[87]

A 'universal sound machine' was advertised that was able to imitate all the following noises: thunder, gunfire, galloping horses, motor-car engines, horns, drums, bells, waterfalls and rain, breaking glass, children crying, dogs barking, cats miaowing, horses neighing and sheep bleating. But if a theatre did not have one of these machines, noises could always be produced by simpler methods. Thunder could be made by shaking sheets of iron or by rolling cylinders filled with bits of metal. Wind could be imitated by spinning a drum against a piece of tightly stretched silk, rain and hail by pouring dry peas on to wrapping paper. The sound of breaking surf could be made by rolling small stones in a box spiked with nails.

> If at the moment when a wave on the screen was about to crash on to the shore you flexed a piece of tin rapidly back and forth with both hands, and at the same time someone else turned the handle of the box, you would get the sound of breaking waves. If you then rapidly tipped the box in the opposite direction the stones would slide down, striking the nails and producing a noise that sounded just like waves ebbing back into the sea, taking pebbles and shells with them.[88]

The smaller cinemas made do with a metal bowl, a toy pistol and a police whistle.

It was mentioned above that special musical scores were written only for premières in the capital cities. We can see from the showing of *The Defence of Sebastopol* [Oborona Sevastopolya, 1911] how the accompaniment might change as a film moved from the centre into the provinces. The music for this film was written by Georgi Kazachenko, who insisted that a gala performance be given in the Moscow conservatoire. A month later, in mid-November 1911, the film was shown in Yalta for Nicholas II, after which it was distributed throughout Russia. An account of the showing in Kineshma shows that in the provinces the musical score (or incidental music performed instead of the original score) took second place to the sound effects:

> The accompanying pianist thumped frenziedly on the bass notes. Behind the screen iron sheets and other objects were hammered and rattled, and real revolver shots rang out. When the cannons opened up, muffled rifles were fired. The auditorium was thick with gunsmoke, and the shots made the viewers jump. The projection beam hardly managed to pierce the smoke and its reflection lit up the whole auditorium.[89]

With the entry of Russia into the war, and the appearance of patriotic war pictures, some sequences began to be shot specifically with sound effects in mind. In the film *Lumbering Russia has Stirred to Defend the Sacred Cause* [Vskolykhnulas' Rus' sermyazhnaya i grud'yu stala za svyatoe delo, 1916], newsreel recordings of explosions and gunfire were inserted, and the naval guns in the picture were mainly depicted firing directly at the audience.[90] The film was distributed with an accompanying sound effects 'script'.

Sound effects occasionally received a mention in reviews. Méliès' film *La Civilisation à travers les âges* [Civilisation Through the Ages, 1907], which was distributed in Russia with the more appropriate title *The Culture of Human Savagery* [Kul'tura chelovecheskogo zverstva], was given a hostile reception by *The Cinematograph Herald*: 'The scenes are coarse and revolting. They are accompanied (presumably for greater realism) by sound effects. For instance, in the scene entitled "Christians at the Stake" you hear a crackling sound supposedly representing the burning of brushwood.'[91]

This and similar comments suggest that sound effects were used for films in the spirit of the Grand Guignol tradition. Sound effects were pure attractions, in both Eisenstein's and Tom Gunning's sense of the word. The fireworks accompanying *The Defence of Sebastopol* in Kineshma and the destroyer's gun firing straight at the viewer in *Lumbering Russia . . .* bring to mind the occasion when, a decade later, Eisenstein exploded firecrackers under the spectators' seats in his 1923 theatre production *Wise Man* [Mudrets], and also the film where the muzzle of a gun was first turned on us – Edwin Porter's *The Great Train Robbery* (Edison, 1903). In spite of the usual complaints that the sound effects were 'just too realistic' – or, rather, *because* these complaints were so common – one can clearly see that sound effects, in fact, subverted the overall realist intent behind the film-making of the 1910s. The problem was that, of all the potential sounds that an attentive viewer could 'hear' in the screen narrative, sound-effects specialists picked out only the most 'traumatic' ones (a slap, for example, or a shot), and passed over those that were less striking, or those that belonged more to what one might call the film's 'diegetic ambience'. The question as to whether pictures ought to be accompanied by sound effects at all was answered by a Simbirsk reader of *The Projector* as follows:

> Pictures should not be accompanied by sound effects, because you get a dissonance that both offends the eye and grates on the ear. When a person on the screen moves his lips we cannot hear what he is saying, but we can hear when he slaps his partner, or when a pistol goes off, and as a rule noises like these are far too loud. Quieter sounds – footsteps, small moving objects, rustling noises, etc. – are not taken into account. I believe that the reproduction of sound effects in pictures ought to be based on the principle of 'speaking pictures' like the 'kinetophone', etc. [92]

THE RECEPTION OF RECORDED SOUND

Edison's kinetophones (kinetoscopes equipped with rubber earphones) were demonstrated in Nizhny Novgorod in the summer of 1896 but were completely wiped out by the effect produced by the Lumières' cinematograph. Although Gaumont's 'Chronomégaphone' was shown in Moscow on 8 October 1906 I have found no critical references to sound in the Russian press before 1908. In 1908 *Cine-Phono* published an article formulating an objection which twenty years later was to become an obstacle to getting audiences used to the talkies: 'One thing really kills the illusion: the sound waves come to us from a place in the theatre different from where the screen is situated.'[93]

In 1913 Thomas Edison made an attempt to revive the kinetophone idea. The updated kinetophone projected motion pictures in a large theatre with synchronous recorded sound.[94] The equipment was demonstrated in the USA, then sold to Europe and Japan. In 1913, alarmed by Edison's initiative, European companies (including Gaumont) renewed their own experiments with sound. As a result the Russian cinema press had occasion to start discussing talkies long before the issue became really critical.

In the event, many observers made the same complaints about the kinetophone and chronomegaphone as about hand-produced sound effects. An observer in Rostov-on-Don (where Edison's kinetophone arrived in 1915) was dissatisfied with the selectivity of mechanical sound: 'the lack of sound when the actors move about spoils the illusion. A dog runs about noiselessly like a disembodied ghost, but his barking is far too loud. People sing and dance; the singing is loud, but you can't hear the shuffling sound of the dancing.'[95] Sound 'portrayed' certain objects, but failed to 'portray' space.

What people mostly complained of was the timbre of the kinetophone. A correspondent of the Moscow *Early Morning* had this to say of a performance in St Petersburg: 'The singing and music were relatively well done, but

ordinary speech sounded ridiculous.'[96] Professor Arabazhin said that the only
sound the machine could faithfully reproduce was that of a dog barking.[97]
Another critic observed that the normal human voice sounded like that of a
ventriloquist, or of a puppeteer.[98] 'These sounds make the viewers laugh, or
put them off, rather than excite them. They are like the guttural and nasal
sounds you hear coming from behind the screen in Punch-and-Judy shows.
Sometimes they remind you of a talking parrot', remarked the drama critic
of *Theatre and Art*.[99]

One other acoustic characteristic, the scratching of the gramophone needle,
evoked the image of an invisible snake: 'Hamlet sings over the skull and his
voice is drowned in the hissing of a snake',[100] wrote Sergei Gorodetsky in a
1910 short story describing what was possibly a scene from Sarah Bernhardt's
Hamlet recorded for one of the first 'gramophone pictures'. The same trope
of reception is found in a 'decadent' verse exercise by the young Fyodor
Otsep, in which the future film director tried to render the hissing sound of
the gramophone needle by an abundance of sibilants and fricatives:

The snake-like hiss of snake-like words
Cannot quench the fires of passion.
The grating wheeze of weasel words
Cannot break the still of death.[101]

The image of the invisible snake links the reception of the human voice
recorded for 'gramophone pictures' to a larger family of sonic metaphors
related to sound machines proper – the gramophone (which Yuri Tynyanov
once suggested sounded like someone being strangled to death), and the
telephone.[102] Here, as Roman Timenchik has shown in his study of telephones in Russian poetry, the image of the hissing snake was supplemented
by the image of a serpentine cable swallowing up its messages.[103]

Chapter 4

The reception of interference

OPTICAL INTERFERENCES: 'RAIN' AND 'FOG'

According to Roman Jakobson's theory, as developed in the writings of Yuri Lotman, there exists a distinction between semiotics as a communications discipline and what Lotman defines as 'cultural semiotics'. The distinction is in the angle of research. The semiotics of communication examines the way people transmit information, and the model situation is *person – text – person*. Within this model the 'best' text is the one that best serves the purpose of communication. The clearer the channel the better the message transmitted along it. Other signals passing along the channel are regarded as 'background interference'.

Cultural semiotics has a different object. It studies texts as they are processed 'through' people. Here the model is *text – person – text*, and the main interest lies in the distortions rather than in the clarity of the 'message'. Cultural semiotics, therefore, investigates the discrepancies between the 'input' and 'output' texts. What for communication is 'background interference' or 'noise' may be turned into 'message' by culture. New texts are often born as misreadings of older ones.

The *text – person – text* angle is applicable in reception studies as well. Reception 'transcends' text by adding something to what the author put into it. Usually it happens by way of internal 'co-authoring': while reading a book the reader invests into it something he or she knows or thinks (or thinks he or she knows) but he or she also indulges in intentional as well as accidental misreadings. The area that we call 'the aesthetic' is extremely labile and is subject to frequent redefinition. It may contract (everyone knows how frequently a film loses its spell when re-released), but it may also expand. The OPOYAZ[1] school of literary history called such expansion 'the valorisation of extra-aesthetic categories' [*kanonizatsiya vneesteticheskogo ryada*]. While the OPOYAZ Formalists applied this notion to major areas and genres of discourse, it can also be attributed to mechanical distortions of each given text. For an art that attached so much importance to its claim to be 'life-like', and was as dependent upon unsophisticated projection techniques as cinema was in its early days, 'semiotic interference' became a factor that could not be too easily ignored. Indeed, in early film reception such mechanical interference was frequently – even typically – misread as part of the aesthetic message rather than as 'background noise'. In this chapter I shall consider those elements which can be called, to use Yuri Lotman's term, 'the expedient irregularities'[2] of silent film culture.

Let us take the 'rain effect' as an example. Every cinemagoer is familiar with the scratch marks on worn prints that show up as specks flickering vertically down the screen.[3] In early films these were particularly trouble-some. A 1916 technical manual explained this involuntary 'animation effect' as follows:

> Since . . . a scratch mark in the corner of the picture is rapidly followed by one in the middle or at the top, it looks as though they are dancing all over the place, sometimes in dense clusters, sometimes scattered all around the image. If there are a lot of these defects the screen will appear to be covered with a fine veil of flickering white specks, or a shower of 'rain'.[4]

The word 'rain' was both a technical term and a common metaphor; it was a minor trope of film reception. Film reviews often contained facetious 'meteorological' references; in a big country like Russia spectators living in far-off regions often had to put up with poor second-hand copies. One Moscow critic, who came across a showing of *Cabiria* (Italy, 1914) in a provincial cinema as late as 1917, wrote with mock surprise:

> One thing puzzled me: was the action taking place indoors or outside in the open air? There was torrential rain everywhere . . . It was explained to me that the picture was a second-hand one, and with second-hand pictures the actors are always getting soaked to the skin . . .[5]

In 1929 Osip Mandelstam used the notion to evoke the 'naive' trick films of the 1900s when 'a chambermaid with a broom could walk up a wall and dry celluloid rain poured down in illusion theatres'.[6] This passage does not necessarily suggest that the prints shown in the 1900s were of inferior quality. Rather the term 'rain' is used here as one might use the term 'patina', to suggest an archaic quality.

Occasionally, a writer would invoke the image of 'celluloid rain' to conjure up a metaphor for a dramatic dimness of vision. The hero of Nabokov's novel *Laughter in the Dark* is waiting for his wife to give birth to a baby when he hears the doctor saying 'it's all over': 'Before Albinus's eyes there appeared a fine rain like the flickering of some very old film . . .'[7]

My next example is closer to film-making – it demonstrates that a film-generated literary trope similar to the one used in Nabokov's novel may 'rebound' back into cinema, this time as a premeditated artistic device rather than as the mechanical 'interference' it had originally been. When the Symbolist writer Fyodor Sologub was working on the script for *Miss Liza*

[Baryshnya Liza] in 1918, and was trying to find a way of representing the heroine's failing sight, the best thing he could think of was the very common 'rain effect' (which he probably imagined could be achieved by hand-scratching the film). In any event, that is how he described the contrast between the sunlit clarity of the actual scene and the way it appeared to Liza, who had ruined her eyesight through the self-inflicted punishment of constant embroidering, night and day: 'It's a bright morning, but Liza can't see anything clearly; it is as though the shapes of things are obscured by heavy rain. In her imagination the whole world seems to be rippling, quavering.'[8] In another scene the intended effect is almost identical to the technical description of 'celluloid rain' cited above: 'She looks about her: the bright day is misty, everything seems to be hidden behind a fine veil.'[9]

If we look back at these examples, we may be able to visualise a logical trajectory formed by different spheres of application of the 'rain effect'. The trajectory consists of four 'generations': unintentional optical interference; a reception trope formed within the sphere of film literature; a literary metaphor that refers to this effect; a text (this time, a film script) that aims to reinstate the 'rain' within the film image, to simulate intentionally the effect unintentionally produced.

The *screen – reception – screen* cycle is, of course, an abstraction and should not be given any chronological interpretation. Besides, the whole schema is too perfect to be true in as much as the cycle can never be traced completely. With Sologub's 'rain', for example (if we have reconstructed his idea correctly), the cycle went no further than the suggestion stage. It is most unlikely that the director for whom Sologub wrote the script, Alexander Sanin, would have agreed to scratch the emulsion as Orson Welles later did in *Citizen Kane* in order to imitate a worn-out print.[10] Nevertheless, the understanding of the way extra-aesthetic factors are valorised and brought into the sphere of 'the aesthetic' may help to interpret those episodes in film history that at first glance may appear to be the products of pure chance.

One of these is the story of soft-focus photography as it came into Soviet films. To use Barry Salt's definition, 'soft focus' is a common expression for image diffusion, for blurring the definition of the film image either by the use of a special lens, or by gauzing, or by means of a diffusion filter, or by throwing the lens out of focus, or by some other technique.[11] Soft focus is the technical trick best suited to achieve the kind of effect that Sologub failed to find when he suggested using 'celluloid rain' to imitate poor-sightedness.

The moment when a blurred, indistinct, diffused image came to be seen as an aesthetic device is recorded with unusual unanimity by cinema historians. Kevin Brownlow claims that soft focus was first used as a deliberate artistic technique in Griffith's *Broken Blossoms* (1918/19).[12] Barry Salt agrees that although soft focus had appeared in the mid-1910s (or possibly earlier), these were isolated instances rather than evidence of systematic practice.[13] Soft focus was received as a sign that film art was coming closer to art in the proper sense of the word. A contemporary critic remarked on 'Billy' Bitzer's (and Hendrik Sartov's) camera work for *Broken Blossoms*:

> The photography is not only perfect, but, with caution, is innovational, and approximates, in its larger lights and softness of close view, the details of bright and dark upon the finest canvases in the Louvres of the world.[14]

In fact what Griffith and his cameramen reproduced on the screen was not a painterly effect but the technique of nineteenth-century 'pictorial' photography with its 'photogravures', 'glycerine' and 'gum' processes, etc. that tried to imitate painting.[15]

Soft focus appeared in Russian cinema almost simultaneously with *Broken Blossoms*, but independently, in a different way, and for a different reason. The effect was first observed in pictures from the Rus company. Some of them were produced as early as 1919, and were shown outside Russia in the early 1920s. Victor Shklovsky, then a Russian émigré in Berlin, noticed one curious aspect in the response of Western viewers to films from the Rus studios. When he returned to the USSR Shklovsky discussed this with his OPOYAZ collaborator, the literary historian Boris Tomashevsky, who then passed it on to the readers of the magazine *The Life of Art* in 1924:

> An out-of-focus shot conventionally represents a disturbed state of mind: grief, delirium, a dream, or a nightmare. In Victor Shklovsky's words this convention, which has become the hallmark of good taste in all the latest Western European and American films, has brought unexpected success to several Russian films where this conventionally 'melancholic', out-of-focus photography is used not only for close-ups but all the way through, from beginning to end.[16]

How this 'conventionally melancholic' effect arose is explained in the memoirs of the chairman of Rus, Moisei Aleinikov. Writing about the conditions under which films were made in 1919, Aleinikov recalled that before filming began expeditions were sent throughout the country (to Kiev and Odessa in particular) to collect any surviving stocks of unexposed film. What stock they managed to find was usually damaged, covered with a tracery of tiny cracks due to bad storage conditions, or 'fogged' due to part exposure. This stock, which earlier would have been condemned as unusable, was used, for example, for Aleksandr Sanin's film *Polikushka* (1919). As Aleinikov recalled, the resulting mistiness of the film had no deleterious effects on the picture, quite the reverse:

> In this case the 'fogged' film helped the cameraman to realise the general stylistic intention behind the film. The critics saw the mistiness as being due to the cameraman's desire to maintain the softness of tone that permeated the whole production.[17]

For his next film, *The Stationmaster* [Kollezhskii registrator, 1925], the cameraman (Yuri Zhelyabuzhsky) used high-quality German stock and tried to capture this ethereal, misty effect by shooting whole scenes through gauze filters.

The reason why Western audiences were won over by the accidental soft-focus effect was because optical interference (the 'fogginess' of the spoiled film stock) was rooted in soil that had been well-prepared in two ways: by Griffith's *Broken Blossoms*, and by the assumed 'vagueness' and 'melancholy softness' of the 'Russian soul', the notion brought into being by Russian nineteenth-century writers and turned by their Western readers into a cross-cultural stereotype.

TREMOR, FLICKERING, BLINKING, VIBRATION

One of the most persistent and irritating forms of interference in early cinema was vibration. This could come from several sources – the projection speed, the type of gate shutter used, the condition of the sprocket holes, etc. – and gave rise to a great deal of criticism from the public and the press. Annoyance, however, was not the only response to an unstable image: a vogue for 'vibration' developed within turn-of-the-century culture. As Christoph Asendorf observes: 'Around about 1910 the idea of vibration, along with certain conceptual variations, was a central theme in aesthetic debate.'[18] Oscillation was a significant element in the 'new sensibility' cultivated in *fin de siècle* literature and art. It was connected – insists Asendorf – with the cultural discovery of such scientific concepts as the behaviour of nervous systems, electricity and the undulatory nature of energy.[19] Hence the cult of 'neurosis' brought about by 'decadent' literature and imported into Russia through the works of Stanisław Przybyszewski, a Polish-German modernist writer extremely popular in Russia. 'Neur-asthenic' roles, the portrayal of languid, enervated, neurotic characters – like Treplev in Chekhov's *The Seagull* – became an established line of business for male actors like Pavel Orlenev in the theatre, or Ivan Mosjoukine in Yermoliev's films.[20]

It was the same in the visual arts. *Art nouveau* ornament defined itself as 'the pulsation of life', and Victor Horta's fragile architecture produced the impression of 'vibrating structures'.[21] Dutch *art nouveau* designers 'were particularly skilful at juxtaposing colour to produce a slight vibration',[22] and the Post-Impressionist painters developed a special technique of multiple cross-hatchings [*multiples hachures entrecroisées*] in order to achieve the same effect.[23] Vibration of light and vibration of 'atmosphere' (understood as both air and mood) was something Stanislavsky was striving to achieve on the stage of the Moscow Art Theatre.[24] This was an age when reviewers typically described the activity of readers, viewers and theatregoers as 'a response to the vibrations of the artist's soul'.

The ground for the 'flickering movies' was also prepared by the doctrines of occult science. Theosophical booklets (theosophy being a bestselling topic in Russia at the turn of the century) highlighted 'vibration' as the first among the three types of motion created by nature.[25] According to W. C. Leadbeater, invisible 'penetrating oscillations' are the way the Cosmic Will is communicated to earthly souls.[26] Those initiated in the refined ecstasy of vibration enjoyed going to the cinema for the same kind of pleasure that visitors to the St Petersburg cabaret The Stray Dog [Brodyachaya sobaka] were said to experience when they all trooped off to the Nicholas bridge where they 'felt the most extraordinary vibrations by leaning with their backs against the railings'.[27]

An obsession with instability, insecurity and irrationality was one of the reasons for the Symbolist poets' intense interest in cinema, a topic that will be discussed in more detail later in this book. The special feeling of 'tremulousness', reinforced by the vibration of the image itself on the screen, was described in 1907 by Remy de Gourmont after he had viewed a 'scenic' film about the Zambesi in which a tiny bush shook in the current: 'that trembling movement, which came from a country so far away, stirred in me a feeling that I can't really describe.'[28] In *The Man Who Was Thursday*, first published a year later, G. K. Chesterton described a forest chosen by the hero as a setting for the duel: 'The inside of the wood was full of shattered sunlight and shaken shadows. They made a sort of shuddering veil, almost recalling the dizziness of the cinematograph.'[29] A few years later this hesitant 'almost' would disappear from descriptions of this kind; cinematic metaphors would become commonplace in such portrayals of natural phenomena.

The 'touching weakness' of Russian writers for cinema would sometimes be used as a weapon in literary debates. In a 1912 attack on his fellow poets, Sergei Gorodetsky pointed to the 'very strange fact of an alliance' between the Symbolists, 'from Andrei Bely to Maximilian Voloshin', and the cinematograph, and to the 'coincidence in their methods of artistic representation: fussily impressionistic on the part of the Decadents, and feverishly vibrant in the cinematograph'.[30] The argument was not new. In a critical essay written in 1908 Andrei Bely himself attacked Stanisław Przybyszewski for the allegedly cinematic 'jerkiness' of his prose: 'convulsive movements of the spirit and the flesh, punctuated by a sequence of cinematographic pictures'.[31] At the same time, according to Bely's later memoirs, his friend Ellis (L. I. Kobylinsky, a minor Symbolist poet), who used to entertain visitors by giving brilliant live imitations of the cinematograph with its jerky movements, 'studied cinema in order to be able to take off these scenes . . . and even managed to capture the way the cinema screen trembled'.[32] For a Symbolist poet, going to the cinema and sharing what a German writer of the 1910s called its 'aesthetics of fever'[33] was like feeling the pulse of modernity itself.

A BREAK IN THE FILM

The most irritating interference of all was when the film broke, and, like the 'celluloid rain', it was a disaster that mainly occurred in provincial cinemas. Before the distribution system was properly introduced into Russia, exhibitors in Moscow and St Petersburg were in the habit of reselling used prints to provincial cinema owners. Distribution companies inherited this unfortunate habit and passed on second-hand copies to less well-off cinemas. The wear and tear increased in proportion to the distance from the centre. Let us take one of the furthermost places, Yakutsk, in eastern Siberia. In 1913, when the metropolitan cinemas were dominated by film palaces with musical winter gardens, *The Yakutian Borderlands* still urged its readers to be patient:

> We are happy to note that Priyutov's cinematographic performances have improved. The pictures are now clearer and more distinct; the film does not break so often, but the lack of lighting during the interruptions . . . alarms the public, . . . there is a lot of stamping and whistling . . . The public must understand that the cinematograph is a new invention . . . Rome wasn't built in a day, gentlemen![34]

In 1910 there occurred an event that received much comment in the film press:

> On 15 November, after the end of a performance in the Kirsanov Theatre of Illusions, the projectionist, N. Melioransky, tried to poison himself. His only pleasure in life was the knowledge that he was a useful member of the local community, which had always been delighted with his excellent work. But the very last night of the season turned into total disaster: one of the pictures, *Cupid's Darts* [Strely amura] was so badly worn that it kept on breaking off inside the projector, each break being greeted by the audience with loud laughter and rude remarks. Not understanding the real reason for the breakdowns, they turned on their former hero and made him the butt of their derision. The proud youth was overcome with shame and went off to poison himself. Luckily his life was saved.[35]

Like vibration, a broken film became an established feature of film reception. The frustration accompanying the event was a popular subject for poets writing in film magazines. One stanza from a poem entitled 'The Film Broke' [Porvalas' lenta] may serve as an example:

The film broke – and in the dark
Boredom, unbidden, hung in the air.
Two empty, hurried, nervous notes
Echoed from the piano's soul.[36]

At the beginning of the 1910s a special gadget appeared in many film projectors: the so-called isolation shutter (as David Shepard tells me, they were called 'heat glasses' in America). The reason for this was that if the projector stopped the hot beam of light could set fire to the broken film. The isolation shutter was a device (two devices, to be accurate: one centrifugal, the other antifrictional) which automatically prevented the beam reaching the film whenever the projector stopped. A transparent barrier, made of heat-absorbing filtering material, came down between the film and the light source. As a result, whenever such an emergency occurred, a grey frozen image would appear on the screen instead of a white square.

The emergency freeze-frame turned out to be an important event in the history of film reception. For some spectators the sudden halt created as unforgettable an impression as the sight of the still image coming to life at the Lumières' demonstrations. A reviewer for *The Theatre Paper* wrote:

> Once, at a private viewing, I saw a picture suddenly stop dead. The technician had halted the machine for some unknown reason and the actors froze in rigid poses on the brightly lit screen. It was a most unusual sight – almost frightening. A funny old woman, a jolly fat man, an elegant dandy, who had all just been playing out some kind of silly nonsense or other, suddenly, as if at the wave of a magic wand, froze in absurd, meaningless poses. It did not even resemble a photograph or a slide show. One could feel something mystical happening ... When the projector beam was obstructed, the actors remained motionless and grew dimmer in the semi-gloom – *you could feel the chill of death emanating from the screen.* But suddenly the projector started up again and the clowning recommenced. Nevertheless the tragic motif of the accidental interruption was not forgotten. It made a deeper impression on me than anything else I had ever seen in the cinematograph.[37]

The critic Mikhail Brailovsky was struck by the changes in tone and light caused by the greyish shutter filter (it was either made out of thin metal mesh or consisted of a water and glycerine bath): it reminded him of Moscow during the general strike of 1905:

> Stop the regular movement of the film through the projector for just one moment and, instead of a living picture, you get a grey, dull, lifeless image – one without perspective or relief. Life on the screen momentarily disappears and dies. And of course we have only recently witnessed how the life of a vast capital city begins to die when the mechanism that moved it is temporarily stopped.[38]

Like the vibrations in Ellis's skits on cinema, a breakage in a film was a popular subject to imitate in home entertainments. Alexander Fevralsky relates what Lidiya Ilyashchenko, one of Meyerhold's actresses, told him about the game they used to play at Fyodor Sologub's literary salon in 1914–15:

After dinner, when all the older, more sedate guests were leaving, Fyodor Kuzmich [Sologub] used to give us younger ones a wink and we would stay behind. Then the real fun would begin . . . The best game was playing cinemas. We would hang up a large sheet, put out the lights and place a bright lamp behind the sheet. We acted between the lamp and the sheet, on which our shadows stood out clearly. Sologub's wife, Anastasia Chebotarevskaya, supplied all the things we needed. Fyodor Kuzmich would put his feet up on the sofa and dictate the 'scripts', which we would act out straight away. We tried to act mainly in profile, as the screen only conveyed silhouettes. Of course we only parodied cinema really. We hammed it up, sometimes in street-theatre style – we were drama students, after all. In one of Sologub's scripts I was Fata Morgana. I put a paper cap shaped like a sugar loaf on my head and tied a long piece of string to it that cast a zig-zag shadow on the screen. Vsevolod Emilevich [Meyerhold] did not take part himself. He sat beside Sologub and sometimes shouted out 'Marvellous!' in that famous voice of his. Sometimes 'the film broke' and we would freeze in the most improbable poses. Sometimes the cinema would start to run backwards (it really used to happen then) and we would all move in the opposite direction, laughing uncontrollably.[39]

One should not be too surprised to find the effect of the broken film simulated in Andrei Bely's 1918 film script for his own novel *Petersburg* (1913). The stylistic feature of the 'break' *(figura obryva*, in Bely's own words) appealed to the author primarily as a literary device. It occupies a special place in his work on Nikolai Gogol, *Gogol's Mastery* [Masterstvo Gogolya]:

The first volume of *Dead Souls* is a pile of 'breaks' heaped up one on top of another; they both represent the author's ideas and stress details that are interpreted in different ways . . . the 'break' sets you thinking by stressing contrasts . . . Every short chapter is a heap of scraps, colourfully painted and strung on a living thread solely by the device of the 'break'.[40]

Having traced the role played by this device in Gogol's prose, Bely turns to his own novel *Petersburg* as an example of how it worked in post-Gogolian literature showing that its narrative, too, was a string of breaks. Another structural analogy of the sudden unmotivated ending, claimed Bely, was provided by the cinematograph:

the fluttering images of unnaturally excited people are chasing someone. The scene ends with a scuffle and a crash. Suddenly the screen is filled with the shape of a triumphant cockerel, and the intertitle: *Pathé – The End*.[41]

When in June 1918 Bely was asked to 'write a script adapting his novel *Petersburg* for the cinema'[42] he obviously saw the 'break' as the most natural compositional device for a film script. The prologue to the script was conceived as a deliberate piling up of 'pictures' (no fewer than eighteen), without any narrative context. The pictures were to acquire significance later on, when each of them would take its own place in the plot. By this method, Bely apparently aimed to evoke a sense of *déja vu* in the more important scenes, a sense of recognition in a new context.[43] Bely had never written for films before, and we can only marvel at his audacity as a scriptwriter (albeit the audacity of a layman) when, for example, at the beginning of Part Two he suggests simply 'repeating' two scenes from the prologue or beginning the narrative from the point where the relevant scene of the prologue had 'broken off':

> Picture 18.
> An exact repeat of picture 9 of the prologue, with all the details . . . But it is not cut off once the viewers have seen it, as it is in the prologue; instead we see the figure of Anna Petrovna standing by the embankment. She has grown older and fatter and is wearing a very worn foreign-looking dress. She is chewing her handkerchief and staring at the windows of a yellow, three-storey house. She cannot make up her mind what to do.[44]

Here, as in the case of the 'rain' in Sologub's script for *Miss Liza*, we can see the author attempting to project his experience as spectator into his attempts at screenwriting. There is nothing strange about this – it is probably the usual way for a beginner to set about writing a film script. What is noteworthy is that, by so doing, both Bely and Sologub were making a statement about the phenomenology of the medium itself. Scratches and 'breaks' belong in the world of reception, not in that of the film itself; incorporated into the film they become metacinematic elements. Both scripts remained unrealised, but, viewed from the perspective of the later development of cinema, Sologub's and Bely's ideas seem to anticipate the metacinematic cinema of the 1960s – for example, Ingmar Bergman or Alain Resnais.

ACOUSTIC INTERFERENCE: 'LIVE ILLUSTRATION'

What external sounds were there to interfere with the film show? In the improvised cinema theatres of the 1900s noises came mainly from outside the building:

> Rows of attentive heads
> Beneath the magic beam.
> But from the door come muffled sounds,
> The noise of carriages and feet,
> A distant, constant, call.[45]

In the 1910s film accompaniment was often overlaid with music coming from an orchestra in the foyer:

It's a holiday and the foyer is full of expectant cinemagoers. The proprietor is joyfully rubbing his hands and orders the orchestra to strike up and keep everyone happy. The sounds of a rollicking tune, clearly audible in the auditorium, mingle with the mournful melody illustrating the death of the heroine on the screen. Not a single voice is raised in protest – after all, this is the cinematograph.[46]

I do not, however, propose to include all external noises in the category of acoustic interferences, only those incidental sounds that happened to affect the reception of the image. The main factor here was the presence or absence of music. Since music was the acoustic norm of a silent film show, the most serious interference with the reception of silent films was silence itself. As Roman Jakobson demonstrated in 1933, music in silent films served as a constant reminder that the acoustic dimension of the action [*das akustische Ding*] was not relevant.[47] The corollary of this was that the absence of music 'switched on' our expectations as to diegetic (i.e. narrative) sound. Skilful accompanists knew how to make use of it. Sometimes music or sound effects were withheld to make the audience 'listen' to the diegesis:

For example, someone picked up a huge pile of plates and began to swing them round and round, until finally – of course – they suddenly fell and smashed without a sound. The audience roared with laughter, but only at seeing something like that happen without hearing any noise.[48]

One of the main things that activated diegetic sound expectations in silent films was the spontaneous reaction of the audience. Here are two reminiscences selected at random from many: one from the actor Alexander Werner, the other from the director Voldemars Puce:

The audience often argued among themselves and discussed the plots noisily, adding their own 'live illustration', which was always unexpected, highly expressive and original.[49]

The viewers were never at a loss for pithy interjections: they shouted, applauded loudly, egged on the heroes and booed the villains. Whenever they thought a picture lacked sound or text they did their best to provide their own sound effects. In the love scenes they would encourage a faint-hearted lover and express their approval of decisive action. When lovers kissed on the screen loud smacking noises resounded all round the auditorium and people tried to time their kisses to synchronise exactly with those on the screen. When this happened there would be laughter and applause throughout the auditorium.[50]

For some observers this kind of response was in itself a fascinating part of the spectacle. This was certainly the case with the Symbolist poet Alexander Blok, whose visits to the cinema were part of his 'urban slumming expeditions'. Blok was captivated both by the city folklore element in films and by the touch of folklore in the responses of the audiences. But another aspect was also important: early cinema (particularly the Pathé company, which dominated the European film market before the First World War) was a powerful catalyst of cultural exchange. Cinema imported images and themes into Russia that were quite new to the Russian mass audience. Cinema auditoria were places where bizarre cross-cultural encounters occurred. In Blok's notebook for 6 March 1908, we find a record of the following incident: 'On the screen a toreador fighting a duel. A woman's voice: "Men are always brawling".'[51] Since the message behind the whole entry is somewhat elusive, it has been discussed by literary historians interested in Blok's attitude to popular culture.[52] At a seminar on Blok held at Tartu in 1980, Roman Timenchik drew attention to the fact that the incident recorded by Blok also featured in Georgi Chulkov's 1908 poem 'A Living Photograph', in which the real incident (witnessed at the same show or heard from Blok) is furnished with a fictional context:

Two bull-fighters duel over a lovely Spanish girl.
Oh, you silly, swarthy landsmen of Cervantes!
But just look at the people bewitched by the scene:
The lad from the shop with his mouth open wide,
The corseted lady fit to explode,
The sullen tart staring, moist-eyed, at the screen.
But the passion-mad toreadors cross their swords
And a high, clear woman's voice rings out:
'Men are always brawling'.[53]

There is a slight incongruity between the mental image invoked by the Russian word for 'brawling' [derutsya] and the scene it was used to describe. What could have fascinated Blok and Chulkov was the ingenuous essentialism of the remark which reduced the refined tradition of the duel with rapiers (the film was apparently an early screen version of *Carmen* or *Blood and Sand*) to a more familiar notion – a straightforward street brawl.

In the 1910s cinemagoing in the larger cities was no longer the prerogative of the urban lower classes, but audience reactions and attitudes remained very much the same. Uninhibited behaviour became part of cinema's specifically democratic style, and cinema thus established for itself a very special place in urban culture. As the press of the day liked to point out, one and the same person behaved quite differently at the cinema and at the theatre:

What a difference there is in the way people behave at the theatre and at the cinema! At the theatre you dare not even whisper; the briefest comment to your neighbour brings angry 'shushings' from those around you. But in the cinema! . . . The chords of the piano, the melancholy, nasal sounds of the harmonium accompanying the tragic passages, the constant murmuring, whispering and calling – all so graphically revealing the character of the audience – blend into a single seamless whole, into one integral 'idea' of cinema: that darkened auditorium with its shadows flickering and fading before your eyes.[54]

We see an extreme form of the public taste for 'live illustration' in a tragic event that took place at the end of 1910. In January 1911 extracts from Pskov newspapers appeared in the cinema press under the heading 'Suicide in the cinema':

On 27 December a shot rang out during a performance of the film *Student Years* at the Modern cinematograph in Pskov. It coincided with the screen suicide of a doctor; he had just identified the body of a drowned girl as that of his first love. The audience assumed that the shot had been arranged by the management in order to heighten the effect of the scene, but it was fired by one M. Bykhovsky, from the town of Krestsy. He was taken to the local hospital, where he died soon after without regaining consciousness. According to the paper *Pskov Life*, a piece of paper was found in his pocket; on it was written: 'Please do not accuse anyone of my death. It was hard to go on living after Lev Tolstoy had passed away. It was hard to carry on fighting for freedom. Goodbye, dear mother, brothers, sister and comrades. M. V. Bykhovsky'.[55]

THE NOISE OF THE PROJECTOR

Despite the nickname that the cinematograph was lovingly accorded in Russia, the cultural image of the 'Velikii Nemoi' [The Great Silent One] was acoustical as well as optical. Together with other members of the noisy family of machines the cinematograph burst into the quiet world of nineteenth-century culture and was noisily greeted by Futurist artists and poets. In the Futurists' disorderly version of the *Gesamtkunstwerk* [total work of art] idea, the main art was to be 'the art of noise',[56] and cinema too was co-opted into the new aesthetic category. Vadim Shershenevich wrote: 'I sink into the noise of the city, into the jingling and tinkling sounds of the cinematograph.'[57] David Burlyuk proclaimed:

The cinematograph occupies a commanding position in contemporary life. Its eternal symbol, Movement, is from now on engraved upon its brow; the cinematograph was the first and only art form capable of keeping abreast of the age and of *resonating in unison with the dawn of the coming twentieth century, with its roaring of motor cars and its wailing of sirens.*[58]

The acoustic core of cinema performance was composed of four elements: musical accompaniment; sound effects; 'live accompaniment'; and, not least, the characteristic sound of the projector itself.

Depending upon the year of manufacture and the type, film projectors covered all ranges of tone, from *forte* to *pianissimo*. Before 1908, when ether–oxygen burners predominated, the noise came mainly from the moving parts of the apparatus, while the light source gave out only a faint crackling sound, which Alexander Blok affectionately likened to a 'tender purring'.[59] In 1908 safety regulations were introduced that insisted that fixed film projectors had to be operated by electricity. The danger of projectors catching fire was to some extent reduced, but the new regulations brought another problem: since their Drummond lamps needed a very high voltage, projectors could not be run off the city grid and had to be provided with their own dynamos, which were appallingly noisy. The journal *Cine-Phono* complained:

> All the machines used in cinema theatres – dynamos, transformers, motor generators, and especially machines for supplying the house lighting – can produce varying degrees of noise, . . . for example, if a commutator is in any way damaged or out of alignment, or not properly polished, the carbon brushes can make a whistling sound; if an alternating current motor in a generator is overloaded it can produce a magnetic 'howl', etc., etc.[60]

The Riga city architect's departmental files on the opening of cinema theatres contain complaints made to the building inspector's office by people who had the misfortune to live in premises adjacent to cinemas. This is a typical document (the first of its kind), drawn up only a month after the new regulations came into force. It is the record of an investigation dated 30 January 1909:

> As a result of a complaint from a Mr Silling, the owner of no. 5 Bocharnoy Street, about the noise made by the electric motor of the Synchrophone cinema theatre in the former Elephant warehouse at no. 10 Theatre Street, which backs on to his premises, I carried out a survey at no. 5 Bocharnoy Street. My findings were as follows: on both the lower and the upper floors one could clearly hear an extremely irritating noise coming from the electric motor located in the corner of the rear wall of the Elephant warehouse. There is also a crack in the wall more than three feet long.[61]

Luckily for the audience, these fire regulations also required that the auditorium be separated from the projection room by a metal partition, which also functioned as a sound insulating system, so that the audience was far less annoyed by the noise than those outside. However, whether *piano* or even *pianissimo*, the reception of the film was always accompanied by the background noise of the projector.

People who wrote about cinema did their best to find words and metaphors to describe such sounds: 'Somewhere, to everybody's alarm, something crackled and spluttered and figures suddenly appeared on the screen.'[62] 'Zzzzzz . . . buzzed the lamp.'[63] 'And the cinematograph went on hissing and hissing, with a dry monotonous crackle.'[64] 'Behind us something was sizzling as if they were frying a wild boar.'[65] 'We heard the monotonous chattering of some kind of strange apparatus; it reminded us of the distant sound of a sewing machine.'[66] 'The "chattering" of machine guns in war stories reminded the reader of the staccato sound of a film projector.'[67] There would be no point in accumulating more examples if some of them did not link the sound of the projector to other aspects of film reception. One such comment referred to non-filmic sound as a substitute for filmic speech. Yuri Tynyanov was convinced that the accompanist's music

> gives the actors' speech the final element it lacks – sound . . . Music gives richness and a subtlety of sound impossible to find in human speech. It helps to reduce the character's speech to a pithy, intense minimum.[68]

In other words, music offered sound to offset speech. As we have already suggested, the absence of music activated diegetic (narrative) sound expectations. There was always a risk that without music actors would be 'dubbed' by the projector. The writer Venyamin Kaverin, recalling the first time he saw a film, recorded exactly this effect:

> It was curious to hear the deserted countess crying to her lover: 'trata-ta-ta'. He tries miserably to excuse himself: 'trata-ta-ta'. Then she loses her temper: 'trata-ta-ta'. He falls sobbing at her feet: 'trata-ta-ta'.[69]

The other aspect of the projection sound is related to an issue that I am going to return to later in the book.[70] Early spectators were subject to the effect of proprioceptive instability, caused by the excess of movement within the frame, which increased to the point of dizziness if the camera happened to be mounted on a moving train or boat, etc. In such cases, a spectator would experience the feeling that it was the auditorium that was moving and that he was being caught up and born away. The illusion was all the more complete when the projector sounded like a moving vehicle. Alexander Khanzhonkov likened the noise of the British-made Urban projector to that of a 'creaky farm cart'.[71] Feofan Shipulinsky referred to a sledge gliding over snow – the comparison is crowned with a famous 'panoramic' stanza from Pushkin's *Eugene Onegin*:

> The whirring [*zhuzhzhanie*] of the film as it runs through the machine is like the noise made by the runners of a troika as it rushes over uneven snow bearing the poet of our imagination who watches
>
> 'Everything flying past: old peasant women and huts,
> Streetlamps, gardens and kids,
> Palaces, sledges and shops,
> Bukharans, hovels and barns,
> Balconies, boulevards, chemists,
> Peasants, Cossacks and towers,
> Flocks of jackdaws on crosses,
> And merchants, and lions on gates.'[72]

One can point to a case when the association between watching a film and going for a drive worked in reciprocal fashion. It concerned Franz Kafka and cinema. In 1911 in Prague Kafka saw a Danish film, *Den hvide Slavehandels sidste Offer* (August Blom, 1911), distributed there as *Die Weisse Sklavin II* [The White Slave Girl II] – its distribution title in England was *In the Hands of Imposters II*. The film was on the underground prostitution industry.[73] It made a deep impression on Kafka, and is mentioned more than once in his letters and diaries. One such entry is in connection with an ordinary car ride: 'The tyres swished on the wet asphalt like a projector in the cinema. Again the *White Slave Girl*'.[74] This episode should be regarded both as a fact of film reception and as a fact belonging to the reception of automobile travel in Austro-Hungarian culture before the First World War.

To sum up, the sound of the silent cinema was a distinct voice in the cacophonous chorus of modernity itself. This is how Luigi Pirandello described this voice in his 1915 novel *Shoot! The Notebooks of Serafino Gubbio, Cinematograph Operator*:

Do you hear it? A hornet that is always buzzing, forbidding, grim, surly, diffused, and never stops. What is it? The hum of the telegraph poles? The endless scream of the trolley wheels along the overhead wire of the electric trams? The urgent throb of all those countless machines, near and far? That of the engine of the motor-car? Of the cinematograph?

The beating of the heart is not felt, nor do we feel the pulsing of our arteries. The worse for us if we did! But this buzzing, this perpetual tickling we do notice, and I say that all this furious haste is not natural, all this flickering and vanishing of images; but that there lies beneath it a machine which seems to pursue it, frantically screaming.

Will it break down?[75]

'THE METRONOME OF WORLD TIME'

Among the many metaphors for projector noise found in Russian film literature of the 1910s, that of ticking clockwork attained the status of ontological allegory. As discussed above in Chapter 2, the figure of the film projectionist was fictionalised as that of the master of human destiny. In Europe this rhetorical apotheosis of the projectionist and the apparatus seems to have been introduced by Ricciotto Canudo: 'That which we call life is the triumphant forms and rhythms brought to life by turning the handle of the film projector.'[76] In Russia Lev Ostroumov claimed he too heard its eternal whirring:

The eternal mechanic cranks the handle,
The machine of being whirrs away . . . [77]

As has been mentioned, this cultural *emploi* was inherited from literature, with its 'clockwork' concept of the universe and its image of the Supreme Clock-Maker.[78] The noise of the projector was associated with the noise of time, all the more readily because the clicking of the film-feed mechanism did indeed resemble the ticking of a clock.

As an element of 'film discourse' as well as a rhetorical figure used in film reviews, this trope of reception acquired particular momentum in film culture of the 1920s – the post-Revolutionary age of high-flown allegories and oratorical overstatements. Two examples out of many may be cited. Mikhail Koltsov's article 'By the Screen' [U ekrana] published in *Pravda* in 1922 begins with this description of what was in fact an ordinary film show in an ordinary cinema: 'the apparatus ticked away like the crazy pendulum of the clock of history'.[79]

Dziga Vertov, Koltsov's friend, included images of an ever-accelerating 'demented' pendulum in the vertiginous finale of *The Man with the Movie Camera* [Chelovek s kinoapparatom, 1929], while the prologue for this film showed a projectionist preparing his machine. In the 'music and sound score' that Vertov designed for *The Man with the Movie Camera* the orchestra was instructed to keep silent while the projectionist was shown. The only notice in Vertov's score opposite the heading 'Prologue' says: 'A clock ticking'.[80] Time, the projectionist, the pendulum and history are interlinked in a circular compositon.

The idea of the 'ticking' of the film projector as measuring the passage of time found its way into a theoretical doctrine of the 1910s, according to which acting for cinema is only successful when attuned to the rhythm of the film camera. This theory, which was propagated in 1918 by the popular *Cinema Paper* [Kinogazeta] (in particular by Pudovkin's future wife, the film journalist Anna Lee), was – as Mikhail Yampolsky suggests – an attempt to adapt to cinema Jaque-Dalcroze's ideas of rhythmic gymnastics: 'the new anthropology of the actor urgently requires the discovery of a rhythmic law of cinema and it is to be found in the natural "metronome" of cinema, the cranking of the camera'.[81] While this was the first attempt at a Constructivist approach to the problem of acting, this theory was also based on the actual experience of the film actors of the 1910s. Brownlow cites Ben Lyon on this topic: 'For the final rehearsal we sometimes asked the cameraman: "Will you give us the camera?" No film – but it was an inspiration to hear that grinding.'[82] Reflecting on cinema in 1949, the Georgian-born actor and director Ivan Perestiani struck a more thoughtful note:

> I am still convinced today that the film actor must listen to the camera. Its ticking is the music of the action. It is a question of a special sense, which is at bottom psychological, that keeps time . . . You must retreat into yourself as deeply as you can, slow down all your feelings, thoughts and desires, and just wait for the command to act. When it comes you must

immediately rise above everything, literally everything. You must stop seeing and feeling anything that puts you off or distracts you. You must shut your ears to everything but the clicking of the camera handle as it counts off your movements perfectly, just like a metronome, and let the camera do the rest.[83]

Here also lies the clue to the reception of projector sound. Vsevolod Meyerhold, who believed that a film actor's real gift lay in the instinct for 'hearing time',[84] likened the hypnotic impact of a cranking camera to a similar effect produced by the projector on the viewer:

The whole essence of the screen is movement. Sitting in the semi-darkened room, we hear the ticking of the projector, and are constantly reminded of the passage of time. It creates a special mood; it makes us aware of our existence in time.[85]

Evidently for Meyerhold, as for the aesthetic intuition of the Symbolist epoch in general, behind the noise of the projector there loomed a more archaic image of time: the monotonously droning axle of the world.[86]

Part II

Chapter 5

Shifting textual boundaries

PERFORMANCE VERSUS FILM

Part I of this book dealt with the reception of cinema as performance. Reception can be defined as the blurring of boundaries. The preceding chapters have attempted to demonstrate just how contingent and mobile the boundaries between the world of the screen and the acoustic, social and architectural spaces around the screen really were. I have argued that each of these spaces was always ready to enter into a 'reception game' with what took place on the screen. The game consisted in making the main semiotic boundary – that between the text and everything that was not the text – diffuse and unstable.

In Part II I am going to deal with the reception of cinema as text as a specific dimension of early film history. Why 'cinema as text' and not 'film as text', a term habitually used in film studies? This chapter will attempt to explain. I will argue that the very notion of 'text' needs to be historicised and redefined in order to make it a subject of reception studies.

As I have already noted, throughout the 1900s we frequently observe an apparently paradoxical situation: cinema and its reception in the cultural consciousness of the age developed along two autonomous lines. This has special relevance to the way the boundaries of the cinematic text were defined. The early film-maker and the early viewer did not share the same concept of text: for those who produced films it was of course the film itself that constituted the text, while for the viewer the actually experienced cinematic text was the performance. In the 1900s one did not go 'to the film', but 'to the cinematograph'.[1] The performances consisted of a number of short unconnected films, but the differences between the pictures comprising the performance were overshadowed by what they all had in common: the fact that they were all part of the new spectacle. In this respect early cinemagoers resembled those European travellers who were convinced that all Chinese looked more or less the same.

In these circumstances viewers had to have a certain semiotic skill in order to differentiate one film from another, and the organiser of the show had to make a special effort to separate them within the performance. In the early years, when cinema was establishing itself in Russia, the Lumière programmes had short intervals between pictures. For example, in an 1898 performance described by Vladimir Tyurin, the pictures were separated acoustically:

> The manager rings a bell; the first living picture vanishes and is replaced by another. Instead of a station we see a broad forest clearing filled with cavalry and artillery . . . Another ring and the clearing gives way to a long avenue with an elderly man on a bench, reading a newspaper.[2]

In the 1900s an avalanche of cinematograph halls swept over Russia and this led to a weakening of the internal articulation within performances. Although the issue of 'an ideally composed programme' was often discussed in cinema journals, in the main cinema proprietors neither observed the 'rules' of programme composition nor felt the need to separate the pictures. Films were shown one after the other, without intervals, and very often they were selected at random.

This had its effect on the viewer's reception of cinema. The point was that even in those cases when images (or, rather, the brief 'single-image films' of the earliest times) were separated by a pause or a bell, they were not perceived as unrelated. Note the phrase '*instead of* a station we see . . .' in the 1898 account cited above, in which the words 'instead of' betray the fact that its author (and, therefore, the average viewer of the Lumière shows) must have had some kind of expectation of duration and continuity. In other words, once the picture was there one was inclined to think it was going to last for a while or at least be followed by a picture with related subject matter. Such expectations were part of the pre-cinematic cultural norm that will be discussed in greater detail in later chapters.

If this is what happened with the average viewer's orientation at the Lumière shows, how able was he to find his way through a torrent of films shown without intervals? As contemporary accounts indicate, the impression made by one picture imposed itself involuntarily upon the next, which might have absolutely no connection with it apart from this accidental juxtaposition. Textual boundaries were washed away by the diffusing energy of reception.

Let us take an example. In Russia in the 1900s the censors banned all pictures of a religious or biblical nature, and also all films portraying members of the Imperial Family.[3] The ban on religious or biblical films was not surprising: the representation of sacred images was prohibited also on the secular stage. It is harder to explain the ban on the cinematic representation of royal figures. Russian state tradition held that the tsar was not a sacred figure and his depiction was not taboo. Indeed, the first film cameramen who came to Russia (Camille Cerf, Alexandre Promio, Félix Mesguich) were expressly invited to film Tsar Nicholas II, and as a result the film collection of the tsarist court contained a large number of reels depicting the sovereign.

The explanation is that in this case censorship rules did not apply to making films but to showing them. The censor's office was worried about the possible cases of 'unfortunate proximity' that might result from showing court newsreels alongside other pictures in the same programme. To understand this anxiety, we can refer to a 1915 article by N. Karzhansky in which the author recalls a film show he had seen earlier in Paris: 'On the white screen the figures of the Kings of Spain and England leapt up one after the other, followed by a glimpse of a dozen scenes of Morocco, some Italian cuirassiers galloping past, and a new German battleship plunging into the water.'[4] Even though the footage containing the two kings appeared in the perfectly decent context of 'current event' newsreels, the unceremonious presentation of the sequence was embarrassing. The 'syntax' of the early film show produced the effect of a visual zeugma.

This was the reason why at the beginning of the 1910s, when Russian distribution companies received permission to show members of the Imperial Family on film, the censor tried to block any possible semantic interference from contiguous footage by a special circular laying down the conditions under which such films had to be shown:

(a) There must be no musical accompaniment and the films must always be shown at a particular place in the programme and quite separate from and not mixed up with the other pictures (i.e. before the showing of any such film the curtain must be lowered, then only episodes from the events may be shown, after which the curtain must again be lowered).

(b) Such pictures must also be separated from other pictures by some form of interval, and the manager of the cinema must take particular care that the pictures be projected by hand, and at a speed that ensures that the movements and gait of those represented on the screen do not give rise to any comment.[5]

As we see from this document, what the censor's office was trying to do was in fact to redefine textual boundaries and make the film and not the film show the 'master unit' of cinema. I am not sure about newsreels of the tsar, but as far as cinema in general was concerned, this kind of redefinition did not occur until the mid-1910s when the period of reception shift was over. Before then the text of cinema was still largely perceived as a potentially endless series of randomly juxtaposed units with blurred boundaries between them.

Is there any evidence that might afford us a glimpse into this 'pre-shift period' of text reception? Some clues may be found in the very form of discourse used in early Russian film literature. In those years there were two ways in which cinema performances were most commonly described, depending on the target message of the description: whether it was the show itself or the impressions it evoked. Some observers would string together separate sentences each starting with 'Vot', a word used to draw someone's attention to something ('Here is', or 'Here we have'), but which in this context we might loosely translate as 'Look!'[6] This 'Look! . . . Look! . . . Look! . . .' way of describing a film show should be seen as an attempt to render verbally the *separateness* of the images on display. The other form of description might be called the 'and . . . and . . . and . . .' type which was often used when the author had in mind to stress the impression of *indiscriminateness* that separate pictures used to produce when shown in a torrent. That is where the 'zeugma effect' can be spotted. In fact, one may even notice that some writers (or fictional film viewers, if we are dealing with a literary work) indulge in a private game of mentally 'editing' contiguous pictures. In Mikhail Kuzmin's short story *A Distinguishing Feature* [Otlichitel'nyi priznak, 1915] the heroine visits the Kinemacolor film theatre[7] and is watching a colour picture show in which 'silken horses swished their tails, butterflies fluttered about, magnified to the size of carriages, and the dark-red inside of a severed pomegranate was almost frightening in its juicy massiveness'.[8] Here we have a spontaneous montage-like association: one of the contiguous images imposes its own dimensional scale on the other. Clearly, the butterflies are compared to a carriage because their relative size is automatically derived from that of the horses in the preceding picture. The chance juxtaposition of the films in the same programme instantly generated a common semantic field. What was more, shown in rapid sequence, shorts tended to merge into the semblance of a causally motivated narrative. Sometimes such unintentional 'phantom narratives' were extremely funny. Could one help inter-relating the consecutive film titles mentioned in a 1909 programme note of the Petersburg Urania film-theatre: *Latest Grand Manoeuvres of German Troops in the Presence of Kaiser Wilhelm*; *Fortifying Medicine*; *I Am Dead (Comic Scenes)*? And such games did not stop at the 'misreading' of programme notes alone. An early poem by Samuel Marshak (1908) plays with the effect produced by the juxtaposition of a French film farce and a German newsreel. In the farce a husband leaves for work and from the top deck of a bus notices someone entering his bedroom. He rushes back as his wife's lover jumps out of the bedroom window right on to the upper deck of the departing bus. The film story (but not the poem) ends with the enraged husband rushing in only to find the wife alone in bed, staring at him in mock surprise. The poem ends with this unexpected epilogue:

> The hussy stares, amazed;
> The husband looks well pleased . . .
> And Kaiser Bill reviews
> His life-guards on parade.[9]

Marshak's *tour de force* makes the reader relive the classic mistake he probably himself made while watching the film: *post hoc ergo propter hoc*.

By substituting causality for consecutiveness (thus turning a cumulative text into a narrative one), the poem transformed the German newsreel into a pompous apotheosis of successful adultery.

Thus, film boundaries were blurred by the reception of performance being experienced as coherent text. Consequently, their diegetic boundaries also became blurred. Well before Lev Kuleshov's theory of 'created geography'[10] the effect of a world without boundaries was created by this practice of showing pictures in random juxtaposition, as a poem by Alexander Krantsfeld demonstrates:

All lumped together: gangsters, dandies,
Camels, cars and vaudeville,
And the god of war, handsome and terrible,
In Pathé's latest news.
All lumped together: Le Prince and Mona Lisa,
Stern Caesar and the ballet,
Ceylon and Moscow, Cairo, London.
No frontiers now in space![11]

In film literature the issue of how this spatio-temporal confusion might be avoided by clever programming has been discussed as a theoretical as well as a practical problem: should the programme be arranged thematically or ought the succession of contrasting impressions to be viewed as a value in its own right?[12]

Those opting for the diversity principle appealed to the experience of spectacle genres like variety theatre and miniature theatre. Indeed, we do come across theatre reviews favouring mixed programmes: 'The repertoire of the Grand Guignol company is very original: powerful realistic drama alongside comedy that borders on slapstick. The public seems to get a particular kick out of seeing these contrasting genres side by side.'[13]

This argument remained valid as far as fictional genres were concerned. Certainly, the multi-film performance *was* something inherited from vaudeville.[14] Yet the 'variety format' in cinema differed from vaudeville in that the latter did not contain 'serious' non-fictional items. Emotional contrast was one thing, but cultural incompatibility was something different. Here programme proximity could incur criticism, and this does not only concern newsreels about the Imperial Family. A cartoon published in 1910 in the humorous magazine *Shut* [The Jester] shows a passer-by staring at a cinema poster advertising a newsreel about Lev Tolstoy programmed together with *Dopey's Adventures* (an André Deed comedy). There is another documented example. In the mid-1910s the well-known Pushkin scholar Nikolai Lerner went to see Goncharov's *The Life and Death of Alexander Pushkin* [Zhizn' i smert' A. S. Pushkina, 1910]. He was shocked, not so much by the vulgarity of this film biography as by the fact that 'the great man' was shown on the screen 'between the moustachioed Kaiser, riding to inspect his regiment of Uhlans, and a French farce involving repeated undressing and kicks up the backside'.[15] On the basis of the historical evidence, then, it would appear that film boundaries were too frail to safe keep culturally incompatible figures in their own diegetic compartments.

FILM VERSUS SHOT

Earlier chapters have described the several changes in exhibition practice that were part of the more general process of cinema's changing cultural identity. Theatre names, architectural space, the social topography of the auditorium, musical accompaniment and other environmental aspects of the performance all underwent change. At the same time the textual dimensions of cinema were changing as well. Primarily, these were changes in repertoire. The process of refocusing the repertoire from trick films to drama was also indicative of cinema's adaptation to traditional forms of culture. Second, there were changes in cinemagoing habits. After Asta Nielsen's *Afgrunden* [The Abyss, Denmark, 1910] and the Italian epic *La caduta di Troia* [The Fall of Troy, 1911] had been shown in Russia, audiences gradually got used to memorising (and reviewers to mentioning) the actual titles of films. People started going to see particular films rather than just 'going to the cinema'. Accordingly, text boundaries were redefined. It was more and more the film itself (now a multi-shot unit) rather than the film performance that was considered the 'master text' of cinema. Text reception was moving towards more classical forms.

Was it an easy transition? On the one hand, incidental (or intentional) misreading of adjacent films as forming a coherent sequence seems to indicate that the viewers were quite prepared to accept the basic theorem of editing: that contiguous images tend to merge into larger units. When ten years later Lev Kuleshov staged his famous experiment with three identical shots of Mosjoukine's face in close-up, where its expression 'changed' when juxtaposed to a plate, a coffin or a playing child, it was an experiment in film reception rather than film practice: all he needed was a few feet of existing footage and an unsuspecting viewer.

On the other hand, as we know, the transition was not a particularly smooth one. It took quite some time for film-makers to institutionalise the few rather simple techniques of continuity and narrative articulation needed for story-telling by means of longer films. Film-makers are probably not the ones to blame. It seems that in order to account for the hidden resistance with which audiences greeted their attempts during the first twenty years after the invention of cinema one has to look into the mechanisms of film reception rather than into those of film-making itself.

One can argue that, as opposed to film-making, film viewing took in a wider cultural background. While in many cases early film-making was a form of tinkering (that is, a process of trial and error: now Edwin Porter does this, the next time he tries that),[16] early film viewing was an intellectual activity more dependent upon cultural stereotypes. Some researchers tend to connect the emergence of longer films based on more complex narrative techniques with the fact that cinema was now addressing more educated bourgeois audiences.[17] Certainly, since both the readdressing of the medium and the restructuring of its narrative forms took place more or less at the same time, there must be some connection between the two events. But, to say the least, this connection was anything but straightforward. On the contrary, a closer look at film literature of the 1910s makes one suspect an inverse correlation: the higher the general culture of the viewer, the more reluctant he is to accept innovation.

Let us take one example. The switch from medium shot to facial close-up, which the uneducated sections of the Russian public had by and large accepted by the end of the 1900s, continued to arouse serious aesthetic objections among theatregoing circles as late as 1913. The theatre critic E. Stark had this to say about close-ups:

> The directors are clearly people with no idea of artistic taste: the slightest hint of emotion in a scene and for some reason they immediately shoot figures and faces enlarged almost to twice life-size. Imagine what it is like to see a huge nose, a vast mouth, monstrous whites of eyes, unnaturally protruding lips, all leering down at you. And when all these bits of a face belonging to a visitor from outer space begin to move, to express profound emotion – well, the sadder the scene is meant to be, the more grotesque and totally ridiculous is the effect.[18]

The notion of 'life-size' that almost invariably figures in scale-related statements in film literature of the early years probably corresponded to the writer's intuitive sense that the distance between actor and spectator in the theatre constituted a cultural norm, and that this cultural norm was felt to be at risk. For a cultured spectator, the 'reality' represented in close-up was oversized and over-emphasised – in a word, over-represented. For one thing, an oversize face provoked the effect of *trompe-l' oeil*: a feeling that the object was 'spilling over' the textual boundaries initially assigned to it. Second, the over-emphasised fragment was 'falling out' of the otherwise continuous syntagmatic chain (the 'life-size' shots that preceded and followed it). This internal tension between the part and the whole created a new focus of ambivalence: sometimes a single shot looked more of a self-contained text than the film itself.[19]

Let us take an earlier example – a newspaper article about cinema that appeared in 1908 and that seems to have been written by the music critic Yu. Engel. It mentions a French farce:

> After seeing off her husband 'she' sends a letter to Paul asking him to drop in. The letter contains all those delightful little lover's phrases prescribed

in the *Young Person's Guide to Letter-Writing* and is actually shown on the screen separately. Paul is round like a flash.[20]

Guided by this description, one can try to reconstruct the montage structure of the sequence in question. It was probably something like this:

1 'She' in full shot is writing a letter.
2 Close-up of the letter to Paul.
3 Full shot: Paul coming into 'her' room.

If we now look again at the way this sequence was presented in Engel's article we will get an idea of how film narrative was perceived by a cultured viewer around 1908. The words 'separately' and 'like a flash' look unusual. They refer to the cuts between shots 1 and 2 and between 2 and 3. These cuts mark shifts in film's narrative: a spatial shift (from the letter-writer to the letter, i.e. enlargement), and a temporal shift. Actions like the posting of the letter, its receipt by Paul, etc., are omitted, i.e. elided. By denoting the ellipsis with the words 'like a flash', Engel seems (or, rather, pretends – this is an ironic description) to be deceived by the way events were presented (the level of discourse) to the point of losing the sense of what is going on (the level of diegesis).

Even more revealing is the use of the phrase 'shown on the screen separately' to describe the close-up of the letter. It does not look ironic; rather, it bears witness to a cultural incompatibility of textures: this close-up is excluded from the flow of events. The author of the article sees the letter as belonging to a separate category – to the world of writing rather than that of images. It is no accident that he supplies the letter-insert with a genealogy: the *Young Person's Guide to Letter-Writing* style. The insert was still perceived as something really inserted ('shown separately') and not as an integral part of the 'life-size' diegesis presented by what were seen as essentially theatrical means.

Why was the viewer, who had been so ready to overlook film boundaries in his earlier belief that whatever was shown in the cinema was first and foremost 'cinema' and only afterwards 'films', so reluctant to ignore boundaries between shots in multi-shot films? As the close-up examples show, editing as narrative (or expressive) textual strategy violated the internal stratifications of received culture. In borrowing the ready-made forms of pre-cinematic narrative culture cinema was forced to resort to several stock cultural themes simultaneously. Taken singly, not one of the forms of traditional art known to culture was able to equip the 'language' of cinema with everything it needed for a coherent narrative.[21] By its very origins this 'language' was heterogeneous. We hardly feel it now, but it could be actually experienced at the beginning of the century when there was still some tension felt between the separate cultural strata on which film narrative rested. It led to a counteraction of forces which actually defined the 'climate' of film reception. In claiming its right to create a new cultural form, cinema aimed at the hybridisation of these genealogically disparate elements, while they, in their turn, offered semantic resistance, so that for the contemporary viewer each element remained attached to its own source: longer shots – to the theatre stage; close-ups – to portrait painting and photography; intertitle – to literature, and so on. This struggle was waged on the 'territory' of each film, and the conflict between the different sub-languages of culture was focused on shot boundaries – on cuts. This goes at least some way to explain the reluctance of cultured audiences to accept some of the 'rules' of film narrative. As in teaching a foreign language the difficulty does not lie in the intelligence of the learner but in the degree of resistance offered by the structures of the native language, so too the reluctance of the early cinema viewer to accept new techniques of narration can be explained not by the coarseness of his cultural sensitivity but by its refinement. For him the centrifugal tendency of heterogeneous shots was stronger than the unity presented by the fact that they were placed together within the boundaries of a single text – the film.

Thus in the area of text reception we see two opposing tendencies. On the one hand we can observe a drive to unite unconnected pictures shown in one programme by concocting a common context for them. But as soon as film-makers themselves attempt to introduce such a context it turns out that cultural reception offers serious resistance. I know of at least one written text that documents both tendencies at the same time. It is a short story by Sergei Gorodetsky (1911), which contains a parodied description of a film performance. Although at the end of the 1900s and the beginning of the 1910s theatres in Russia were still showing multi-film programmes, many of their entries were actually multi-shot films. This was a transitional period in which both versions of text definition ('cinema as text' and 'film as text') remained active. This is how Gorodetsky described the show:

> A rajah is riding on a tall elephant under date palms and banana trees, his face suddenly becomes enormous. The skin is ripped off a yard-long banana, the fruit slithers through his thick lips. A river, people are diving into the water. A staircase. A room. A man with St Vitus's dance is reading a newspaper. Some people burst in, tear it away, tumble over and over. Hamlet sings to the skull and his voice is enveloped in the hissing of a snake. Suddenly – the two Pathé cockerels. Darkness. A boy runs across a field and through a forest, swims across a river, and shins up a tree; from the tree he dashes into a house – the house bursts into flames; he scrambles out through the chimney, and after him tumble crazy fat men, head over heels, and an old woman in baggy trousers flapping at the ankles, one after the other. They'll never ever catch him, but the boy will never ever get away.[22]

As a literary endeavour this passage reveals Gorodetsky's interest in what would be later called 'the stream of consciousness' (this interest was shared by other modernist writers in Russia around 1911 – Andrei Bely in particular). This explains its asyntactic constructions and the intentionally erratic style. However, a significant point about this short story is that the eccentricities of literary style are motivated by subject matter: the narrator is sitting in the cinema. So, in a way, one may regard this passage not only as an attempt to draw a landscape of the mind but also as a literary image of film reception. What was it like? On the one hand, this is an 'and . . . and . . . and' type of film description: Gorodetsky is trying to de-emphasise the boundaries between the individual plots. Take a typical boundary: the Pathé trade mark, two cockerels, which usually appeared at the beginning and the end of Pathé films. Gorodetsky mentions the trade mark but does not make clear whether it belongs to the film that ends or to the one that begins: 'Suddenly – the two Pathé cockerels. Darkness. A boy running . . .'. 'Suddenly'can mean both 'suddenly the Pathé film starts' and 'suddenly *Hamlet* ends' (the latter version is prompted by a hint at a pause between the two subjects – 'Darkness'). Throughout the passage, the content of one film seems to ride on the same wave of intonation into that of the next. It creates the impression of a single text, a foolish tale in which the separate parts fuse into senseless cohesion.

On the other hand, the shots that evidently belong to one and the same film are rendered in deliberately discontinuous manner ('A staircase. A room'). The use of the word 'suddenly' in the first sentence is particularly significant because it suggests a jump in what we normally perceive as a continuous transition to a closer shot: 'his face suddenly becomes enormous'. The metamorphosis of the banana that turns into a 'yard-long' object is presented as an event more startling than all the crazy incidents shown thereafter.

This brings us back again to the general problem of the cinematic text, its boundaries and cultural stratification. As many film historians of recent years have pointed out, the development of the narrative structures of cinema does not consist of a series of inventions and improvements but is the more complex outcome of the struggle between a number of hidden and multi-directional forces. The problem does not lie in the development of a new 'language' but in the extent of its cultural adaptibility. Around 1910 the centre stage of film history was dominated by the collision between the received understanding of cultural boundaries and the conception of text and its boundaries that cinema offered.

Chapter 6

The reception of the moving image

The preceding discussion addressed the issue of boundaries between films within the performance. This chapter will deal with text reception at the level of the image and will concentrate on two problems: the forefront boundary of the moving image as defined by the historical viewer, and what was perceived as its temporal boundary – the moment when the image 'disappeared from the screen', to repeat the expression used in those days. In short, the chapter will focus on the screen and the cut. I will argue that both the status of the screen and the status of the cut are historically specific.

ORIGINS OF THE MYTH

Testing the status of the screen was very much what the first Lumière films were all about. As Kevin Brownlow has observed, what struck the early cinema viewer most of all was 'head-on' movement, i.e. movement towards the camera.[1] This movement was conceived at its potential extreme. The first viewers of *The Arrival of a Train at La Ciotat Station* [L'Arrivée du train en gare de la Ciotat, 1895] were not sure where the limits of the space that the train intended to transcend really lay. For us the true meaning of *The Arrival of a Train* is lost for ever; it could be apprehended only by a viewer with no prior experience of cinema whatsoever, since its effect was wholly dependent on the unclear cognitive status of the screen.

With its habitual attention to origins, historiographical tradition highlights this film and dwells on the assumed panic it caused among those who first saw it. Tom Gunning was right to question the accuracy of this history-made 'origin myth' and the validity of its sources.[2] There was probably no panic at seeing the train, although a British 1896 account published in *The Sketch* refers to the sense of a shared 'uneasiness':

> In the distance there is some smoke, then the engine of the express is seen, and in a few seconds the train rushes in so quickly that, in common with most of the people in the front rows of the stalls, I shift uneasily in my seat and think of railway accidents.[3]

As Schivelbusch's study observes, the fear of railway accidents was part of nineteenth-century cultural sensibility, so the anxiety cannot be categorised as 'naive'.[4] Perhaps there never was such a thing as a truly 'naive' spectator. The fear the first viewers experienced was a sophisticated, 'cultural' kind of *Angst* prepared (as Gunning has shown) and mediated (as I am going to argue) by rich layers of pre-cinematic culture.

However, the historiographical origin myth persists, and one wonders where its own origins lie. To be more specific, when exactly did the train arriving at La Ciotat station become canonised as one of cinema's central 'unforgettable' and 'unrepeatable' impressions? What was the effect of this 'primal scene' (to use Gunning's term once again) on subsequent film practice?

Looking at Russian sources, *The Arrival of a Train* was singled out as epitomising cinema's 'Golden Age' as early as 1907. The editorial printed on the first page of the first number of the first Russian cinema journal *Cine-Phono* clearly situates 'the first picture ever made' in a miraculous historical past:

> It was about fifteen [*sic*!] years ago that moving pictures were shown for the first time and the impression they made was so great that everybody remembers the time when they first saw a train rushing across the white screen as something quite miraculous.[5]

While the motivation behind it was simple editorial rhetoric ('Look, cinema already has its history, so why not publish a cinema magazine?'), the statement is important. All that a film history needs is there: its own existence is announced and the first film named. By 1913 the origin myth had already acquired its element of 'hysteria'; a contributor to a theatre magazine (not a cinema journal) recalled:

> I remember that evening very clearly: it was one of the most powerful experiences of my life. When the train came rushing towards me from the screen, when three or four hundred people spilled out on to the station platform, and when the train pulled out again, I began to scream. No one hauled me up for disturbing the peace for the simple reason that everyone else was screaming too.[6]

Of course, the emotional tone of memoir texts depends primarily on the person who wrote them. However, if one discards this circumstance for a minute, one cannot help thinking that, as time goes by, the mythology surrounding *The Arrival of a Train* became more entrenched. Recollections written down in the early 1950s by the film director Yevgeni Ivanov-Barkov, who as a child visited a film booth in his native Kostroma, give a characteristically overstated scene, with the panic component already present:

> The engine came nearer and nearer; it was rushing straight towards us . . . closer and closer! . . . A huge steel monster! . . . It was hurtling towards us! It was terrifying! Straight at us! AT US! A piercing scream, Oh! . . . OH! . . . Panic! People leaped up. Some rushed towards the exit. Total darkness.[7]

ANNA KARENINA AND THE ARRIVAL OF A TRAIN AT LA CIOTAT STATION

Did the train myth affect film practice? In 1919 Ilya N. Ignatov, after closely following the progress of Russian cinema for ten years, recalled with some bewilderment the reaction of the Russian press to Gardin's 1914 film version of Tolstoy's *Anna Karenina*. He remarked that, if the papers were to be believed, 'it was not only that the film marked a great step forward in the development of cinema, but that the film possessed certain special qualities that had a stronger influence on the viewer than even the novel itself had on its readers.'[8] This was, indeed, an uncommon response, given the cult status that Tolstoy enjoyed in Russia, even among those who could not read.

Reviewers singled out *Anna Karenina* for its 'psychology', but of course this was not the quality that caused its contemporaries to rate the film as meriting comparison with the novel. On the contrary, it was precisely the psychological treatment of the role of Anna (played by the Moscow Art Theatre actress Maria Germanova) that provoked the greatest division of opinions. People within the Moscow Art Theatre called it sacrilege. Konstantin Stanislavsky's wife, Maria Lilina, remarked somewhat ironically that Germanova was incomparably better in *The Wanton Wife* [Zhena vakkhanka, 1915] than in *Anna Karenina*,[9] and Maria Kallash, in a letter to Olga Knipper-Chekhov dated 31 May 1914 that played up to rivalries within the theatre world, waxed indignant: 'Anna Karenina comes across as being exactly like Vasilisa in Gorky's *Lower Depths* [Na dne]. I wasn't expecting very much, but all the same I didn't imagine that it would be such a mockery of Tolstoy.'[10]

The setting attracted similar criticism. Kallash's letter refers to 'such incongruities as a plush teddy bear and other ultra-modern toys that Anna brings for her son'.[11] A review by the writer Dmitri Filosofov was, on the whole, sympathetic, but also drew attention to anachronism, this time of the gratuitously modern locomotive – Anna's suicide weapon: 'it was not at all like the engines of the late 1870s . . . they used to have huge funnels that widened out towards the top.'[12]

Where the film most notably parted company with Tolstoy's novel was in Gardin's treatment of Anna's suicide, and it was this scene above all that seems to have persuaded critics that the film had some special quality that enabled it to bear comparison with the novel. Only the first reel of *Anna Karenina* survives, so we have to refer to production stills and contemporary descriptions in order to reconstruct the way the scene was staged. Fortunately, an article by a reporter present at the location shooting appeared in the Moscow theatre periodical *Footlights and Life* in 1914. The article was entitled 'The Suicide of Anna Karenina' and it explained to its readers what special effects had been used (dummy substitution plus reverse shooting) to make the suicide scene look real. Among other interesting technicalities the

9 *Anna Karenina* [1914]: the tragic heroine contemplates her destiny (production still)

reporter mentioned that the film ended somewhat differently from the novel: in the novel Anna threw herself from the platform under the second carriage, not under the approaching engine as she did in the film. The reporter did not really object to this: 'that is the way they do it in cinema.'[13] Neither did any of the other reviewers find this a problem, not even those who were so alert to the non-period teddy bear and the anachronistic locomotive. Gardin's ending must have been really effective to be able to justify the liberty the director had taken with the source in treating the novel's crucial scene.

Can Gardin's modification be identified as specifically cinematic? Technically speaking, it cannot. A similar treatment of the suicide scene had already been tested on the theatre stage before 1895. A poster advertising a stage production of *Anna Karenina* in the Moscow Skomorokh Theatre announced: 'In the last act a railway engine (specially constructed in L. A. Fyodorov's workshop) will cross the entire stage, and Anna Karenina will throw herself under it.'[14] The necessary stage machinery for such thrilling effects had been developed for the nineteenth-century American melodrama, the genre that surely inspired the Skomorokh idea.[15] Ivan Shcheglov, who had seen the performance, wrote:

> but it was Fyodorov's engine that turned out to be the biggest disappointment for the audience. It not only failed to run Anna Karenina over (she let out a scream even before it appeared), but it did not even succeed in crossing the whole stage as promised; it got hopelessly stuck between the first stage wing and the garden table at which Levin, Kitty and their guests had been drinking toasts 'To Russia' at the beginning of the act.[16]

However, the iconography of the suicide *mise-en-scène* used in Gardin's film was clearly not theatrical. A glance at the production still published by the illustrated weekly *Sparks* for 1914[17] shows the train in exactly the same position relative to the camera as in the Lumières' *The Arrival of a Train*, the only difference being that between the camera and the approaching engine we see the figure of Anna Karenina kneeling by the rails. Of course, Gardin can hardly be suspected of imitating Lumière. Still, I do not think we can dismiss the similarity as purely coincidental; it is probably more a question of the formative influence of the first impressions created by cinema, or, to be more specific, of the emotional memory attached to them. All the more so because, as I have mentioned in the Introduction, the associative link between Tolstoy's *Anna Karenina* and the Lumière cinema was potentially established long before Gardin made his film. Two notable figures in Russian culture, Maxim Gorky and Vladimir Stasov, both left behind emotional contemporary accounts of the Lumière train effect. The way Gorky described it turns the Lumière train into something like a Grand-Guignol *coup de théâtre*:

10 Satirical views of cinema
  (*a*) M. Mikhailov's 1910 caricature of cinema's 'impossible juxtapositions': Lev
  Tolstoy and Glupyshkin (the Russian name for the French comedian, André
  Deed)
  (*b*) P. W.'s view of a 'typical' scene from a 1910 film, the 'dance of the
  Apaches'
  (*c*) I. Stepanov's 1913 depiction of the 'embarrassed' viewer stealing incog-
  nito into the 'electric theatre'

СПОРЪ ТЕАТРА СЪ КИНЕМАТОГРАФОМЪ.

Театръ. Въ театрѣ можно видѣть красивыя плечи.

Кинем. А въ кинематографѣ, пользуясь темнотой, можно ихъ обнимать.

Театръ. Въ театрѣ слушаешь хорошіе голоса.

Кинем. А въ кинематографѣ вы можете сами бесѣдовать.

11 'Cinema's dispute with theatre', from the journal *Theatre and Art*, 1914

  (*a*) *Theatre:* In the theatre you can view beautiful shoulders.
    Cinema: But in the cinema, thanks to the darkness, you can put your arm round them.
  (*b*) *Theatre:* In the theatre you can hear excellent voices.
    Cinema: But in the cinema you can talk yourself.

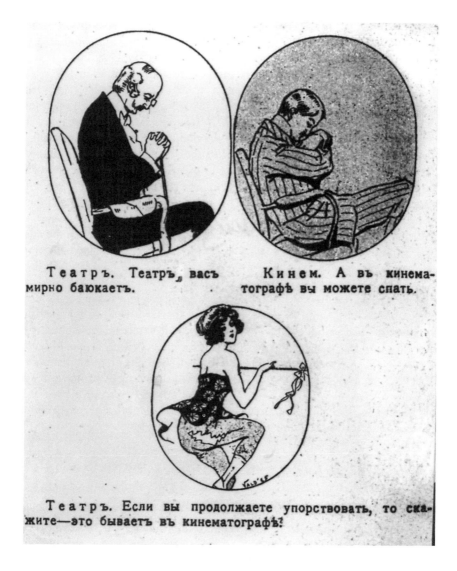

Театръ. Театръ, васъ мирно баюкаетъ.

Кинем. А въ кинематографѣ вы можете спать.

Театръ. Если вы продолжаете упорствовать, то скажите—это бываетъ въ кинематографѣ?

(c) *Theatre:* The theatre lulls you gently to sleep.
   Cinema: But in the cinema you can sleep.
(d) *Theatre:* If you go on being obstinate, can you see this happen in the cinema?

It darts like an arrow straight towards you – watch out! It seems as though it is about to rush into the darkness where you are sitting and reduce you to a mangled sack of skin, full of crumpled flesh and splintered bones, and destroy this hall and this building . . . and transform them into fragments and dust.[18]

Stasov was an art critic rather than a writer, and his description is not particularly colourful, but he does register the cultural analogy prompted by the effect. The reference Stasov makes is to Tolstoy's novel, naturally; permit me to cite again a passage from his enthusiastic letter written in 1896: 'All of a sudden a whole railway train comes rushing out of the picture towards you; it gets bigger and bigger, and you think it's going to run you over, just like in *Anna Karenina* – it's incredible.'[19] This association occurred despite the fact that the novel does not actually contain any image of an onrushing locomotive: as I have just mentioned, Tolstoy's Anna throws herself under a passing carriage. It seems as though the Lumière film both evoked the scene and reshaped it in Stasov's mind. The film and the ending of *Anna Karenina* became pseudomorphically related. Can we really associate a passing remark made in 1896 in a private letter with something that took place in the film industry eighteen years later? Two considerations may help make the case look stronger. First, Tolstoy's *Anna Karenina* had been an immediate best-seller – the novel was even more successful than *War and Peace*. Given this, as well as the fact that everyone in Russia's cities must have seen the Lumières' film, we may surmise that Stasov's reaction must have been shared by the public in general. Second, time does not seem to have dimmed the vividness of that initial shock. On the contrary, if someone remembering it in 1913 could say 'I began to scream, and everyone else was screaming too', it proves that by the time *Anna Karenina* was filmed, the emotional memory of being scared by *The Arrival of a Train* turned the past event into an image of collective hysteria. After the Lumières one might almost have been able to predict that if *Anna Karenina* were ever to be made into a film the suicide scene would follow the Lumières rather than Tolstoy.

THE ARRIVAL OF A TRAIN: DISTORTED SPACE AND YAWNING FOREGROUND

Of course, the impression made by *The Arrival of a Train* could not be repeated by later film-makers, however hard they may have tried.[20] Similarly, there is no point in scrutinising other films released by the Lumières in order to establish their initial impact. One can say that it was not so much the Lumières as the viewer personally who authored the train effect. The film survives but we have lost its viewer.

Can we hope to reconstruct the figure of the 'first viewer' by assembling scraps of non-filmic evidence? In fact, such an attempt was the whole point of 'the origin myth' I have discussed earlier in this chapter. From 1907 on (or did it start earlier?) memoirists and film historians began trying to construct a figure of the 'naive viewer', someone who believed in the reality of what was, in fact, a mere image. Should we take for granted the viewer implied by the screenwriter Alexander Voznesensky when he recalled the calming assurances that the management felt compelled to issue at the entrance to the cinema: 'It is a real train, but it cannot come off the wall'?[21] The fictional nature of such a figure has been exposed by Christian Metz and Tom Gunning.[22] An alternative approach should probably focus on the reconstruction of the cognitive experience of the first viewers. While the 'naive viewer' is a historiographic fiction, the 'innocent' viewer, that is, a viewer with untrained cognitive habits, can be proposed as a historically more helpful figure.

Not only did the reactions of a person totally unfamiliar with moving images belong to a different emotional register, his 'reading of space' was different from ours. Was moving photography perceived as something so life-like as to be confused with reality? Yes and no. While all accounts of a first visit to the cinematograph stressed how 'life-like' it seemed, some also mentioned that the space on the screen looked distorted.

Two accounts published in 1896 complained that the screen perspective was 'not right'. O. Winter wrote in an English newspaper in May 1896:

> The disproportion of foreground and background adds to your embar-rassment, and although you know that the scene has a mechanical and intimate correspondence with truth, you recognise its essential and inherent falsity . . . The most delicate instrument [the Lumières' camera] is forced to render every incident at the same pace and with the same prominence, only reserving to itself the monstrous privilege of enlarging the foreground beyond recognition.[23]

While specialists in cognitive psychology and perspectival research may have their own explanation of this effect,[24] a Russian press review of 1896, quoted in his memoirs by the cameraman Alexander Digmelov, tended to explain it by positing the excessive clarity of background images. Background objects – argued the reviewer – had to be portrayed with a certain indistinctness (called aerial perspective in classical art theory) in order to signal that they were further away:

> were it not for the unfortunate *lack of aerial perspective*, which makes the background figures seem incredibly tiny, while those at the front are grotesquely enlarged, the Lumière cinematograph could fool even the sharpest eye. [my emphasis][25]

The 'lack of aerial perspective' signalled that the image was perceived as being all too clear, with too many things in it to see. In fact, the Lumière films contradicted a basic convention, almost a reflex drilled into the European viewer by the canons of post-Renaissance painting: the image should have one focus, the centrepiece pre-selected by the artist and signalled to the onlooker by obscuring other, less important details, either by deliberate overlapping or by the indistinctness of aerial perspective or by some other definition-reducing technique. Some nineteenth-century artists questioned the convention by giving equal weight to all parts of the painting (like Pierre Puvis de Chavannes), by denouncing aerial perspective (like Ferdinand Hodler) or by giving too much realism to peripheral details (the Pre-Raphaelites). In such cases the cultural norm of realism (which is always lower than the contemporary technique of representation is able to offer) was exceeded, which, paradoxically, resulted in loss of image credibility. The uncentred image refused to guide the gaze, and was perceived as cold, neutral and uninhabited. The neutrality of treatment made the world of the image look metaphysical and dreamlike.[26] The effect was similar to that of the *trompe-l'oeil*, to hyper-realist painting, or – to return to the Lumières – to the impact of the moving image upon the first film viewers: the image was too perfect to be true.

In terms of its reception, *The Arrival of a Train* fell into two parts: before and after the train stopped. Before it stopped, the viewer reacted to the engine bearing down on him. As soon as it stopped, the second 'attraction' was on display: the crowd swarming on the station platform. Georges Sadoul has observed the importance of this moment: 'Twenty doors all opened at once and the whole composition suddenly changed.'[27] Because of this constantly shifting overlapping, the moving image must have looked as though it was randomly generated, the embodiment of chaos. We only have to imagine what an inexperienced viewer might have felt seeing figures hurrying along a platform (towards the camera) and *overtaking* one another, i.e. in turn overlapping others and being themselves overlapped, to sympathise with the English reviewer, Winter, who complained feelingly:

> A railway station, for instance, is a picture with a thousand shifting focuses . . . Both the cinematograph and the Pre-Raphaelite suffer from the same vice. The one and the other are incapable of selection.[28]

However, what made the image look really strange was the effect of disappearing figures. The great majority of accounts mention the fear of the train bearing down upon the viewer. We are not given much information about what happened at the Lumière shows when this tension was resolved. In this respect L. R. Kogan's recollection is important because it registered a quite separate moment of 'attraction' in the Lumière film: the cognitive (or should we say, 'geometric'?) riddle that confronted the viewer as soon as the locomotive was out of frame – 'where has the engine gone?' According to Kogan's memoirs, 'a train appears in the distance coming with great speed right towards the auditorium. There is an involuntary commotion in the audience, a cry of alarm, *then laughter*: the engine and the carriages have slipped away somewhere to the side [my emphasis]'.[29] For the viewer who did not yet have any cognitive model helping him to account for the disappearance of the locomotive, it was easier to imagine that the train swerved away at the last minute than to place it mentally (as we do now) in a topologically ambivalent 'buffer zone' which we sense simultaneously behind our backs (a signal coming from the camera's field of vision) and, as it were, between us and the screen (a proprioceptive awareness that the position of the viewer and the camera's field of vision do not coincide).[30]

Disappearing figures turned the screen into an uncanny kind of 'black hole' swallowing up everything coming near its edge. Gorky was particularly hypnotised by this quicksand effect. Writing about what seems to be *La Place des Cordeliers* (1895) (titles are not mentioned in his articles), Gorky observed: 'The carriages come straight out towards you, straight out into the darkness where you are sitting . . . [Life is] in motion, alive, vibrant; it comes into the foreground of the picture and then just vanishes.'[31] Gorky had published two articles on the Lumière Cinematograph, and in both of them he dwelled upon the bizarre phenomenology of the screen as a singular zone of non-being that the characters could not surmount and that turned them to nothingness.

THE TEMPORAL BOUNDARY OF THE MOVING IMAGE

For the first viewers of the Lumière films the sensation that the world behind the screen suddenly 'broke off' into the darkness of the auditorium merged with a similar kind of sensation caused by the abrupt closures of most of the Lumière films. Because of the size of the Lumière camera, the first films were all the same length: 17 metres (= 50 seconds). This meant that the ending of the film could not be thoroughly pre-planned. To use Noël Burch's lapidary definition, 'the film (the shot) ended when there was no film left in the camera.'[32] *The Arrival of a Train* was a film with a clearly defined beginning, but with a dangling ending.[33] For Gorky, who was so fascinated by the disappearance of objects in the foreground ('the engine vanishes silently', people on the platform 'come into the foreground and disappear'), this series of disappearances was concluded by the equally unaccountable disappearance of the whole picture from the screen: 'grey figures descend in silence from the carriages, they greet one another silently and make no noise when they laugh; they walk, run, bustle about, get excited – all without a sound . . . and vanish. And then a new picture appears.'[34]

The innocent viewer greeted this rapid change of pictures with the same air of cognitive bewilderment with which he received the yawning void of a screen that devoured all the figures that approached it. For the less philosophically minded it was the sight of images magically appearing rather than vanishing that counted, but the main effect remained unaltered: the whole thing looked more dreamlike than real. Henry Tyrrell, reviewing the Lumière programme for *The Illustrated American* (1896), remarked that

> Sea-waves dash against a pier, or roll in and break languidly on the sandy beach, as in a dream; and the emotion produced upon the spectator is far more vivid than the real scene would be, because of the startling suddenness with which it is conjured up and changed, there in the theatre, by the magic wand of electricity.[35]

Although, technically speaking, the change of pictures at the Lumière shows was effected by breaks between reels rather than by cuts in the classical sense, we are clearly dealing with the prototype of the cut. As Tom Gunning has suggested in his recent paper on temporality in early films, the attractive potential of picture change discovered by the viewer of the first shows was intentionally maximised by the generation of film-makers that emerged immediately after the Lumière brothers:

> The act of display on which the cinema of attractions is founded presents itself as a temporal irruption rather than a temporal development. While every attraction would have a temporal unfolding of its own and some . . . might cause viewers to develop expectations while watching them, these temporal developments would be secondary to the sudden appearance and then disappearance of the view itself. In this sense Méliès's transformations become emblematic examples of the cinema of attraction, endlessly replaying the effect of surprise and appearance, as would a series of brief actualities of the Lumière sort, appearing one after another.[36]

It may be added that the phenomenology of the 'magic cut' had been inherited by the Lumières' shows (and their spectators) from the pre-cinema period of screen practice. An important part of the nineteenth-century fascination with the art of the magic lantern was that, unlike any other kind of images known to the European mind, lantern pictures were not permanently attached to their material bearer, the canvas. The lantern was called magic not so much because it produced images as because it produced them as in the twinkling of an eye and on the very same surface. In 1803 or 1804 the Russian poet Gavriil Derzhavin wrote a longish poem 'The Lantern', which seems to have set a paradigm for the magic lantern metaphor in nineteenth-century Russian literature. In a repetitive manner eight stanzas, each corresponding to one slide in a magic lantern, follow the same pattern. Each stanza is introduced by the words 'Appear, and Be' [Yavis'! I byst'], followed by a dramatic description of the image itself (a lion pouncing on a lamb, a rebel reaching for the crown, a lover touching the private parts of his sweetheart and unaware of Death's scythe looming over him, etc.) and, as soon as the description seems to have reached its climax, the stanza invariably breaks off with the words: 'Vanish! Vanished' [Ischezn'! Ischez].

Predictably, the concluding strophe summarises the lesson: should we, who are no more than guests at the Great Lanternist's feast, crave for the things He shows us or humbly admire their beauty and praise the One who knows our time to vanish?[37] The tradition was taken over by Alexander Pushkin, in whose poems the image of the magic lantern was de-allegorised and turned into a metaphor of transience, of fleeting moods, 'of things that disappear as suddenly and unaccountably as they had come into being.'[38] The magic lantern metaphor has been used in a similar sense by Marina Tsvetayeva, whose first book of poetry was called *The Magic Lantern* [Vol'shebnyi fonar', 1912] and, as a later tribute to the tradition, by Vladimir Nabokov in *Ada*: 'Eighty years quickly passed – a matter of changing a slide in a magic lantern.'[39] It was the same cultural tradition that prompted Gorky's melancholy (or, shall we say, 'literary *Angst*') in his second article on the Lumières (published in Odessa in 1896), when he chose the following words to describe a simple change of reels:

A strange life is being enacted before you, it's real, alive, bustling ... And suddenly it vanishes. There's just a piece of white cloth in a wide, black frame, and it doesn't look as if there had been anything on it at all . . . It gives you a strange, eerie feeling.[40]

UNRELIABLE REALITY

In an earlier chapter I mentioned the Symbolist writers' fascination with what were generally considered to be defects in the cinematic image: vibration, celluloid rain, breaks in film. Andrei Bely's interest in abrupt endings ('crash endings', as he called them), and his idea of exploiting a break in the film as a scenario device, were part of the specifically Symbolist game that approached modernity as a puzzle containing a secret prophecy. At the same time, eccentric as it was, the Symbolist response reflected some universal features of early film reception. In 1908 Bely published an essay entitled 'Theatre and the Modern Drama', in which he made the following remark: 'There is indeed myth-making in the cinematograph: a man sneezes and bursts.'[41] But what kind of 'myth-making' did he mean?

Before I address this question directly, let me briefly summarise the above analysis of texts referring to the Lumière cinematograph. The impression that moving images left on their first spectators was a unique combination of mutually exclusive effects. On the one hand, the Lumières' audiences were struck by what they believed to be the excessive naturalism of the image. The spectator of the 1890s felt that within the new medium the habitual balance between image and object was tilted in favour of the latter.

On the other hand, to repeat a contemporary account already quoted, 'although you know that the scene has a mechanical and intimate correspondence with the truth, you recognize its essential and inherent falsity'.[42]

The increasing visual realism of the image went side by side with, and was undermined by, the acute sensation of its ephemerality. The surprising thing about the locomotive was not just that it seemed menacingly real but that it vanished into thin air once it left the frame. The effect of diegetic objects vanishing from the field of the image was reinforced by the perplexing transience of the image. Hyper-realistic in their visuality, cinematographic images could at any moment 'burst like a bubble'. Life on the screen was very real but not very reliable.

This feature of early film reception made the cinema a particularly interesting medium for the Symbolists. The impermanence, the ephemerality, of the material world, conceived as a thin visible integument covering the body of the unknown, was a recurrent Symbolist motif. On 26 December 1908 Alexander Blok made the following remark in his notebook: 'Element and culture. The feeling of catastrophe, disease, anxiety, rupture (mankind like a person standing next to a bomb). The bomb was planted by history, and it has disrupted everything.'[43] The end of history, the death of culture, and a mystical fear of the future were central to the Symbolist universe. This future was channelled through Blok's 'blue abyss' of the modern city, and the cinema was its most unambiguous token. Russian Symbolism was essentially eschatological, and the 'crisis of culture', or the 'end of history', intuited by Blok and proclaimed in Bely's essays, were just two versions of that basic Symbolist theme: the end of the world. Blok's definition of mankind as 'a person standing next to a bomb' echoed Andrei Bely's definition of reality as 'a cake-walk over the abyss'. The cinema with its flickering, vibrating, unstable image was a perfect symbol for such a representation of the world, as was the bomb, the central metaphor of Andrei Bely's novel *Petersburg*, first published in serial form in 1913/14. Small wonder then that the Méliès (and Méliès-inspired) series of trick films based on exploding characters were subject to an eschatological reading in Symbolist literary texts. In his 1907 essay, 'The City', Andrei Bely described two films that to his mind reflected the inner nature of modern life. He did not mention the titles, but the first one sounds very much like Walter R. Booth's *The '?' Motorist* (Hepworth, 1906), an English version of the Méliès space fantasies:

Someone is chasing after someone else. A motor car, a bicycle, a policeman are flying in pursuit. Crrump! The car smashes through a wall and drives through someone's peaceful living room. Crunch! It smashes through the wall and calmly drives on down the street.[44] It's funny, but it's really not at all funny. Walls and peaceful domesticity cannot protect us from the arrival of the unknown, can they? And now that same car, to the accompaniment of a waltz, is rushing up a wall in defiance of the laws of gravity; is being chased by a policeman, also defying the laws of gravity. Higher and higher. Excelsior! The motor car zooms up into the sky. Meteors fly past, but around them is nothing but empty space . . . The city, which has swallowed up the fields and grabbed all the riches of the earth, is just a motor car suspended in a void . . . Electric lights cascade from billboards, but this is the rain of meteors flashing through the ether. And the driver – Death in a top hat – is baring his teeth and rushing towards us.[45]

Bely's eschatological reading of the trick cinema ('walls cannot protect us from the unknown') is even more salient in his description of what seems to be Lewin Fitzhamon's film *That Fatal Sneeze* (Hepworth, 1907). It is this or a similar film that made Bely think of 'myth-making in the cinematograph':

An old man has sprinkled something in front of a child. The child sneezes. He makes his way into the room where the old man is sleeping: he sprinkles some powder. The old man gets up and sneezes. The wall collapses. He runs out into the street – and sneezes: the shop window displays come crashing down, the lamp-posts fall over, the houses fall apart. He sneezes. The earth begins to fall apart. He sneezes, and finally explodes in a cloud of smoke.[46]

For Bely this was a perfect representation of the end of the world in its modern (i.e. unheroic, bathetic and ironic) version. On the one hand, the English film, its shaking and swaying camera conveying the effect of a seismic cataclysm, must have looked like a visual parallel to the biblical prophecy:

. . . the foundations of the earth do shake.
    The earth is utterly broken down, the earth is clean dissolved, the earth is moved exceedingly.
    The earth shall reel to and fro like a drunkard, and shall be removed like a cottage; and the transgression thereof shall be heavy upon it; and it shall fall, and not rise again.[47]

On the other hand, the film made this prophecy work on the level of immediate, present-day reality. For Bely, the way the world ends was not with a bang, nor even with a whimper, but with a sneeze:

Man is a cloud of smoke. He catches a cold, he sneezes and bursts; the smoke disperses . . . The cinematograph reigns in the city, reigns over the earth. In Moscow, Paris, New York, Bombay, on the same day, maybe at the very same hour, thousands of people come to see a man who sneezes – who sneezes and explodes. The cinematograph has crossed the borders of reality. More than the preachings of scholars and wise men, this has demonstrated to everyone what reality is: it is a lady suffering from a cold who sneezes and explodes. And we, who hold on to her: where are we?[48]

This cinematic motif, the motif of an unreliable reality, was transformed by Bely into the leitmotif of his famous novel *Petersburg*. Its story line is strikingly similar to that of Fitzhamon's film *That Fatal Sneeze*. In the film a boy makes his father explode (or is it his uncle, as some sources claim?)[49] by pouring sneezing powder over him while he is sleeping in his bedroom.

In Bely's novel a young man, Nikolai (Kolenka) Ableukhov, who is a former member of a terrorist group, has two obsessions: that he must blow up his father, a senator, with a time bomb; and that he has swallowed the bomb himself and hears it ticking inside him, about to blast him to smithereens. This is how Nikolai Ableukhov plans to kill his father:

> He would smuggle the sardine tin [which contained the bomb] into his father's bedroom and place it under his pillow, or, better still, under the mattress. Later –
> 'Good night, papa!'
> 'Good night, Kolenka!'
> Then he would go to his own room, undress quickly and pull the bedclothes over his head . . .
> His heart thumping, he would lie there trembling in the soft bed, listening, straining, longing for the bang that would shatter the silence, tear apart the bed, the table, the walls, and also perhaps . . .
> He would hear the familiar shuffling of slippers as his father went to the lavatory . . .
> Waiting, waiting . . .
> . . .
> Half an hour to go. The greenish first light of dawn, turning to blue, then grey, and the candle light growing dim; only fifteen minutes left. And now the candle goes out . . .
> Every minute an eternity . . . He would strike a match – only five minutes had passed! He would try to calm himself down, tell himself that *it* would only happen after ten more slow revolutions of time, try to deceive himself . . .
> – but then that inimitable, unmistakable, drawn-out sound –
> – the Explosion!
> Thrusting his bare legs into his drawers, or even just in his night shirt –
> he would leap, out of the warm bed, his face white and twisted – Yes, Yes, Yes! – and would rush barefoot into the darkening corridor, straight as an arrow to that unmistakable sound, breathing in that special odour, that acrid smell of burning and gas, and . . . of something else, something more horrible than either . . .
> . . .
> He would run in, choking and coughing, and struggle through the black hole in the wall made by the explosion.
> And there, beyond the hole . . . where the demolished bedroom had been, a grim flame would reveal – nothing: just swirling clouds of smoke.[50]

True, there is no sneeze motif in the novel – although the father does suffer from chronic flatulence – but for Bely, the images of the 'exploding man', be it the manic sneezer in *That Fatal Sneeze*[51] or the bomb-ridden gas-filled Ableukhov, are symbolic of the great Nothingness we carry within ourselves:

An indecent something had taken a nothing into itself, swelling up from
time eternal –

> – as the stomach swells from the expansion of gases, a
> complaint from which all the Ableukhovs suffered –
> – to time eternal.[52]

THE EMPTY SCREEN (A BLANK SHOT)

Let us take another look at the way Gorky described his response to a
vanishing image: 'There is' – he wrote – 'just a piece of white cloth in a wide,
black frame, and it doesn't look as if there had been anything on it at all . . .
It gives you a strange, eerie feeling.'[53] For Gorky, even after the last picture
had vanished, the show was still not over. The piece of white cloth seemed
almost to have been an integral part of the attraction, in the same way as the
effect of the slide change in the magic lantern had been a legitimate part of
the transience allegory for Derzhavin.

Would it be going too far, then, to suggest that the effect of 'a cut to an
empty screen' was, if not exactly premeditated, then taken into account by
early film-makers? If so, it will help to explain why quite a number of early
films ended with an explosion or a cataclysm of some kind – the kind of
closure (or, rather, as Noël Burch called it, 'non-closure'[54]) that Andrei Bely
simply referred to as 'crash endings'.[55] The single-shot film *How It Feels to
be Run Over* (Cecil Hepworth, 1900), about a motor car that crashes full-tilt
into the screen, concluded with the intertitle 'Oh. Mother will be pleased!'
This presumably referred to the last thought that flashed through the victim's
mind, but to someone like Gorky the subsequent blank screen (as the film ran
out through the projector gate) would probably be read as representing the
ensuing post-crash silence. Interestingly, while the attraction of directly
addressing (or assaulting) the screen and the viewer did not last long in fiction
films, it found a natural refuge in the sensational travel scenes shot by Félix
Mesguich in the mid-1900s. One of these, described in his memoirs, might
have included the cut-to-screen effect. This is Mesguich's account of the joke
played on him by the King of Spain when he was shooting what later became
King Alfonso XIII Out Hunting [Le Roi Alphonse XIII à la chasse]:

> I tracked him [the king] while he aimed directly at the camera, and carried
> on filming without even flinching. He came nearer and nearer; now he was
> looking straight into the lens, he couldn't get any closer: 'I hope I haven't
> missed?' he said . . . [Each time the film was shown] the audience got
> noticeably excited as their sovereign got bigger and bigger. First the king's
> face and then his eyes and mouth grew to enormous proportions, com-
> pletely filling the thirty-square-metre screen.[56]

Quasi-newsreels that portrayed dramatic hunting incidents in various parts
of the world were a popular subject and a good pretext for sensational trick

photography. Mesguich, naturally, shot a film about bear hunting in Russia. It was filmed in a real hunting forest but with the bear played by one of the hunters in a bear's skin. Of course, Mesguich knew how to convince the viewer that the cameraman, too, had been in serious danger. Sometimes such pictures came with their own legend. One of these was taken for granted by Feofan Shipulinsky whose book on film history described a picture 'filmed by an anonymous cameraman' during a safari in Africa:

> He positioned his camera alongside the bait, but, when the enraged lion pounced, it crushed both him and the camera. Paralysed with fear, he carried on cranking the handle right up to the last moment. He died, but a few weeks later audiences could see the pouncing lion filling the whole of the screen.[57]

A dramatic pause (an empty screen) would be an eloquent closure for such films. If this hypothesis is correct, and something like a 'blank shot', or an empty screen position, did exist as an aesthetic factor in early film viewing, maybe even film-making, it might help to interpret an otherwise quite baffling idea Andrei Bely had in 1918 for a film based on his novel *Petersburg*. If it had ever been shot, it would certainly have been the first really avant-garde movie in film history. As I mentioned earlier (Part I, Chapter 4), Bely based his project on what he considered to be a highly effective artistic device, the 'break' (or 'rupture') [*figura obryva*]. Time and again throughout the scenario we come across the instruction 'the film breaks off'. Bely neither explained nor seems to have given a thought to what these 'breaks' meant in technical terms, but, since each of them is semantically overdetermined, it is possible that something like a blank shot is implied. This is how Bely's script presents the sequence (conceived as a succession of scenes in silhouette) in which the terrorist Alexander Ivanovich attempts to assassinate the senator:

> Tableau 22.
> In the dim cosmic space we glimpse the outline of a flying brougham. The brougham stops. The shadowy figure of Apollon Apollonovich Ableukhov [the senator] jumps out. Suddenly the dim outline of Alexander Ivanovich appears. In his hand he is holding a parcel. He rushes towards Apollon Apollonovich and throws the parcel at him. It falls at Apollon Apollonovich's feet. There is a blinding flash and a dreadful, hollow, explosion.
> (The picture breaks off)[58]

AWARENESS OF THE SCREEN

Unlike the modern spectator, the early viewer was very screen-conscious. In his memoirs Ivanov-Barkov described the metamorphosis of the screen from rectangle on the wall to window on the world as an attraction in its own right:

Suddenly a blueish, flickering rectangle flashed up in front of us ... And then something miraculous that we had never seen before: the walls of the booth instantly vanished and the rectangle turned into a window thrown wide open, right on to one of the most famous cities in the world – Paris! ... Live people – walking, running, rushing in all directions! One of them came right up to us, said something, gave us a wave and hurried on.[59]

The screen appeared as an ambiguous and elusive membrane, a boundary between 'us' and 'them' that – at the same time – insisted that no boundary existed at all.

As we know from a number of accounts, this curious surface appealed to the sense of touch. Most memoirists explain it by referring to the realism of the medium: 'The picture show made such an amazing impression on me that after the train scene I got up to take a look behind the screen.'[60] Of course such a response may well have been prompted by straightforward curiosity, and perhaps it is only a myth that the 'naive' spectator wondered 'how they managed to get Paris behind that screen?' When we see a rabbit produced out of a hat we are more intrigued by the hat than by the rabbit. The desire to touch must have been caused by the substance of the screen rather than by the image on it. What magic stuff was it made of? What did it feel like? Was it waterproof? The ladies watching the Lumière film *A Boat Leaving Harbour* [Barque sortant du port, 1895] gathered up their skirts, and after the performance was over anybody who wanted to was allowed to touch the screen.[61] The paradox of the screen was that its surface seemed at once penetrable and impenetrable, substantial and immaterial, transparent and opaque.

Early accounts are often more rewarding than memoirs. Stasov's letter of 1896 describing *A Boat Leaving Harbour* indicated the very subtle way awareness of the screen interfered with the perception of the image; one feels its rectangle engraved into the scene:

Imagine that you suddenly have the open sea in front of you, no shore at all: the shore is the bottom edge of the picture right in front of where we are sitting in our chairs and armchairs ... And the waves are getting bigger and bigger all the time, they are rolling in from far out and coming on right up to you ... on and on, leaping up and crashing down, and the lines of surf are breaking right against the front edge of the picture.[62]

Stasov's way of describing the film (actually, of misreading it) clearly reveals the perception 'error' the contemporary viewer made while watching the Lumière films: a discursive component of the image ('the front edge of the picture') was 'mistaken' for its diegetic component – the missing shore. As the last chapter of this book will argue, such 'misprojections' of discourse upon diegesis were a universal rule of early film reception. Of course, we can only call it 'misreading' in a very relative sense. No one was ever really deceived by early films but, rather, as Gunning has shown, the spectator was willingly misled by the optical games they offered.[63]

Very soon, however, acute awareness of the screen gave way to its opposite. While the very first exhibitors exposed the screen to touch, in the early 1910s we observe the tendency to conceal the screen, to cover it with a curtain. As I tried to show earlier in the book, this new attitude towards cinema's technological anatomy was part of its ongoing cultural absorption. The exhibitors' desire to make their theatres conform to the received cultural norm coincided with the film-makers' growing inclination to tell conventional stories in a conventional manner. The screen was not only covered up, it was suppressed as a factor of text reception.

A SHADOW ON THE SCREEN

According to some popular theories of the human psyche, suppression does not mean forgetting: one way or another, what has been suppressed is bound to re-emerge. The following examples suggest that there were moments in Russian film culture when screen awareness resurfaced.

The recurrent image of a cinema spectator accidentally caught in the beam of the projector has been identified by Roman Timenchik in three works by minor Russian poets of the 1900s–1910s. The reason why this particular kind of haphazard effect – observed, I am sure, rather than invented by the poets – has attracted the three authors is obvious: it presented a perfect metaphor for a fleeting intersection of fantasy and reality. Ada Chumachenko's poem written in 1911 pictures a little girl's head in the dark auditorium as it is suddenly brightly illuminated by the chance 'backlight':

Now and then, in the golden ray
Of the thin cold light that falls
From somewhere behind us
On to the white square of the screen,
Would flash the profile of a child
Absorbed by the tale,
Its locks of golden hair
And its gentle, pensive gaze.[64]

In the other two poems the interest was focused on the shadow that a spectator caught in the beam of the projector cast over the image on the screen. A poem by Alexander Roslavlev (1907) stresses the oxymoron of a figure in the next seat to you imposing its profile over an exotic image:

Egypt's scorching sun . . .
Alexandria . . . The Nile . . .
Suddenly
A shadow rises on the screen –
And the pyramid's in shade.[65]

Finally there is Maria Moravskaya's long ballad 'The Girl With the Bright Torch', a poem about an usherette in love with a violin player in the cinema orchestra, who is, in his turn, in love with the star on the screen, and who hardly ever notices

> How often on the wonders of fabled lands
> Shown on the trembling screen
> The accidental shadow falls
> Of the girl with her bright torch![66]

Moravskaya's poem had been written in 1915, a time when the cinema was already in its age of realistic illusionism. The poem questions the fundamental convention of illusionism – the 'transparency' of the screen. The poor usherette is a real girl in love with somebody as real as herself. Her 'accidental shadow' betrays the true nature of the screen. It is exposed as a dull wall rather than a window opening out on 'the wonders of fabled lands'. Yet, real as she is, the usherette can only flash across the 'screen lands' as an immaterial silhouette. Narrative involvement notwithstanding, the feeling that the viewer's real self had no part in the world on the other side of the screen was at the core of the viewer's sensibility in the 1910s.

THE UTTERANCE, PAST AND PRESENT

As with some of the other topics discussed by modern film theory,[67] the problem of cinematic utterance has its prehistory in film literature of the 1910s. What do film theorists mean by 'utterance', and why does it present a problem? According to Emile Benveniste, a linguistic utterance [*l'énonciation*] can either belong to the dimension of discourse (to the 'here and now'), thus implicitly acknowledging the presence of the speaker and his inter-locutor(s), or can exclude the immediate situation and those present and hence be situated in the dimension of history (the 'then and there'), for which the circumstance of the utterance is irrelevant to the situation to which it refers. The 'plane of history' excludes the pronouns 'I' and 'you'; the events it refers to require only the past tense, etc.; whereas an utterance belonging to the 'plane of discourse' can be recognised by the fact that it implies an 'I' and a 'you', i.e. participants in the given act of speech.[68] Although Benveniste's famous distinction may be relatively simple and instrumental when applied to language, it turns into a theoretical problem when applied to literature and to art. The performing arts, as it happens, are the trickiest. The tacit convention of dramatic theatre, for example, corresponds to the plane of history as presented in oral discourse. Although in terms of real time and real space the performers and the audience they address participate in the same 'speech act', the presence of the audience and the very fact of it being addressed is not acknowledged, as the well-known concept of 'the fourth wall' developed by Stanislavsky testifies. At the same time, any given play is presented in conformity with stage conventions as a unique event, taking place currently, exclusively, as it were, in the present tense. At first sight this set of theatre conventions does not look drastically different from the rules of the game as accepted by cinemagoers today. But for the viewers of the 1910s the screen and the stage, in terms of presence, must have seemed diametrically opposed, and some time and effort were required before this feeling was overcome. Take Stanislavsky's attitude to cinema, for example. His method of acting involved paying homage to what he called the 'gift of public solitude', i.e. ignoring the presence of the audience and creating a sort of psychological 'fourth wall' that ruled out any hint of direct address to the audience, whether by acting, direction or stage design. We might assume that in this respect the type of performance he developed was rather similar to what cinema viewers experienced. Yet even Stanislavsky had difficulty in making the transition to cinema. Whenever he was approached with an offer to make a film, he would turn it down, alleging that the 'fourth wall of the screen' frightened him. As he put it in 1914:

> Theatre is alive only because of the ceaseless exchange of spiritual energy between spectator and actor, because of the invisible sympathetic strings that exist between actor and spectator. The cinematograph will never have this, because the live actor is missing, because his spiritual impulse is confined by mechanical means. In the theatre a living being alarms us, consoles us, makes us happy or unhappy, while everyone and everything in the cinematograph is *as if* alive.[69]

Indeed, the strange idea of absent actors addressing absent viewers was difficult to swallow. In terms of the theory of utterance, film performance was rather unlike anything theatre viewers and actors had been used to. In Christian Metz's words, 'During the showing of the film the audience is in the presence of the acting, but the actor himself is absent; during the shooting, when the actor is present, the audience is absent.'[70]

In the attempt to overcome the feeling of mechanicism and lifelessness associated with the medium of cinema, a unique genre of hybrid performances was born. In 1914 the newspaper *The Day* started a discussion, which was taken up by theatre periodicals and, of course, cinema trade papers, about whether or not screen action could possibly be combined with acting on stage.[71] The paper's critic invited his readers to imagine the philosophical dialogues from Dostoyevsky's *Crime and Punishment* being presented by 'live' actors while Raskolnikov's confused wanderings through the grey streets of St Petersburg before he kills the old lady are being shown on the screen above.[72]

The great Russian stage actor Pavel Orlenev was more enthusiastic about the idea than anyone else. In 1914 he declared he was going to put on hybrid versions of Dostoyevsky and Ibsen. Theatre critics, however, were sceptical about the project. A reviewer for *The Theatre Paper* warned his readers:

He [Orlenev] proposes to produce Ibsen's *Brand* in such a way that some of the scenes would be played by live actors, and some presented cinematographically. I am sorry for Orlenev, who is sincere in his enthusiasm, because I can see the whole thing turning into an unmitigated disaster: you cannot combine live and dead material, you cannot link the excitement of real living action with the impersonal coldness of the screen.[73]

The critic's worst fears were realised; the result was the opposite of what Orlenev intended. Instead of eliminating the contrast between stage conventions and those of the screen, Orlenev's textual mutants only heightened it. In his memoirs Orlenev himself admits that the experiment was a failure, although it ran to full houses for more than three months and made good money.[74] The review in *The Theatre* was succinct: 'the second half, printed on soulless film, is as colourless as the first half, the spoken part, is vivid.'[75]

Film histories relate that early film actors, especially in comic genres, would sometimes turn towards the camera and give it a wink. I am not sure how this particular mannerism was received but, as a general rule, the harder films tried to address the viewer directly, the more the viewer seemed to be aware of the one-way character of this contact. As the poet Konstantin Ldov remarked in a poem of the 1910s, 'Film characters are not just mute, they are also blind.'[76] This phenomenological aspect of early cinema is described with almost archaeological authenticity in Thomas Mann's *The Magic Mountain*. In Mann's novel the residents of an Alpine sanatorium excitedly watch a scenic short showing a young Moroccan girl, her firm breasts half-exposed, smiling and waving to them:

[Catching a casual glance from the screen] . . . the audience stared, taken aback, into the face of the charming apparition. It seemed to see and saw not, it was not moved by the glances bent upon it, its smile and nod were not of the present but of the past, so that the impulse to respond was baffled and lost in a feeling of impotence.[77]

For some observers the awareness that the event which seemed to be unfolding right in front of their eyes had, in fact, taken place in another time and space, must itself have been an aesthetic experience. In one of Virginia Woolf's essays we find a vivid introspective analysis of this feeling. She suggests that objects represented in films, compared with the way they are represented in photographs,

have become not more beautiful, in the sense in which pictures are beautiful, but shall we call it (our vocabulary is miserably insufficient) more real, or real with a different reality from that which we perceive in daily life? We behold them as they are when we are not there. We see life as it is when we have no part in it. As we gaze we seem to be removed from the pettiness of actual existence. The horse will not knock us down. The King will not grasp our hands. The wave will not wet our feet.[78]

In Russian literature the metaphor of cinema as 'a world without me' was used to portray two psychological landscapes traditionally important for Russian culture: the world as seen through the eyes of an émigré and the world as seen by the dead. In Nabokov's novel *Mary* [Mashenka, 1926] Ganin, a white émigré in Berlin, 'imagined that the foreign town passing before him was only a moving snapshot'.[79] And the émigré writer Alexander Kuprin, writing from Paris, complained that 'nothing that happens here seems real; it's as if everything is taking place on a cinema screen. I'm not living in it, you understand'.[80]

The other mental landscape, life as if seen through the eyes of the dead, was linked with the uncanny but commonly observed feeling one experiences at seeing one's own face on the screen. In the Introduction to this book I have mentioned Alexei Tolstoy's and Leonid Andreyev's instinctive revulsion at seeing themselves in early newsreels. The uneasiness characteristic of such an experience has been portrayed in Luigi Pirandello's novel *Shoot!*, in a passage describing what the fictional actress Varia Nesteroff used to feel while she was watching herself on the screen: 'She sees there someone who is herself but whom she does not know.'[81] Ganin, the fictional film extra in Nabokov's *Mary*, recognises himself on the screen 'with a deep shudder of shame', but also with 'a sense of the fleeting evanescence of human life',[82] and feels compelled to leave the theatre.

Strange encounters of this kind used to invoke a tenet canonised by the Russian Orthodox Church. Within the Orthodox tradition it is believed that, before they go to Heaven, the souls of the dead hover over the earth for forty days and in that time they review their former lives. Needless to say, watching screen characters in the knowledge that they were no longer there was immediately seized upon as the closest equivalent of this *post mortem* view of earthly life. As the *Cine-Journal*'s film correspondent wrote in 1917: '[Being in the cinema] is like the soul detaching itself from the body and looking down to see the body imitating the presence of the soul by mechanically copying and repeating certain gestures.'[83] This same association formed the theme of a poem by a major Symbolist writer, Vyacheslav Ivanov:

So all my life
Is on a moving ribbon.
Clear evidence – no lies –
Of the life I lived.

But, actor, could you bear
To see yourself,
From the darkness,
Without daring to intervene?

Too dreadful, is it? But

Before the fiendish torments start
There awaits us in the darkened hall
That cinema beyond the grave.[84]

Chapter 7

The reception of narrative categories

While the preceding chapter dealt with the reception of the cinematic image, the ensuing discussion will focus on the question of textual reception, the reception of cinematic narrative.

Narrative is a kind of language, even if we decide that cinema is not. Language systems may be approached from two perspectives, that of the speaker and that of the listener. Similarly, the history of cinema narrative can be studied from the viewpoint of either the film-maker or the filmgoer. The difference lies in the context of the study. In the first case, the focus is on production forces and their effect on film narrative (the situation of the film industry, the growth of technology, legal debates, export and import considerations, etc.); in the second, the focus is on film narrative and intrinsic cultural norms.

This chapter, as well as the next one, will attempt to consider what narration in early films looked like from the point of view of the narrative norms implicitly shared by film viewers (and reviewers) of the 1910s. In these years an odd dialogue grew up between received cultural expectations and the particular kind of narration that cinema offered its audiences. More often than not, this dialogue resembled a battle. Film editing and the moving camera were not heralded as welcome, long-awaited innovations; neither was the facial close-up: bringing the actor's face right up close was initially received as a violation of good taste, and cinema narrative had to overcome this instinctive revulsion.

The concept of the 'narrative norm' mentioned above refers neither to a model construction nor to a criterion of the correctness of a cinema text. Strictly speaking, before the process of initial narrative integration was completed, no firmly established concept of 'correct' cinematic narrative really existed. Although the influence of non-cinematic standards decreased steadily, for about twenty years after the Lumière brothers cinema was still measured against standards that automatically defined its texts as essentially anomalous – irrespective of whether such an anomaly was perceived as a defect or welcomed as an innovation.

IMAGES OF CINEMATIC NARRATIVE: THE CHASE

The earliest narrative-related comments one can spot in Russian film literature refer to chase films. British films were the first to feature multi-shot chases, starting from 1900. According to Gunning, from 1904 on the chase form became one of the staples of international cinema.[1] In June 1905 the Russian literary and theatrical journal *The Spectator* published a paragraph in response to this new genre of photoplays. It recorded the 'strange temporality' of chases – a sensation probably shared by other contemporary spectators:

> You see men and women running and jumping over various obstacles (fences, ditches, etc.), and swimming across rivers. They run for two, three, nine, fifteen minutes, they run so fast and for so long that you, who cannot keep running for more than one minute, begin to feel dizzy and exhausted . . . You feel that if they go on like this any longer you will faint; your feeble body recoils at the very sight of any exercise beyond its own capability. But you realise that the running and jumping crowd on the screen can carry on like this for an hour, two hours, a day, two days, as long as they like.[2]

In 1907 the chase craze reached its climax on Russian screens: 'It's funny, but is it really funny?'[3] reflected Andrei Bely after seeing the vertical wall chase in Walter R. Booth's *The '?' Motorist*. In that same year Kornei Chukovsky declared that, apart from two or three underwater pastorals (see p. 174) and the bedroom farce, the only subject the cinematograph really cared for was the manhunt:

> A counterfeiter is fleeing from the police: he crawls along a roof, followed by the police; he tumbles down a hill, followed by the police; he crosses rivers, lakes, seas, oceans – the police hot on his heels. Everyone is shooting, laying traps and snares and setting ambushes. This is all a source of great enthusiasm among the audience.
>
> A police spy is dashing off to report some robbers, the robbers in hot pursuit. A madman has escaped from an asylum, the warders in hot pursuit. A bridegroom is fleeing from an ugly bride, her folks in hot pursuit. You know, I haven't seen a single cinema show without a human being hunted by other humans. The human steeplechase, the eternal *La Course des belles-mères* [Mother-in-law Race], that's the sole passion of our civilised Papuans.[4]

Reviewers' interest in the chase abated with the decline of the genre itself, and after 1910 it was mentioned only in retrospect as a narrative form specific to cinema. But what aspects of the chase seemed peculiar to the contemporary viewer? Intially, two chase patterns were used in the cinema of the 1900s: in-frame chases and cross-frame chases. The in-frame chase was a marginal form employed by Georges Méliès before 1906 (it was probably transferred directly from his stage practice).[5] Similarly to the way it is done in modern computer games, both the pursuers and the pursued exited one side of the frame only to enter the same space from the other side. This circular pattern of pursuit was connected with the fact that Méliès continued to use interior staging and building sets for exterior scenes.

Outdoor chases were based on an opposite principle. As soon as the pursuer(s) and the pursued were out of frame, the shot changed, and they entered a new space only to leave it for the next. As a rule, the same diagonal was used to cross each frame. Since the chase sequence was the central piece of chase films, the action usually went on for quite a while with no significant escalation other than the adding of new characters to the pursuing mob. Unlike circular indoor chases, the outdoor chase was expressly linear. To quote Tom Gunning again, 'although the chase format stretched a narrative action over a number of shots, it maintained a strict homology between the continuity of the action portrayed and the linearity of its portrayal'.[6]

The first thing about chase sequences that struck Russian observers was that this linearity was taken to absurd limits, and chase narratives were consequently perceived as being understructured. Repetitions of one and the same pattern instead of built-up tension made the chase look potentially endless. Narrative progression was replaced by movement for movement's sake.

In order to exemplify the universality of this response, I will permit myself to quote a passage from the short story by Sergei Gorodetsky already cited on a different occasion. It was evidently the writer's intention to use cinema as a basis for a philosophical metaphor of the human condition. In early films, however long a chase sequence might have lasted, it always came to its logical conclusion. Despite this fact, Gorodetsky insists on the eternal impossibility of halting the chase (or stopping the wheel of human suffering, if we wish to read the metaphor as a metaphor):

a boy runs across a field and through a forest, swims across a river and shins up a tree; from the tree he dashes into a house – the house bursts into flames; he scrambles out through the chimney, and after him tumble crazy fat men, head over heels, and an old woman in baggy trousers flapping at the ankles, one after the other. They'll never ever catch him, but the boy will never ever get away.[7]

Although it is not explicitly asserted in either of the quoted passages, one feels that both tend to say more than they claim (or mean) to say. In fact, the subject here is not so much the chase itself as cinema in general. The images of chase narrative were part of the more general image of cinematic textuality discussed in the Introduction to this book. If we were able to question the authors of these sketches on this point, the answers would probably run as follows: 'The chasing crowd on the screen is tireless because cinema is a *mechanism* that, unlike an *organism*, does not know what fatigue is'; or,

'These chases are interminable because of the endless celluloid ribbon on which they were recorded'; or, 'The chase will never stop because the projectionist will make it run again and again, until the film breaks', etc. Early film reception was essentialist in its logic.

IMAGES OF CINEMATIC NARRATIVE: THE PROBLEM OF COHERENCE

In the 1910s cinema fully entered its period of narrative integration. This meant that film-makers were concerned to 'normalise' film narrative, or, to put it in the more precise terms proposed by Tom Gunning, were developing 'the narrator system' customised for the specific needs of storytelling by means of cinema.[8]

Yet, was this system 'normal' from the point of view of the contemporary spectator? Certainly not, or at least not for the Russian spectator of the 1910s. For him, the film story progressed in fits and starts, sometimes indulging in unjustified temporal leaps, sometimes slowing the action down exactly where it ought to have been boldly passed over. This can be seen clearly in the extended metaphor that a 1911 observer used when attempting to define the way cinema tells its stories:

> Theatre is a broad, placid river. The cinematograph is a headlong torrent, leaping down the hillside. It has burst forth somewhere up above, and rushes along, splashing drops of icy water, churning up white foam, seizing broken twigs and branches and whirling, spinning them along and hurling them back torn to shreds.[9]

Critical articles characterised cinema's attempts at narrative as 'unbalanced', 'mechanical', 'spasmodic', 'gratuitous', 'purposeless', 'faulty'. Even though these epithets were mostly used to criticise story lines of particular films, they could easily be readdressed – as one can see today – to the narrator system in general. It was, in fact, an 'ugly duckling' effect: films and film-makers were held responsible for what was soon going to turn into a new and powerful method of telling stories. For example, a critic in *The Projector*, reviewing Władysław Starewicz's *In the Fire of Passions and Sufferings* [V ogne strastei i stradanii, 1916], pointed out what he saw as the film's narrative paradox: 'The action is drawn out in places. But at the same time you get the feeling that some important scenes have been left out – for example, there is no concert scene, and all you get is the ovation that follows'.[10] If we try to 'restore' the criticised sequence in our mind's eye (no copy of the film has survived), we can feel how different our present-day criteria of narrative coherence are from those deployed by the critic of the 1910s. The film *In the Fire of Passions and Sufferings* was dedicated to the memory of the singer A. D. Vyaltseva and was initially conceived as her biography. Concerts of vocal music were not the most rewarding subjects for silent film, and it is obvious why Starewicz preferred ellipsis to 'mute' singing. The applause must have been the film's signal for the beginning of a sequence that took place off-stage. For the present-day viewer such transitions are perfectly legitimate. The contemporary critic, however, felt acutely the need for a causal link that would motivate the ovation (after all, any applause is always *caused* by something!). To use a term derived from David Bordwell's poetics, the narrative was diagnosed as lacking compositional motivation.[11]

But diagnoses like this are only a part of the picture: there were those who found narrative anomalies fascinating. What is most surprising is that some critics found that screen adaptation had a wholesome effect on the classical works of Russian literature. In the Russian cinema of the 1900s the role of screen versions of the literary classics corresponded, in narrative terms, to the role of Passion films in European cinema. As Noël Burch has argued,[12] these films had no narrative problems to solve because the story of Christ's life was universally known. The same more or less applies to the screen versions of famous Russian nineteenth-century novels. Alexander Khanzhonkov, one of the pioneers of this genre, recalled:

> We selected the most striking scenes [from the classics] without bothering too much about whether the selection made sense as it stood, probably in the hope that the viewer could not be unfamiliar with such popular classics.[13]

Of course, this meant that narrative links between the selected scenes were omitted in the first place. The basic convention of the nineteenth-century novel, the coherence of the story, was sacrificed as soon as the novel was transferred to the screen. To see how cinema critics reacted to this abandonment of literary convention let us compare two responses to Peter Chardynin's screen version of Nikolai Goncharov's novel *The Abyss* [Obryv, 1913]. The journal of the teaching profession, *The Education Herald*, was, of course, dismissive: 'what is left of the novel? At most a few of the author's asides and a sequence of bad pictures.'[14] *The Theatre Paper*, on the other hand, was almost ecstatic: 'These [pictures] are like quotations – [they are] so rich, so full of flavour and atmosphere.'[15]

Both reviews remark on the same thing, the way the film departed from the narrative norm, but in the second response the anomalous story construction is interpreted as innovation. The point is that for the theatre reviewer the lack of compositional motivation was compensated for by what she interpreted (and welcomed) as intertextual motivation. The year 1913 was the high point of modernism in Russian literature, and, with all the respect there was for the nineteenth-century novel, its heavy narrative rules were felt to be something of a burden. The very fragmentary nature of the screen version was treated as a way of modernising the source. The fragment was 'liberated' and inscribed in a modern narrative perspective. Thus, little by little and almost without realising it, cinema was gaining ground as an alternative narrative model, a part of the twentieth-century poetics of quotation, of allusion and of intertextual reference.

THE IMAGE OF THE SPECTATOR

In the first part of this book I have tried to sketch a collective portrait of the 'spectator' as seen through the prism of early film literature. I tried to observe his habits of cinema attendance, the tricks he used to conceal (or motivate) addiction, his attempts to keep up the mask of a casual *flâneur*. My argument was that there existed a vague image of the 'model cinema spectator' and that empirical spectators were more or less aware of this image. However, that was the portrait of 'the spectator as cinemagoer'. The question that now arises is whether there was also an image of 'the spectator as film viewer'.

In a sense, we can say that early films shaped their own viewer, and that on the whole this viewer defined his role as opposed to that of the theatregoer. As we know from the evidence discussed in Part I, the very act of visiting a cinema theatre was perceived as a chance encounter rather than a pre-arranged event. What happened to his self-perception once the spectator was in and the lights went down? The impression of a chance encounter was reinforced by the structure (or, rather, by the 'unstructured' quality) of what he saw on the screen. According to the undeniable law of text reception formulated by Jan Mukařovský in 1943, the lack of textual unity is always interpreted by the recipient as a token of unintentionality. In other words, a well-organised text is perceived as a *sign*, while its opposite – a text that reveals itself to be 'spontaneous' or 'understructured' – is seen as a *thing*.[16] Faced with the kind of narrative that, as one critic complained, looked rather like 'an incomprehensible kaleidoscope of individual phenomena, whose internal coherence is totally inaccesible',[17] the viewer felt thrust out of his role as the consumer of art; he felt that he was a witness to something unpremeditated, rather than the adressee of a meaningful artistic communication. The text of cinema had more of a 'thing' than a 'sign' about it, and the internal position of the film viewer vis-à-vis the film was closer to that of an 'observer'.

Thus, the decrease in intentionality within the text predicated a change within the mode of text reception. This basic displacement accumulated minor motivations that seemed to reinforce and diversify the new image of the cinema viewer as opposed to the theatre viewer. The prevalence of outdoor scenes over scenes staged in interiors[18] tended to locate this image in the street rather than indoors. Panning and tracking shots endowed it with mobility. As an observer, the film viewer was believed to be exceptionally perceptive to detail. In 1913 one of the contributors to *The Cinema Theatre and Life* (probably Alexander Anoshchenko) thus portrayed the image of the new spectator induced by the new spectacle:

Before the eyes of the ideal cinematograph viewer flash some pictures that are important and some that are trivial, some that are significant and some that are completely superfluous to the action. In front of him there is enacted not a drama in the theatrical sense of the word but a sequence of episodic events or *a drama as perceived by a casual passer-by*: not an intensification of conflictual passions, not a 'fatal duel', not strictly self-contained action, but a tangled story of everyday life in its externals, with a thousand trivialities and a million unimportant details.[19]

Anoshchenko's 'casual passer-by' (the phrase was underlined by the author himself) was a role induced by textual necessity. It had to be conjured up in order to motivate 'externally' what cinematic narrative failed to motivate by internal (compositional) means: the lack of textual unity. The image of the film viewer helped the empirical viewer to justify the lack of intentionality, and to explain the abundance of details that – he felt – had not been deliberately 'selected' but simply 'happened to be there'. In that capacity the image corresponded to the model of aesthetic perception (behaviour) that was later studied by Walter Benjamin, but on the basis of material from an earlier period: 'the vision of a city lounger' [*der Blick des Flaneurs*].[20] For many, this 'vision' was a source of enjoyment, and so was the mask of the casual film viewer. Here I have to make another reference to aspects of the filmgoer's behaviour discussed in Part I, Chapter 1. The motif of an unpremeditated, spontaneous, sudden, unplanned decision, together with the motif of aimless urban perambulations, was part of the conscious strategy of cinemagoing. Planning his cinematographic saunterings as improvisations, Alexander Blok sought to capture the impression of 'coming across' cinema unawares, to 'experience' it as a manifestation of the physiognomy of the modern city. In France, the homeland of *flânerie*, André Breton, strolling from cinema to cinema without ever sitting through the whole performance, turned his viewing experience into a chain of accidental, unpremeditated impressions. A. Flaker maintains that Osip Mandelstam cultivated a similar method of looking at paintings:

When he gives his impressions of the 'French masters' Mandelstam does not describe the pictures in detail. He does not pause in front of each individual canvas, but 'wanders amongst them' as if he is sauntering along a boulevard, i.e. he employs 'an idler's vision', something that allows him to convey his immediate impressions in condensed metaphoric and associative form.[21]

'An idler's vision' became a universal allegory that fostered unordered impressions and promoted them to the rank of aesthetic experience. This new experience was found to be not just different from theatre aesthetics but opposed to it, as the new and the daring is opposed to the respectable and the slightly old-fashioned. One can sense an element of challenge in the image of the film viewer as defined by Anoshchenko in 1913:

Between him and the spectator in the theatre there is nothing, or almost nothing, in common, just as there is nothing in common between someone casually sauntering down a street and taking in all the diversity of moments passing into eternity, and someone lost in the religious contemplation of an eternity fixed in a timeless work of art.[22]

THE IMAGE OF THE NARRATOR?

Does the narrator in fiction film exist as an ever-present (although not always visible) figure 'behind' the text or is he a 'phantom figure' cued by the text only when the text needs it? Opinions differ. David Bordwell claims that

> in watching films, we are seldom aware of being told something by an entity resembling a human being . . . To give every film a narrator or implied author is to indulge in an anthropomorphic fiction . . . The narration, appealing to historical norms of viewing, creates the narrator.[23]

Tom Gunning objects that the concept of narrator is inherent in the very semiotic nature of the text as a message addressed to somebody by somebody, and has the following to say about the experience of the spectator thus addressed:

> We experience the text as an intentional object, designed to have certain effects on us. More than a random set of cues, the narrator embodies the design organising narrative discourse, and the intention that unifies its effects . . . As a series of intentions the term *narrator* recalls the narrative's nature as a unified manufactured object, the product of human labor.[24]

In his book on film narrative as compared to narration in literature André Gaudreault made an attempt to transfer the question of the narrator to the plane of film history. Since this question is related to the issue of authorship, Gaudreault made a study of court cases arising from disputes connected with early film copyright. This approach helped him to trace the emergence of the 'proto-theoretic' notion of authorship in relation to cinema as well as – and this is exactly the point at which the figure of the 'owner' turns into that of the 'author' – to pinpoint the moment when the judge was forced to admit that not only the pictures but also the order in which the pictures are shown should be covered by copyright law. This particular decision (passed as early as 1902) marked the beginning of the process by which cinema, conceived as an art of 'showing', was redefined as the art of 'telling stories'. The concept of the author was coupled with the concept of the narrator.[25]

After Gaudreault's excellent excursus into the legal history of production, it seemed tempting to see whether any such narrator figure was also to be found in the 'proto-theoretic' discussion (to use Gaudreault's term) of reception history. The result is less rewarding than one would expect. While there was much talk about 'who made it', it is almost impossible to make a distinction between the narrator and the author (which is so easy to make in theory). There are only three points one can make without risking a far-fetched conclusion.

In trying to specify the image of the narrative as such, contemporary observers sometimes used anthropomorphic metaphors. More often than not, these were tropes that had to do with the realm of language, speech, telling, etc., so, in a sense, these figures may be considered as obscure allegories of the narrator. However, such metaphors, as a rule, imply the idea of a defect in the speech faculties of this supposed 'narrator' or in his manner of telling stories. This makes them applicable to more things than the level of narration alone. The closest example at hand is the generic idiom used for cinema in Russia: *Velikii Nemoi* [The Great Silent One]. Of course, it can be applied to the narrator who has to explain himself by help of intertitles instead of spoken words, but the name also defines the entire medium as well as its 'speechless' characters. The same concerns the less idiomatic but often-found zoomorphic metaphor of fish. Cinema as 'alien' can be interpreted as referring to the figure of the narrator (intensive gesturing and no language), but it is obvious that the metaphor's primary motivation was cinema's genesis and its technical nature. Cinema as 'child' primarily points to the age of the medium and the age of its most faithful devotees, and only secondarily to its 'infantile' and 'naive' narrative. Even the anthropomorphic metaphor used directly to designate the imbalanced pace of the cinema narrative that gave it, in the eyes of *The Theatre Paper*'s reviewer, 'the same freedom of action that the tsar's jester had',[26] cannot be fully attributed as a generalised image of the cinema narrator. In the diffuse light of film reception all images blur and overlap.

What one *does* spot in early film literature is the change of verbs used to describe what film stories do. At a certain point (c. 1910, roughly) we can observe that the expression 'the film shows . . .' is gradually replaced by 'the film tells . . .'. This confirms that the transition from the cinema of attraction to that of narrative integration, as both Gaudreault and Gunning suggest, was linked to the reorientation of the entire textual strategy of the medium from 'showing' [*monstration*] to 'telling' [*narration*], or – to put it in Bordwell's terms – the change of wording indicates that, at the very least, the early film critics changed their conception of film narrative from 'mimetic' to 'diegetic'. Sometimes you can actually feel how difficult the transition from attractions to narration was by the way these words were misapplied. I cannot find a better example than the one already cited earlier, Yuli Engel's newspaper article of 1908. In it he mentioned a French film where he described the heroine's letter to her lover as being 'actually *shown* on the screen separately'.[27] In Engel's rendering one can almost sense a puppeteer hidden behind the screen and 'showing' things to you. It indicates that, as a film viewer, Engel was still in the period of *monstrations* while the cinema was already *telling* stories. A later critic would probably say something like 'the letter appeared on the screen *telling* us . . .'. Generally, the 'telling' mode is felt to be somewhat more 'impersonal', maybe because stories, unless they are marked as fantastic, claim to be part of 'real life' (whereas tricks and magic do not). Be that as it may, when reviewers started to apply the verb 'tell' in relation to film stories, they usually used the expression 'the film tells'.

Can we, then, claim that the figure of the narrator was synthesised by the viewer only when it was intentionally cued by the film-maker? This would probably be too sweeping. I think a distinction should be made between intentionality as part of the film-maker's design and the intentionality of the text in Mukařovský's sense. As early film history demonstrates, the question of the message ('what is this film trying to tell me?') and, in a somewhat less clear fashion, the question of the message sender ('who is addressing me with this message?') becomes a relevant part of text reception when this or that film comes up with innovative or unusual traits of narrative structure. In *The Defence of Sebastopol* [Oborona Sevastopolya, 1911] Vasili Goncharov experimented with cross-cutting dancing scenes with battle scenes (it was the first attempt at cross-cutting in a Russian film), and the device was immediately recorded in a 1911 article by Pavel Nilus as a step towards more personal discourse: 'the germ of the impact [that this film has on us] lies in the rapid alternation of impressions which is presented as a value in itself.'[28] The question 'who is the narrator?' is not explicitly posed here, but the critic is on the verge of it. The film is clearly read as a sign which is designed to reach us, and the viewer's response may well acquire an interpersonal dimension.

THE RHETORICAL AUTHOR: *THE COMING HAM*

The issue of 'the sender' takes on a more definite form when it is moved on to the firm ground of authorship. The urge to 'peep behind the screen' to see who is behind all this was there from the days of the Lumière brothers: an attraction makes us want to see the conjuror. In the 1900s the function of the 'author' was often transferred to the figure of the projectionist (actual instances when the showman was also the cameraman of the films he showed were practically unknown in Russia after 1902). This trait of 'naive' reception was immortalised in 1929 in a funny scene from *The Black Sail* [Chernyi parus] by Sergei Yutkevich. In this film Eisenstein's *Battleship Potemkin* is shown in a far-off fishing village to young people who had evidently never seen a film before. After the show, the villagers rush to the projectionist and toss him in the air. Authorship was attributed to the *monstrateur* in the very first meaning of this word.

In less straightforward cases the image of the author was constructed proceeding from the assumptions the viewer made on the basis of what he saw on the screen. Technically speaking, throughout the 1900s whenever there was a need to refer to the author, the term 'the manufacturers of these pictures' (usually in the plural) was used. However, some writers felt that anonymity was itself a significant fact about the cinema, and used this 'blank spot' in order to construct a notion that I suggest calling 'the rhetorical author'. What does the term mean? As a person living in a big city in 1907, Andrei Bely was perfectly aware that films were products made by specialists who were employed by commercial companies in France and elsewhere. Yet, as a Symbolist writer, Bely was convinced that the same moving pictures shown on every street corner in Moscow, London and Paris were *not* produced by any particular human being because they were the outgrowth of the self-generating medium of the 'city', just as mushrooms are not 'produced' by the damp forest but are an organic part of it. Authorship (or, in this case, the absence of authorship) is constructed rhetorically.

The rhetorical author constitutes an important dimension of film reception because this figure is 'co-produced' by forces embedded within the traditional culture and the in-coming data provided by the new medium. Therefore I suggest that we pause to dwell upon one of the earliest versions of the rhetorical author (constructed in 1907/8) even if the topic demands some extensive quoting and may seem to take the reader out of his way. This rhetorical author was composed from the Méliès-produced and Méliès-influenced Pathé trick films massively imported into Russia in the late 1900s and the vernacular cultural idiom – the Symbolist allegory of 'the coming Ham'.

The 1900s – the decade during which Russian audiences became familiar with Méliès's film style – were the years when Russian culture was dominated by Symbolist images and patterns of thought. As I have tried to show in the previous chapter when discussing Andrei Bely's visionary idea of cinema as the ultimate prophecy, the Symbolist mind explored apocalyptic thought and 'endist' ideas, such as the 'end of history' and the 'death of culture'. Within the Symbolist frame of reference, genuine culture was believed to be exposed to danger on two fronts: from the East it was menaced by the 'yellow peril', variously seen to reside in 'pan-Mongolism', 'Chinese positivism' or Japanese imperialism, while in the West there loomed the threat of Europe's 'conglomerated mediocrity',[29] i.e. the danger of being overwhelmed by material philistinism. In 1906 Dmitri Merezhkovsky, a major Symbolist philosopher, published his famous essay *The Coming Ham* [Gryadushchii Kham] in which he argued that the 'yellow blood' of soulless positivism was forcing itself into the blue blood of culture. The biblical Ham (cursed by his father Noah to be his brothers' slave) represents philistinism and lack of principle.'[30] For Merezhkovsky, Ham is an apocalyptic figure: the philistine come to power.[31] By 1908 the grotesque image of 'the coming Ham' was already used as a critical catchword applied to the philistine, narrow-minded and sordid features of contemporary life. A niche for Méliès-type cinema in the temple of Russian culture had already been prepared.

Two texts of the period manifested this type of reading of the Méliès style. One of them was was the essay by Kornei Chukovsky that has already been mentioned earlier in this chapter, the other was an article by Ivan Shcheglov, a moralist interested in popular education.[32] In both articles, the central idea was tied to exclusivity: 'high art' exclusivity in Chukovsky's essay, and national exclusivity in Shcheglov's case. In those early years of Russian film-making, the cinema was still perceived as a 'foreign gadget'. As often happens in Russia, Shcheglov's concern for 'the simple people' took the form of suspicion of everything coming from the West that could 'spoil' them. In his attitude towards what we might call 'Mélièsian' aesthetics one can also see a touch of a typically Russian contempt for the vulgarity of French theatre culture. Shcheglov starts by mentioning a certain Bertha Kukelvan, a singer of easy virtue who (the author relates) was hissed off the stage by a working-class audience. Then Shcheglov gives an account of a film show consisting, presumably, of Pathé remakes of Méliès film stories:

> There they are, the wonders of modern astronomy shown on the screen for you. Wonders indeed! An old fellow, the astronomer, who is obviously dissatisfied with his earth-bound research, invents a wonderful balloon which takes the scientist to the stars he had so often admired from afar through his telescope. As he comes closer, they turn out to be even more interesting. As soon as our brave astronomer approaches the first one, a lasciviously smiling head looks out, belonging to no one but the same Bertha Kukelvan. And one by one, coquettes peep out of each star. Isn't this a truly astronomical discovery! Small wonder that the poor scientist loses his head and his balance and falls head over heels back to his observatory.[33]
>
> A similar wonderful adventure also happens to a young man who goes fishing. For some reason, there are no fish in the sea, but instead enormous pearl shells, again with a coquette in each shell, and again – Bertha Kukelvan.[34]
>
> Next they show some magic flowers and magic butterflies on the screen. Each rosebud conceals the same Bertha Kukelvan, and the colourful butterflies, as soon as they are touched, turn into half-naked dancers with the familiar Kukelvan looks . . . [35]
>
> Even the touching poetry of the Easter holidays is not forgotten. In comes a gentleman dressed in a tail-coat and top-hat (probably, just back from his Easter visits) and takes out of his tail-coat and trouser pockets half a dozen big Easter eggs. With a blissful smile, he smashes them all: cheep-cheep-cheep . . . a baby Kukelvan hatches out of each egg. The little Kukelvans preen their feathers and start dancing the 'matschisch' on this very Easter table.[36]

Although Shcheglov's article was quite in tune with the theme of 'the coming Ham', it does not refer directly to this figure as a possible 'author' of the films it mentions. Kornei Chukovsky, however, does explicitly locate the 'pictures of the cinematograph' within this Symbolist idiom. Chukovsky's article is about 'the Hottentots, Kaffirs and Papuans of our modern cities', another common metaphor in turn-of-the-century essays. In his view, cinematic fairy scenes provide a source of folklore for city savages. Unlike the nationalist Shcheglov, Chukovsky – a literary critic of élitist orientation – is not xenophobic: for him, the new aesthetics brought by the cinema was rather a kind of international epidemic of aggressive low-brow culture:

> True, all these pictures were made abroad, and if they manifest any ideology at all, this ideology is foreign, not Russian. All right – but Hegel, Darwin, Nietzsche, Marx, Zola and Wedekind also manifested foreign ideology; did this prevent each of these thinkers creating powerful movements within Russian society? Certainly not. For the open-minded Russian, that *citoyen du monde*, cinema has become almost as native, almost as much of a national phenomenon, as were, successively, Russian Hegelianism, Darwinism, Marxism, Nietzscheanism. Take Maeterlinck and Knut Hamsun: are they not Russian writers now? The same is true for the cinema. If you want to see what is happening to Russia now, forget newspapers and magazines, rush to see *La Course des belles-mères.*[37]

After three pages of critical analysis of this and a number of other Pathé chase comedies, Chukovsky turns to the fairy tale film, 'this Hottentot poetry of the modern city':

> How I love these cinema tales! See how the green water flows past! See the long fronds of sea-weed streaming out and swirling in the current! See the darting fish with their shimmering scales! Look at the giant shells scattered around! We can see the very depths of the ocean. And there, that shell in the middle is opening up and a rose is growing out of it! Look, look, the rose is turning into a woman! The woman, getting on a bit and wearing orange tights, jumps out of the shell, and sashays along the ocean floor, swinging her hips with the knowing swagger of a *café-chantant étoile.*
>
> The pianist starts the matschisch, and in a flash all the shells open, with a rose emerging from each one. The roses turn instantly into girls of different colours – orange, lilac, crimson, brown – and they flicker so much that it hurts your eyes. After a while, they adopt different poses, but they do not have to hold them for very long because a diver appears on the sea bed. The sight takes his breath away, and – still wearing all his diving gear – he rushes towards them with open arms: first to the crimson girl, but she turns into a rose; then to the lilac one, and she does the same. Every girl he rushes towards turns into a huge paper rose, still swaying seductively. Broken-hearted, he dances the matschisch, and the photoplay is over.
>
> What I like about this play is that it is all so healthy, no one could ever call it morbid. All you need to create masterpieces like this is the constitution of an ox and the psychology of a horse.
>
> The author was given infinite power: power to transport us to the bed of the ocean, power to turn people into flowers and flowers into people. But

with all this infinity of power, he could think of creating nothing grander than an underwater *café-chantant*.

Why such poverty of the imagination? Why is it that our human society, which has created so many religions and Utopias, so many ancient and medieval cultures rich in legends and myths, has come so suddenly to the end of the road? Where have all the Utopias, myths and legends gone? Why, when it wants to recreate them, can our age find nothing in its soul but the matschisch at the bottom of the sea? Where are you, *The Thousand and One Nights* of modern man? Take any tale of the cinema: in *A Trip to the Moon* the door of the moon opens, and out comes a brown star, swinging her hips across the clouds as if she were on stage; in *The Visiting Gnomes* a door opens in a mountain and here she comes again, the same star with the same walk, but a different colour. *The Shoemaker's Dream, The Astronomer's Dream, The Fisherman's Dream* ... whatever the dream it's always the same. Up in Heaven, down on Earth, under the sea ... everywhere the same hopeless star, the same inconceivable poverty of imagination.[38]

Chukovsky then wonders who could possibly be the author of these pictures and, answering his own rhetorical question, he constructs a rhetorical author. He starts by entering upon a lengthy explanation parodying the socio-economic arguments of a popular Marxist booklet:

You may have noticed that the image of a cockerel appears on the screen in every cinematograph as soon as the picture is over – it doesn't matter whether the picture is sad or amusing. This cockerel is the trade mark of the company that produces stories for the cinematograph. Unlike other tales and stories, the tales and stories of the cinematograph have a trade mark – like our galoshes, our shoes, our samovars, our cigarettes, matches, knives. Its ballads, legends and myths are market commodities, mass-produced, commercial products. Therefore, even if none of these pictures is able to express our individual souls, as commodities they give voice to our social milieu, and a very definite kind of voice, too.

Because nowadays commodities struggle for existence, and because only those that are accommodated to the consumer survive, the art of accommodation has become so refined that every ornament on manufactured calico and each tiniest flower on manufactured wallpaper can be considered the creation of the consumer himself. Likewise the pictures manufactured for the market of the cinematograph can be considered the creation of the audience that patronises it ... *La Course des belles-mères* has no author, it reflects no one individual soul; it has been created by its own spectators and therefore it reflects the ideology of these spectators better than any book could possibly do. Books are written by writers, and writers have their whims and tempers. Gogol, say, or Dostoyevsky were so skilful in revealing the whims and fancies of their individual souls that no Marxist, even a well-trained one, is able to force them into the Procrustean bed of ideology. However much you try, something will always stick out, a tuft of hair or something, and either you cut the tuft off, or you break the bed. Here, in the cinematograph, you see nothing of the kind. Here the milieu and its ideological mirror image coincide to the utmost degree. Because it is here and only here that we witness the new perfect form of collective creation.[39]

Following this line of argument, Chukovsky constructs an image of the 'collective author', who is also 'the collective viewer' of his own creation. Culture ends with the mass entertainment that John Stuart Mill's 'conglomerated mediocrity' itself creates, claims Chukovsky. The new technology of the cinematograph offers a perfect vehicle for such 'consumer-creativity': the screen, upon which 'the imaginative poverty' of 'the coming Ham' is directly projected by the viewing audience. At this point Chukovsky's author-cum-viewer converges with Andrei Bely's conception of the essential anonymity of authentic cinema authorship.

Chapter 8

The reception of narrative devices

While the previous chapter dealt with general narrative categories (narrative coherence, the sender and the recipient of the narrative discourse) as perceived or constructed by contemporary observers, this chapter will concentrate on the reception of the specific devices that constituted cinema's narrative system. As I have noted, this analysis will take as its starting point the notion of pre-cinematic (or, rather, extra-cinematic) narrative norms. But, before passing to a discussion of the actual aspects of film narrative as perceived against the narrative norms of the 1910s, I have to admit that these norms, as presented here, are not based on any kind of independent research. As far as I know, no research into them has been undertaken. My use of the notion is purely operational. I derive 'norm' *ad hoc*, by way of summing up reception-registered deviations from it. At first sight, such a method may appear faulty – in fact, it is not: this is more or less what anyone does in order to reconstruct expectational horizons. Early film spectators had certain expectations as to what constituted narrative norms: ellipses should be provided with conventional marks (the rule of narrative continuity); narrative elements should be subdivided into 'main' and 'auxiliary' (the rule of narrative focus); certain elements of the text should be repeatable, while others should not be (the rule of narrative economy); the pre-textual reality (the 'text of life') should be represented with varying degrees of mimetic precision (the rule of selectivity). Such expectations were far from being a rigid code of rules, but they give us some idea of the narrative norms to which cinema was expected – but failed – to conform. The list of narrative devices highlighted here does not pretend to be complete; it is not derived from an exhaustive analysis of actual films. There is a discussion of camera movement but there is no section on cross-cutting. Although, of course, part of the responsibility for any lacunae should lie on me as a researcher, the choice of what to discuss and what to ignore was largely dictated by the particular angle of my research. A historian may be expected to be encyclopaedic, but not the history itself – and certainly not the contemporary viewer. Some things were just not noticed or mentioned at the time. Other things *were* noticed and mentioned, but from the opposite point of view than that of the film-maker of the day. For example, production histories of film style discuss the various means of securing continuity because continuity was such a key problem in film-making. As to the viewer, he rather responded to discontinuity, which therefore defined my focus of research. In terms of saliency, reception is related to production as mould to cast. Therefore, no notes on reception can give a plausible historical picture unless they are complemented by the stylistic history of film-making.[1]

THE RECEPTION OF NARRATIVE DEVICES: ELLIPSIS

Whatever its length, 'clumsy' ellipsis (lapsed time) was received as an anomaly exclusively characteristic of cinema. We may recall Yuli Engel's 1908 article, where he observed that the lover 'was round in a flash' after the letter had been sent to him. This became a standing joke in the 1910s. In his original and ironic catechism of the diegetic 'peculiarities' of cinema Georg German wrote in 1914: 'Why does love move so fast? The girl behind the counter or the cash register has hardly set eyes on the young lord before she is sitting in front of him, abandoned and grief-stricken, with the baby in her arms.'[2] Another reviewer for *The Theatre Paper*, writing about Yevgeni Bauer's film *Leon Drey* (1915), exclaimed with mock bewilderment: 'What kind of a man is this Leon Drey, who kisses a different woman in each tableau and betrays the heroine of the previous one?'[3] In both cases the irony manifests a rejection of the new ('jerky') narrative conventions or, rather, cinema's inability to live up to older narrative norms.

Films on topical themes were sometimes hurriedly made, and in such cases ellipses in construction became particularly glaring. One film that suffered from this defect was *Dark Forces: Grigori Rasputin and His Associates* [Temnye sily: Grigorii Rasputin i ego spodvizhniki, 1917], which was shot in a few days immediately after the February Revolution. No copy of the film has survived, but a review in *The Petersburg Newsletter* parodied the film's ragged plot:

> Rasputin is shown life-size, but it's appallingly badly done . . . Rasputin stealing horses. Rasputin calling on the wife of the local governor. A few completely meaningless scenes, and then a car, a house on the Moika, the river Neva, and one overshoe on the embankment.[4]

The single black overshoe lying by a hole in the ice after Rasputin's dead body had been thrown into the Neva did actually figure in press descriptions of the scene of the crime, and in the memoirs of those involved in the assassination. The film director Sergei Veselovsky was probably conscious of the metonymic effect this 'grisly detail' potentially entailed (a narrative device later made famous by the pince-nez in *The Battleship Potemkin*). However, in 1917 this cinematic *pars pro toto* struck the reviewer as simply comic. *The Petersburg Newsletter* critic refused to recognise narrative economy and suspected that the depiction of the overshoe instead of the 'real scene' was motivated by considerations of economy in the more basic sense of the word. In his eyes it turned into a detail symbolising the essentially elliptical nature of cinema narrative: 'meaningless scenes' instead of biography; a 'ragged plot' instead of the main thing; a senseless overshoe instead of the depiction of the murder.

Small ellipses (or temporary omissions within a scene) were even more of a problem for narrative continuity. The best way to see how smooth narrative transitions turned into jolts is to study writers' attempts at creating screen versions of their own books. If we look at Andrei Bely's own script for a film version of his novel *Petersburg*, or at Sologub's screen version of his play *Miss Liza* [Baryshnya Liza], both dating from 1918, we can actually feel how the apparently simple task of creating ellipses in a visual text led these professional writers into unexpected difficulties. For example, in order to elide the scene in *Miss Liza* where the heroine was getting dressed in the morning, Sologub was not able to think of anything better than a kind of a time-lapse title normally used to indicate years or months:

> 7 [. . .] Liza shivered all over and, quickly throwing back the blanket, jumped out of bed.
> 8 The same room a few minutes later.
> Liza is hurrying to finish dressing.[5]

Andrei Bely encountered a similar problem in his script, a scene where one of the characters was to be shown shaving himself before committing suicide. In the novel the shaving scene looks completely normal from the narrative point of view:

> He shaved his chin and neck, but the razor accidentally sliced off a bit of his moustache. Now he had to shave it all off. If they were to break the door down and find him with only half a moustache . . . and . . . like that, too . . . So Sergei Sergeyevich Likhutin shaved himself clean. Now he looked a total idiot.[6]

In his script Bely proposed the following cinematic equivalent of a 'paragraph':

> peering into the mirror, he suddenly nicks his moustache with the razor; his face immediately looks foolish; seeing himself with a lop-sided moustache, he gives a sly wink; (the picture breaks off for a second and flashes up again immediately).
> A clean-shaven Serg[ei] Serg[eyevich] is standing in front of the mirror, looking like an idiot exposed.[7]

Since cinema narrative lacked the equivalent of verbal forms used to describe completed action ('she had got dressed', 'he had finished shaving', etc.), recourse had to be made either to portraying the action at length, or to infringing the narrative continuum by inserting an ellipsis into the middle of the scene. Transformed into the film narrative language of the 1910s, perfect tenses asked for a jump cut.

DISCONTINUITY CUES

Why were cinema ellipses considered to present a problem for text reception? In cinema, the 'exit' from one shot and 'entry' into another are often open to two interpretations: the spaces can be seen either as adjacent or as separated by a distance. This ambiguity is removed if these spaces are marked, either by obvious signs of proximity (no one is surprised if a character opens a front door and the next frame shows him already in a hallway) or by clear signs of mutual distance, temporal and spatial.

What signs were used as indicators of ellipsis and how were they received? The classical time-lapse marks were fades and irises, mainly used to elide erotic scenes. By 1915 this usage became so widespread that the word 'iris' [*diafragma*] became a critical catchword for this kind of moment. 'Good direction is only needed for psychological dramas', stated an ironical review of a Russian screen version of Octave Mirbeau's *Diary of a Chambermaid* [Dnevnik gornichnoy, 1916], 'all that the "real story" needs is an iris.'[8] The same applies to fade-ins. Here is a sarcastic description another reviewer gave of *The Husband* [Muzh], a film made in 1915 after a play by Mikhail Artsybashev, the novelist whose literary name was made by the so-called 'problem of sex':

> Scene one: Duganovich, the hero of the film, sleek and well-fed, embraces a cocotte and kisses her. Then he leads her to the sofa . . . and darkness falls. Scene two: Duganovich embraces the wife of his assistant. Undressing. Couch. Darkness. Scene three: Duganovich embraces his sister-in-law. Parlour. Kisses. Darkness. Scene four: the same character embraces a chambermaid amidst fur coats. Darkness falls even without as much as a single kiss.[9]

Another common way to cover up an ellipsis was to insert an intertitle. According to Alfred Hitchcock (who started as title writer for a British studio), the favourite intertitle of silent cinema was 'Came the dawn'.[10] However, as Nikolai Izvolov has pointed out in his recent dissertation, this observation probably applies mainly to films produced in the 1920s.[11] In the 1910s, when prints were as a rule released in tinted versions, the dawn was more likely to be indicated by the change of tint from blue (commonly used for night) to pink. Colour, then, was yet another frequent signal for ellipsis.

It can be argued that some of these signals were historically specific. Today, when we watch narrative films of the 1910s, we are sometimes puzzled by what we tend to misread as the lack of narrative clarity. Here is an example drawn from my own experience of film restoration undertaken with a group of colleagues at the Gosfilmofond archives in Moscow in 1988. In Peter Chardynin's film *Chrysanthemums* [Khrizantemy, 1914] the heroine (Vera Coralli) leaves her lover's room after a final showdown and in the next shot collapses grief-stricken on a chair. The modern viewer reads this cut as continuous: after she has closed the door to his study, she is too distressed to leave his house. It becomes clear only later that Vera had returned to her own house, and that the scene in which she collapses actually belongs to a different place and time in the story. Since the print of *Chrysanthemums* comes to us from studio negatives (negative prints did not have intertitles and, of course, were not tinted), there is no easy way to establish if this ambiguity is a property of the film itself or of its archival copy.[12] Theoretically, the ellipsis could have been cued by means of an intertitle, by means of tint change (different interiors were as a rule differently tinted) or, perhaps, by the insertion of a so-called 'passage shot' (Vera walking, riding or driving home) that has subsequently been lost from the footage. I shall return to the question of 'passage shots' when discussing the effect of 'fermata' on the reception of film narrative.

But there is also a possibility that what we today misread as continuity was read as discontinuity in 1914. We may assume that the historical viewer was more sensitive to certain types of discontinuity signals than we are to the same signals nowadays. Since I am not sure that it can be sufficiently documented, I make this assumption on a speculative rather than an empirical basis. As is known from textual studies of early narrative cinema (Barry Salt, Tom Gunning), the initial rules for marking continuity were more rigorous than the ones that came later. For example, exits and entrances, as well as directions of characters entering and leaving the frame, had to be co-ordinated and matched with cuts.[13] In some Russian film scripts of the 1910s 'exits' and 'entrances' meticulously marked for continuity sequences were also accompanied by 'directions': if a character was supposed to move in continuous space, he had to exit to the right of a frame and reappear from the left (or vice versa). Hence, one may assume that in cases where such rules were not observed (e.g. cut before exit or left/right confusion) the viewer would automatically read the sequence (or cut) as discontinuous. In *Chrysanthemums* Vera moves to the right almost as far as the shot will allow, then turns to the door in the back wall and exits through it heading leftwards. In the next shot (already home) she enters from the left side of the frame. In terms of directions this is a mismatch. Could it be that while for us a match on action is enough to validate continuity between shots, the 1914 generation of spectators may have required the match on action to be complemented with a directions match? If this hypothesis is sound, one may say that the narrative competence of the early viewer was more firmly based on the presumption of discontinuity than ours is.

Be that as it may, it is significant that early film scripts, as well as indicating exits and entrances and marking them with 'left' or 'right', avoided giving these indications at the starting and ending points of a continuity sequence. Here is an example from Czesław Sabinski's shooting script for *See The Post Coach Rushing* [Vot mchitsya troika pochtovaya, 1914], in which only the first entry lacks directions and the last cut (which takes us away to another sequence) lacks an 'exit':

9 A general view of the fête. Ivan and Masha come out of the crowd at the tent. They look back and both exit right . . .

10 Ivan and Masha appear on the street from the left with their backs to the camera. They walk past laughing and joking and disappear right . . .

11 Ivan and Masha are walking from the left towards the house of the village elder, their backs to the camera. They stop . . . Masha says goodbye. Ivan embraces Masha and kisses her.[14]

A distinction can be drawn between transition inserts (like intertitles and passages) and in-frame indicators of ellipsis (like directions, change of tint, etc.). Some ways of controlling narrative through manipulation of in-frame diegetic elements were quite specific. If we take, for example, a closer look at shot 11 of the shooting script cited above, we will see that the end of the continuity sequence was signalled by mutual gestures of parting. On the surface, these gestures were simply part of the characters' story-motivated behaviour. At the same time, they served as diegetic signals of discontinuity. Parting gestures, welcoming gestures, comings, goings, arrivals, departures, and the like, belonged to those few diegetic elements that, apart from their surface role in the story, had a covert function within the narrator system. These agents in the service of syntax could be detected by the suspicious frequency with which they would show up at certain points of the diegesis. This made film stories look really bizarre. 'Why do people who live in castles do little else but shake hands and smoke cigars?', queried Georg German, with assumed naivety, in the article describing what we may define as the aggregate diegesis of cinema around 1914. 'Can every estate owner really be a professional hand-shaker?'[15]

Some observers pointed to the syntagmatic role of the motor car: 'The plot of a cinema drama has the right to be as absurd as it likes, as long as the linkage between its component parts is guaranteed by a crazy car ride', wrote a reviewer for *The Theatre Paper* in 1914;[16] while the paper's regular film correspondent, reviewing Bauer's *Silent Witnesses* [Nemye svideteli, 1914], pointed out that the device of switching from one scene to another was poorly done, with no clear narrative perspective: 'there were a number of blank spots and gaps, . . . the action was monotonous; people arrived, departed, got into a car, got out of a car, and that was that.'[17]

In this respect, in-frame discontinuity cues (greetings and farewells, arrivals and departures) functioned in a similar way to letters and telephone conversations. 'Why are cinema's *dramatis personae* always writing letters?', wondered the same Georg German with the same air of innocent surprise.[18]

Indeed, letters took the lion's share of all written texts that figured in early films: to send a letter was the easiest way to 'communicate' between distant shots. The same applied to telephone calls, which were particularly useful because, unlike letters, which helped to establish links over time ('Paul is round in a flash'), they established simultaneous action over physical distance. Therefore, as Eileen Bowser observes, 'for some film-makers, the literal "link between spaces" of the sounds of a telephone call may have been needed to stimulate . . . alternative editing.'[19] Like letter-writing, telephone conversations were overexploited in early film practice – a fact that has not passed unrecorded in literature.[20] Like letters and telephone conversations, greetings and farewells signposted the narrative relationship between shots, the only difference being that the letter and the telephone performed a conjunctional role, drawing shots separated in time and space into a single narrative block, while gestures of greeting were more like signs of narrative disjuncture.

Some contemporary remarks make one think that by the second half of the 1910s in-frame transition markers were regarded as somewhat obsolete. In 1916 a reviewer for the journal *Pegasus* praised Nikander Turkin's film *Tanya Skvortsova – Student* [Kursistka Tanya Skvortsova, 1916] for a successful ellipsis: 'It cleverly avoided yet another train departure with much waving and saluting from passengers and people seeing them off. The square in front of the station was shown, and then just the train itself, pulling out of the station.'[21] In-frame transition markers (hand-shakes, goodbye gestures, etc.) were gradually replaced by transition inserts (a shot of a train, for example). A skilfully done transition insert was well received, since it was not only a fresh device of cinema narrative but a device that also brought the narrative technique of cinema closer to the demands of the narrative norm. The playwright Ilya Surguchov, who regularly reviewed films for the journal *The Wings* [Kulisy], praised one such carry-over from one scene to another in Bauer's *The Lie* [Lozh', 1917]:

> The departure for the holidays is very cleverly done . . . particularly the scene where the train suddenly appears, rushing through a small wood. This really injects life into the stereotyped 'train departure' sequence and highlights the truthfulness of the events that follow.[22]

This last remark is particularly interesting, since the 'truthfulness of events' is seen to be dependent on their position in the narrative perspective of the text.

Towards the 1920s transition inserts became the normal way of coping with story ellipses. A straight cut from a 'goodbye' pantomime to greetings in the next shot looked old-fashioned. The point was that while in-frame cues warned the viewer that a discontinuous cut was approaching, transition inserts created a semblance of continuity. Therefore the shift can be explained by the general tendency to smooth the course of film narrative, to turn the 'mountain creek' into the 'wide river'. In film literature of the 1920s transition inserts were to be recognised as revealing the 'innate nature' of cinema narration, something that Béla Balázs called 'visual continuity'.[23] Boris Eichenbaum also agreed:

> The movement of a film is built on the principle of temporal and spatial linkage ... If a character walks out of a house, then in the next shot he cannot be shown entering another house; this contradicts both time and space. Hence the need for so-called 'link-shots', which in the hands of inexperienced directors tend to weigh down the film by introducing irrelevant, and therefore meaningless, details.[24]

He continues: 'In other words, the significance of space in cinema lies more in its contribution to style (syntax) than in its role in the plot.'[25]

FERMATA

Let us now pause to consider those 'irrelevant and meaningless details' that Eichenbaum warned inexperienced directors against, and attempt to define this aspect of cinema narrative against the background of the narrative norm.

Like any kind of narrative, cinema narrative presupposes the existence of a pre-textual reality, which it is claiming to represent. What does this axiom entail from the point of view of the narrative norm? The 'correct' narrative had to observe narrative economy. Every detail of pre-textual reality did not have to be delineated with equal meticulousness. The narrative was felt to be flexible and economical when it was able to dwell longer on the more important details, while only mentioning the trivial in passing. In other words, a narration was recognised as economic if the degree of realism with which this or that detail was represented varied according to its centrality within the story. Too much realism in details created the effect of *trompe-l'oeil* which impaired the realism of the entire text.

As contemporary reports suggest, it was exactly the principle of narrative economy that was denied to early cinema narrative by the pre-set and unvarying way in which it represented reality. Let us imagine an automatic narrating machine that reproduces every detail, both important and trivial, with equal meticulousness. From the first days of its existence, the image of cinematic text was close to that of such a narrative automaton. We have seen this image emerge in O. Winter's essay of 1896 which condemned film images for their lack of focus and inability to select. Of course, Winter's 'case' against the Lumières had to be confined to the discussion of individual images. However, the impression that cinematic images were too faithful to be true was so strong that the term 'cinematograph' was instantly turned into a metaphor employed by literary critics to describe what they earlier used to call the 'photographism' of realistic prose. One can provide a number of examples from literary criticism of the 1910s; but it would perhaps be better to quote a review that dates back to 1897 and which gives the following description of Anton Chekhov's plays:

There is something quite particular in this writer's manner: he seems to make myriads of snapshots and then display them with astonishing life-likeness . . . But there exist complex cases that the cinematograph fails to register. What we need is more than exactitude and fidelity of images: [to tell a story] you have to select moments that are typical and characteristic for each dramatic character.[26]

As soon as cinema transformed itself into a narrative vehicle, it was accused of doing exactly the same to the accepted norms of storytelling: the general opinion was that cinema failed to distinguish the important from the trivial.

Let us look at the way in which this presumption inflected the reception of transition inserts. Joyce E. Jesionowski claims that the British film-maker Cecil Hepworth was the first to use the accumulation of spaces to indicate 'how long' it takes the character to get where he is going.[27] According to Barry Salt's chronology, it was around 1907 that Pathé's directors began to use corridors and staircases in their 'comings' and 'goings' scenes.[28] Although these transition inserts helped to establish continuity, they were also felt to burden the narrative with 'unnecessary and meaningless' footage. In other words, in their attempts to 'normalise' film narrative, the Pathé film-makers were caught between two norms: any step towards conforming to the norm of narrative coherence was also a step away from the norm of narrative economy.

Salt quotes the following extract from the autobiography of Albert Smith, one of the founders of the American Vitagraph company:

No one complained about this until it became evident that Pathé was using its goings and comings over and over again. The stories varied, but sandwiched in between would be the same goings and comings. This aroused a two-horned complaint: the audiences were getting tired of the same goings and comings, often having little relation to the story, and secondly the buyers weren't going to pay fifteen cents a foot for this surplusage. They said the story was better without the goings and comings, and so they began to scissor them out of the picture, paying Pathé only for what was left.[29]

The problem with transition inserts was that, in order to serve their purpose as linkages, they had to be somehow 'downgraded' to the level of auxiliary elements – and there was no easy way to signal to the viewer that 'passages' recorded with the same impartial precision as 'main scenes' were less important. This is, essentially, what Boris Eichenbaum meant when pointing out (twenty years later) that in the hands of inexperienced directors 'link-shots' weigh down the film by introducing irrelevant and meaningless details.

However, as we know from some sources quoted earlier, resistance to transition inserts went hand in hand with fascination. One has to bear in mind that reception is always ambivalent in its assessments. Like any cultural anomaly, deviations from the narrative norm were not necessarily seen as a defect. By some observers passages were recognised as an aesthetic resource for developing something like cinema's own unique manner of storytelling.

In his recent paper on cinema's temporality, Tom Gunning points to a dual nature of plot unfolding in the cinema of the 1910s. There was always some tension between the viewer's involvement in the story line (what will happen next?) and the satiation of visual pleasure through the excess of spectacle. Gunning links the latter level of enjoyment to the vestiges of 'the cinema of attractions', the period when the whole *raison d'être* of cinema lay in its spectacularity and ability to astonish:

> In spite of (indeed because of) the structural differences between the temporality and visual pleasure offered by attractions and those structured by narrative, the two ways of addressing the spectator can frequently interrelate within the same text. Rather than a developing configuration of narrative, the attraction offers a jolt of pure presence, soliciting surprise, astonishment, or pure curiosity instead of following the enigmas on which narrative depends.[30]

Gunning's observation can not only be confirmed by what we find in Russian film literature of the 1910s, it can also be extended to cover filmic elements not necessarily connected with the world of the cinema of attractions. By strange coincidence, transition inserts, initially born out of necessity in order to linearise narrative, turned out to be a powerful source of visual pleasure. Surplus footage, unnecessary details, 'flattening out' of the difference between the key story line and auxiliary sections (a kind of cinematic 'spondee') all had their admirers as well as adversaries.

As an example, let us take two diametric opinions concerning the way the characters of a film were introduced to the audience. This usually took the form of a series of non-narrative 'portraits' included among the credit titles. How were they received? Opinions differed – some viewers clearly found these 'overtures' off-putting:

> At the start of the performance the *prima donna* of the piece appears on the screen. From behind the slowly parting curtains a massive female emerges, getting bigger and bigger all the time. Her already huge physiognomy swells to vast proportions and turns slowly from right to left, making mysterious and languid eyes and adopting a nauseatingly 'passionate' expression. This is followed by the face of the hero, drawn and clean shaven, insanity staring from his wide-open eyes; the same slow moving of the head from right to left and a specially expressive, but this time 'pathological', gaze. Then the action begins.[31]

On the other hand, some people claimed that it was the scenes situated outside the actual story line that gave cinema its own particular narrative plasticity and beauty. An important aspect of this rhetoric was that films were held to be unconsciously beautiful; beautiful, as it were, 'without knowing it', much as African art or the Primitivist painters were once described. The device of presenting introductory portraits of characters was sometimes cited in support of the argument that cinema as a medium was far superior to the 'silly stories' it was made to tell. In 1911 Pavel Nilus (an artist based in Odessa) owned up to an 'illicit' aesthetic experience:

> We are so in love with everyday life that we are fascinated by seeing people on the screen, not just by the story line. I recall seeing a picture where the director, for some reason or other, found it necessary to introduce the individual characters. It only took a few minutes, but you ought to have seen how delighted the audience was to see the living portraits of those charming, smiling actors and actresses. It struck me then that the directors of this new genre had not yet realised what power they had, that they had not yet understood what gripped audiences and what left them unmoved.[32]

Two cultural references made by contemporary observers, one to music and the other to book illustrations, may help explain the fascination with these (and similar) para-narrative segments of narrative films. When Fyodor Sologub prepared 'production notes' for Alexander Sanin, the suggested director for his 1918 screen version of *Miss Liza* [Baryshnya Liza], he particularly stressed the importance of including pictures that did not actually form part of the story line:

> Bearing in mind the actress who is to play the main role [Olga Gzovskaya], it would be a very good idea to highlight the plastic and mimetic moments of the part. The author has therefore thought it necessary to mark on the script some pictures that show M[iss] L[iza] in various moods, but always equally enchantingly. I think the best place for the first of these pictures would be right at the beginning – as a living vignette, just like the little cameo illustrations one finds in books of that period.[33]

By 'books of that period' Sologub meant books of the beginning of the nineteenth century, in which the action of his scenario was set. His long story *Miss Liza* and the theatre version on which the writer had based the film script were both stylisations of the nineteenth-century sentimental novel, so there is no wonder that Sologub wanted the film to be stylised as well. However, the 'living vignette' reference makes one think that what Sologub also had in mind was to establish a kind of internal correspondence between cinema and the archaic illustrated story. The feature in common would be 'naivety' (the naivety of a literary archaism and the naivety of the newly fashionable cinema) and a love of digression and unnecessary detail – a narrative style that Sologub defined as a 'living vignette'.

Another idea was to define this style by association with music. Two philologists of the 1920s, Boris Eichenbaum and Karoł Irzykowski, suggested – quite independently of each other – the same term to denote elements of cinema narrative that lay outside the story line itself: this was the musical sign *fermata*, which indicates that the length of a note (or pause) may be extended at the performer's discretion. In Irzykowski's definition these were 'ligature scenes', seemingly unimportant, but which should be played 'without haste': 'it is easy to see that directors like them, and that they don't see them just as a part of the content that has to be shown purely for the sake of coherence.'[34] Although Eichenbaum's notion of the cinematic *fermata* is of a slightly different order, he too sees the narrative pause as one of the key elements in cinema stylistics: 'The flow of time appears to stop, the film holds its breath – the viewer is plunged into contemplation.'[35]

THE CLOSE-UP

As research into the history of film narrative refines its tools, most general terms, formerly pivotal for generations of cinema historians, become less and less easy to use. The 'close-up' presents a problem both as a notion and as a technical term. Technically speaking, the term 'close-up' refers only to the scale of framing which includes face or face plus shoulders, and one is expected to give specific gradations when other distances are involved ('big close-up', 'medium close-up', 'medium shot', etc.). Whatever relevance they may have for the history of production, it is not always possible (or necessary) to make these distinctions when narrative devices are regarded from the point of view of their reception. Diffuse terms are sometimes more useful for the study of reception. While film-makers had to enlarge objects in order to set new semantic parameters of the narrative system, the viewers responded to the 'semantic gesture'[36] of *enlargement* rather than to the parameters as such. Therefore, in using the term 'close-up', I shall stress closing in as a gesture, an act of *changing* the scale of representation, and not any of the terminal states of this change.

As to close-up as a theoretical notion, it has by now stratified into categories specified according to: (*a*) the part of the diegesis it represents; (*b*) the spatial articulation it entails; and (*c*) its mode of address.

Barry Salt distinguishes between 'the true Close-Up and the Insert, [which is] a close shot of some object or part of an actor's body *other than the face*'.[37] As Salt shows, insert chronology goes back to the early 1900s. The areas of application are also different: inserts (a letter, an egg in *La Poule aux oeufs d'or* [The Hen that Laid the Golden Eggs, 1905]) serve to supply basic story line information, while facial close-ups – as Kristin Thompson's analysis of the correlative development of acting and framing demonstrates – provide access to character psychology.[38]

Narrative articulation of the diegetic space differs depending on whether a closer shot is *cut into* the longer view that preceded it (thus actually 'bringing us closer' to a character or detail) or adds to the diegetic space of this view (change of angle, cutaway, cross-cutting, etc.). As Tom Gunning argues, the cut-in as used by Griffith in character-oriented narratives was one of the key devices that helped to formulate the narrative system as early as 1908.[39]

Gunning also argues that, although cutting-in to a closer view of a previous shot (as well as other ways of closing in) was occasionally used before Griffith, the mode of address of early close-ups was essentially different. They functioned rather as 'scarcely narrativised attractions' in which the change of a shot scale was interesting *per se*.[40]

Historically, close-ups also differed according to the degree of their integration into the diegesis. So-called 'emblematic shots'[41] attached to the beginning or end of a film were intended to betoken the gist of the story rather than present a part of it. The best-known example is the case of Erwin Porter's gunman whose close-up was offered to exhibitors as a separate reel supplementing *The Great Train Robbery* (1903).[42] As one can see from the detailed film descriptions in Félix Mesguich's memoirs, emblematic close-ups were used as routine closures in Eclair's 'scenic pictures' of the mid-1900s. Since all the films made by this travelling cameraman were 'foreign views' centred on exotic and sensationalist subject matter, bringing it close to the viewer's eyes was the purest case of scopic attraction. The final scene of Mesguich's documentary on pearl divers (1909) showed black faces bending over a shining pearl, and *Fishing Cormorants* [Les Cormorans pêcheurs, c. 1908] 'ended with an amusing scene that caused laughter in those present at the shooting. I did not fail to present it in close-up (preceded by the following intertitle): "A cormorant opens its beak and spits the fish out." '[43] The future palaeontology of cinematic devices will probably name the emblematic shot as the most archaic.

Some marginal cases one observes in Russian films and film literature show how dynamic the categories within the above matrix were. Undeniably, the letter insert served as a vehicle for functional narrative information while facial close-ups channelled character state and psychology. As I have already mentioned, this disguised functionality affected the credibility of the aggregate diegesis of the early cinema. First, there were simply too many letters per film. Second, as some viewers complained, these letters were too rapidly written – particularly compared to the time it took the audience to read them.[44] Third, they all looked too much the same. In 1910 the trade journal *Cine-Phono* published a viewer's complaint that deserves to be quoted because it betrays the growing demand for character-motivated narrative. The correspondence bears the title *Graphology in the Cinematograph*:

Have you never noticed that the handwriting of the captions used in pictures produced, say, by the company 'A' is always large, while film company 'B' always uses small letters; furthermore, haven't you noticed that the Father writing to his Daughter and the Daughter answering her Father's letter have the same handwriting, while it is perfectly clear that the 16-year-old teenager and the old professor would not be able to pen the same letters even if they tried. That is why the handwriting used by *personae* in cinematographic dramas should be in character, instead of the artistically unsatisfactory practice of using one employee in the company who mechanically copies all the letters.[45]

Did complaints like this have any effect on film practice?

At least in one respect the situation in Russia did improve. In Alexander Blok's personal diary we come across an entry made on 19 May 1916, apropos a new tendency observed in Russian films: 'Much attention is paid to psychology (so far not always successfully). Letters are written more slowly, etc.'[46] But it seems that spectators still did not really care very much about handwriting. At least, no Russian film company heeded the request to customise the written style of letter inserts in accordance with age, gender and character traits. Even in the obvious cases when a shaking hand might easily help to suggest a shattered emotional state, credibility was sacrificed to readability. In his 1928 poem on cinema (written in Russian while the author was living in Berlin) Vladimir Nabokov ironically presented a list of its intrinsic diegetic fallacies, the fallacy of neat letters among them:

Letters hastily written in the night.
Danger . . . Trepidation . . . The pen
Scurries across the page . . .
But what a legible hand!
What clerkly penmanship![47]

The only Russian silent film I know of that used personalised handwritten inserts was Grigori Kozintsev's and Leonid Trauberg's 1926 screen version of Nikolai Gogol's *The Overcoat* – and these were used only because it was a film about an office clerk.[48] An earlier (1918) and quite remarkable attempt to give handwriting a dramatic dimension probably also ought to be mentioned, although I am not sure that the director would have carried it out if the film had actually been made. In the 'production notes' for his scenario *Miss Liza* [Baryshnya Liza], a part of which has been quoted earlier, Fyodor Sologub included a painstaking graphological instruction (I should remind you that the action is set in the beginning of the nineteenth century, when the epistolary novel was a legitimate literary form):

Letters should be written in hand, using a goose-quill. Beautiful archaic calligraphy should be observed. Alexis has large, sprawling handwriting, with decisive pressures and thick flourishes, rather slanted. Liza's is upright, thin, all in ligatures, not too perfectly lined, with rounded characters.[49]

Once again, Sologub establishes a cross-century correspondence between cinema narrative, with its craze for letter-writing, and the mannerisms of the novelistic narrative fashionable a hundred years earlier.

This barely discernible drive (if only in tendency) to filter narrative psychology into letter inserts was paralleled by the more manifest meta-morphosis of intertitles. In the mid-1910s explanatory intertitles were giving way to dialogue titles which channelled essentially the same narrative information through character motivation.[50] Again, trade journal contributors tried to speed it up:

> Worried parents are bending over the baby's bed, feeling his forehead, and so on. It's quite clear what's going on, isn't it? But no, the manufacturers [of films] think that you might not understand them, and that if they do not insert the explanatory caption 'The child is ill . . .' you might think that the parents are seeing whether the baby is ready to be served for dinner. These kind of 'narrative phrases' should be replaced by short, clear exclamations; for example one of the characters could say: . . . 'Goodness gracious . . . The baby has a temperature . . .'[51]

Needless to say, the narrative intertitle 'the child is ill . . .' had to be accompanied by a long shot, whereas a dialogue title begged for a facial close-up. The face was the main vehicle for narrative psychology.

However, some marginal cases cause us to suspect that even as late as the 1910s the close-up shot of a face could be occasionally used for purposes other than character motivation. I have mentioned the emblematic close-up, the archaic pre-narrative device that did not last much longer than 1906. Nevertheless, vestiges of emblematic usage can be spotted in some films in the period of narrative integration. A print of the German film *Der Mutter Augen* [The Mother's Eyes, 1913] preserved in Japan contains an extreme close-up of a pair of eyes, which at that time could only be used as an emblematic counterpart of the main title.[52] I do not know whether this film was ever shown in Russia, but one way or another, the idea must have occurred to more than one film-maker, because the actress Nina Gofman, who once starred in A. Besstuzhev's film *Black Eyes* [Ochi chernye . . . ochi strastnye . . ., 1916; no extant copy] recalls exactly the same kind of shot in the Russian film: 'The picture began in close-up, just eyes filling the screen: at first laughing and flirting, then gradually becoming more sombre and finally weeping.'[53] The film owes its title (and, probably, also its story line) to the gypsy song 'Black Eyes', famous for its unique amalgam of joy and sorrow. As described by Nina Gofman, the eyes close-up looks like a visual header designed to mime the emotional trajectory of the eponymous song, while an orchestra (or pianist) played the tune as an overture to the film. The 'psychology' is apparently there, but the usage is clearly extra-narrative, closer to Porter's emblematic gunman with his pistol aimed at the viewer, than to a regular close-up in a 1916 film. Before concluding that there was a fleeting craze for 'eyes emblems' in the cinema of the 1910s – a development that might have anticipated the symbolic eyes in extreme close-up in some famous films of the 1920s – we should have to view more films of the period with the word 'eyes' in their titles.

The above examples may refer to exceptional cases, but the practice they illustrate was not unique. Late emblematic close-ups were not used only to introduce the title theme; ending a story with a close-up of the protagonist's face was fairly common in Russian films. The face of Nikolai Rimsky lost in thoughts about his deceased mistress in *The Bells Ring out, Telling their Simple Tale* [Kolokol'chiki-bubenchiki zvenyat, prostodush-nuyu rasskazyvayut byl'. . ., 1916], or the dead face of Mikhail Salarov lying on the front stairs of his mistress's house in *Child of the Big City* [Ditya bol'shogo goroda, 1914], may be seen as emblematic parallels to the title 'The End'.[54]

LEGENDS OF ORIGIN

What was the chronology of the facial close-up in early Russian cinema? An examination of existing archival holdings is not very rewarding; only about ten per cent of all Russian film output of the 1910s has survived, and – even worse – this percentage does not equally represent the output of the various studios. Khanzhonkov's studio style is fairly well known, while we have almost no idea of the close-up policy of, say, the directors working for Thiemann and Reinhardt studio.

Memoir sources are interesting but particularly unreliable with regard to close-ups. Since, in the 1920s, the close-up came to be regarded as the cornerstone of film poetics, film-makers have been keen to stress in their memoirs that they first came across this important device as early as the 1910s. Anecdotal explanations were concocted as to how the close-up came about and who 'invented' it. One such explanation linked closer framing with bad acting. That is how the historical myth was born that associated close-up with the names of Yevgeni Bauer and the famous Russian film star Vera Kholodnaya. It was the memoir essay written by the set designer and director Czesław Sabinski that launched a theory avidly repeated by many writers. Sabinski maintained that:

> American shot dimensions and montage procedures infected Russian cinema and became *de rigueur*. Early on Bauer used close-up photography in his *Song of Triumphant Love* [Pesn' torzhestvuyushchei lyubvi, 1915] in order to reveal Vera Kholodnaya's innermost feelings. As a matter of fact Vera Kholodnaya did not know how to convey complex psychological nuances, and Bauer had to break the whole scene down into separate, unconnected, moments. For instance: (1) laughter; (2) a calm mask; (3) grief; (4) tears; (5) sobbing. Landscapes, vases, clouds, etc. were sandwiched between these disconnected psychological fragments to act as 'padding'. As a result of all these tricks the novice actress came across as a precious artistic force in her own right.[55]

We can dismiss this talk of Vera Kholodnaya as an actress without talent, but there is some substance to Sabinski's comments. Apparently the stunningly beautiful Vera Kholodnaya was indeed shot in close-up more often than other actresses, and when she appeared in close-up less than usual the critics noticed that something was lacking: 'V. Kholodnaya's acting in the main role was no better than average; perhaps the director was guilty of not taking many close-ups, which are so effective with this actress, and of giving us only very short scenes.'[56]

Possible implications for the quality of their acting notwithstanding, some other actresses claimed that they were the pioneers of close-up. According to our memoir sources, we would have to allow at least three other candidates for the 'first close-up in the history of Russian cinema'. Nina Gofman alleged that the big close-up of her eyes looking straight at the audience in *Black Eyes* was the first. Zoya Barantsevich claimed this distinction for her picture *Tanya Skvortsova – Student*; fragments of the picture have survived, but there are no close-ups among them.

> This was the first time extreme close-up was used; Tanya's face almost filled the whole screen. For some reason or other no one had dared to attempt this before, perhaps they didn't trust the technology, or perhaps the actors refused to do it? But I can clearly remember the conversations we had about it; some actors were confused and frightened by such a novel idea, even some directors were nervous about it, and couldn't decide whether it was a good thing or not.[57]

In Vera Pavlova's memoirs we come across a similar account, this time concerning Boris Chaikovsky's film *A Ballerina's Romance* [Roman baleriny, 1916]:

> I cried when I first saw myself on the screen. I was upset and annoyed that nothing I had tried to do or show had come out right. I didn't like my gestures or the way I moved. I just wanted to tear up some of the takes and re-do them. Even so, it wasn't all dreadful, and one shot, that of the big face of a dog and my tearful face taken in close-up, was really outstanding.[58]

There is one interesting thing about these reminiscences – all three actresses were writing about films made in 1916. But neither the reviews of *Tanya Skvortsova – Student* nor of *A Ballerina's Romance* mentioned that these films incorporated any new techniques, and this is not surprising: by 1916 it was not unusual to see a face filling the whole space of the screen in a Russian film. Nevertheless, in one sense the reminiscences were not mistaken; although technically the close-up had been invented years before, 1916 *was* important: it was the year when film-makers and film critics suddenly realised that, far from being just an occasional device, the close-up was turning into something dangerously central to the narrator system.

RESISTANCE TO CLOSE-UP: FACE VERSUS SPACE

Kristin Thompson quotes a French film-maker, Victorin Jasset, who in 1911 explained American experimental close framings as attempts to 'sacrifice the decor' in order to achieve better character presentation.[59] Even though facial close-ups provided the psychological narrative motivation so desired by Russian critics, by 1916 the latter were deeply divided over the issue. A Russian reviewer of Otis Turner's *Business is Business* (Universal, 1915), shown in Russia in 1916 under the title *The Slave of Profit* [Rab nazhivy], was full of praise for the close-up:

> Having correctly reasoned that in a psychological [photo]play the viewer's attention should be concentrated on the *actor's facial expression* (because the depth of emotion in the soul can only be revealed through the face) the director makes lavish use of the foreground in almost every scene. He is not content, however, simply to shoot actors in foreground, but deploys the following technique. He positions two actors (seated, of course), as close as he can to the camera lens, and gets them to mime the dialogue. All we see on the screen are the two actors, much enlarged, and we cannot help but catch their every facial expression. To enhance the effect, the director masks off part of the frame with a diaphragm so that when one of the actors mimes his bit of the dialogue we see only him and not the other one . . . One cannot but admire this technique: all superfluous details are removed from the viewer's field of vision, and all he sees is the actor's face. Clearly, there is no device better suited for a *psychological* picture.[60]

Opponents of the close-up argued that the 'superfluous details' were too much of a sacrifice; that close-ups reduced the need for background sets and had been deliberately introduced in order to cut production costs. In his essay *Uncrumpled Pillows* Ilya Surguchov, for instance, genuinely supposed that American film-makers used the same bad sets for all their films. Western films, he wrote, can be recognised by the uncrumpled pillows betraying the essential artificiality of the unlived-in rooms in which they are set:

> They were aware that their rooms were sloppy fakes, and so they decided to film the faces in 'close-up' and to have the actors looking directly 'into the camera'. They hoped that the audience would remember the beauty of the faces and the 'acting', and that for a few seconds they would not notice the lifelessness of the décor; but afterwards that only made the falseness of the room even more glaringly obvious.[61]

For some film-makers the choice between decorative space and the close-up was an extremely difficult one to make. It certainly was for Yevgeni Bauer, whose reputation was based on his genius as a set designer. He reached the peak of his art in 1916 in an ambitious high-budget production, *A Life for A Life*,[62] with lavish interiors filmed in very long shot with the overhead space sometimes twice the height of the characters. As far as we can judge by his other films made that same year, Bauer was quite excited by the narrative possibilities of the close-up, but at the same time the written sources suggest that he was also somewhat alarmed at the consequent sacrifice of décor. Contemporaries were acutely conscious of the dilemma. *The Cinematograph Herald*, the Khanzhonkov-owned trade journal that always fostered Bauer's career, expressed it in a sympathetic review of *Nelly Raintseva* (1916):

> Bauer's latest productions – as well as *Nelly Raintseva* we also have in mind *Oh if only I could Express it in Music* . . . [O esli b mog vyrazit' v zvukakh – no extant copy] – show that he has made a firm decision to favour 'genre pictures' and now prefers spirited portraits to the lifeless beauty of décor.
>
> Big faces at the expense of decorative background: this is the director's new artistic choice. And we must do Bauer justice; his hand did not falter as he implemented this new principle in his latest productions.
>
> Maybe he was just a little bit upset when, after having put so much into his brilliant set design for *Nelly Raintseva*, he had to push it further to the background, to cover it (quite literally!) with actors' bodies. Maybe the former Bauer, the architect of colonnaded halls and winter gardens, was indeed upset, but as a genuine artist he must be satisfied by this production . . . The close-up principle is a dangerous principle, you can pursue it only if you can have good performers. Ye. F. Bauer is aware of it, and in terms of performance *Nelly Raintseva* cannot be overestimated.[63]

The shift from space-centred narrative to that centred on the faces of the characters involved a noticeable change in the mode of narration. As I have mentioned earlier, any innovative device immediately increased the intentionality of the text in the eyes of the beholder. All the more so in the case of the close-up. By its very nature – 'behold!' – the close-up was seen as a deixis, the textual gesture implying direct address. The new, space-free narrative mode was felt as subjective in contrast to the objective mode of the earlier space-bound narration. Some observers (film-makers included, presumably) did not seem too happy about this turn of events. Paradoxically, there were reviewers who, despite all the technical evidence, saw the close-up as a step back towards the aesthetics of the theatre, in the sense that closer framing (like the theatre's premeditated, artful means of focusing the spectator's attention) also revealed too much authorial presence. On this point Valentin Turkin's review in *The Cinema Paper* of Peter Chardynin's *Still, Sadness, Still ...* [Molchi, grust', molchi, 1918] is revealing:

> American shots, which give separate moments of the general scenes in close-up, are no help at all. Close-ups used like this do nothing to mitigate the theatricality of the screen production, they even emphasise its conventionality and failure to convince. It's as if they were saying 'In case

you people couldn't make that out from a distance, you can have it close-up as well.' It may at first glance seem paradoxical, but you can easily pick out a director suffering from a surfeit of theatricality by his attachment to the use of explanatory American shots.[64]

CLOSE-UP AND NORM

Closer framing of characters was also resisted on the basis of general aesthetic principles. The credibility of the type of narrative based on closer framing was undermined – I shall argue – by traditional norms of proxemic behaviour and by the traditional notion of spatial homogeneity.

Some Russian critics were convinced that, beautiful as they might be, facial close-ups looked grotesque.[65] Articles were published depicting the repulsive naturalism of gigantic heads. As Yuri Lotman suggests, these reactions recalled (sometimes explicitly) the famous passage in *Gulliver's Travels* describing the hero's disgust as he looks at a giantess breastfeeding her child.[66]

There is one peculiarity common to such articles: none of them refers to the insertion of a non-facial detail; the attack is aimed exclusively at facial close-ups. This leads me to think that the response may have been conditioned by proxemic norms. As some studies in cultural anthropology have shown, distances between people are related to (indeed, dictated by) the chosen genre of interpersonal communication. Edward T. Hall distinguishes between four classes of 'informal distance': public (10 to 22 feet), social-consultive (4 to 10 feet), personal (1.5 to 4 feet) and intimate (less than 1.5 feet), which – as the author stresses – are valid for 'middle-class Americans of North European origin'.[67] While there is no point in directly applying the rules of social behaviour in modern society to the medium of an earlier epoch and a less clearly specified cultural field, I do not see why this cannot be done with reserve (especially since anthropologists themselves readily take their examples from art and literature). Here are some aspects of proxemics that may help us understand the calamities of early film reception. Experiments show that at the 'intimate' distance (around one foot) the field of *clear vision* takes in the eyes, nostrils and mouth, and at the 'personal' distance extends to cover the whole face, and so on.[68] We may assume that, by isolating a face or a part of it, close-up framing created a kind of surrogate field of vision anthropologically associated with, say, 'intimate' distance, thus forcibly imposing intimacy on the unprepared viewer. Hall's chart shows that at this distance *detail vision* reveals the finest facial hairs and the smallest eye vessels – something that immediately makes us think of Swift's complaint about the unbearable sight of the giantess's skin as well as routine protests against the revolting details brought to us by the close-up (once again, the *trompe-l'oeil* quality of the image being the hardest obstacle to overcome). Furthermore, as proxemics demonstrates, there is an element of normality 'built into' our perception of sizes and distances. From more than 2 feet away we see the human head as being of 'normal' size, while at a closer distance we perceive its size as 'over normal'. This may well be the norm responsible for facial close-ups being perceived as grotesquely out of proportion.

Again, however helpful to us this ongoing research in proxemics might seem to be, I wish to warn against applying proxemic categories too simplistically to the history of film reception, a field that perhaps calls for entirely different taxonomies of communication genres. Yet we should be aware that, just as the language of poetry is dependent on natural language, so must cinema be related to in-set visual and kinesthetic patterns of cultural behaviour.

Returning to the rejection of close-up by film critics of the 1910s, we should assume that the new cinematic proxemics was most probably measured against the proxemic norm of the theatre. This norm can be defined as a *proxemic constant*: for any given text (spectacle, concert, etc.) the distance between the spectator and the space where the event is taking place is a constant value. That this value is coded anew every time (by the price of the ticket, the size of the auditorium or other circumstances) is another matter, but, once given, the proximity of the viewer to the event remains the same. The early viewer brought a similar kind of assumption to the cinema, an assumption that was not challenged until the transformation of space-bound narration into the anthropocentric narrator system began to take place. To quote an exact definition given at the beginning of the 1920s by Alexander Arkatov, the great merit of this transformation was that it 'replaced the man gesticulating and moving in space with "flying" spaces changing each other'.[69] Indeed, the new system offered a different, mobile geometry of narrative space. The constancy of the viewing distance was no longer one of its axioms. As film directors started their experiments with framing, the former proxemic constant was turned into a variable value.

The new rules of the game were not easy to learn. Initially, the new construction of narrative space was perceived as its deconstruction. Barry Salt's apt term 'scene dissection' reveals that the process involved a degree of violence; the old monolithic diegesis resisted intrusion.

Some early mentions of 'enlarged images' preserve this air of a dismantled system, of lost unity and integrity. How long did the period of transition last? Let me refer once again to the expression used in 1908 by Yuli Engel in describing a letter insert: 'the letter . . . is actually shown on the screen separately.'[70] Alongside other historically specific aspects discussed earlier in connection with this word, 'separately' shows that the insert was received as having lapsed out of the old system, without yet being recognised as part of a new system. The same expression was used in a similar context as late as 1917, the very year when the new narrative forms became firmly established,[71] in a derogatory review of Sergei Veselovsky's (or N. Arbatov's) film *Kings of the Stock Exchange* [Tsari birzhi, 1916]: 'The actors playing

Velinsky and Nadya, badly made up around the eyes, often pull terrible faces. The director ought not to have fastened the audience's attention on these grimaces, which are shown separately from the rest of the picture and much enlarged.'[72] This does not sound just like criticism of a lack of continuity in editing; the critic is targeting close framing as such. Exactly as with inserts a decade earlier, the 1917 reviewer felt that close-ups simply did not cohere with the encompassing space.

Another difficulty presented by the new conception of narrative space was the mobile camera angle. In Engel's phrase 'shown separately', it isn't just the word 'separately' that sounds strange today; 'shown' is equally odd. Since the distance between the viewer and the object was now seen to be a variable value, the viewer had to learn that, paradoxically, it was not that the larger picture had been dismantled and that the close-up had been 'served up' for more detailed scrutiny, but the reverse: the viewer or, rather, his disembodied self was able to glide unnoticed within the space of the picture to a position nearer the object portrayed. In 1911 the critic Alexander Kosorotov, in an attempt to impart the effect of a close-up, where

> 'a gigantic head suddenly filled the whole scene, with the slightest movement of the blood-vessels, the tiniest flickering of the eyes, the twitching of the lips, all startlingly clear', described this device as 'ripping the main moments out of the general scene and bringing them closer.'[73]

In this description you can sense that the new mode of narrative is perceived as the work of a maniacal showman destroying the diegesis in order to construct a story.

THE RULE OF MISREADING

In the mind of the modern viewer, a distinction exists between the story diegesis (things and events the film is about) and the story discourse (the way things and events are cinematically presented). Theoretically speaking, nothing is changed within the structure of an event itself whether it is rendered by means of one long shot or by several close-ups, or by a static or a moving camera, etc. – or, at least, that is what the viewer automatically assumes as he watches the film. Ability to distinguish between discourse and diegesis is a mandatory part of the viewer's cinematic competence. We do not assume that somebody is round 'in a flash' because there was a time lapse in discourse, or that close-ups exist 'separately' from the rest of the picture. In other words, the tacit convention between the film-maker and the film viewer, upon which the correct reading of the cinematic text is based, says: *structural changes at the level of film discourse do not predicate spatio-temporal changes within the diegesis.*

The restructuring of cinematic narrative as it approached its 'classical' form (i.e. the form familiar to us now) mainly concerned discursive aspects of the film story. Yet this reform had to face up to the risk of the newly structured narrative being misread by a section of the viewers it addressed. This historically specific misreading always followed the same track: discursive alterations were taken for diegetic ones. We can, therefore, suggest a rule that may help us in our diagnosis of the historical misreading of narrative: *the early viewer tended to project discourse upon diegesis.* This may have served to enhance the impact of the former but certainly undermined the credibility of the latter.

COMING INTO THE FOREGROUND

Basically, the semantic gesture of discursive figure enlargement could be conveyed in three different ways: by the cut-in; by bringing the camera closer to the character; and by bringing the character nearer to the camera. As we have seen, the first method was prone to misreading. Let us now consider the viewer's responses to the other two. Our evidence will be selected from contemporary literary sources.

We may start with the episode from Thomas Mann's novel *The Magic Mountain* that was mentioned in Chapter 6 in connection with our discussion on the surface of the screen: the scene in the 'bioscope'. Of the pictures shown at that performance, the one the characters remember is the one where

A young Moroccan woman, in a costume of striped silk, with trappings in the shape of chains, bracelets and rings, her swelling breasts half bared, was suddenly brought so close to the camera as to be life-sized [*ward plötzlich in Lebensgrösse angenähert*]; one could see the dilated nostrils, the eyes full of animal life, the features in play as she showed her white teeth in a laugh, and held one of her hands, with its blanched nails, for a shade to her eyes, while with the other she waved to the audience.[74]

Another source is the following scene in Samuel Marshak's 1908 poem 'At the Cinematograph':

The cinematograph. A Berlin street.
(Flickerings, flashes, flecks and ants.)
We meet two portly gentlemen,
With slim briefcases in their hands.
They stop. Crazily, like froth,
A motor car flies past.
The two instantly grow huge,
Descend and vanish off the screen.[75]

The shots described in Mann's novel and Marshak's poem look similar in several respects. Both are obviously 'exotic' scenic pictures: Berlin scenes for Russian audiences; Morocco shown for Germans. As described, both films were (and were received as) self-contained attractions. The Moroccan picture exhibits an erotically loaded tourist attraction, while the Berlin film belongs to the popular genre of 'busy city' street scenes. Both also play what we might call a 'size game' and both Marshak and Mann seem to stress this aspect in the films they refer to. In the period described, the movement of a character towards the camera could easily form an attraction in its own right. In Mann's novel the bare-breasted Moroccan girl steps into the zone of 'intimate' proxemics (as Edward T. Hall would have it) displaying the 'animal life' of her eyes and dilated nostrils. Such spatial effects formed the basis of Félix Mesguich's minature 'actuality' films, one of which – Katisha's Smile [Le Sourire de Katicha], shot in Java in the mid-1900s – was so similar to the picture described by Mann that one is almost tempted to think of it as the original source of the 'bioscope' scene in the novel. In his memoirs, Mesguich recalled this picture, and how it was greeted everywhere with rapturous enthusiasm:

> I had overcranked my camera slightly to achieve a slow-motion effect. Katisha came out of the river, right to the foreground; her breasts were bare. She wrapped a sarong around her with a swift gesture and tied it beneath her breasts. Her figure got bigger and bigger, her dark eyes opened wide; then there was a row of teeth chewing betel juice. There was laughing and joking in the hall, and Katisha vanished from the screen to the shout of 'What a mouth!'[76]

The 'size attraction' in Marshak's poem is of a more formal nature. The Berlin film lures the viewer into a game of volumes by juxtaposing a very long shot – a mesmerising 'crowd' view[77] with tiny humans described as 'flecks and ants' – with two figures coming out of deep space, pausing to cross a street, then approaching the foreground until they almost fill the screen and finally disappear below what seems to be the bottom edge of the frame – the cameraman was probably shooting from an overhead position.

Was there anything like spatial paradox that made similar 'size games' specially entertaining? As some other sources indicate, in the 1900s the proportion between enlarged objects in the foreground and reduced objects in the background was sometimes perceived as discrepant. Kornei Chukovsky's 1908 article thus describes the chase comedy The Mother-in-Law Race [La Course des belles-mères]: 'Closer and closer [the mother-in-law] comes, bigger and bigger she grows on the screen. But there, in the far distance, some tiny dots – her unfortunate rivals – jump and flicker.'[78] Both Mann and Marshak are describing abrupt movement into the foreground: Mann has 'suddenly'; Marshak 'instantly'. It looks almost as if they were referring to cut-ins. To all appearances, movement out of the background towards the viewer was seen as being quite precipitous.

However, the main attraction in watching this kind of movement seems to have been the possibility of a dual reading of depth cues. Chukovsky's formula 'the closer she comes, the bigger she gets' provides a clue. Unlike us today, contemporary observers never failed to notice both the size of the figure being blown up and the distance being reduced. Mann writes that the Moroccan girl 'was suddenly brought so close to the camera as to be life-sized'. One may mention a number of similar descriptions, but a scene from Vladimir Nabokov's novel *The Defence* (1929) can perhaps serve as the purest example of the point I wish to make. Although the action takes place in the 1920s, Luzhin, Nabokov's grown-up chess-obsessed protagonist, is taken to the cinema for the first time in his life. Nabokov then gives an 'alienated' description of a standard feature film of the time as seen through the eyes of a 'naive' viewer with no mastery of cinema narrative and no experience of reading images in movement. When one of the characters notices his daughter, and in the next shot comes forward to meet her at the door, Luzhin sees that suddenly 'everything changed [that is how Nabokov refers to a cut], and the father, growing in size, walked towards the spectators'.[79] A standard shot from a standard film is described in the same manner as the first viewers described the Lumières' train. What is peculiar about this kind of space reading? The modern viewer reads the change in size only as an unambiguous depth cue. This reading habit is so firmly established within us that we readily let ourselves be deceived by animated films when, by making a figure grow bigger, they make us believe in spatial depth. The early perception worked rather the other way round. Although enlargement *was* understood as coming closer, it also remained enlargement. In his poem, Marshak dispenses entirely with the 'depth' dimension and gives only the two-dimensional misreading of the event ('two gentlemen instantly grow huge') – perhaps for him the unreal (not to say surreal) illusion of real figures being blown up provided the poetic justification for the whole stanza. Depth cues are discursive signals, and we read them as such, while early viewers were able to project them upon the diegesis. As a result, photographed moving images could be enjoyed as we enjoy animated cartoons – by just admiring the tricky aspect of image formation. The early viewers had only to mentally switch off depth reading for a moving object to acquire a magical ability to change its size. An ordinary actuality film turned into an entertaining spectacle.

Thus we can say that, for a person of the beginning of the century, enlargement caused by movement out of the background of a shot was a kind of spatial attraction, whose appeal was that the viewer could arbitrarily change the code for reading space ('enlargement versus approach'); or, more accurately, he could simultaneously experience the duality of this code and the interchangeability of the interpretations it offered.

PROPRIOCEPTION

A third method of enlargement, 'track-in', where the camera is brought nearer to the object, was rarely used in the 1900s.[80] In trick films the track-in technique was sometimes employed for effects like Méliès' expanding heads. Outside the trick genre, head-on camera movement was used for proprioceptive attraction effects, primarily in 'phantom rides'.

Why 'proprioceptive'? Tracking 'into' (or out of) the pro-filmic space incited in an inexperienced viewer a special type of sensory involvement. In the 1900s the camera moving down the line of sight provoked the physical sensation of the viewer personally having become part of this movement. This effect was exploited by early exhibitors. As we know from Charles Musser's and Tom Gunning's ongoing research into the practice and reception of the travel genre in early cinema, certain shows offered special kinds of films that both simulated and stimulated the illusion of being (literally) carried away. Regular shows sometimes used the travel attraction as an effective closure. Gunning quotes the example of an American cinema show that ended in this way:

> Showman Lyman Howe often ended his program of films with an attraction called *The Runaway Train* in which a wildly overcranked projector caused a film taken from a train in the Alps to plunge down inclines and across bridges, creating a sensation in the audience.[81]

Modern first-time-effect attractions like IMAX Theatres, The Omni Theatre in the Museum of Science in Boston, or Star Track in Disneyland may help the inquisitive reader to experience the sensations felt by Howe's spectators.

Similar effects addressed the viewer's sense of spatial identity – 'proprioception', to borrow a term from experimental psychology.[82] It seems that, in order to arouse a proprioceptive illusion, the camera movement had to satisfy at least two conditions: it had to be unusual and iconically motivated. Novelty, 'the first-time-in-my-life' aspect of the experience, was the main necessary precondition for proprioceptive experiments to work. Proprioceptive illusions were projective: the viewer projected a novel experience on to a habitual one. The other precondition was iconicity: the habitual experience had to be recognised in the novel one. For example, in order to make the viewer feel sea-sick, one had actually to locate a camera on a pitching and rolling boat. The programme note of the Petrograd cinema Saturn in April 1910 advertised this strange entertainment as the coda of the performance (like Lyman Howe with *The Runaway Train*):

> Dramas, comedies, comic sketches and magical tricks all take place on the screen. Each picture has its own effect on the viewer and we have a unique opportunity to observe them. The finale is just as entertaining. You see shots of a stormy sea on the screen, and you really feel seasick! This doesn't put viewers off – it actually brings them in.[83]

Proprioceptive effects were occasionally used in fiction films – provided that the camera movements that induced them were both unusual as a cinema experience and familiar as something one had experienced in 'real life'. In Edwin Porter's *Dream of a Rarebit Fiend* (1906), the frame starts to sway as the drunk returns home. When the Earth is rocked by the manic sneezer in Hepworth's *That Fatal Sneeze* (1907), the frame rocks too. It begins to spin round as the poisoned hero of the Italian film *Tigris* (Vincenzo C. Denizot, 1913) looks at the dancing party. The famous subjective spin in Murnau's *The Last Laugh* [Der Letzte Mann, 1924] might have also worked (or have been intended to work) partly as a proprioceptive attraction.

Travel notes by the writer Alexander Koiransky published in 1907 in a weekly newspaper contain the first Russian comments on the proprioceptive power of the film medium. Koriansky's essay was a reversal of what Musser would later term as 'spectator-as-passenger convention'. Its author tells of his train trip from Paris to Moscow via Cologne and Berlin. There was some time to kill in Paris before his departure, and in the German cities between trains. That is how Koiransky discovered cinema. He spent three hours in a Paris film theatre and, as he finally takes a coach to the station, he cannot get rid of his residual impressions:

> Getting on the coach I took care that the porter did not put a basket on my head, as I had just seen in the cinema. The coach pulled off. The streets of Paris glided past me, almost without flickering.[84]

The feeling that he was still at the cinema grew even stronger when Koiransky got on the train:

> The wheels clattered and the train gathered speed, shaking and flickering, like the film in the cinematograph; from time to time it emitted a whistle, a kilometre or so long. People, unknown and unwanted, came and went: fellow-travellers in the night. As on the screen, the night life twinkled and shimmered nervously in the bright electric light cast by the big stations. And again the wheels clattered, and the train, swaying and jumping, rushed on into the frosty darkness.[85]

Of course, Koiransky's free hours in Cologne and Berlin were also spent in the cinema, and when he finally got home, Moscow's Arbat Street greeted him with the flickering lights of cinema façades. Cinema was turning the planet into unending travel.

Koiransky was describing a rail journey at night. But vistas rushing past carriage windows must also have reminded daytime travellers of cinema. Why this should be so is well explained by Wolfgang Schivelbusch in *The Railway Journey: Trains and Travel in the 19th Century*, chapter four of which deals with panoramic vision as an experience developed specifically by travelling on trains.[86] Besides, a 1917 review of a painting of the view from a train window by the Italian Futurist painter Gino Severini, cited in an article by Edward Eiken, shows the cinema/train association clearly realised as a dual image of 'modern sensibility':

The sensation of movement is expressed: its direction indicated and the fragmentary impressions of eyesight are suggested as one sits in a train and sees the outside objects fleeting by in constant change. The picture represents a mingling of cinematograph effects and those of kaleidoscopic vision.[87]

In the 1910s the early proprioceptive response to cinematic images had passed, but the trope linking viewing to travelling remained, reinforced by other data. In 1913 another author coined this metaphor: 'the automobile of the modern cinema floats over the surface of life accompanied by the music of a brass siren.'[88] An ephemeral image of the Flying Dutchman was used twice with slightly different motivations, once (1913) as a well-nigh cosmic metaphor synonymous to that of the Wandering Jew:

the cinema spectator, the traveller, [shuttles] from coast to coast and from planet to planet, driven, like the Flying Dutchman, by a yearning for the stars, across the tragic sea of everyday life . . . He flies past, observing life only in its reflection, in its outward gestures.[89]

On the second occasion (in 1914) the same trope, from the pen of a different author, was motivated by the cinema's ability to preserve our image beyond the grave:

No, the reason we love the 'Crazy Kinemo' is not because of its rapid movement; we love it because its trembling ghosts bring to life the legend of the Flying Dutchman tossed by the waves in the wilderness of the ocean, with her cargo of passengers rejected by life and unwanted by death.[90]

TRACK-IN

Thus, in the 1910s movement down the line of sight was mainly used in order to activate proprioceptive associations of mobility. Even less ambitious intentions would have been dramatic enough for the early viewer: Gunning mentions two films released by Biograph in 1903 and 1904, whose primary motivation was the surprise presumably caused by a track-in towards the character's face.[91] We may assume that part of the fascination of such track-ins was similar to that of watching figures being 'blown up' as they approached the foreground area. This can be supported by a fragment from Luís Buñuel's memoirs in which he recalls his first childhood impression of cinema. The thrill of the track-in is explained there as an 'odd' combination of ambivalent sensory data: 'getting larger' and 'getting nearer'.

I shall never forget my horror, which was shared by the whole audience, when I saw a 'track-in' for the first time in my life. A head bore down upon us from the screen, getting larger and larger, as if it was going to swallow us up. I could not for one moment imagine that it was the camera that was being brought closer to the head – or that the latter was being magnified by some kind of trick photography, like Méliès used. What we saw before us was a head getting nearer, becoming monstrously enlarged. And, like the apostle Thomas, we believed what we saw.[92]

The biblical allusion is particularly apt here because it was exactly the contradiction between the irresistible realism of the image and the unbelievable things happening to it that trapped the viewer's cognitive ability.

In the 1910s tracking shots were gradually integrated into the narrative. The narrative strategy of tracking differed according to the camera's trajectory. The 'Cabiria movement' (called so after the eponymous Italian film by Giovanni Pastrone, 1914) was a slow lateral (or lateral-diagonal) travelling shot unmotivated by figure movement within the frame. Its aim was to reveal the proportions of the sets and to bring out the three-dimensional quality (called 'stereoscopy' at the time) of action space. This kind of tracking, because of the success of Pastrone's film, influenced a number of film-makers in the West.[93]

Although Cabiria was equally successful in Russia, the 'Cabiria movement' does not appear to have exercised any significant influence on Russian film-makers. Extant films by Yevgeni Bauer never use lateral tracking as a device to reveal the scale of their sets. For this purpose Bauer preferred to use tracking-out motivated by the character's repositionings within the space of the action. After Death [Posle smerti, 1915] provides a well-known example of a three-minute track-out accompanied by a small-scale pan reframing the characters as he makes detours in order to introduce the other visitors to the party.

Bauer's favourite camera movement, though, was the track-in. While in the Western cinema the track-in was rarely used,[94] thanks to Bauer it became fairly popular in Russian films. In his Child of the Big City [Ditya bol'shogo goroda, 1914] the camera tracks in for almost two minutes over the whole restaurant towards the 'Indian dancer'. After Death – as well as the above-mentioned long track-out – contains a remarkable track-in to the face of the heroine reciting poetry that shows her face slowly filling the whole screen. In Boris Chaikovsky's The Devil's Wheel [Chertovo koleso, 1916] there are two track-ins: one from long shot to medium, and then a fast zoom-in to the heroine after she has committed suicide. In Bauer's The Alarm [Nabat, 1917] there is a track-in to the face of the hero Radin, showing him deep in thought.[95] One could at least double the number of examples from surviving Russian films.

In the spring of 1991 Paolo Cherchi Usai mentioned to me his theory of camera movement in the 1910s, which I find extremely convincing and particularly applicable to Bauer. Cherchi Usai defined the 'Cabiria movement' (or, rather, the 'Cabiria-type movement') as a camera gesture that 'invited' the viewer into the diegesis, that 'introduced' him to the space of the film. Cherchi Usai calls this type of tracking shot a 'come with me' camera movement.[96] The lateral camera movement is the film-maker's address to the viewer. Bauer's 'in' and 'out' tracking shots, on the other hand, look as if they addressed the character personally rather than the viewer. The track-in 'gesture' may be sympathetic or aggressive, but it is always interpersonal rather than space-bound.

This historical phenomenology of tracking helps to understand its reception in the 1910s. The track-in energised the diegesis. Essentially, this effect can be explained by the same rule of misreading that one finds working in other cases of early text reception. A purely discursive procedure, the track-in was misread as a propensity of the diegetic world. Of course, in the 1910s no viewers still believed that the head was actually getting bigger, instead of getting nearer. But the attendant effect of 'a head bearing down upon us from the screen', described in Buñuel's memoirs, was still very much there. The track-in imparted extra energy to the subject, which made it impending, menacing, even aggressive. In the 1910s these connotations were still part of the track-in and not only conditioned its reception but also determined its usage. Who today would be impressed by such a narrative cliché of recent Soviet cinema as a zoom-in to the face of the main character as a way of ending a scene? We read it at best as a conventional sign of closure. The viewer of the 1910s, however, did respond to track-ins. Reviewers occasionally mentioned them and some maintained that the device was a melodramatic *tour de force* – too robust to be in good taste. For example, a reviewer of Vladimir Kasyanov's *The Seventh Commandment* [Sed'maya zapoved', 1915] clearly implied that the drama of the final track-in was overdone:

> The last scene takes place in a brothel, at night. A gang of drunken sailors are carousing with the girls. One of them . . . suddenly realises that the girl he had just gone upstairs with is his long-lost sister. He seizes a kitchen knife and holds it to his throat. His sister falls on her knees in front of him, and her face bears down upon the viewer, her staring eyes supposedly conveying horror and madness.[97]

In an age when a face approached by the camera was described as 'bearing down upon the viewer', the track-in played the role of a transformer of energy: the energy of the moving camera was converted into the energy of the face, figure, or detail that was coming towards the viewer.

The self-contained power of the track-in was probably responsible for what we sometimes tend to mistake as editing errors in films of the 1910s. Today, when the track-in is a purely discursive element, it carries out exclusively narratological and syntagmatic tasks. The classical norms of editing continuity demand that if shot B of the scene ABC is the only one containing camera movement, tracking should start after the A/B cut and stop before the B/C cut. In other words, a cut from stasis to movement within a scene is considered a mismatch. Another norm implies that the respective camera positions for shots A, B and C should be mutually co-ordinated before the cuts are executed. The terminal point of camera travel in B predicates its position in C. From the point of view of these standards, camera movement in films of the 1910s often looks pointless. A track-in down a long aisle of wedding tables on to the figures of the newlyweds in Bauer's *A Life for a Life* [Zhizn' za zhizn', 1916], brilliantly executed by the cameraman Boris Zavelyov, leaves a modern viewer dissatisfied. The tracking is broken off halfway into medium close-up by a cut, after which the camera 'recoils' to a longer shot, as if leaving the track-in hanging in mid-air.[98] But did the early viewer see it as a mismatch? I should assume that the syntagmatic function of the track-in was not part of his expectations; camera movement was perceived as a property of the individual shot rather than of a more general spatial and narrative design. In the cinema of the 1910s the track-in was not there so much to assist the story; it was required for another purpose: to provide sterescopy of vision and to activate the space within the shot.

TRAILING A MOVING FIGURE

As we see from the above examples, the viewer's proprioceptive involvement was just one of two possible ways of misreading the camera movement. The alternative proprioceptive response was disinvolvement. The viewer would rather believe in the mobility of the world around him than accept the convention of a mobile point of view. The viewer did not travel mentally in space: close-up, 'detaching itself from the general background', came to *him*. His point of view did not shift towards the face on the screen; the face 'bore down' on *him*. His sense of spatial identity was still controlled by the proxemic norm of theatre with the viewer's bodily self undetached from his 'mental self' (no occult allusions implied!).

On these grounds some critics found camera movement irritating. Just as they condemned close-up as 'theatrical', so they considered experiments with camera movement contrived and uncinematic. An example drawn from the production and reception history of Yakov Protazanov's *The Queen of Spades* [Pikovaya dama, 1916] illustrates how discrepant the film-maker's and film viewer's aesthetic positions sometimes were. While, as Kristin Thompson observes, 'following a moving subject was undoubtedly the most common application of the tracking shot during the silent period',[99] one should probably add 'in exterior scenes' to make this statement applicable to Russian films of the 1910s. If we exclude short-range trailing pans, used rather as a means of reframing than as a self-conscious device in this period, extended tracking within a set required great skill and involved considerable set construction costs as well as some form of mobile camera mounting (outdoors, motor cars were used).[100] As Paolo Cherchi Usai has argued in connection with Bauer's manner of tracking, a track-out following an advancing character – such as a minute-long backward track in *The Deceived Pickpocket* [Le Pickpocket mystifié, Pathé, 1911] – was the exception rather than the rule.[101] Indeed, a similar three-minute-long tracking shot in Bauer's *After Death* has an unmistakable *tour de force* air about it. Yakov Protazanov (who was then working for Yermoliev and was considered Bauer's most serious competitor in terms of 'quality pictures') was impressed, and in *The Queen of Spades* went for an exploit that was obviously meant to out-Bauer. Vladimir Ballyuzek, the set designer for *The Queen of Spades*, recalls how they designed a tracking shot for a scene that, unfortunately, has not survived in any of the extant prints of the film. His description of the event itself seems accurate enough, although he appears to have exaggerated the part he played in it:

> I wanted the entire scene in which Liza writes a letter giving a detailed description of the lay-out of the countess's house to be filmed differently from the way it is staged in the theatre. I thought it would be more interesting from the cinematic point of view to show the hero passing through the endless suites of rooms in that musty mansion. Particularly since there are buildings like that still remaining in some parts of Moscow. I recall how long I had to argue in favour of this idea, which horrified some of those involved in the production. I was helped out by Mosjoukine, who agreed to walk through a long succession of strange rooms as Liza was writing about them, with his back to the camera and the audience. To film this scene I made a special device out of two bicycles. The camera followed closely behind German (Mosjoukine), revealing a vista of endless drawing-rooms in the old mansion. The moving camera allowed the viewer to share German's feelings on surveying those unfamiliar surroundings for the first time.[102]

Interestingly, although in the two films the cameras moved in opposite directions – with the camera following behind Mosjoukine in *The Queen of Spades*, while in *After Death* it backed away as the leading character was introduced into a huge drawing-room full of other guests – the story motivation in both films was similar: the hero was being shown entering a strange house.

We have no information that might tell us how audiences received the tracking shot in Bauer's film, but the one in *The Queen of Spades* gave rise to at least one complaint that things like that undermined the credibility of the space of action. In 1916 *Theatre* magazine published a review that condemned this particular camera movement as a flaw in the film:

> In one place, where German is passing through a suite of rooms, the cameraman follows him, and as a result you see rooms moving on the screen, something that conflicts sharply with the general impression of artistic truthfulness.[103]

An analogy drawn from the world of flying might help to clarify the difference between the way the early viewer experienced spatial movement and the way it is experienced by the modern viewers. Just as someone new to flying imagines that it is the ground that is tilting when the plane turns, not the aeroplane, so might the inexperienced cinema viewer feel that it was the landscape that was moving and not the camera. However, if you ask a pilot or a frequent flyer (as I have done) the answer will show that, with time, the perception of one's body in space adjusts to its real physical position.

IMAGES OF MOVEMENT

The effect of an inverted perception of movement launched two chains of associations that linked this sensory illusion with non-cinematic culture. The first chain led from tracking shots to the turntable stage. The revolving stage was introduced into the European theatre roughly at the same time that cinema was invented,[104] and its effect, of course, was quite similar to lateral tracking. The similarity was noticed, and caused reciprocal comments from both theatre critics and film reviewers. Because everyone compared it with cinema – observed the theatre critic Alexander Kugel in 1913 – the rotating stage gave rise to general disillusionment: 'The cinematograph conveys such a powerful "sense of place" that it reduces even the wittiest and complex stage techniques to baby talk.'[105]

Conversely, in a 1914 review of Giovanni Pastrone's *Cabiria* a New York critic wrote: 'Among the photographic novelties is one frequently used with fine effect. Scenes are slowly brought to the foreground or moved from side to side, quite as though they were being played on a movable stage.'[106]

Because the revolving stage (an expensive technical innovation) was not widely used in Russian theatres of the 1910s, camera movement was sometimes compared with a more traditional stage technique: movable background scenery. For example, in 1911 the St Petersburg Distorting Mirror Theatre put on a parody of the cinematograph, including the whole paraphernalia of a cinema performance, from the droning 'reader' to the flickering illumination. The reviewer for *Theatre and Art* expressed the following wish:

Mr Malshet [the actor] does a very funny impression of running – a favourite cinematograph activity. The way he rushes around, taking tiny steps, is particularly good. The effect could be enhanced if the décor of the 'chase scene' could also be made to move.'[107]

What the reviewer had in mind was the use of a spinning background to mimic the trailing pan.

The other chain of association linked cinema with nineteenth-century classical literature. It traced the idea of the moving camera to the famous description of Nevsky Avenue (the main street in St Petersburg) in Nikolai Gogol's short story *Nevsky Avenue* [Nevskii prospekt], written in 1834. A shy, susceptible young artist falls head over heels in love with an enchanting young girl he glimpses on the street;

> a mist seemed to spread itself before his eyes. The pavement, he felt, was moving at a terrific speed under him; the carriages with their galloping horses stood still; the bridge stretched and was about to break in the centre of its arch; the houses were upside down; a sentry-box came reeling towards him . . . And all this was produced by a single glance, by one turn of a pretty head.[108]

This passage resonated through Russian twentieth-century modernist literature. It was used in literary debates in order to prove that the germ of non-realist technique was already present in nineteenth-century realist prose. In particular, Gogol's proto-modernist vision of Nevsky Avenue was frequently alluded to in Symbolist and Futurist works. To use the term devised by literary historians for a tight intertextual cluster of motifs common to the two centuries, Gogol's description was part of 'the Petersburg text' (or 'the Petersburg myth') of Russian literature.

Andrei Bely was one of those Symbolist writers who cultivated the Gogolesque style and Gogol's vision of St Petersburg. His own novel *Petersburg* is saturated with allusions to *Nevsky Avenue*. In his book *Gogol's Mastery* [Masterstvo Gogolya] Bely wrote:

> It is typical of Gogol that he sees a 'crowd of walls' flickering past, just as we see them from a tram, with houses leaping up, revealing or shutting out the view: '. . . the pavement was flying above him, carriages with galloping horses seemed to stand still.' This is how the artist [Yuri] Annenkov sees the world; Gogol reaches right out to the boldest perceptions of Futurist writing.[109]

In identifying Gogol as the precursor of 'the boldest perceptions of Futurist writing' Bely had in mind the Futurists' fascination with the ideas of relativity of time, space and movement, and the strange distortions of vision that such fascination could engender. Here is a specific example – a typically Futurist reversal of movement in a poem by Sergei Tretyakov written in 1913:

> I thrust the street away with my feet,
> But, believe me, I am not moving!
> I want to walk in the sweat of my brow –
> Oh, so desperately – until I die.[110]

It is easy to imagine just how readily such inverse representations of movement clustered round moving backgrounds, revolving stages as well as trailing pans in films.

To return to Andrei Bely, his interest in movement reversal on stage, in literature and in films had a profound philosophical motivation. The revolving stage was a subject of heated debate in the theatrical world at the beginning of the century. Some people were highly sceptical about the universal fascination with this mechanical novelty (a common argument against it was that it reduced the sense of depth on the stage). Bely, too, was among its critics, but his objections were of a metaphysical rather than a visual order – Bely sensed that the revolving stage was associated with, as it were, the 'wrong' kind of movement: 'wrong', that is, in a cultural and philosophical sense.[111] These ideas were formulated in his 1912 article called 'Circular Movement'. According to Bely, circular movement (movement on the spot) was just as 'false' and 'illusory' as the movement of contemporary aesthetic and philosophical ideas in general. He maintained that the Symbolists' programme to restore to theatre the greatness of medieval pageants and the ritual plays of the antique world failed to live up to these models:

> That is the way the self-satisfied stage has been revolving: not from theatre to mystery-play, but from day-dreams about mystery . . . *to the mystery of the backstage anecdote*. And the spectator, summoned to a 'Dionysian drama' but left unmoved by the stage, began to revolve backwards: from Ibsen to melodrama, to the cinematograph and to cabaret . . . The contemporary stage has failed to grip the spectator; contemporary philosophy has failed to grasp life; the rotating philosophical machinery of the brain corresponds to the machinery of this circular movement of the stage.[112]

Circular movement presented as disguised immobility is one of the clues to Bely's novel *Petersburg*, which was, in essence, a novel about what Bely called the 'Buddhist' (i.e., self-contained, inert, self-centred, materialist) aspect of existence. Nina Berberova recalls Bely's comment regarding the 'architectonics' of his novel: '*Petersburg*, no matter what Berdyaev said, is a circle. Not a cube, but a wheel.'[113] The revolving stage, Gogol's frozen carriages and the 'crowd of walls' running past them, the 'rotating machinery of the brain', and occult references were all part of a powerful semantic field spinning round the textual axis of the novel.

As mentioned earlier, in 1918 Bely wrote a film script of *Petersburg*. This scenario is in many respects as unusual a film script as its source is unusual as a novel. It is conceived as a detailed literary treatment rather than anything resembling a real shooting script, and it is extraordinary in the way it indicates where the director should use a moving point of view.

Each time the moving point of view is referred to in the same manner: the character remains motionless while the world around him or her is set in motion. When the cityscape is depicted as seen through the window of a moving brougham, Bely's description suddenly looks similar to Gogol's famous portrayal of Nevsky Avenue:

> The screen shows the interior of Apol[lon] Apol[lonovich] Ableukhov's carriage; you can see out through the window; there are glimpses of passers-by and houses drifting past; in the carriage are sitting Apol. Apol. and Anna Petrovna.[114]

And earlier:

> Fleeting glimpses of Nevsky Avenue. There is a droshky in the foreground
> of the screen; it seems stationary, because it is moving . . . The droshky
> turns off Nevsky Avenue in the direction of Pavlovsk Palace. Pavlovsk
> Palace goes past to one side. [115]

Accordingly, when Bely wants to signal to the future film-maker that a trailing
pan should be used on a character, he refers to the character as 'walking on
the spot'. One is almost forced to assume (although, of course, there is no way
to prove the point) that for Bely the cinematic pan fell into the same category
as the revolving stage: both were symbols of futile, unreal movement. If
this was so it becomes easier to explain why he was so particular about
indicating the scenes in which camera movement should be used: it may have
been Bely's intention to make them 'walk on the spot' in order to reveal the
fallacy of their motion. The Senator walks on the spot in his huge apartment:
'[Apollon Apollonovich] passes by in the direction of the hall. The walls
move: Apol. Apol. can be seen crossing the hall.'[116] A terrorist runs on the
spot trying vainly to flee from the bronze equestrian statue of Peter the Great
– a traditional symbol of destiny in Russian literature:

> Empty streets. Alexander Ivanovich, going out of his mind, is running
> through the city. More empty streets. The shadow of the Bronze Horseman
> can be seen gliding through the streets after him. The background changes.
> The streets are moving. The Bronze Horseman is flying through the streets
> of St Petersburg.[117]

Here the dreamlike impossibility of escape is juxtaposed with the uncanny
mobility of the statue come to life. The Gogolesque quality of inverted
movement is even more evident in the scene that the writer himself described
as a 'semi-fantastic picture'.[118] Thunderstruck by a letter suggesting that he
commit patricide,

> N. A. [Nikolai Apollonovich] stands up and goes for a walk, his chin sunk
> on to his chest. Everything is concentrated on his facial movements . . .
> The street begins to move. Fantastic shadows of houses float past, with the
> openings of alleys and cross-streets cut into them . . . the panorama
> constantly changes, getting mistier and mistier. Now a procession (N. A.
> accompanied by demons) sets off against the background of a fence: or
> rather – a vision of a fence. Ghostly pictures loom through the fence.[119]

In other words (words that we might have used had Bely's script been shot
and available for analysis), Nikolai Apollonovich stands up and comes into
the foreground; the camera trails him as the exterior background turns into
floating silhouettes and gradually goes out of focus; he keeps walking as this
indiscriminate moving background turns into a fence with figures of demons
superimposed on it; the images of the demons on the fence pursue the

character. Again, the futility of running – this time from one's own darker self – is conveyed by extended panning.

Extended indeed, because this long walk on the spot goes on and on. Demons give way to diverse scenes from Nikolai Apollonovich's life, which he sees in his mind's eye on the passing fence. This endless fence (in fact, an inner scrolling screen through which the stream of his consciousness is conveyed) takes Nikolai Apollonovich to his father Apollon Apollonovich, the Senator, whom his terrorist friends – and indeed, his subconscious patricidal drive – compel him to kill. The boundary between the space of visions and that of reality becomes indiscriminate. For a minute, the viewer is forced to believe that the planned patricide *is* taking place, only to discover that the whole event was no more than a fantasy of the son's feverish imagination. This is how Bely intended this scene to be shot:

N. A. begins to bang frenziedly on the door to the 'unmentionable place' [the lavatory, where his father, A. A., is trying to save himself from the son. Trans.]; and, receiving no reply, hurls his bomb. [We see] the smoke of the explosion (the sound of the explosion can be heard too). When the smoke clears there is no corridor and no N. A. on the fence, where the picture still flickers, only the door leading to the 'unmentionable place' stands out clearly. The door is thrown open, and A. A., clad only in his underwear, his colourless eyes glittering like molten stones, leaps off the surface of the fence and lands right beside N. A., who is standing in front of the fence contemplating the misty images in his mind. The picture fades from the fence.[120]

12　Film posters
(a) *A Wild Force* [Dikaya sila, 1916]
(b) *Life is a Moment, Art is Forever*
[Zhizn' – mig, Iskusstvo – vechno,
1916], starring Ivan Mosjoukine
(c) *The Abyss* [Bezdna, 1917]

(d) *Married by Satan* [Venchal ikh Satana, 1917]
(e) *The Autumn of a Woman* [Osen' zhenshchiny, 1917]
(f) *We Are Not Guilty of Their Blood!* [V ikh krovi my nepovinny! 1917]

Postscript

This book is about a specific period in film history and about its specific spectator. In 1965 Jack T. Munsey remarked on the first four years of cinema: 'As I reflect on the initial reactions to the motion picture, I cannot help but think of MacLuhan's assertion that "Medium is message." It has a ring of truth to it, at least during this earliest of phases.'[1]

I think that if we try to historicise the viewer we can extend this phase well into the 1910s. This thought came to me as I was reading Eileen Bowser's *The Transformation of Cinema* – the part where she is discussing the reception of the close-up and quotes a 1909 review referring to foreground action as being enacted 'by a race of giants and giantesses'. Bowser argues that, unlike people today, the historical spectator was sensitive to the film medium: 'What is to us a very small change in camera position may have seemed striking to that audience. In fact, the contemporary comments on these changes, or the memories of those who experienced them at the time, when filtered through a modern conception of a close camera position, have led to distortions or actual mistakes in the history of use of the close-up.'[2]

In this book I have tried to revive a historical spectator not yet deadened to the novelty of cinematic discourse – the medium-sensitive film viewer. But, having historicised the viewer, should we not think of doing the same with the figure of the film-maker? Let me quote a passage from Viktor Shklovsky's 1923 article 'Chaplin the Cop' that has been puzzling me ever since I read it. In it Shklovsky describes a gag from *Easy Street* which, however, does not look like a gag to me:

A terrible strongman appears on the scene [of action]. Chaplin pretends not to be scared. Chaplin walks away, the strongman follows him. They are moving away from the audience, but the scene is shot so that they seem to be constantly drawing nearer, backs ahead. This funny trick had been used before in one of Chaplin's early films showing him chasing a car on a motorcycle. Probably, the scene was shot from another car overtaking them. The resulting impression was that the motorcycle with Chaplin on it was pulling backwards towards the audience. The evident contradiction between the real direction of movement and the way we perceive it photographically causes laughter in the audience.[3]

I am sure no modern viewer would ever read this as a 'contradiction'. However, what puzzles me is not merely the fact that the audiences Shklovsky referred to were amused by a tracking shot, but rather, did Chaplin intentionally use tracking as a gag? And, if so, how many gags and subtleties envisaged by early film-makers are lost on the present-day generation of filmgoers?

The issue had been raised by the 'cinema of attractions' theory that I have repeatedly alluded to in this book. To pose the problem in a more general way, having agreed to discuss film history in terms of medium-sensitive spectators, can we also speak of medium-oriented messages? Or of a medium-specific period in film history? These questions exceed the limits of this book; however, I am convinced that by historicising the viewer we are taking a step towards a truer history of film.

Notes

FOREWORD

1 J. Staiger, *Interpreting Movies: Studies in the Historical Reception of American Cinema* (Princeton, NJ, 1992); R. E. Pearson and W. Uricchio, '"How to Be a Stage Napoleon": Vitagraph's Vision of History', *Persistence of Vision*, 1991, no. 9, pp. 75–89; W. Uricchio and R. E. Pearson, 'Films of Quality, High Art Films and Films de Luxe: Intertextuality and Reading Positions in the Vitagraph Films', *Journal of Films and Video*, winter 1989, vol. 41, no. 4, pp. 15–31; B. Klinger, 'Digressions at the Cinema: Reception and Mass Culture', *Cinema Journal*, summer 1989, no. 28, pp. 3–19, and *idem*, 'Much Ado about Excess: Genre, Mise-en-scène and the Woman in *Written on the Wind*', *Wide Angle*, vol. 11, no. 4, pp. 4–22; S. Neal, 'Melo Talk: On the Meaning and Use of the Term "Melodrama" in the American Trade Press' (Paper delivered to the BFI Melodrama Conference, London, 1992); M. Hansen, *Babel and Babylon: Spectatorship in American Silent Film* (Cambridge, MA, 1991).

INTRODUCTION

1 *Petrogradskii kino-zhurnal* [The Petrograd Cinema Journal], 1916, no. 1, p. 11.
2 See: A. D. Digmelov, '50 let nazad' [50 Years Ago], p. 3. Typescript in the V. Vishnevsky archive, GFF.
3 I. Yakovlev, 'Son nayavu' [A Daydream], *Novoe vremya* [New Times], no. 7155, 29 Jan. [10 Feb.] 1896, p. 2.
4 A. M. Gor'kii, 'Beglye zametki' [Fleeting Notes], *Nizhegorodskii listok* [The Nizhny Novgorod Newsletter], no. 182, 4 July 1896, p. 3. English translation from: R. Taylor and I. Christie (eds), *The Film Factory: Russian and Soviet Cinema in Documents 1896–1939* (London and Cambridge, MA, 1988), p. 25. This review (translated by Leda Swan) is also to be found in J. Leyda, *Kino: A History of the Russian and Soviet Film* (New York, 1973), pp. 407–9.
5 Ibid.
6 K. Irzykowski, *X muza* [The Tenth Muse] (Warsaw, 1957), p. 127.
7 Ibid., p. 128.
8 A. Blok, *Sobranie sochinenii* [Collected Works] (Moscow, Leningrad, 1962–3), vol. 8, p. 251.
9 'Stasov o kinematografe' [Stasov on the Cinematograph]. Excerpted in *Iskusstvo kino* [The Art of Cinema], 1957, no. 3, p. 128.
10 Yu. Tsivian, 'Portraits, Mirrors, Death: On Some Decadent Clichés in Early

Russian Films.' Paper presented to the *Painted Portraits in Cinema* conference, The Louvre Museum, April 1991. IRIS, 1992, nos 14–15, pp. 67–84.

11 O. V. Vysotskaya, 'Moi vospominaniya' [My Memoirs]. Unpublished mSS, IRLI (MSS division), no. 41, p. 42 verso. I am indebted to Roman Timenchik for this excerpt.

12 L. Andreev, 'O kino' [On Cinema], *Cine-Phono*, 1909, no. 1, p. 10.

13 D. G. Rossetti, *The Collected Works*, ed. W. M. Rossetti (London, 1886), vol. 1. Cited after: T. Ziolkowski, *Disenchanted Images* (Princeton, NJ, 1977), p. 107.

14 *Le Portrait mystérieux* [The Mysterious Portrait, 1899]; *L'Auberge du bon repos* [Comfort Inn, 1903]; *Le Portrait spirite* [The Ghostly Portrait, 1905]; *Le Menuet liliputien* [Liliputian Minuet, 1905]; *Les Affiches en goguette* [Posters on the Spree, 1906]; *Ali Borbouyou et Ali Boeuf-à-l'huile* [Ali Borbouyou and Ali Fried-Beef, 1907]; *Tricky Painter's Fate*, 1908.

15 Leyda, *Kino*, p. 408.

16 A. S. Pushkin, *Polnoe sobranie sochinenii* [Complete Works] (Moscow, 1937–49), vol. 2, part 1, poem no. 253.

17 M. Artsybashev, *Teni utra* [Morning Shadows] (Moscow, 1990), p. 95.

18 Z. Gippius, *Chertova kukla* [The Devil's Doll] (Moscow, 1911), p. 35.

19 Taylor and Christie, *The Film Factory*, p. 25.

20 Prince Senegambii [Fedor Otsep], 'Kinematograf i obryad zhizni' [The Cinematograph and the Ritual of Life], *Kine-zhurnal* [The Cinema Journal], 1917, no. 1/2, p. 68.

21 Z. Gippius, 'Naverno' [Probably], *Vershiny* [Peaks], 1914, no. 4, p. 10.

22 H. Bergson, *Creative Evolution* (A. Mitchell trans., New York, 1911), pp. 302–7.

23 V. Gei, 'Dva ritma' [Two Rhythms], *Teatral'naya gazeta* [The Theatre Newspaper], 1917, no. 4, p. 10.

24 Robert Schmutzler calls this quality of *art nouveau* 'biological romanticism' or 'biological historicism'. See: R. Schmutzler, *Art Nouveau* (New York, 1962), p. 250.

25 'Pisateli o kinematografe' [Writers on the Cinematograph], *Vestnik kinematografii* [The Cinematograph Herald], 1914, no. 88/8, p. 18.

26 A. Krainii [Z. Gippius], 'Sinema' [Cinema], *Zveno* [The Link] (Paris), 1926, no. 204, p. 3.

27 M. Voloshin, *Liki tvorchestva* [Faces of Creativity] (Leningrad, 1988), p. 118.

28 O. Mandel'shtam, *Razgovor o Dante* [A Conversation about Dante] (Moscow, 1967), p. 6.

29 J. Delandes, J. Richard, *Histoire comparée du cinéma* [A Comparative History of Cinema] (Tournai, 1968), vol. 2, p. 185.

30 L. Senelick, 'Boris Geyer and Cabaretic Playwriting', in: R. Russell and A. Barratt (eds), *Russian Theatre in the Age of Modernism* (New York, 1990), p. 45.

31 *Teatral'naya gazeta*, 1914, no. 19, p. 11. For notes on *Silent Witnesses* see: Yu. Tsivian (research), P. C. Usai, L. Codelli, C. Montanaro and D. Robinson (eds), *Silent Witnesses: Russian Films 1908–1919* (London, Pordenone, 1989), p. 230.

32 *Proektor* [The Projector], 1916, no. 21, p. 12.

33 O. Mandel'shtam, 'Sokhrani moyu rech'. . .' [Preserve My Speech. . .], *Mandel'shtamovskii sbornik* [Essays on Mandelshtam] (Moscow, 1991), p. 11.

34 Schmutzler, *Art Nouveau*, p. 11.

35 *Novoe vremya*, no. 13580, 1 (14) Jan., 1914, p. 14.

36 F. M., 'Tri kinematografa' [Three Cinematographs], *Cine-Phono*, 1914, no. 11, p. 22.

CHAPTER 1

1 The first cinema performances in Riga were given at Salamon's circus. (V. Pūce, 'Kinojauniba' [A Childhood at the Cinema], *Literatura un Māksla* [Literature and Art], 3 Sept. 1982, p. 16).

2 V. B. Chaikovskii, *Mladencheskie gody russkogo kino* [Infant Years of the Russian Cinema] (Moscow, 1928), p. 10.

3 I. N. Ignatov, 'Kinematograf v Rossii: Proshloe i budushchee' [The Cinematograph in Russia: Its Past and Future], TsGALI, 221/1, p. 3.

4 A. L. Pasternak, *Vospominaniya* [Memoirs] (Munich, 1933), p. 132.

5 A. Verner [Werner], 'Beglye zametki' [Fleeting Notes], p. 1. Typescript in the V. Vishnevsky archive, GFF.

6 Chaikovskii, *Mladencheskie gody*, pp. 12–13.

7 M. Ya. Landesman, *Tak pochinalosya kino: Rospovidi pro dozhovtnevii kinematograf* [That's How Cinema Began: Stories about the Cinematograph before the October Revolution] (Kiev, 1972), p. 31.

8 *Volshebnyi fonar': katalog na 1901–1903* [The Magic Lantern: Catalogue for 1901–1903] (Yekaterinograd, n.d.).

9 Lolo [Munshtein], 'Teatr elektricheskii i teatr dramaticheskii' [The Electric Theatre and the Dramatic Theatre], *Teatr* [Theatre], no. 1752, 18–19 Oct. 1915, p. 11.

10 V. Svyatlovskii, 'Vasil'evskii ostrov' [Vasilevsky Island], in: *Sedye goroda* [Grey Cities] (St Petersburg, 1912), p. 45.

11 A. Akhropov, *Tadzhikskoe kino* [The Tadzhik Cinema] (Dushanbe, 1971), p. 6.

12 R. Musil, 'Ansätze zu neuer Aesthetik: Bemerkungen über eine Dramaturgie des Films' [Towards a New Aesthetic. Notes on the Dramatic Theory of Film], *Der Neue Merkur* [The New Mercury], (Munich), 1924–25, no. 8, p. 489.

13 R. Sieburth, 'The Music of the Future', in: D. Hollier (ed.), *A New History of French Literature* (London, 1989), p. 797.

14 M. A. Voloshin, 'Mysli o teatre' [Thoughts on Theatre], *Apollon* [Apollo], 1910, no. 5, pp. 39–40.

15 N. Shebuev, *Negativy* [Negatives] (Moscow, 1903), p. 112.

16 See pp. 109–13, 149–54.

17 A. Koiranskii, 'Kintop' [Ger. das Kintopp: 'The Flicks'], *Nash ponedel'nik* [Our Monday Paper], no. 2, 26 Nov. 1907, p. 5.

18 Quoted from: G. Struve, *Russkaya literatura v izgnanii* [Russian Literature in Exile] (New York, 1956), p. 312.

19 Chaikovskii, *Mladencheskie gody*, p. 15.

20 F. K. Sologub, 'V kinematografe' [At the Cinematograph], IRLI, 289/1/2, p. 279.

21 R. Garms [Harms], *Filosofiya fil'ma* [The Philosophy of Film] (Leningrad, 1927), p. 70. The original title of Harms's book was *Philosophie des Films: Seine aesthetischen und Metaphysischen Grundlagen* [The Philosophy of Film: Its Aesthetic and Metaphysical Principles] (Leipzig, 1926).

22 'Kazn' Cholgosha v kinematografe' [The Execution of Czołgosz in the Cinematograph], *Novoe vremya*, 1902, no. 20, p. 637.

23 S. M. Volkonskii, *Rodina: Moi vospominaniya* [Motherland: My Memories] (No place of publication, n. d.), p. 224.

24 L. Andreyev, 'Pis'mo o teatre' [A Letter on Theatre], *Polnoe sobranie sochinenii* [Complete Works] (St Petersburg, 1913), vol. 8, pp. 305–16. For an English translation see: R. Taylor and I. Christie (eds), *The Film Factory: Russian and Soviet Cinema in Documents 1896–1939* (London, 1988), pp. 27–31.

25 M. Brailovskii, 'Velikii Nemoi' [The Great Silent], *Cine-Phono*, 1914, no. 3, p. 25.

26 *Hätte ich das Kino! Die Schriftsteller und der Stummfilm* [If Only I Had Cinema! Writers and the Silent Film] (Munich, 1976), pp. 69–70.

27 P. Boborykin, 'Besedy o teatre' [Conversations on Theatre], *Russkoe slovo* [The Russian Word], no. 142, 21 July 1913, p. 2.

28 Koiranskii, 'Kintop', p. 5.

29 L. O. [L. Ostroumov?], 'Lenta zhizni' [The Ribbon of Life], *Pegas* [Pegasus], 1916, no. 4, p. 52.

30 A. Benua [Benois], 'O kinematografe' [On the Cinematograph], *Aleksandr Benua razmyshlyaet* [Alexander Benois Reflects] (Moscow, 1968), p. 108. That Benois's term for cinema was also the name of a famous French nude model was coincidental.

31 S. Gorodetskii, 'Zhiznopis' [Biograph], *Kinematograf* [The Cinematograph], 1915, no. 2, p. 3.

32 M. Swartz, 'An Overview of Cinema on the Fairgrounds', *Journal of Popular Film and Television*, 1982, vol. 15, no. 3, p. 105.

33 A. Gaudreault, T. Gunning, 'Le Cinéma des premiers temps: un défi à l'histoire du cinéma?' [Cinema in its Early Years: A Challenge to Cinema History?] in: J. Aumont, A. Gaudreault and M. Marie (eds), *Histoire du cinéma: Nouvelles approches* [Cinema History: New Approaches] (Paris, 1989), pp. 49–63.

34 T. Gunning, 'An Aesthetic of Astonishment: Early Film and the (In)credulous Spectator', *Art and Text*, spring 1989, no. 34, pp. 31–45.

35 Chaikovskii, *Mladencheskie gody*, pp. 20–1.

36 B. V. Dushen, 'Beglye vospominaniya' [Fleeting Memoirs], p. 2. Typescript in the V. Vishnevsky archive, GFF.

37 N. I. Orlov, 'Pervye kino'smki v Rossii' [The First Film Shootings in Russia], pp. 1–3. Typescript in the V. Vishnevsky archive, GFF.

38 Garms, *Filosofiya fil'ma*, p. 67.

39 Swartz, 'An Overview', p. 108.

40 Dushen, 'Beglye', p. 2; Ignatov, 'Kinematograf', p. 50.

41 T. Vechorka, *Magnolii* [Magnolias] (Tiflis, 1916), p. 9.

42 Ignatov, 'Kinematograf', p. 50.

43 L. Ya. Gurevich [N. Repnin], 'Teatral'nye ocherki' [Theatre Essays], *Slovo* [The Word], no. 297, 6 Nov. 1907.

44 'Flanyor', 'Kinematografiya' [Cinematography], *Zhizn'* [Life], no. 1, 5 Jan. 1909. The Moscow floods were the subject of a Pathé newsreel made by Georges Meyer.

45 Ibid.

46 N. M. Zorkaya, *Na rubezhe stoletii: u istokov massovogo iskusstva v Rossii 1900–1910 godov* [At the Turn of the Century: The Sources of Mass Art in Russia] (Moscow, 1976), p. 134; M. A. Beketova, *Aleksandr Blok: Biograficheskii ocherk* [Alexander Blok: A Biographical Essay] (Petrograd, 1922), pp. 260–1.

47 Ignatov, 'Kinematograf', p. 3.

48 M. Blonskii, 'Druzheskii sovet' [Friendly Advice], *Kinoteatr i zhizn'* [The Cinema Theatre and Life], 1914, no. 6, p. 2.

49 Volkonskii, *Rodina*, p. 244.

50 E. Maurin, *Kinematograf v prakticheskoi zhizni* [The Cinematograph in Practical Life] (Petrograd, 1916), p. 134.

51 Ibid., p. 137.

52 A. B., 'Kinematograf' [The Cinematograph], *Bogema* [Bohemia], 1915, no. 5/6, p. 7.

53 P. Nilus, 'Torzhestvo sovremennogo kinematografa' [The Triumph of the Modern Cinematograph], *Proektor* [The Projector], 1917, no 1/2, p. 4.

54 Pūce, 'Kinojauniba', 17 Sept. 1982, p. 16.

55 TsGALI, 989/1/153.

56 I. Sel'vinskii, *Ulyalaevshchina* [Ulyalaev's Band] (Moscow, 1927), p. 83.

57 Ignatov, 'Kinematograf', p. 90.

58 Sologub, 'V kinematografe', p. 279.

59 A. Blok, 'Na zheleznoi doroge' [On the Railway], *Sobranie sochinenii v shesti tomakh* [Collected Works in Six Volumes] (Leningrad, 1980), vol. 2, p. 154.

60 I. Lukash, 'Teatr ulitsy' [The Theatre of the Street], *Sovremennoe slovo* [The Modern Word], no. 2539, 25 April 1918, p. 1.

61 L. Kirby, 'The Urban Spectator and the Crowd in Early American Train Films', *Iris*, summer 1990, no. 11, p. 52.

62 Chaikovskii, *Mladencheskie gody*, p. 10.

63 Maurin, *Kinematograf*, p. 127.

64 'Vliyanie kinematografa na zrenie: Beseda s prof. L. G. Bellyarminovym' [The Effect of the Cinematograph on the Eyes: An Interview with Prof. L. G. Bellyarminov], *Peterburgskaya gazeta* [The Petersburg Newspaper], no. 8, 9 Jan. 1908, p. 2. See also: N. V., 'Kinematograf i zrenie' [The Cinematograph and Sight], *Cine-Phono*, 1909/10, no. 22, p. 9; G. Tel'berg, 'Vliyanie kinematografa na zrenie. (Mnenie prof. Kazanskogo universiteta G. Agababova)' [The Effect of the Cinematograph on the Eyes. (The Opinion of Prof. G. Agababov of Kazan University)], *Cine-Phono*, 1909/10, no. 3, p. 12; Dr. Yu. S. Vainshtein, 'Vreden li kinematograf dlya zreniya. (Iz doklada sdelannogo na zasedanii obshchestva vrachei)' [Is the Cinematograph Bad for the Eyes. (From a paper presented at a conference of the Russian Medical Association)], *Vestnik kinematografii* [Cinematograph Herald], 1912, no. 31, pp. 18–20; 'Kinematograf i zdorov'e' [The Cinematograph and Health], *Zhurnal za sem' dnei* [The Seven-Day Magazine], 1913, no. 38, pp. 817–18.

65 T. Gunning, ' Heard Over the Phone: The Lonely Villa and the de Lorde Tradition of the Terrors of Technology'. Paper delivered to the SCS Conference, Washington, DC, 1990.

66 Ya. A. Zhdanov, 'Po Rossii s kinogovoryashchimi kartinami' [Around Russia with Talking Pictures], p. 9. Typescript in the Soviet Film Section of VGIK.

67 Maurin, *Kinematograf*, p. 12.

68 Quoted after: M. Ratgaus, 'Kuzmin – kinozritel'' [Kuzmin as Film Spectator], *Kinovedcheskie zapiski* [Film Studies Notes], 1992, no. 13, p. 61.

69 E. Altenloh, *Zur Soziologie des Kino: Die Kino-Unternehmung und die sozialen Schichten ihrer Besucher* [Towards a Sociology of Cinema: The Cinema Business and the Social Strata of its Visitors] (Jena, 1914).

70 Review of the above, *Cine-Phono*, 1914, no. 13, p. 35.

71 Ignatov, 'Kinematograf', p. 2.

72 Koiranskii, 'Kintop', p. 5.

73 A. Serafimovich, 'Mashinnoe nadvigaetsya' [The Machine Age Approaches], *Russkie vedomosti* [The Russian Gazette], 1 Jan. 1912. This translation is taken from R. Taylor, *The Politics of the Soviet Cinema, 1917–1929* (Cambridge, 1979), p. 7.

74 K. and O. Koval'skie, 'O kinemo-teatrakh' [On Cinema Theatres], *Studiya* [The Studio], 1912, no. 25, p. 8. 'Glupyshkin' (or sometimes 'Durashkin') ['Dopey'] was the Russian name for the French-born film comedian of early Italian cinema, André Deed, known in Italian as 'Cretinetti' and in English as 'Foolshead' or 'Dopey'. Max Linder (1883–1925) was an early French film comedian who was particularly popular in Russia.

75 Gurevich, 'Teatral'nye ocherki'.

76 A. Belyi, 'Sinematograf', in: *Arabeski* [Arabesques] (Moscow, 1911).

77 After Bely's article it became customary for those attacking the idea of the essentially collective nature (*sobornost*) of the new theatre to buttress their

arguments with references to cinema. A distant echo of this approach can be seen in Boris Eikhenbaum's article, 'Problemy kinostilistiki' [Problems of Cinema Stylistics], in: *Poetika kino* (Moscow, Leningrad, 1927). For English translations of *Poetika kino* see: R. Taylor (ed.), *The Poetics of Cinema: Russian Poetics in Translation*, no. 9 (Oxford, 1982); and H. Eagle (ed.), *Russian Formalist Film Theory* (Ann Arbor, MI, 1981).

78 Belyi, 'Sinematograf', p. 349.

79 G. I. Chulkov, 'Zhivaya fotografiya' [A Living Photograph], *Zolotoe runo* [The Golden Fleece], 1908, no. 6, p. 11.

80 S. Lyubosh, *Vestnik kinomatografii*, 1913, no. 9, p. 3.

81 A. R. Kugel', *Utverzhdenie teatra* [Consolidating the Theatre] (Moscow, 1923), p. 181.

82 M. Gor'kii, 'Beglye zametki' [Fleeting Notes], *Nizhegorodskii listok*, no. 182, 4 July 1896, p. 3.

83 'Iz provintsial'nykh gazet' [From the Provincial Papers], *Novoe slovo* [New Word], 1896, no. 11, p. 189.

84 M. Gorkii, 'Otomstil . . .' [Revenge], *Polnoe sobranie sochinenii* [Complete Works] (Moscow, 1969), vol. 2, p. 500.

85 Prince Senegambii, 'Kinematograf i obryad zhizni' [The Cinematograph and the Ritual of Life], *Kine-zhurnal*, 1917, no. 1/2, p. 87.

86 M. Hansen, *Babel and Babylon: Spectatorship in American Silent Film* (Cambridge, MA, 1991), pp. 232, 353.

87 Homo Novus [A. Kugel'], 'Zametki' [Notes], *Teatr i iskusstvo* [Theatre and Art], 1913, no. 35, p. 682.

88 Zorkaya, *Na rubezhe*, pp. 127–30.

89 V. Mazurkevich, 'Kinematograf' [The Cinematograph], *Vsya teatral'no-muzy-kal'naya Rossiya* [All Theatrical and Musical Russia], (Petrograd, 1914–15), p. 102.

90 K. Varlamov, 'Kak ya smotryu na kinematograf' [How I Look at the Cinematograph], *Kino-teatr i zhizn'* [The Cinema Theatre and Life], 1913, no. 5.

91 Programme of the Renaissance cinema, St Petersburg, 2–8 May 1909. The RKM collection.

92 Chaikovskii, *Mladencheskie gody*, p. 11.

93 Garms, *Filosofiya*, p. 71.

94 Ignatov, 'Kinematograf', p. 11.

95 S. Cavell, *The World Viewed: Reflections on the Ontology of Film* (New York, 1971), p. 11.

96 A. Belyi, 'Gorod' [The City], *Nash ponedel'nik* [Our Monday Paper], 9 Nov. 1907, no. 1.

97 Voloshin, 'Mysli'.

98 A. Blok, *Pis'ma Aleksandra Bloka k E. P. Ivanovu* [Letters of Alexander Blok to E. P. Ivanov] (Moscow, Leningrad, 1936), pp. 31, 32.

99 R. Abel, 'American Film and the French Literary Avant-Garde (1914–1924)', *Contemporary Literature*, 1975, vol. 17, no. 1, p. 104.

100 Ibid.

101 G. Sadoul, *Vseobshchaya istoriya kino* [A General History of Cinema] (Moscow, 1958–82), vol. 2, p. 206.

102 A. Kaes (ed.), *Kino-Debatte* [Cinema Debate] (Munich, 1978), p. 72.

103 'Pis'mo v redaktsiyu' [A Letter to the Editor], *Vestnik kinematografii*, 1913, no. 17, p. 19.

104 Programme of the Saturn cinema, St Petersburg, 21 April, 1913. The RKM Collection.

105 A. Bukhov, 'Max Linder', *Sinii zhurnal* [The Blue Journal], 1912, no. 42, p. 18.

106 A. Bukhov, 'O kinematograficheskikh avtorakh' [On Cinematograph Authors], *Kinematograf* [The Cinematograph], 1915, no. 1, p. 9.

107 Protei [Proteus], 'Kinematografy' [Cinematographs], *Teatr i zhizn'* [Theatre and Life], 1913, no. 4, p. 2.

108 Ignatov, 'Kinematograf', p. 11.

109 Ibid., p. 3.

110 E. Panofsky, 'Style and Medium in the Motion Pictures', in: G. Mast and M. Cohen (eds), *Film Theory and Criticism* (New York, 1985), p. 216.

111 N. Lopatin, 'Kinematograf' [The Cinematograph], *Cine-Phono*, 1915, no. 27, p. 19.

112 Prince Senegambii, 'Kinematograf i teatr' [The Cinematograph and the Theatre], *Kine-zhurnal*, 1916, no. 1/2, pp. 69, 70.

113 Ibid., p. 70.

114 Lopatin, 'Kinematograf', p. 19.

115 P. Tavrichanin, 'Iskusstvo i kinematograf' [Art and Cinema], *Vestnik kinematografii*, 1912, no. 52, p. 3.

116 Lopatin, 'Kinematograf', p. 19.

117 K. Chukovskii, *Nat Pinkerton i sovremennaya literatura* [Nat Pinkerton and Contemporary Literature] (Moscow, 1908).

118 TsGALI, 416/1/203, p. 13.

119 L. Dobychin, 'Gorod En' [The Town of N], *Rodnik* [The Spring], 1988, no. 10 (22), p. 79.

120 L. May, *Screening Out the Past: The Birth of Mass Culture and the Motion Picture Industry* (New York, Oxford, 1980), p. 158.

121 'Khronika' [Chronicle of Events], *Vestnik kinematografii*, 1913, no. 18, p. 18.

122 'Eks-korol' Manuel' na pokoe' [Ex-King Manuel in Retirement], *Vestnik kinematografii*, 1913, no. 85/86, p. 39.

123 Chaikovskii, *Mladencheskie gody*, pp. 13, 14.

124 'Sinematograf', [The Cinematograph], *Cine-Phono*, 1912/13, no. 13, p. 25.

125 Koiranskii, 'Kintop', p. 5.

126 *Kino*, 1929, no. 39, p. 3.

127 M. Boitler, 'Kakim dolzhen byt' ideal'nyi kinoteatr?', *Kino*, 1928, no. 40, p. 3.

128 V. Muromskii, 'O kinematografe' [On the Cinematograph], *Den'* [The Day], 4 Nov. 1913.

129 A. Mackintosh, *Symbolism and Art Nouveau* (London, 1975), p. 54.

130 E. Beskin, 'Listki' [Jottings], *Teatral'naya gazeta* [The Theatre Paper], 1916, no. 1, p. 8.

131 *Zhurnal zhurnalov* [The Journal of Journals], 1915, no. 2, p. 10.

132 B. Salt, *Film Style and Technology: History and Analysis* (London, 1984), p. 120.

133 Arno [Arnaud?], 'Kinematograf' [The Cinematograph], *Moskovskie vedomosti*, 1917, no. 53, p. 2.

134 Ignatov, 'Kinematograf', p. 59.

135 Maurin, *Kinematograf*, p. 124.

136 W. Schivelbusch, *Disenchanted Night: The Industrialization of Light in the Nineteenth Century* (Berkeley, 1988), p. 148.

137 M. A. Rashkovskaya, 'Poet v mire, mir v poete' [The Poet in the World, the World in the Poet], *Vstrechi s proshlym* [Meetings with the Past] (Moscow, 1982), no. 4, p. 144.

CHAPTER 2

1 M. Hansen, *Babel and Babylon: Spectatorship in American Silent Film* (Cambridge, MA, 1991), p. 4. See p. 297 for a bibliography on 'apparatus theory'.

2   J.-L. Boudry, 'Le Dispositif' [The Apparatus], *Communications* (Paris), 1975, no. 23, pp. 56–72. The reference is to Plato's *Republic*, book VII. Socrates puts it to Glaucon that for men chained in a cave, and able to see only the shadows of objects cast on a wall, it is the shadows that represent reality, not the objects themselves.

3   K. Bal'mont, *Stikhotvoreniya* [Poems] (Moscow, 1969), p. 96.

4   V. Bryusov, *Vesy* [The Scales], 1904, no. 11, p. 50.

5   F. Sologub, 'Netlennoe plemya' [The Imperishable Race], *Teatr i iskusstvo* [Theatre and Art], 1912, no. 51, p. 1021.

6   A. Krantsfel'd, 'Velikii nemoi' [The Great Silent], *Teatr i kino* [Theatre and Cinema] (Odessa), 1916, no. 1, p. 17.

7   R. Timenchik, 'K simvolike tramvaya v russkoi poezii' [On the Symbolism of the Tram in Russian Poetry], *Semiotika: Trudy po znakovym sistemam XXI* [Semiotics: Transactions on Sign Systems XXI] (Tartu, 1987), p. 138. Also by the same author: 'K simvolike telefona v russkoi poezii' [On the Symbolism of the Telephone in Russian Poetry], *Semiotika XXII*, (Tartu, 1988), p. 157.

8   K. Chukovskii, *Nat Pinkerton i sovremennaya literatura* [Nat Pinkerton and Contemporary Literature] (Moscow, 1908), p. 5.

9   V. B. Chaikovskii, *Mladencheskie gody russkogo kino* [Infant Years of the Russian Cinema] (Moscow, 1928), p. 10.

10 A. Norman [Vitte], 'Fantomy' [Phantoms], in: *Poemy: Stat'i o teatre* [Poems: Articles on Theatre] (Tashkent, 1920), p. 9.

11 N. U-el', 'Zhizn' – kinematograf' [Life is a Cinematograph], *Vestnik kinemato-grafii* [The Cinematograph Herald], 1912, no. 50, p. 16.

12 On 4 May 1897 140 people died when a marquee caught fire at the annual Charity Bazaar on the Rue Jean Goujon just off the Champs Elysées. The alleged cause was the negligence of the projectionist, who tried to relight the ether-gas projection lamp with a match. The tragedy caused a great stir throughout Europe and America (the victims were mainly from the upper classes; there were many children among them) and led to safer projection techniques, stricter fire precautions in public places, and to a search for less flammable film. (P. Hugnes, M. Marnin, *Le Cinéma français: Le Muët* [French Cinema: The Silent Film] (Paris, 1986), pp. 44–5).

13 E. Maurin, *Kinematograf v prakticheskoi zhizni* [The Cinematograph in Practical Life] (Petrograd, 1916), p. 122.

14 *Nasha nedelya* [Our Week], 1911, no. 5, p. 23.

15 Yu. Krichevskii, 'V kinematografe' [At the Cinematograph], *Nevod* [The Dragnet] (Petrograd, 1918), p. 22.

16 K. Brownlow, 'Silent Films: What was the Right Speed?', *Sight and Sound*, summer 1980, pp. 164–7; B. Salt, *Film Style and Technology* (London, 1984), p. 203.

17 Yu. Tsiv'yan, 'Dmitrii Kirsanov, ili poetika pauzy' [Dmitrii Kirsanov, or the Poetics of the Pause], *Kino* (Riga), 1981, no. 7, pp. 28–9.

18 D. Kirsanoff, 'Les problèmes de la photogénie', *Cinéa-ciné pour tous* [Cinema for All], 1926, no. 62, pp. 9–10.

19 G. K. Chesterton, 'On the Movies', in: *Generally Speaking: A Book of Essays* (London, 1937), p. 234.

20 S. M. Eizenshtein, *Izbrannye proizvedeniya v 6 tomakh* [Selected Works in 6 volumes] (Moscow, 1964–71), vol. 1, p. 321. This translation taken from: Sergei Eisenstein, *Immoral Memories. An Autobiography*, (translated by Herbert Marshall) (London, 1985), p. 88.

21 V. Gei, 'Dva ritma' [Two Rhythms], *Teatral'naya gazeta* [The Theatre Paper], 1917, no. 4, p. 10.

22 'Mel'kanie' [Flickering], *Cine-Phono*, 1912/13, no. 13, p. 23.

23 I. Petrovskii, 'Kinodrama ili kinopovest" [Cine-drama or Cine-story], *Proektor* [The Projector], 1916, nos 18, 19 & 20, pp. 2–3. Ivan Ilyich Mozzhukhin [Mosjoukine] (1889–1939) played romantic leads, emigrated in 1920 and then worked mainly in France. Olga Vladimirovna Gzovskaya (1884–1962) was an actress in the Moscow Art Theatre before becoming a popular film actress. Vladimir Vasilyevich Maximov (1880–1937), a very popular romantic actor, also appeared in many Soviet films. Vitold Alfonsovich Polonsky (1879–1919) was one of the most popular pre-Revolutionary romantic actors.

24 I. Mozzhukhin, 'V chem defekt?' [What's wrong?], *Teatral'naya Gazeta* [The Theatre Paper], 1914, no. 30, p. 13.

25 N. Shpikovskii, 'A vse-taki khorosh' [But He's a Good Guy Nonetheless], *Sovetskii ekran* [The Soviet Screen], 1925, no. 26 (30), p. 16.

26 Aleko, 'V chem gore?' [What's the Problem?], *Pegas*, 1915, no. 2, p. 59.

27 On the question of cinematic tempo in the rendering of historical material by Tynyanov and FEKS see: Yu. M. Lotman, Yu. G. Tsivian, 'SVD: zhanr melodramy i istoriya' [SVD: The Genre of Melodrama and History], in: *Tyn'yanovskii sbornik: Pervye Tyn'yanovskie chteniya* [Essays in Honour of Yu. N. Tyn'yanov: First Tyn'yanov Readings] (Riga, 1984), pp. 69–72.

28 TsGIAL, 733/182/166, p. 31 verso.

29 N. A. Savvin, 'Kinematograf na sluzhbe u istorii i istorii literatury' [The Cinematograph at the Service of History and the History of Literature], *Vestnik vospitaniya* [The Education Herald], 1914, no. 8, pp. 195–6. For notes on *Princess Tarakanova* and *The Year 1812* see: Yu. Tsiv'yan (research), P. C. Usai, L. Codelli, C. Montanaro and D. Robinson (eds), *Silent Witnesses: Russian Films 1908–1919* (London, Pordenone, 1989), pp. 96 and 158.

30 *Zhizn' i sud* [Life and the Lawcourts], 1915, no. 18, p. 15.

31 TsGIAL, 766/22/33.

32 G. C. Pratt, *Spellbound in Darkness: A History of the Silent Film* (New York, 1973), p. 18.

33 V. Tyurin, *Zhivaya fotografiya* [A Living Photograph] (St Petersburg, 1898), p. 5.

34 R. Garms (Harms), *Filosofiya fil'ma* [The Philosphy of Film] (Leningrad, 1927), p. 53.

35 Ibid., pp. 53–4.

36 For the description of magical effects produced by reverse diving see H. Münsterberg, *The Film. A Psychological Study: The Silent Photoplay in 1916* (New York, 1972), p. 15. This work was first published in 1916 with the title *The Photoplay: A Psychological Study.*

37 B. Salt, *Film Style and Technology* (London, 1984), p. 47.

38 LGITMIK Archives, lecture IV.

39 A. Koiranskii, 'Kintop', *Nash ponedel'nik* [Our Monday Paper], no. 2, 26 Nov. 1907, p. 5.

40 R. Tun, 'Problema vremeni v kino' [The Problem of Time in Cinema], *Kino-zhurnal A. R. K.* [A. R. K. Cinema Journal], 1925, no. 3, p. 24.

41 N. A. Umov, 'Kharakternye cherty i zadachi sovremennoi estestvenno-nauchnoi mysli: Rech' na obshchem sobranii chlenov II Mendeleevskogo s"ezda (21 Dek. 1911)' [Characteristic Features and Tasks of Contemporary Thought in the Natural Sciences: A Speech given at the Plenary Session of the Second Mendeleyev Congress (21 Dec. 1911)], *Dnevnik vtorogo Mendeleevskogo s"ezda po obshchei i prikladnoi khimii i fizike v Sankt-Peterburge* [Journal of the Second Mendeleyev Congress on General and Applied Chemistry and Physics in St Petersburg], 1911, vol. 5, pp. 19–21. I am indebted to Georgi Levinton for bringing this source to my attention.

42 Ibid.
43 Azr. [A. Zenger?], 'Kinematograf' [The Cinematograph], *Zritel'* [The Spectator], 1905, no. 6, p. 7. The passage refers to the film described above by Alexander Koiransky.
44 M. 'Iz pesen XX veka' [From the Songs of the XX Century], *Vestnik kinematografii*, 1911, no. 1, p. 2.
45 V. V. Khlebnikov, *Stikhotvoreniya, poemy, dramy, proza* [Verse, Poems, Drama, Prose] (Moscow, 1986), p. 333. For an English translation by E. J. Brown see: *Velimir Khlebnikov: Snake Train*, ed. Gay Kern (Ann Arbor, MI, 1976), pp. 125–31.
46 I. N. Ignatov, 'Kinematograf v Rossii: Proshloe i budushchee' [The Cinematograph in Russia: Its Past and Future], TsGALI, 221/1/3, p. 16.
47 V. Gaidarov, *V teatre i kino* [In Theatre and Cinema] (Moscow, 1966), p. 89.
48 V. V. Mayakovskii, *Sobranie sochinenii v 8 tomakh* [Collected Works in 8 vols] (Moscow, 1968), vol. 1, p. 183. There is an English translation of the whole poem in: V. Mayakovskii, *Selected Works in Three Volumes* (Moscow, 1986), vol. II, pp. 49–50. The poem is also sometimes translated as 'War and the Universe'. Although in modern Russian the title 'Voina i mir' is spelt the same way as Tolstoy's epic *War and Peace* [Voina i mir], in the old, pre-Soviet orthography the two possible meanings ('world'/'universe' and 'peace') were distinguished by different forms of the letter 'i' in the word 'mir'.
49 On Mayakovsky's use of the 'reversed-time' stunt in connection with cinema see: T. Miczka, 'Filmowe eksperimenty Włodzimierza Majakowskiego' [The Film Experiments of Vladimir Mayakovsky], *Kino* (Warsaw), vol. 8, 1979. It has been noted that Mayakovsky's poem could probably not have been written before the age of cinema: E. J. Brown, *Mayakovsky: A Poet in the Revolution* (Princeton, NJ, 1973, p. 319.
50 Mavich [M. Vavich?], 'Postnye temy' [Lenten Themes], *Cine-Phono*, 1914, no. 1, pp. 23–4. A reference to Khlebnikov's poem mentioned in note 44.
51 M. B. Yampol'skii, 'Zvezdnyi yazyk kino' [Cinema's Language of the Stars], *Kino* (Riga), 1985, no. 10, pp. 28–9.
52 Eizenshtein, *Izbrannye*, vol. 1, p. 321. The translation is from *Immoral Memories*, pp. 88–9.
53 Eizenshtein, *Izbrannye*, vol. 3, p. 605.
54 J. Leyda, *Kino: A History of the Russian and Soviet Film* (New York, 1973), p. 85.
55 S. Yablonskii, 'Kinematograf' [The Cinematograph], *Russkoe slovo* [Russian Word], no. 269, 6 Dec. 1906, p. 3.
56 A. Averchenko, *Dyuzhina nozhei v spinu revolyutsii* [A Dozen Knives in the Back of the Revolution] (Paris, 1921), p. 9.
57 Ibid., pp. 10–12. The dates of the four pre-Revolutionary Russian Dumas [parliaments] were: 1906, 1907, 1907–11, and 1912–17.

CHAPTER 3

1 A. Prokopenko, 'Kuprin i kino' [Kuprin and Cinema], *Iskusstvo kino* [The Art of Cinema], 1960, no. 8, pp. 119–20.
2 L. L. Sabaneev, 'Ekran i muzyka' [Screen and Music], *Teatral'naya gazeta* [The Theatre Paper], 1914, no. 27, p. 12.
3 Cited in: E. Simeon, 'Music in German Cinema before 1918', in: P. C. Usai and L. Codelli (eds), *Before Caligari: German Cinema, 1895–1920* (Pordenone, 1990), p. 90.

4   Sabaneev, 'Ekran i muzyka', p. 12.
5   Martin Marks in a talk given at SCS Annual Conference held at the University of Southern California, 25 May 1991.
6   K. S. Stanislavskii, *Sobranie sochinenii* [Collected Works] (Moscow, 1960), vol. 7, p. 614. Yevgeni Bagrationovich Vakhtangov (1883–1922), director, actor and drama teacher, famous for his 'psychological' expressionist style, remained active in the theatre after the October Revolution.
7   D. Robinson, *Music of the Shadows* (Pordenone, 1990), p. 8.
8   C. Musser, *Before the Nickelodeon. Edwin S. Porter and the Edison Manufacturing Company* (Berkeley, Los Angeles, London, 1991), pp. 54–5.
9   B. V. Dushen, 'Beglye vospominaniya' [Fleeting Memoirs], p. 1. Typescript in the V. Vishnevsky archives, GFF.
10 B. Likhachev, *Kino v Rossii* [Cinema in Russia] (Leningrad, 1927), p. 34.
11 A. Anoshchenko, 'Iz poluzabytoi epokhi' [From a Half-forgotten Age], pp. 1–2. Typescript in the V. Vishnevsky archives, GFF. Alexander Dmitrievich Anoshchenko-Anod was a piano accompanist, film journalist, director, scriptwriter and lecturer at GIK.
12 Ibid.
13 E. Z. [Efim Zozulya?], 'Mucheniki kinematografa' [Martyrs of the Cinematograph], *Vsemirnaya panorama* [World Panorama], 1912, no. 257 (12), p. 13.
14 S. Sel'skii, 'Muzykal'naya improvizatsiya v kinematografe' [Musical Improvisation in the Cinematograph], *Kinematograf* (Rostov-on-Don), 1915, no. 4/5, p. 11.
15 Anoshchenko, 'Iz poluzabytoi epokhi', p. 13.
16 Cited in: Yu. Tsivian (research), P. C. Usai, L. Codelli, C. Montanaro and D. Robinson (eds), *Silent Witnesses: Russian Films, 1908–1919* (London, Pordenone 1989), p. 96.
17 A. L., 'Muzyka v kinematografe' [Music in the Cinematograph], *Kine-Zhurnal* [The Cinema Journal], 1911, no. 2, pp. 8–9.
18 Sabaneev, 'Ekran i muzyka', p. 12.
19 K. Brownlow, *The Parade's Gone By . . .* (London, 1968), p. 338.
20 'Koe-chto o muzykal'noi illyustratsii' [A Thing or Two About Musical Illustration], *Vestnik kinematografii* [Cinematograph Herald], 1913, no. 17, p. 19.
21 Yu. N. Tyn'yanov, *Poetika. Istoriya literatury. Kino* [Poetics. Literary History. Cinema] (Moscow, 1977), p. 322.
22 E. Panofsky, 'Style and Medium in the Motion Pictures', in: G. Mast and M. Cohen (eds), *Film Theory and Criticism* (New York, 1985), p. 156.
23 R. Garms [Harms], *Filosofiya fil'ma* [The Philosophy of Film] (Leningrad, 1927), p. 79.
24 T. W. Adorno, H. Eisler, *Komposition für den Film* [Composing for Film] (Munich, 1969), p. 333.
25 M. Hansen, *Babel and Babylon: Spectatorship in American Silent Film* (Cambridge, MA, 1991), p. 43.
26 A. Belyi, *Arabeski* (Moscow, 1911), p. 350.
27 G. I. Chulkov, 'Zhivaya fotografiya' [Living Photograph], *Zolotoe runo* [The Golden Fleece], 1908, no. 6, p. 11.
28 V. B. Chaikovskii, *Mladencheskie gody russkogo kino* [Infant Years of the Russian Cinema] (Moscow, 1928), p. 16.
29 Panofsky, 'Style and Medium', p. 156.
30 I. Khudyakov, 'Novaya otrasl' iskusstva' [A New Brand of Art], *Vestnik kinematografii*, 1911, no. 9, p. 11.
31 O. Leonidov, *Stikhi* [Verses] (Moscow, 1914), p. 41.
32 Dushen, 'Beglye', p. 2.
33 A. V. Goldobin, B. M. Azancheev, *Pianist-illyustrator kinematograficheskikh*

kartin [Accompanying Cinematograph Pictures on the Piano] (Kostroma, 1912), p. 419.

34 This conference was held at the Institute of Language and Literature of the Latvian Academy of Sciences on 14 April 1986. The point was made by Anita Rozkalne.

35 Sabaneev, 'Ekran i muzyka', p. 12.

36 L. G., 'Organichnost' kinematografa' [The Organic Nature of the Cinematograph], *Teatral'naya gazeta*, 1914, no. 29, p. 5.

37 D. S. Merezhkovskii, 'O kinematografe' [On the Cinematograph], *Vestnik kinematografii*, 1914, no. 88/8, p. 18. See pp. 8–9.

38 M. S-ev [L. Sabaneev?], 'Muzyka v elektro-teatrakh' [Music in Electric Theatres], *Vestnik kinematografii*, 1914, no. 3/83, p. 11.

39 Chaikovskii, *Mladencheskie gody*, p. 16.

40 S-ev, 'Muzyka'.

41 Ibid.

42 L. G., 'Organichnost'', p. 5.

43 Khudyakov, 'Novaya otrasl'', no. 9, p. 11.

44 Anoshchenko, 'Iz poluzabytoi epokhi', p. 7. A 1913 review gives an idea of Khudyakov's skills as composer and conductor: 'Last week Khanzhonkov's cinema showed Władisław Starewicz's *The Terrible Vengeance* [Strashnaya mest', 1913], with musical illustration by I. N. Khudyakov. Mr Khudyakov is a talented and experienced improvisator, and this was his debut as an orchestral illustrator. It has to be said that his work was highly successful. The illustration, which followed Mikhail Glinka's compositional style, sounded superb under Mr Khudyakov's baton, with regard to both rhythm and nuance. The melodic themes, adapted from Ukrainian folk songs, fitted the characters perfectly, and the chromatic style beautifully captured the way the wizard slithered and twisted, and glided through objects. The scene showing the Poles in a tavern was strikingly illustrated with a mazurka. The audience were quite taken with Mr Khudyakov's innovation and applauded him warmly' (*Kino-teatr i zhizn'* [The Cinema Theatre and Life], 1913, no. 5, p. 11).

45 I. Khudyakov, *Opyt rukovodstva k illyustratsii sinematograficheskikh kartin* [A Preliminary Manual for Illustrating Cinematographic Pictures] (Moscow, 1912).

46 Khudyakov, 'Novaya otrasl'', p. 11.

47 Sabaneev, 'Kino-muzyka', p. 4.

48 L. L. Sabaneev, *Vospominaniya o Skryabine* [Memories of Scriabin] (Moscow, 1925), p. 80.

49 Sabaneev, 'Kino-muzyka', p. 4.

50 Anoshchenko, 'Iz poluzabytoi epokhi', pp. 7–8.

51 Khudyakov, 'Novaya otrasl'', p. 11.

52 For notes on *Stenka Razin* see: Tsivian *et al.* (eds), *Silent Witnesses*, p. 56.

53 B. S. Likhachev, *Kino v Rossii* [Cinema in Russia] (Leningrad, 1927), p. 51.

54 J. Leyda, *Kino: A History of the Russian and Soviet Film* (New York, 1973), p. 35.

55 M. Oms, 'Une esthétique d'opera' [An Aesthetic of Opera], *Cahiers de la Cinémathèque: Le cinéma muët italien* [Cinémathèque Notes: The Italian Silent Cinema] (n. d.), no. 26/7, p. 133.

56 By looking at such close-ups, one can reconstruct what music was played for Yakov Protazanov's *Satan Triumphant* [Satana likuyushchii, 1917]; Sigismund Veselovsky's *The Bells Ring Out, Telling their Simple Tale* [Kolokol'chiki-bubenchiki zvenyat, prostodushnuyu rasskazyvayut byl' . . ., 1918]; Alexander Uralsky's *Fantasy and Life* [Mechta i zhizn', 1918]. For notes on these films see: Tsivian *et al.* (eds), *Silent Witnesses*, pp. 328, 422, 474. Earlier score close-ups

for cueing the right song were used by D. W. Griffith in *Pippa Passes* (USA, 1909).

57 I. N. Perestiani, *Vospominaniya* [Recollections]. TsMK archives, pp. 12–13.

58 I. N. Ignatov, 'Kinematograf v Rossii: Proshloye i budushchee' [The Cinematograph in Russia: Its Past and Future], TsGALI, 221/1/3, p. 110.

59 Perestiani, *Vospominaniya*, p. 11.

60 Sabaneev, 'Kino-muzyka', p. 4.

61 In an article on the psychology of musical reception in general, Sabaneyev wrote: 'Music is distinguished by a high degree of "associativeness". When musical motifs or phrases are repeated, one clearly recalls the circumstances in which one first heard them. In its ability to recapture past experience music is rivalled only by the sense of smell. Such recollections are entirely involuntary, and in all my experience – which is confirmed by the experiences of others – they come quite out of the blue; sometimes it is only afterwards that you realise what caused them: a fleeting musical phrase or a snatch of tune that you did not really notice hearing. This is something that is perhaps more strongly developed in the less musically aware, since such instinctive psychological phenomena are generally more vivid for those who receive them in a less analytical manner. It is a precious source of experiences when listening to music. Everything comes back in great detail, and when it is unexpected one has only the music to thank for the pleasure. The non-analytical mind of the layman is unable to determine where the purely musical impression ends and the experience created by the associations evoked by the music begins'(L. L. Sabaneev, 'O publike' [About the Audience], *Teatral'naya gazeta*, 1915, no. 38, p. 11).

62 A. Stavritskii, 'Sol' v royali' [The Piano is the Point], *Kino* (Moscow), no. 49 (273), 4 Dec. 1928, p. 3. For notes on *Still, Sadness, Still . . .* see: Tsivian *et al.*, *Silent Witnesses*, p. 478.

63 *Birzhevye vedomosti* [Exchange Gazette], no. 15224, 1 Nov. 1915.

64 Vsevolod Yevgrafovich Cheshikhin (1865–1934), well-known music critic and music historian. The composer Vyacheslav Aleksandrovich Bulychev (1872–1959).

65 Anoshchenko, 'Iz poluzabytoi epokhi', p. 17.

66 Ibid.

67 Khudyakov, 'Novaya otrasl'', no. 9, p. 11.

68 Anoshchenko, 'Iz poluzabytoi epokhi', p. 2.

69 Film histories mention similar publications in the West: '1912: *The Pictures* (London) began publishing suggested musical selections for the week's releases' (D. Robinson, *Music of the Shadows: The Use of Musical Accompaniment with Silent Films, 1896–1936*, supplement to *Griffithiana*, October 1990, no. 38/9, p. 26, see also pp. 8–16); 'By 1913 handbooks such as the Sam Fox Moving Picture Music volume printed music under topical headlines such as "Indian", "Oriental", "Spanish" or "Mexican"' (J. Staiger, 'The Hollywood Mode of Production to 1930', in: D. Bordwell, K. Thompson and J. Staiger, *The Classical Hollywood Cinema: Film Style and Mode of Production* (London, 1988), pp. 107–8).

70 A. Averchenko, 'Kinematograf', *Satirikon*, 1908, no. 30, p. 51.

71 E. Z., 'Mucheniki', p. 13.

72 K. Argamakov, 'O fortep'yannykh improvizatsiyakh' [On Piano Improvisations], *Cine-Phono*, 1913/14, no. 4, p. 24. For notes on *Eugene Onegin* see: Tsivian *et al.*, *Silent Witnesses*, p. 128.

73 Stavritskii, 'Sol' v royali', p. 3.

74 L. E. Ostroumov, 'Moya druzhba s Velikim Nemym' [My Friendship with the

Great Silent]. Typescript in the V. Vishnevsky archive, GFF, p. 2.
75 For details and illustrations of film colouring see: P. C. Usai, *Una Passione infiammabile: Guida allo studio del cinema muto* [An Inflammable Passion: A Guide to Studying the Silent Cinema] (Turin, 1991), pp. 9–11; table of colours.
76 Anoshchenko, 'Iz poluzabytoi epokhi', p. 2.
77 Ibid., p. 14.
78 Ibid., p. 8.
79 P. P. Muratov, 'Kinematograf' [The Cinematograph], *Sovremennye zapiski* [Contemporary Notes], 1925, no. XXVI, p. 294.
80 E. Faure, 'The Art of Cineplastics', in: D. Talbot (ed.) *Film: An Anthology* (Berkeley, 1969), p. 6.
81 'Stasov o kinematografe. Publikatsiya A. Shifmana' [Stasov on the Cinematograph. Prepared for publication by A. Shifman], *Iskusstvo kino* [The Art of Cinema], 1957, no. 3, p. 128.
82 Muratov, 'Kinematograf', p. 224.
83 Anoshchenko, 'Iz poluzabytoi epokhi', p. 15.
84 Ibid., p. 14.
85 Muratov, 'Kinematograf', pp. 294–5.
86 Ibid., p. 295.
87 Chaikovskii, *Mladencheskie gody*, p. 17.
88 Maurin, *Kinematograf*, p. 182.
89 V. Stepanov, 'Kino v Kineshme' [The Cinema in Kineshma], p. 4. TsMK Archives.
90 For notes on *Lumbering Russia . . .* see: Tsivian *et al.* (eds), *Silent Witnesses*, p. 254.
91 'Kul'tura chelovecheskogo zverstva' [The Culture of Human Savagery], *Vestnik kinematografii*, 1912, no. 54, p. 5.
92 'Pochtovyi yashchik' [Post Box], *Proektor* [The Projector], 1916, no. 11/12, p. 17.
93 *Cine-Phono*, 1908, no. 1, p. 11.
94 Musser, *Before the Nickelodeon*, pp. 471–2.
95 'O kinetofone' [On the Kinetophone], *Kinematograf* (Rostov-on-Don), 1915, no. 2/3, p. 6.
96 'Kinetofon', p. 13.
97 Ibid., p. 14.
98 N. Driesen, 'Kinematograf' [The Cinematograph], *Zhizn'* [Life] (Berlin), 1920, no. 10, p. 24.
99 P. Gnedich, 'Sovremennoe' [The Modern], *Teatr i iskusstvo* [Theatre and Art], 1913, no. 45, p. 911.
100 S. Gorodetskii, 'Volk' [The Wolf], in: *Povesti i rasskazy* [Tales and Stories] (St Petersburg, 1910), p. 147.
101 F. Otsep [F. Mashkov] 'Stikhi i kino' [Verse and Cinema], *Proektor*, 1916, no. 7/8, pp. 16–17, supplement.
102 Tyn'yanov, *Poetika*, p. 321.
103 R. Timenchik. 'K simvolike telefona v russkoi poezii' [On the Symbolism of the Telephone in Russian Poetry], *Semiotika XXII*, (Tartu, 1988), pp. 156, 161–2.

CHAPTER 4

1 OPOYAZ: The Society for the Study of Poetic Language [Obshchestvo izucheniya poeticheskogo yazyka]. A group founded by the leading Russian Formalists before the October Revolution and given official recognition between 1919 and 1923.

2 Yu. M. Lotman, 'Fenomen kul'tury' [The Phenomenon of Culture], *Trudy po znakovym sistemam* [Works on Semiotic Systems], no. 10 (Tartu, 1978), p. 5.

3 Tom Gunning tells me that in the early 1910s the Vitagraph company actually had a machine that could simulate rain by scratching slanting parallel lines on to prints.

4 E. Maurin, *Kinematograf v prakticheskoi zhizni* [The Cinematograph in Practical Life] (Petrograd, 1916), p. 154.

5 N. L-skii, '*Kabiriya* v provintsii' [*Cabiria* in the Provinces], *Cine-Phono*, 1917, no. 9/10, p. 53.

6 O. Mandel'shtam, 'Kukla s millionami' [The Doll with Millions], *Pamir*, 1986, no. 10, p. 170.

7 V. Nabokov, *Laughter in the Dark* (London, 1961), p. 12. The novel was originally published in Russian with the title *Kamera obskura* (Paris, 1933). An English translation entitled *Camera Obscura* appeared in 1936 and Nabokov published his own translation, *Laughter in the Dark*, in 1938.

8 RLI, 289/1, no. 184, p. 43.

9 Ibid., p. 33.

10 On Sologub's script see: N. Nusinova and Yu. Tsiv'yan, 'Sologub – stsenarist' [Sologub the Scriptwriter], *Al'manakh kinostsenariev* [An Almanac of Film-scripts], 1989, no. 2, pp. 151–7. For the French translation of the script and the introductory article by the same authors see: *La Licorne*, 1989, no. 17, pp. 221–61.

11 B. Salt, *Film Style and Technology: History and Analysis* (London, 1984), pp. 389, 393.

12 K. Brownlow, 'Lillian Gish', *Films and Filming*, Nov. 1983, p. 21.

13 Salt, *Film Style and Technology*, p. 156.

14 G. C. Pratt, *Spellbound in Darkness: A History of the Silent Film* (New York, 1973), p. 251.

15 Salt, *Film Style and Technology*, p. 40.

16 B. Tomashevskii [B. G.], 'Glupye zheny' [Foolish Wives], *Zhizn' iskusstva* [The Life of Art], 1924, no. 10, p. 16.

17 M. N. Aleinikov, *Puti sovetskogo kino i MKhAT* [The Course of Soviet Cinema and the Moscow Art Theatre] (Moscow, 1947), p. 90. For notes on *Polikushka* and *The Stationmaster* see: Yu. Tsivian (research), P. C. Usai, L. Codelli, C. Montanaro and D. Robinson (eds), *Silent Witnesses: Russian Films, 1908–1919* (London, Pordenone, 1989), pp. 500, 510.

18 Ch. Asendorf, *Ströme und Strahlen: Das langsame Verschwinden der Materie um 1900* [Currents and Rays: The Slow Disappearance of Matter around 1900] (Giessen, 1989), p. 154.

19 Ibid., pp. 23, 79–83, 154–63.

20 Iosif Nikolaevich Yermoliev (1889–1962), one of six major Russian film producers; emigrated in 1920 to France, where he founded a new studio.

21 R. Schmutsler, *Art Nouveau* (New York, 1962), p. 9.

22 A. Mackintosh, *Symbolism and Art Nouveau* (London, 1975), p. 55.

23 *Autour de Levy-Dhurmer. Visionnaires et Intimistes en 1900* [Around Levy-Dhurmer: Visionaries and 'Intimistes' in 1900] (Paris, 1973), p. 61.

24 On 'vibrating' sets for Chekhov's *Uncle Vanya* see: Yu. Nekhoroshev, *Khudozhnik V. A. Simov* [The Artist V. A. Simov] (Moscow, 1984), p. 65.

25 The two lesser types of motion were rectilineal and circular. See the Russian translation of F. Ch. Barlet, *L'Occultisme. Définition. Méthode. Classification. Applications* (Paris, 1909), viz. F. Kh. Barle, *Okkul'tizm* [Occultism] (St Petersburg, 1991, first edition 1911), p. 43.

26 Lidbiter [C. W. Leadbeater], *Mental'nyi plan* [The Mental Plane] (Riga, 1937; St Petersburg, 1991), p. 78.

27 A. E. Parnis, R. D. Timenchik, 'Programmy "Brodyachei sobaki"' [The Programmes of the 'Stray Dog'], in: *Pamyatniki kul'tury: Novye otkrytiya* [Cultural Texts: New Discoveries] (Leningrad, 1985), p. 162.

28 R. de Gourmont, 'Cinématographe' [The Cinematograph], *Mercure de France* [The Mercury of France], 1 Sept. 1907, p. 142.

29 G. K. Chesterton, *The Man Who Was Thursday* [1908] (London, 1976), p. 126.

30 S. Gorodetskii, 'Tragediya i sovremennost" [Tragedy and Modernity], *Novaya Studiya* [The New Studio], 1912, no. 5, p. 9.

31 A. Bely, 'Prorok bezlichiya' [The Prophet of Facelessness], in: *Arabeski* [Arabesques] (Moscow, 1911), p. 5.

32 A. Belyi, *Nachalo veka* [The Beginning of the Century] (Moscow, Leningrad, 1933), p. 49.

33 A. Kaes (ed.), *Kino-Debatte* [Cinema Debate] (Munich, 1978), p. 7.

34 A. A. Kletskin, *Kino v zhizni yakutyan* [Cinema in the Life of the Yakutians] (Yakutsk, 1973), p. 10.

35 D. L., 'Samoubiistvo mekhanika' [The Suicide of a Projectionist], *Cine-Phono*, 1910/11, no. 5, p. 11.

36 N. U-el', 'Porvalas' lenta' [The Film Broke], *Vestnik kinematografii* [Cinematograph Herald], 1913, no. 2, p. 16.

37 V. Gei, 'Paradoksy tenei' [The Paradoxes of Shadows], *Teatral'naya gazeta* [The Theatre Paper], 1916, no. 8, p. 10.

38 M. Brailovskii, 'Kino-kul'tura' [Cinema Culture], *Cine-Phono*, 1913/14, no. 1, p. 16.

39 A. Fevral'skii, *Puti k sintezu: Meierkhol'd i kino* [Paths to Synthesis: Meyerhold and Cinema] (Moscow, 1978), pp. 11, 12.

40 A. Belyi, *Masterstvo Gogolya* [Gogol's Mastery] (Moscow, Leningrad, 1934), p. 93.

41 A. Belyi, *Rudol'f Shteiner i Gete v mirovozzrenii sovremennosti* [Rudolf Steiner and Goethe in Contemporary Thought] (Moscow, 1917), p. 328.

42 TsGALI, 989/1/5, p. 41.

43 In the prologue Bely intended just to suggest the settings of the action. As in the novel, he began with a deliberately confused topography of St Petersburg, including interiors (for example, of the office of a 'certain Government Ministry', where later, in the first part of the script, two of the main protagonists would meet).

44 A. Belyi, 'Peterburg; Kinostsenarii po romanu' [Petersburg: A Film Script from the Novel]. GBL, 516/3/37, p. 39.

45 A. Roslavlev, 'V kinematografe' [At the Cinematograph], in: *V Bashne* [In the Tower] (St Petersburg, 1907), p. 61.

46 I. Khudyakov, *Opyt rukovodstva k illyustratsii sinematograficheskikh kartin: S ukazaniem na 1000 tem* [A Preliminary Manual for Illustrating Cinematographic Pictures: With an Index of 1000 Themes] (Moscow, 1912), p. 11.

47 R. Jakobson, 'Verfall des Films?' [The Decline of Film?], *Sprache im technischen Zeitalter* [Language in the Age of Technology], 1968, no. 27, pp. 187–8.

48 R. Garms [Harms], *Filosofiya fil'ma* [The Philosophy of Film] (Leningrad, 1927), p. 24.

49 A. Verner [Werner], 'Beglye zametki' [Fleeting Notes], p. 1. Typescript in the V. Vishnevsky archive, GFF.

50 V. Puce, 'Kinojauniba' [A Childhood at the Cinema], *Literatura un Maksla* [Literature and Art], 10 Sept. 1982, p. 16.

51 A. A. Blok, *Sobranie sochinenii v 8 tomakh* [Collected Works in 8 volumes] (Moscow, Leningrad, 1960–3), vol. 8, p. 103.

52 Some years later Blok mentioned the incident again in a letter to Maxim Gorky's wife, the actress Maria Andreyeva: 'A girl in a film once came out with a very coquettish remark: "Men are always fighting", she said' (ibid., p. 525). In the letter, as opposed to the note in the diary, this observation is placed in context. Blok was writing about one of Alexander Amfiteatrov's plays, which was 'full of brawling and fighting'. Yuri Lotman, remarking that 'Pushkin also used to like watching fights' categorised the woman's comment as belonging to the 'folklore type' of audience reaction (Yu. M. Lotman, 'Blok i narodnaya kul'tura goroda' [Blok and the Popular Culture of the City], in: *Mir A. Bloka: Blokovskii sbornik, IV* [The World of Alexander Blok: Essays on Blok, IV] (Tartu, 1981), pp. 10, 24).

53 G. I. Chulkov, 'Zhivaya fotografiya' [A Living Photograph], *Zolotoe runo* [The Golden Fleece], 1908, no. 6, p. 11.

54 Knyaz' [Prince] Senegambii, 'Kinematograf i teatr' [The Cinematograph and the Theatre], *Kine-zhurnal* [The Cinema Journal], 1916, nos 1/2, p. 70.

55 'Samoubiistvo v kinematografe' [Suicide in the Cinematograph], *Kine-zhurnal,* 1911, no. 1, pp. 11–12. The film *Student Years* [V studencheskie gody, 1910] was adapted from Leonid Andreyev's play *The Days of Our Life* [Dni nashei zhizni].

56 See the chapter on Luigi Russolo and the 'Art of Noise' in: M. Kirby, *Futurist Performance* (New York, 1971), pp. 33–40. In a 1913 manifesto the Italian Futurist Carlo Carra insisted that Futurist art was the 'plastic equivalent of the sounds, noises and smells that we come across in theatres, music halls and cinematographs' (U. Apollonio (ed.), *Futurist Manifestos* (New York, 1973), p. 114).

57 V. Shershenevich, *Avtomobil'ya postup'* [The Tread of the Motor Car] (Moscow, 1916), p. 20.

58 D. Burlyuk, 'Futurist v kinematografe' [A Futurist in the Cinematograph], *Kine-zhurnal*, 1913, no. 22, p. 22.

59 A. A. Blok, *Sobranie sochinenii v 6 tomakh* [Collected Works in 6 volumes] (Leningrad, 1981), vol. 2, p. 12.

60 *Cine-Phono*, 1914, no. 18, p. 27.

61 GAP, group 2, no. 27.

62 Fon-Lik, 'Plody kul'tury' [The Fruits of Culture], *Kinematografiya*, no. 1, 5 Jan. 1909, p. 11.

63 Teffi, 'V stereo-foto-kine-mato-skopo-bio-fono i proch.-grafe' [At the Stereo-foto-etc. etc.-graph], *Satirikon*, 1908, no. 33, p. 5.

64 *Birzhevye vedomosti (vechernyi vypusk)* [Exchange Gazette (Evening Edition)], no. 13501, 17 April 1913.

65 K. Paustovsky. *Razlivy rek* [Flooded Rivers] (Moscow, 1973), p. 54.

66 E. A. Ivanov-Barkov, 'Vospominaniya' [Recollections], TsGALI, 2970/1/52, p. 102.

67 A. B., 'Kinematograf', *Bogema* [Bohemia], 1915, no. 5/6, p. 54.

68 Yu. N. Tyn'yanov, *Poetika. Istoriya literatury. Kino* [Poetics. Literary History. Cinema] (Moscow, 1977), pp. 321–2.

69 V. Kaverin, 'Razgovory o kino' [Conversations on Cinema], *Zhizn' iskusstva,* 1924, no. 1, p. 27. There is a possible literary reference behind this description. In Chekhov's *Three Sisters* Vershinin and Masha exchange 'tra-ta-tas' and 'tra-ra-ras' in a comic duet, and this in turn derives from an actual event, as we see from Alexander Kugel's recollections of his meetings with Chekhov: 'As everybody knows, he had a large note book, in which he jotted down everything that struck him as important, or that suddenly came into his mind, with no system or order – just as raw material. When he was listening, or smiling, or dropping remarks to which he expected an answer, I had the impression that all the time he was

collecting material for his note book. That's where the famous "Tra-ta-ta" in *Three Sisters* came from. There was a lively party going on, with plenty of cognac . . . An actress was improvising, using this sound to imitate or express wild passion. It was the cognac talking; it was a "cognac improvisation"' (A. R. Kugel', *List'ya s dereva* [Leaves from a Tree] (Leningrad, 1926), pp. 67–8).

70 See p. 201 ff.

71 A. A. Khanzhonkov, *Pervye gody russkoy kinematografii* [The First Years of Russian Cinematography] (Moscow, Leningrad, 1937), p. 16.

72 F. Shipulinsky, 'Dusha kino' [The Soul of Cinema], in: *Kinematograf: Sbornik statei* [The Cinematograph: A Collection of Essays] (Moscow, 1919), p. 20.

73 M. Engberg, 'What did Kafka See When He Went to the Cinema on the 26.8.1911 in Prague? On Franz Kafka and the Danish Film *In the Hands of Impostors II*', *Programme Notes of the Bologna Film Festival – 'Cinema Regained'* (Bologna, 1990).

74 W. Jahn, 'Kafka und die Anfänge des Kinos' [Kafka and the Beginnings of Cinema], *Jahrbücher der deutschen Schillergesellschaft* [Annals of the German Schiller Society] (Stuttgart, 1962), vol. 6, p. 355.

75 L. Pirandello, *Shoot! The Notebooks of Serafino Gubbio, Cinematograph Operator* [Translated by C. K. Scott Moncrieff] (New York, 1926), p. 11.

76 Cited in: R. Boussinot, *L'Encyclopédie du cinéma* (Paris, 1980), vol. 1, p. 237.

77 L. O. [L. Ostroumov], 'Lenta zhizni' [The Ribbon of Life], *Pegas* [Pegasus], 1916, no. 4, p. 52.

78 R. Timenchik, 'K simvolike tramvaya v russkoi poezii' [On the Symbolism of the Tram in Russian Poetry], *Semiotika: Trudy po znakovym sistemam XXI* [Semiotics: Transactions on Sign Systems XXI] (Tartu, 1987), p. 138.

79 M. Kol'tsov, 'U ekrana' [By the Screen], *Pravda*, 1922, no. 269.

80 TsGALI, 2091/1/28.

81 M. Yampolskii, 'Kuleshov's Experiments and the New Anthropology of the Actor', in: R. Taylor and I. Christie (eds), *Inside the Film Factory: New Approaches to Russian and Soviet Cinema* (London, New York, 1991), pp. 40–1.

82 K. Brownlow, *The Parade's Gone By . . .* (London, 1968), p. 341.

83 I. Perestiani, *Vospominaniya* [Memoirs], pp. 13, 28. TsMK.

84 V. E. Meierkhol'd, 'Portret Doriana Greya' [The Picture of Dorian Gray], *Iz istorii kino* [From the History of Cinema] (Moscow, 1965), no. 7, p. 23.

85 Ibid, p. 24.

86 On the sound of the 'axle of the world' in Symbolist literature see: N. V. Skvortsova, 'Aleksandr Blok v stat'e Andreya Belogo "Khimery"' [Alexander Blok in Andrei Bely's Article 'Chimeras'], *Mir A. Bloka: Blokovskii sbornik* [The World of A. Blok: Essays on Blok], no. 5 (Tartu, 1985), p. 88.

CHAPTER 5

1 This, as Miriam Hansen suggests, long remained the rule for American spectators: 'Surveys throughout most of the 1920s suggest that only a small fraction (10 percent of the survey) of moviegoers had come to see the feature, the overwhelming majority (68 percent) had come for the "event"' (M. Hansen, *Babel and Babylon: Spectatorship in American Silent Film* (Cambridge, MA, 1991), p. 99).

2 V. Tyurin, *Zhivaya fotografiya* [A Living Photograph] (St Petersburg, 1898), p. 4.

3 See: Yu. Tsivian, 'Censure Bans on Religious Subjects in Russian Films', in: R.

Cosandey, A. Gaudreault and T. Gunning (eds) *An Invention of The Devil's: Religion and Early Cinema* (Lausanne, 1992), pp. 71–80.

4 N. Karzhanskii, 'V kinematografe. (Iz knigi *Parizh*)' [At the Cinematograph. (From the book *Paris*)], *Rampa i zhizn'* [Footlights and Life], 1915, no. 32, p. 6.

5 TsGIAL, 776/22/33.

6 Cf. this 1908 description of a typically varied performance (I cite here only the beginnings of paragraphs): 'Look! English boxers . . . Look! *The Witnessing Child* . . . Look! "Tortures of the Inquisition" shown in full detail . . . Look! The favourite topic of comic cinema, the adventures of a crook . . . Look! Another trick film, something perfectly fit for children . . .' (Yu. Engel' [Signed Yu. E.], 'O kinematografe' [On the Cinematograph], *Russkie vedomosti* [The Russian Gazette], no. 275, 27 Nov. 1908).

7 Kinemacolor was an early colour reproduction technique invented by the English photographer George Albert Smith as well as the name of the cinemas where these colour films were shown.

8 M. Kuzmin, 'Otlichitel'nyi priznak' [A Distinguishing Feature], *Sinema* (Rostov-on-Don), 1915, no. 8/9, p. 14.

9 S. Ya. Marshak [Signed 'Doktor Friken'], 'V kinematografe' [At the Cinematograph], *Satirikon*, 1908, no. 12, p. 7.

10 Kuleshov's experiment was based on joining together shots filmed on different locations.

11 A. Krantsfel'd, 'Velikii nemoi' [The Great Silent], *Teatr i kino* [Theatre and Cinema] (Odessa), 1916, no. 1, p. 17. Le Prince was the name of a French comic actor.

12 In German sources, for example, there is a difference of opinion on this point between H. Lehmann and Rudolf Harms. The latter wrote: 'Lehmann is scathing about the practice of showing a comic picture after a serious one, or of mixing up documentary and feature films. It seems, however, that this is precisely what the general public prefers: a continuous sequence of films that differ in mood and content' (R. Garms [Harms], *Filosofiya fil'ma* [The Philosophy of Film] (Leningrad, 1927), pp. 72–3). Harms was referring to Lehmann's *Die Kinematographie, ihre Grundlagen und ihre Anwendungen* [The Cinematograph, its Basic Principles and Applications] (Leipzig, 1919).

13 'Artisticheskoe spravochnoe byuro' [Information Bureau of the Arts], *Rech'* [Speech], no. 1, 5 Feb. 1910, p. 5.

14 See: T. Gunning, *D. W. Griffith and the Origins of American Narrative Film: The Early Years at Biograph* (Urbana, Chicago, 1991), p. 86.

15 N. Lerner, 'Pushkin v kinomatografe' [Pushkin in the Cinematograph], *Zhurnal zhurnalov* [The Journal of Journals], 1915, no. 26, p. 18. For notes on *The Life and Death of Alexander Pushkin* see: Yu. Tsivian (research), P. C. Usai, L. Codelli, C. Montanaro, D. Robinson (eds), *Silent Witnesses: Russian Films, 1908–1919* (London, Pordenone, 1989), p. 90.

16 N. Burch, 'Porter, or Ambivalence', *Screen*, 1978/9, vol. 19, no. 4, pp. 91–106. See also: C. Musser, *Before the Nickelodeon: Edwin S. Porter and the Edison Manufacturing Company* (Berkeley, Los Angeles, London, 1991), pp. 212–34.

17 See the discussion of 'pros' and 'contras' on this issue as applied to American films of around 1907 in: C. Musser, 'The Nickelodeon Era Begins: Establishing the Framework for Hollywood's Mode of Representation', *Framework 22/23* (autumn 1983), p. 10.

18 E. Stark, 'S nogami na stole' [Feet on the Table], *Teatr i iskusstvo* [Theatre and Art], 1913, no. 39, p. 770.

19 'The tension between scenes perceived as self-contained wholes on the one hand

and their potential as part of a more complex sequence on the other is a partial explanation for narrative structures [prior to mid-1907]' (Musser, 'The Nickelodeon Era Begins', p. 4).

20 Yu. Engel' [Signed Yu. E.], 'O kinematografe' [On the Cinematograph], *Russkie vedomosti*, no. 275, 27 Nov. 1908.

21 The comic paper, an advanced pre-cinematic form of illustrated narrative, was virtually unknown in Russia. The extent to which the magic lantern show had evolved its own cultural identity has yet to be researched. On cinema and pre-cinematic culture see: J. Fell, *Film and the Narrative Tradition* (Oklahoma City, 1974).

22 S. Gorodetskii, 'Volk' [The Wolf], in: *Povesti i Rasskazy* [Stories and Tales] (St Petersburg, 1910), pp. 146–7.

CHAPTER 6

1 K. Brownlow, *The Parade's Gone By* . . . (London, 1968), p. 6.

2 T. Gunning, 'An Aesthetic of Astonishment: Early Film and the (In)credulous Spectator', *Art and Text*, no. 34, spring 1989, pp. 31–6.

3 *The Sketch*, 18 March 1896, p. 323.

4 W. Schivelbusch, *The Railway Journey: Trains and Travel in the 19th Century* (New York, 1979), pp. 135–57.

5 *Cine-Phono*, 1907, no. 1, p. 1.

6 Protei [Proteus], 'Kinematografy' [Cinematographs], *Teatr i zhizn'* [Theatre and Life], no. 4, 4 May 1913, p. 2.

7 E. A. Ivanov-Barkov, 'Vospominaniya' [Memoirs], TsGALI, 2970/1/52, pp. 108–9.

8 I. N. Ignatov, 'Kinematograf v Rossii: Proshloe i budushchee' [The Cinematograph in Russia: Its Past and Future] TsGALI, 221/1/3, p. 74. For notes on *Anna Karenina* see: Y. Tsivian (research), P. C. Usai, L. Codelli, C. Montanaro and D. Robinson (eds), *Silent Witnesses. Russian Films, 1908–1919* (London, Pordenone, 1989), p. 210.

9 M. P. Lilina, 'O kino' [On Cinema], *Teatr*, 1915, no. 1752, p. 8.

10 Muzei MKhaTa [Moscow Art Theatre Museum], Arkhiv Knipper–Chekhovoi [Knipper–Chekhov Archive], file no. 2388.

11 Ibid.

12 D. V. Filosofov, 'Anna Karenina Tret'ya' [Anna Karenina the Third], *Zhivoi ekran* [The Living Screen], 1914, no. 21/2, p. 20.

13 de-Nei, 'Samoubiistvo Anny Kareninoi' [Anna Karenina's Suicide], *Rampa i zhizn'* [Footlights and Life], 1914, no. 20, p. 13.

14 Quoted in: I. Shcheglov, *O narodnom teatre* [On Popular Theatre] (Moscow, 1895), p. 107. A skomorokh was a traditional Russian itinerant minstrel-cum-clown.

15 A poster for Augustin Daly's melodrama *Under the Gaslight*, reproduced on p. 23 of J. Fell's *Film and the Narrative Tradition* (Oklahoma City, 1974), gives a fairly good idea of how the 'skomorokh version' of Anna Karenina's suicide must have looked.

16 Shcheglov, *O narodnom teatre*, p. 109.

17 *Iskry* [Sparks], 1914, no. 20, pp. 156–7. The snapshot was taken from a position close to where the camera was sited, as you can see if you compare the still with de-Nei's account in *Footlights and Life*.

18 M. Gor'kii, 'Beglye zametki' [Fleeting Notes], *Nizhegorodskii listok* [The Nizhn Novgorod Newsletter], no. 182, 4 July 1896, p. 3. Translated in: R. Taylor and I.

Christie (eds) *The Film Factory: Russian and Soviet Cinema in Documents 1896–1939* (London, Cambridge, MA, 1988), pp. 25–6.

19 'Stasov o kinematografe.' Publikatsiya A. Shifmana. [Stasov on the Cinematograph. Prepared for publication by A. Shifman]. Excerpted in *Iskusstvo kino* [The Art of Cinema], 1957, no. 3, p. 128.

20 The concluding frame of *The Battleship Potemkin* is very well known. The battleship bears down upon the viewer, 'splitting' the screen (the original idea was that the screen really should burst). Vertov thought that Eisenstein stole the idea from him, and was not slow in letting everybody know it: '*Leninskaya kinopravda* [Leninist Cine-Pravda] begins with moments from the struggle of the insurrectionary proletariat, the middle of the picture is built around the death of the leader, and the picture ends on a note of victory and high spirits, with shots of the train of revolution bearing down on the auditorium and then rushing on over the heads of the audience. *Potemkin* also begins with the struggle of the insurgents, the middle is built around the death of Vakulinchuk, and the film likewise ends on a note of victory and high spirits, with shots of the battleship bearing down upon the auditorium. But I only mention this in passing . . .' (D. Vertov, 'Za stoprotsentnyi kinoglaz' [For a One-Hundred-Percent Cine-Eye], in: *Istoriya stanovleniya sovetskogo kino* [A History of How Soviet Cinema Came into Being] (Moscow, 1986), p. 64).

Vertov seemed to have forgotten that his 'train of revolution' effect was itself a reprise of *The Arrival* of the Lumière train. Incidentally, Eisenstein was nettled by Vertov's insinuations and was fond of reminding people that the *Cine-Eye* group's methods had not advanced much beyond the newsreels of the Lumières' day. (See: S. M. Eizenshtein, 'Vse my rabotaem na odnu i tu zhe auditoriyu . . .' Publikatsiya N. Kleimana. ['We are All Working for the Same Audience . . .' Prepared for publication by N. Kleiman], *Iskusstvo kino*, 1988, no. 1.)

21 A. Voznesenskii, 'Kinodetstvo. (Glava iz "Knigi nochei")' [A Childhood at the Moving Pictures. (A Chapter from 'A Book of Nights')], *Iskusstvo kino*, 1985, no. 11, p. 78.

22 C. Metz, *The Imaginary Signifier: Psychoanalysis and the Cinema* (Bloomington, 1982), pp. 72–3. For Gunning's polemics with Metz see his 'An Aesthetic of Astonishment,' pp. 32, 42.

23 O. Winter, 'The Cinematograph', *Sight and Sound*, autumn 1982, pp. 294–5.

24 The most likely explanation is that this was due to the persistence of habits of vision that were not accustomed to, and not activated by, the flickering impulses of screen movement. At a seminar on film reception conducted at the British Film Institute in 1990, Geoffrey Nowell-Smith suggested that the observer's ability to read perspective could also have been dependent on where he or she sat in the auditorium.

25 A. D. Digmelov, '50 let nazad' [Fifty Years ago], p. 2. Typescript in the V. Vishnevsky archive, GFF.

26 The effect is convincingly analysed in: A. Mackintosh, *Symbolism and Art Nouveau* (London, 1975).

27 G. Sadoul, *Louis Lumière* (Paris, 1964), p. 48.

28 Winter, 'The Cinematograph', p. 295. Compare with what Gunning has to say on crowd views as focuses of attraction: 'New centers of interest bob into the frame unexpectedly, while others depart beyond reclamation. The receptive spectator approaches these images with the global curiosity about its "many interesting phases", a curiosity that is being endlessly incited and never completely satiated. The street is filled with endless attractions' (T. Gunning, 'The Book that Refuses to Be Read: Images of the City in Early Cinema', forthcoming).

29 L. R. Kogan, *Vospominaniya* [Memoirs], pt 2, no. 1, 1894–7. GPB, 1035/35, p. 39.

30 If it really was the Lumière film that Kogan was remembering, and not another film in which the train actually does cut away at the last moment, one may assume that the early viewer constructed the space within the shot as curving within the diegetic area close to the screen. The gradient of depth that the growing size of the locomotive signalled while it was within the field of the image disappeared as soon as the locomotive was out of field – and the space immediately 'flattened'. If this hypothesis is valid (which only a specialist in visual perception can tell), it can be confirmed by a similar effect described in a contemporary account of the Lumière film *La Place des Cordeliers* (1895): 'One of the carriages, drawn by galloping horses, was coming straight at us. A woman sitting next to me was so frightened that she jumped to her feet . . . and wouldn't sit down *until the carriage had turned round and disappeared* [my emphasis]' (quoted in: Sadoul, *Louis Lumière*, p. 32).

31 Gor'kii, 'Beglye zametki', p. 3.

32 N. Burch, 'A Primitive Mode of Representation?' in: T. Elsaesser and A. Barker (eds), *Early Cinema: Space Frame Narrative* (London, 1990), p. 222.

33 See M. Deutelbaum, 'Structural Patterning in the Lumière Films', in: *Film before Griffith* (London, Los Angeles, 1983), p. 306.

34 Gor'kii, 'Beglye zametki', p. 3.

35 G. C. Pratt, *Spellbound in Darkness: A History of the Silent Film* (New York, 1973), p.17.

36 T. Gunning, 'Now You See It, Now You Don't: The Temporality of the Cinema of Attractions.' Paper presented at the SCS conference, May 1991, p. 9.

37 G. Derzhavin, 'Fonar'' [The Lantern], in: *Sochineniya Derzhavina* [Derzhavin's Works] (St Petersburg, 1865), pp. 465–9.

38 V. Khodasevich. *Poeticheskoe khoziaistvo Pushkina* [Pushkin's Poetic Apparatus] (Leningrad, 1924) p. 28.

39 V. Nabokov, *Ada* (London, 1969), p. 458.

40 Gor'kii, 'Beglye zametki', p. 3,

41 A. Belyi, 'Teatr i sovremennaya drama' [Theatre and Contemporary Drama], in: *Kniga o novom teatre* [A Book on the New Theatre] (Moscow, 1908), p. 274.

42 Winter, 'The Cinematograph', p. 294.

43 A. Blok, *Zapisnye knizhki* [Notebooks] (Moscow, 1965), p. 127.

44 There are no sequences of cars smashing through walls in *The '?' Motorist*, only a shot where a car comes through a ceiling. The 'wall-smashing' trick was devised by Méliès for *Voyage à travers l'impossible* [Journey Towards the Impossible, 1904].

45 A. Belyi, 'Gorod' [The City], *Nash ponedel'nik* [Our Monday Paper], no. 1, 9 Nov. 1907, p. 2.

46 Ibid.

47 Isaiah 24: 18–20.

48 Belyi, 'Gorod', p. 2.

49 *British Film Catalogue (1895–1970)* (London, 1973).

50 A. Belyi, *Peterburg* (Moscow, 1978), pp. 259–60. For other English versions of this passage see: Andrey Biely, *St Petersburg* [Introduced by George Reavey and translated by John Cournos] (New York, 1959), pp. 250–1; and Andrei Bely, *Petersburg* [Translated, annotated and introduced by Robert A. Maguire amd John Malmstad] (Bloomington, London, 1978), pp. 226–7.

51 Tom Gunning has kindly drawn my attention to the pre-cinematic series of comic strips, *Little Sammy Sneeze*, as a possible source and an evident parallel to the

film – as well as to other comic cartoons dealing with exploding characters. Sneezing (found in a number of similar films) was just one variant of the 'exploding man' motif in early cinema. There was also *A Giant Hiccup* [Riesenschlucker, Gaumont, 1909?], a grotesque 'scare-it-away' film. In more serious realistic films the theme would most likely involve anarchists and bombs. For Bely the image of the 'exploding man' – in addition to its eschatological symbolism mentioned above – echoed the fable of the frog who wanted to become larger than the bull, and Dostoyevsky's idea (see his novel *The Possessed* [Besy, 1873]) of revolutionary thought as a mental disease that turns the fanatic's brain into ever-expanding matter. Roman Timenchik has suggested that a possible source for Bely's novel *Petersburg* was G. K. Chesterton's novel *The Man Who Was Thursday* (1908), which contains an image of the terrorist as a person whose head is filled with dynamite.

52 Belyi, *Peterburg*, p. 259.
53 Gorkii, 'Beglye zametki', p. 3.
54 Burch, 'A Primitive Mode of Representation?', p. 222.
55 A. Belyi, *Na perevale: Berlin* [At the Turning Point: Berlin] (Petrograd, Moscow, 1923), p. 328.
56 F. Mesguich, *Tours de manivelle: Souvenirs d'un chasseur d'images* [Cranking the Handle: Memories of an Image Hunter] (Paris, 1933), p. 84.
57 F. Shipulinskii, *Istoriya kino* [The History of Cinema] (Moscow, 1934), p. 66.
58 A. Belyi, 'Peterburg; Kinostsenarii po romanu' [Petersburg: A Film Script from the Novel]. GBL, 516/3/37, p. 14.
59 Ivanov-Barkov, 'Vospominaniya', p. 105.
60 Ya. A. Zhdanov, 'Po Rossii s kinogovoryashchimi kartinami' [Around Russia with Talking Pictures], p. 1. Typescript in the Soviet Cinema Section of VGIK.
61 This fact is referred to in: D. Vaughan, 'Let There Be Lumière', in: T. Elsaesser and A. Barker (eds), *Early Cinema: Space, Frame, Narrative* (London, 1990), pp. 63–75.
62 'Stasov o kinematografe', pp. 127–28.
63 Gunning, 'An Aesthetic of Astonishment', pp. 31–45.
64 A. Chumachenko, 'V kinematografe' [At the Cinematograph], *Vestnik kinematografii* [Cinematograph Herald], 1911, no. 7, pp. 15–16.
65 A. Roslavlev, 'V kinematografe' [At the Cinematograph], in: *V bashne* [In the Tower] (St Petersburg, 1907), pp. 61–2.
66 M. Moravskaya, 'Devushka s fonarikom' [The Girl with the Torch], *Russkie zapiski* [Russian Notes], 1915, no. 10, p. 52.
67 See the discussion of the 'Plato cave' model as a platform for the theory of cinematic apparatus and as a trope of early film reception in Part I Chapter 2 above.
68 E. Benveniste, *Obshchaya lingvistika* [General Linguistics] (Moscow, 1974), pp. 270–2.
69 *Cine-Phono*, 1914, no. 16, p. 23. See also *Peterburgskii Kur'er* [The Petersburg Courier], no. 75, 5 April 1914.
70 Metz, *The Imaginary Signifier*, p. 117.
71 For a more detailed history of this genre and on parallel experiments in Western cinema see my article 'Early Russian Cinema: Some Observations', in: R. Taylor and I. Christie (eds), *Inside the Film Factory: New Approaches to Russian and Soviet Cinema* (London, New York, 1991), pp. 24–30.
72 Quoted from: *Cine-Phono*, 1914, no. 3, p. 23.
73 E. Beskin, 'Ne tovarishchi' [No Bedfellows], *Teatral'naya gazeta* [The Theatre Paper], 1914, no. 47, p. 3.

74 P. Orlenev, *Zhizn' i tvorchestvo russkogo aktera Pavla Orleneva, opisannye im samim* [The Life and Work of the Russian Actor Pavel Orlenev as Described by Himself] (Leningrad, Moscow, 1961), pp. 251–2.

75 *Teatr*, 1915, no. 1684, p. 3.

76 Communicated by Roman Timenchik.

77 T. Mann, *The Magic Mountain* [English translation by H. T. Lowe-Porter] (Harmondsworth, 1965), p. 318.

78 V. Woolf, 'The Movies', *New Republic*, 4 Aug. 1926, p. 308.

79 V. U. Nabokov, *Mary* (London, 1971), p. 82. This is a translation of *Mashenka* (Berlin, 1926). On cinema in connection with the opposition of 'existence' and 'non-existence' in *Mary* see: Yu. I. Levin, 'Zametki o "Mashen'ke" V. V. Nabokova' [Notes on Nabokov's *Mary*], *Russian Literature*, 1985, V–XVIII, nos 21–30, pp. 21–7.

80 'Neopublikovannoe pis'mo Kuprina' [An Unpublished letter by Kuprin], *Russkie novosti* [Russian News], no. 37, 25 Jan. 1946, p. 4. For Kuprin on cinema see also: Yu. Tsiv'yan, 'K genezisu russkogo stilya v kinematografe' [On the Origins of the Russian Style in Cinema], *Wiener Slawistischer Almanach* [Viennese Slavic Almanac], 1984, vol. 14, p. 266.

81 L. Pirandello, *Shoot! The Notes of Serafino Gubbio, Cinematograph Operator* [English translation by C. K. Scott Moncrieff] (New York, 1926), p. 61.

82 Nabokov, *Mary*, pp. 30–1. A possible intertextual link between these two scenes is analysed in: G. Moses, '"Speculation" on Pirandello, and Nabokov on "Specularity"', in: *Pirandello 1986: Atti del simposio internationale in Berkeley* (Rome, 1987), pp. 135–47.

83 Prince Senegambii, 'Kinematograf i obryad zhizni' [The Cinematograph and the Ritual of Life], *Kine-zhurnal* [Cine-Journal], 1917, no. 1/2, p. 69.

84 V. I. Ivanov, *Stikhotvoreniya i poemy* [Verses and Poems] (Leningrad, 1978), p. 312.

CHAPTER 7

1 T. Gunning, *D. W. Griffith and the Origins of American Narrative Film: Early Years at Biograph* (Urbana, Chicago, 1991), p. 67.

2 Azr [Aleksei Zinger], 'Kinematograf' [The Cinematograph] *Zritel'* [The Spectator], 1905, no. 6, p. 6.

3 A. Belyi, 'Gorod' [The City], *Nash ponedel'nik* [Our Monday Paper], no. 1, 9 Nov. 1907, p. 2.

4 K. Chukovskii, *Nat Pinkerton i sovremennaya literatura* [Nat Pinkerton and Modern Literature] (Moscow, 1908), p. 7.

5 Méliès dropped this pattern for the more conventional cross-frame chases in *Les Incendiaires* [The Fire-Raisers, 1906]. For details on this and earlier chase sequences in Méliès see: *Analyse catalographique des films de Georges Méliès* [Analytical Catalogue of the Films of Georges Méliès] (Paris, 1981), p. 126 and before.

6 Gunning, *D. W. Griffith*, p. 77.

7 S. Gorodetskii, 'Volk' [The Wolf], in: *Povesti i Rasskazy* [Stories and Tales] (St Petersburg, 1910), pp. 146–7.

8 Gunning, *D. W. Griffith*, pp. 188–232.

9 'Teatral'nost' i kinematografichnost' [Theatre and Cinema Specificity], *Vestnik kinematografii* [Cinematograph Herald], 1911, no. 7, p. 12.

10 'V ogne strastei i stradanii' [In the Fire of Passions and Sufferings], *Proektor* [The Projector], 1916, no. 6, p. 12.

11 D. Bordwell, 'The Classical Hollywood Style, 1917–60', in: D. Bordwell, J. Staiger and K. Thompson, *The Classical Hollywood Cinema: Film Style and Mode of Production to 1960* (London, 1985), pp. 19–21.

12 N. Burch, 'Passion, poursuite: la linéarisation' [Passion, Pursuit: Linearisation], *Communications*, 1983, no. 38, p. 31.

13 A. A. Khanzhonkov, *Pervye gody Russkoi kinematografii* [The First Years of Russian Cinema] (Moscow, Leningrad, 1937), p. 37.

14 N. A. Savvin, 'Kinematograf na sluzhbe u istorii i istorii literatury' [Cinema at the Service of History and Literary History], *Vestnik vospitaniya* [The Education Herald], 1914, no. 8, p. 200.

15 *Teatral'naya gazeta* [The Theatre Paper], 1913, no. 1, p. 11.

16 J. Mukařovský, 'Záměrnost a nezáměrnost v umění' [Intentionality and Unintentionality in Art], in his: *Studii z estetiky* (Prague, 1966), translated in J. Burbank and P. Steiner (eds), *Structure, Sign and Function: Selected Essays by Jan Mukařovský* (New Haven, CT, London, 1978), pp. 89–128. The lecture was originally given to the Prague Linguistic Circle on 26 May 1943.

17 'Tat'yana Repina', *Obozrenie teatrov* [The Review of Theatres], no. 2842, 11 Aug. 1915, p. 8.

18 Of course, I do not insist that in early cinema outdoor scenes prevailed over indoor scenes in any statistical sense. No statement of this kind can be made without specifying period, genre, and also which scenes one calls 'outdoor' – those shot in exteriors or set in exteriors? However, one can argue that from the point of view of the spectator used to pre-cinematic conventions, the aggregate diegesis of cinema of the 1900s–1910s was all about the outdoors.

19 Geinim [A. Anoshchenko?], 'Novoe iskusstvo' [A New Art], *Kino-teatr i zhizn'* [The Cinema Theatre and Life], 1913, no. 1, p. 2.

20 W. Benjamin, *Allegorien kultureller Erfahrung* [Allegories of Cultural Experience] (Leipzig, 1984), pp. 445ff.

21 A. Flaker, 'Puteshestvie v stranu zhivopisi (Mandel'shtam o frantsuzskoi zhivopisi)' [A Journey into the Land of Painting (Mandelshtam on French Painting)], *Wiener Slawistischer Almanach* [Viennese Slavic Almanac], 1984, no. 14, pp. 171–2.

22 Geinim, ibid.

23 D. Bordwell. *Narration in the Fiction Film* (Madison, 1985), p. 62.

24 Gunning, *D. W. Griffith*, pp. 24–5.

25 A. Gaudreault, *Du Littéraire au filmique: Système du récit* [From the Literary to the Filmic: The Narrative System] (Québec, 1988), pp. 133–46.

26 -skii, 'Kino-epos', *Teatral'naya gazeta*, 1914, no. 52, p. 8.

27 Yu. Engel' [Signed Yu. E.], 'O kinematografe' [On the Cinematograph], *Russkie vedomosti* [The Russian Gazette], no. 275, 27 Nov. 1908.

28 P. Nilus, 'Novyi vid iskusstva' [A New Art Form], *Cine-Phono*, 1911, no. 9, p. 9.

29 This English term was borrowed by Dmitri Merezhkovsky from Alexander Hertsen, who, in his turn, had borrowed it from John Stuart Mill.

30 C. H. Bedford, *The Seeker: D. S. Merezhkovskiy* (Lawrence, Manhatten, Wichita, 1975), pp. 126, 189. In Russian the word 'ham' [*kham*] has come to mean 'cad', or 'boor'.

31 B. G. Rosenthal, *D. S. Merezhkovsky and the Silver Age: The Development of a Revolutionary Mentality* (The Hague, 1975), pp. 165–6.

32 Chukovskii, *Nat Pinkerton*. I. L. Shcheglov, 'Teatr illyuzii i Berta Kukel'van' [The Theatre of Illusions and Berta Kukelvan], in: *Narod i teatr* [Theatre and the People] (St Petersburg, 1911).

33 Shcheglov, 'Teatr illyuzii', p. 352. I am indebted to Tom Gunning for his letter of 25 November 1991, suggesting some titles by which these films might be identified. Here Gunning suggests the Pathé film *Voyage autour d'une étoile* (1906).

34 Ibid., p. 352. Tom Gunning suggests this is the Pathé film *Le Pêcheur de perles* (1907 or 1908). Karl Brown mentions a Méliès film with a similar story that was shown in the United States under the title *The Birth of a Pearl* (*American Film*, September 1985, p. 55).

35 Ibid., p. 353. Tom Gunning suggests the Pathé films *La Peine de Talion* (c. 1906) or *The Butterfly's Metamorphosis* (1904).

36 Ibid., p. 353. The last film mentioned was probably the Pathé fairy tale *Easter Eggs*, announced in *Cine-Phono* in 1907, no. 1, p. 5.

37 Chukovskii, *Nat Pinkerton*, p. 2.

38 Ibid., pp. 21–3.

39 Ibid., pp. 25–6.

CHAPTER 8

1 I would recommend Barry Salt, *Film Style and Technology* (London, 1984), and Kristin Thompson, 'The Foundations of Classical Style, 1909–28', in: D. Bordwell, J. Staiger and K. Thompson, *The Classical Hollywood Cinema: Film Style and Mode of Production to 1960* (London, 1985), pp. 155–240.

2 'Georg German o kino' [Georg German on Cinema], *Teatral'naya gazeta* [The Theatre Paper], no. 23, 8 July 1914, p. 12.

3 *'Leon Drey'*, *Teatral'naya gazeta*, 1915, no. 33, p. 15. For notes on this film see: Yu. Tsivian (research), P. C. Usai, L. Codelli, C. Montanaro and D. Robinson (eds), *Silent Witnesses: Russian Films, 1908–1919* (London, Pordenone, 1989), pp. 268–71.

4 *Peterburgskii listok* [The Petersburg Newsletter], 19 March 1917.

5 F. K. Sologub, *'Baryshnya Liza*: Stsenarii' [*Miss Liza*: A Script], IRLI, 289/1/ 184, p. 3.

6 A. Belyi, *Peterburg* (Moscow, 1978), pp. 161, 162.

7 A. Belyi, *'Peterburg*: Kinostsenarii po romanu' [Petersburg: A Film-script from the Novel], Manuscript Department, GBL, 516/3/37, pp. 43 verso–44.

8 *Pegas* [Pegasus], 1916, no. 4, p. 89. Octave Mirbeau (1850–1917), French novelist and dramatist.

9 *Vestnik kinematografii* [Cinematograph Herald], 1915, no. 106/3, p. 26.

10 *Hitchcock – Truffaut* (New York, 1969), p. 19.

11 N. Izvolov, *Vzaimodeistvie esteticheskikh i vne-esteticheskikh faktorov v evolyutsii kinematografa rannikh let* [The Interrelationship of Aesthetic and Non-aesthetic Factors in the Early Days of Cinema] (Unpublished doctoral dissertation, VGIK, Moscow, 1991), p. 77.

12 Some negatives have tinting codes and positions for intertitles scratched on the celluloid, but not *Chrysanthemums*. For notes on this film see: Tsivian *et al.* (eds), *Silent Witnesses*, pp. 248–9.

13 Cf. Tom Gunning on chase films: 'The pattern is consistent: a character is chased by a group of characters from one location to the next. Each shot presents the chased character running at some distance from the pursuing mob. The shot is held until first the pursued, and then the pursuers, exit from the frame. The next shot begins with the entrance of the pursued, and the movement through the frame begins all over again' (T. Gunning, *D. W. Griffith and the Origins of American Narrative Film: Early Years at Biograph* (Urbana, Chicago, 1991), p. 67).

14 C. Sabinski, *'Vot mchitsya troika pochtovaya* (Otryvok iz rezhisserskogo

stsenariya)' [See the Post Coach Rushing (Extract from the director's script)], *Iz Istorii kino* [From the History of Cinema] (Moscow, 1960), no. 3, pp. 158–9.

15 'Georg German o kino', p. 12.

16 -skii, 'Kino-epos' [A Cinema Epic], *Teatral'naya gazeta*, 1914, no. 52, p. 8.

17 -y [M. Kallash?], '*Nemye svideteli*' [Silent Witnesses], *Teatral'naya gazeta*, 1914, no. 19, p. 11. For notes on this film see: Tsivian *et al.* (eds), *Silent Witnesses*, pp. 230–1.

18 'Georg German o kino', p. 12.

19 E. Bowser, *History of the American Cinema, Volume 2, The Transformation of Cinema, 1907–1915*. (New York, 1990), p. 71.

20 I have in mind Vladimir Nabokov's Humbert Humbert: 'With people in movies I seem to share the services of the machina telephonica and its sudden god' (V. Nabokov, *Lolita* (London, 1959), p. 201).

21 *Pegas* [Pegasus], 1916, no. 3, p. 78. For notes on *Tanya Skvortsova* see: Tsivian *et al.* (eds), *Silent Witnesses*, pp. 334–6.

22 I. Surguchov [Signed I. S.], '*Lozh*'' [The Lie], *Kulisy* [The Wings], 1917, no. 23, p. 15.

23 B. Balázs, *Kul'tura kino* [The Culture of Cinema] (Moscow, Leningrad, 1925), p. 25.

24 B. M. Eikhenbaum, 'Problemy kinostilistiki' [Problems of Cinema Stylistics], in: *Poetika kino* [Cinema Poetics] (Moscow, Leningrad, 1927), pp. 34, 35.

25 Eikhenbaum, 'Problemy kinostilistiki', p. 44.

26 T. Polker, 'Dramaticheskie sochineniya A. P. Chekhova' [The Dramatic Works of A. P. Chekhov], *Russkie vedomosti* [Russian Herald], 3 Oct. 1897.

27 J. E. Jesionowski, *Thinking in Pictures: Dramatic Structure in D. W. Griffith's Biograph Films* (Berkeley, Los Angeles, London, 1987), p. 14.

28 Salt, *Film Style and Technology*, p. 109.

29 Ibid., p. 109.

30 T. Gunning, 'Now You See It, Now You Don't: the Temporality of the Cinema of Attractions'. Paper presented at the SCS Conference, May 1991, p. 16.

31 *Moskovskie vedomosti* [The Moscow Gazette], 16 March 1916.

32 P. Nilus, 'Novyi vid iskusstva' [A New Art Form], *Cine-Phono*, 1911, no. 9, p. 10.

33 Sologub, '*Baryshnya Liza*: Stsenarii', p. 1.

34 K. Irzykowski, *X Muza* [The Tenth Muse] (Warsaw, 1957), p. 50.

35 B. M. Eikhenbaum, 'Literatura i kinematograf' [Literature and Cinema], *Sovetskii ekran* [The Soviet Screen], 1926, no. 42, p. 45.

36 The term 'semantic gesture' was introduced by Jan Mukařovský in his study 'Záměrnost a nezáměrnost v umění' [Intentionality and Unintentionality in Art], see his: *Studii z estetiky* (Prague, 1966).

37 Salt, *Film Style*, p. 63.

38 Thompson, 'The Foundations', pp. 189–92.

39 Gunning, *D. W. Griffith*.

40 Ibid., pp. 78–81.

41 The term was introduced by Salt (*Film Style*, p. 387) and is now widely used.

42 On emblematic shots in Porter's films and elsewhere see: C. Musser. *Before the Nickelodeon: Edwin S. Porter and the Edison Manufacturing Company* (Berkeley, 1991), pp. 264–5; see also Index.

43 F. Mesguich, *Tours de manivelle: Souvenirs d'un chasseur d'images* [Cranking the Handle: Memories of an Image Hunter] (Paris, 1933), pp. 168–9; 269.

44 S. Vermel', 'Zhizn' ekrana' [Screen Life], *Iskusstvo* [Art], 1917, no. 1/2, p. 31.

45 *Cine-Phono*, 1910, no. 9, p. 13. Impersonal letter inserts lived on into the 1920s.

Sixteen years later Rudolf Harms repeated exactly the same request in his *Philosophie des Films: Seine aesthetischen und metaphysischen Grundlagen* [The Philosphy of Film: Its Aesthetic and Metaphysical Principles] (Leipzig, 1926). The reference is to the Russian translation: R. Garms, *Filosofiya Fil'ma* (Leningrad, 1927), p. 102.

46 Alexander Blok, *Sobranie sochinenii v 6 tomakh* [Collected Works in 6 Volumes] (Leningrad, 1981), vol. 5, p. 204.

47 V. Sirin [V. V. Nabokov], 'Kinematograf' [The Cinematograph], *Rul'* [The Rudder], 1928, no. 2433.

48 See my article about the use of handwriting in this film: Yu. Tsiv'yan, 'Paleogrami v fil'me *Shinel'* [Paleograms in the film *The Overcoat*], in: *Vtorye Tyn'yanovskie chteniya* [The Second Tynyanov Readings] (Riga, 1986), pp. 14–27.

49 Sologub, '*Baryshnya Liza*: Stsenarii', p. 1.

50 See Thompson, 'The Foundations', p. 188.

51 P. B., 'Nuzhny li nadpisi v kinematograficheskikh kartinakh?' [Do Cinema Pictures Need Intertitles?], *Proektor* [Projector], 1916, no. 17, p. 2.

52 I have not seen the film except for this frame enlargement published in: *FC 89. Cinema: Lost and Found – From the Collection of Komira Tomijiro*, 2 November 1991, p. 31. Hiroshi Komatsu (who has seen the print) tells me I am right in assuming that this was an emblematic close-up. I am indebted to Hiroshi Komatsu for sending me this frame enlargement.

53 N. Gofman, 'Kak ya byla Son'koi Zolotoi-Ruchkoi' [How I Played Sonka Golden-Hand], TsMK archives, p. 16.

54 For notes on *The Bells Ring out, Telling their Simple Tale* and *Child of the Big City* see: Tsivian *et al.* (eds), *Silent Witnesses*, pp. 328–32; 216.

55 Ch. Sabinskii, 'Iz zapisok starogo kinomastera' [From the Notes of an Old Master of Cinema], TsMK archives, p. 11.

56 'Kriticheskoe obozrenie' [Critical Review], *Proektor*, 1915, no. 3, p. 16.

57 Z. Barantsevich, 'Fil'my, lyudi, vstrechi' [Films, People, Encounters], TsMK archives, p. 8.

58 V. Pavlova, 'Zabytoe iskusstvo' [A Forgotten Art], TsMK archives, p. 5. For notes on *A Ballerina's Romance* see: Tsivian *et al.* (eds), *Silent Witnesses*, pp. 358–60.

59 Thompson, 'The Foundations', p. 190. In Russian film articles of the 1910s what we now identify as the American influence was often referred to as just 'Western': the country of origin was usually absent from credits.

60 *Proektor*, 1916, no. 9, p. 14.

61 I. Surguchov, 'Nesmyatye podushki (o kino-rezhisserakh)' [Uncrumpled Pillows (On Film Directors)], *Kulisy* [The Wings], 1917, no. 26/7, p. 12.

62 For notes on *Life for Life* see: Tsivian *et al.* (eds), *Silent Witnesses*, pp. 326–8.

63 *Vestnik kinematografii*, 1916, no. 122, p. 17. For notes on *Nelly Raintseva* see: Tsivian *et al.* (eds), *Silent Witnesses*, pp. 346–9.

64 V. Turkin, review in *Kinogazeta* [The Cinema Paper], 1918, no. 23, p. 14.

65 For an example see the 1914 article by Stark quoted in Part II Chapter 5 (see p. 131). The response was probably universal. For American parallels see Thompson, 'The Foundations', p. 191.

66 The idea is discussed and illustrated with corresponding texts in: Yu. Lotman, Yu. Tsivian, *Dialogi s ekranom* [Dialogues with the Screen] (Alexandra Publishers, Tallinn, Estonia, forthcoming).

67 E. T. Hall, 'Proxemics', *Current Anthropology*, April-June 1968, vol. 9, no. 2/3, p. 92.

68 Ibid. I have to stress that, in contrast to my summary, the actual data given by Hall are complex and specified according to different gradations of visual perception (peripheral vision, scanning, etc.).

69 A. Arkatov, 'Segodnyashnee kino (Opyt analiza)' [Cinema Today (An Attempt at an Analysis)], in: *Teatr i zhizn'* [Theatre and Life], Berlin, 1922.
70 Yu. Engel' [Signed: Yu. E.], 'O kinematografe' [On The Cinematograph], *Russkie vedomosti*, no. 275, 27 Nov. 1908.
71 Thompson, 'The Foundations', p. 231.
72 '*Tsari birzhi*' [Kings of the Stock Exchange], *Kulisy* [The Wings], 1917, no. 9/10, pp. 15, 16. For notes on this film see: Tsivian *et al.* (eds), *Silent Witnesses*, pp. 368–71.
73 A. Kosorotov, 'Monumental'nost'' [Monumentality], *Teatr i iskusstvo* [Theatre and Art], 1911, no. 38, p. 702.
74 T. Mann, *The Magic Mountain* [English translation by H. T. Lowe-Porter] (Harmondsworth, 1965), pp. 317–18.
75 S. Ya. Marshak [Signed 'Doctor Friken'], 'V kinematografe' [At the Cinematograph], *Satirikon*, 1908, no. 12, p. 7.
76 Mesguich, *Tours de manivelle*, p. 213.
77 The fascination with 'busy city streets' and 'crowd effects' [*effets de foules*] in early cinema is analysed in: T. Gunning, 'The Book that Refuses to Be Read: Images of the City in Early Cinema', forthcoming, pp. 4–5.
78 K. Chukovskii, *Nat Pinkerton i soviemennaya literatura* [Nat Pinkerton and Contemporary Literature] (Moscow, 1908), p. 12.
79 V. Nabokov, *The Defence* (London, 1964), p. 151. The translation is by Michael Scammell in collaboration with the author.
80 Salt, *Film Style*, pp. 78, 79.
81 T. Gunning, 'An Unseen Energy Swallows Space', in J. L. Fell (ed.), *Film Before Griffith* (Berkeley, London, 1983), p. 364.
82 Of the sources available in English one can recommend M. Cole, S. Scribner, *Culture & Thought: A Psychological Introduction* (New York, London, Sydney, Toronto, 1974). In his paper '"The Whole World Within Reach": Travel Images Without Borders', delivered at the 2nd DOMITOR Colloquium in Lausanne (June 1992), Gunning suggested the term 'kinesthesia' which is probably a better term because it places the travel attraction within the context of traditional landscape painting.
83 The RKM collection.
84 A. Koiranskii, 'Kintop' [The Flicks], *Nash ponedel'nik* [Our Monday Paper], no. 2, 26 Nov. 1907, p. 4.
85 Ibid.
86 W. Schivelbusch, *The Railway Journey: Trains and Travel in the 19th Century* (New York, 1979), pp. 57–72.
87 Quoted in: E. Eiken, 'The Cinema and Italian Futurist Painting', *Art Journal*, winter 1981, no. 41, p. 353.
88 Geinim [A. Anoshchenko?], 'Novoe iskusstvo' [A New Art], *Kino-teatr i zhizn'* [The Cinema Theatre and Life], 1913, no. 1, p. 4.
89 Ibid., p. 2.
90 L. Voitolovskii, 'Chudesnyi Gost'' [The Miraculous Visitor], *Vestnik Kinematografii*, 1914, no. 85/5, p. 17.
91 Gunning. *D. W. Griffith*, p. 42.
92 L. Buñuel, *Mon dernier soupir* [My Last Sigh] (Paris, 1982), p. 42.
93 Thompson, 'The Foundations', pp. 228–9.
94 Ibid.
95 For notes on these four films see: Tsivian *et al.* (eds), *Silent Witnesses*, pp. 216–18, 286–90, 372–4 and 410–13 respectively.
96 This part of Paolo Cherchi Usai's explanation was illustrated with a gracious,

delightfully inviting gesture that probably only someone born in Italy could ever hope to repeat!

97 'Mopassan po-russki' [Maupassant, Russian style], *Obozrenie teatrov* [The Theatre Review], no. 2856/2857, p. 17. The film was based on Tolstoy's story *Fransuaza* [Françoise], which was itself an adaptation of Maupassant's *Le Port* [The Port]. See: L. N. Tolstoi, *Polnoe sobranie sochinenii* [Complete Works] (Moscow, 1936), vol. 27, pp. 251–8 and pp. 671–7.

98 For notes on *A Life for a Life* see: Tsivian *et al.* (eds), *Silent Witnesses*, pp. 326–8.

99 Thompson, 'The Foundations', p. 228.

100 On the use of exterior 'trailing pans' in Biograph films by Griffith see: J. E. Jesionowski, *Thinking in Pictures: Dramatic Structure in D. W. Griffith's Biograph Films* (Berkeley, Los Angeles, London, 1987), pp. 89–90 and Gunning, *D. W. Griffith*, pp. 210–18.

101 P. C. Usai, 'On the concept of "influence" in Early Cinema'. Paper delivered at the 2nd DOMITOR Colloquium in Lausanne, June 1992. The film was shown at the Colloquium.

102 V. Ballyuzek, 'Na s'emkakh "Pikovoi damy"' [Shooting *The Queen of Spades*], in: *Iz istorii kino, 7* [From The History of Cinema, 7] (Moscow, 1968), p. 102.

103 *Teatr* [The Theatre], 1916, no. 1835, p. 10. For notes on *The Queen of Spades* see: Tsivian *et al.* (eds), *Silent Witnesses*, pp. 352–6.

104 It was invented in Germany in 1986 and was used in Russia in the Maly Theatre in 1900.

105 A. R. Kugel', *Utverzhdenie teatra* [Establishing the Theatre] (Moscow, 1923), p. 186. The passage cited comes from an article written in 1913.

106 Quoted in G. C. Pratt, *Spellbound in Darkness: A History of the Silent Film* (New York, 1973), p. 126.

107 'Krivoe zerkalo' [The Distorting Mirror], *Teatr i iskusstvo* [Theatre and Art], 1911, no. 7, p. 148.

108 N. V. Gogol', *Tales of Good and Evil* [Translated by David Magarshak] (New York, 1957), pp. 171–2.

109 A. Belyi, *Masterstvo Gogolya* [Gogol's Mastery] (Moscow, Leningrad, 1934), pp. 309–10.

110 S. Tret'yakov, *Zheleznaya pauza* [The Iron Interval] (Vladivostok, 1919), p. 8.

111 A. Maguire and J. E. Malmstad write: 'Circular thinking embraces not "eternity" but only a small part of the vast "circle". It can be expressed only conventionally, as dogma, that is, as motionless circular thinking; and dogmas, Bely argues, arise in time, and are grounded in particular ways of apprehending the world, that is, in experience. (A. Maguire, J. E. Malmstad, '*Petersburg*', in: J. E. Malmstad (ed.), *Andrey Bely: Spirit of Symbolism* (Ithaca, London, 1987), p. 99).

112 A. Belyi, 'Krugovoe dvizhenie' [Circular Movement], *Trudy i dni* [Labours and Days], 1912, no. 4/5, p. 63.

113 N. Berberova, 'A Memoir and a Comment: The Circle of *Petersburg*', in: G. Janecek (ed.) *Andrey Bely: A Critical Review* (Lexington, 1978), p. 116.

114 Belyi, '*Peterburg*: Kinostsenarii po romanu', p. 99 verso.

115 Ibid., p. 95.

116 Ibid., p. 38.

117 Ibid., p. 88.

118 Ibid., p. 55.

119 Ibid., p. 56.

120 Ibid., pp. 57 verso, 58.

POSTSCRIPT

1 J. T. Munsey, 'From a Toy to a Necessity: A Study of Some Early Reactions to the Motion Picture', *Society of Cinematologists: Cinema Journal*, 1965, vol. V, p. 99.
2 E. Bowser, *History of the American Cinema, Volume 2, The Transformation of Cinema, 1907–1915* (New York, 1990), p. 94.
3 V. Shklovskii (ed.), *Chaplin* (Berlin, 1923), pp. 43–4.

Bibliography

UNPUBLISHED ARCHIVE MATERIALS AND DISSERTATIONS

Anoshchenko, A., 'Iz poluzabytoi epokhi' [From a Half-forgotten age]. Typescript in the V. Vishnevsky archives, GFF.

Barantsevich, Z., 'Fil'my, lyudi, vstrechi' [Films, People, Encounters], TsMK archives.

Belyi, A., contract for the film script 'Petersburg', TsGALI, 989/1/5.

Belyi, A., 'Peterburg; Kinostsenarii po romanu' [Petersburg: A Film Script from the Novel]. GBL, 516/3/37.

Digmelov, A. D., '50 let nazad' [50 Years Ago], p. 3. Typescript in the V. Vishnevsky archive, GFF.

Dushen, B. V., 'Beglye vospominaniya' [Fleeting Memoirs]. Typescript in the V. Vishnevsky archive, GFF.

Gofman, N., 'Kak ya byla Son'koi Zolotoi-Ruchkoi' [How I Played Sonka Golden-Hand], TsMK archives.

Ignatov, I. N., 'Kinematograf v Rossii: Proshloe i budushchee' [The Cinematograph in Russia: Its Past and Future], TsGALI, 221/1.

Ivanov-Barkov, E. A., 'Vospominaniya' [Memoirs], TsGALI, 2970/1/52.

Izvolov, N., *Vzaimodeistvie esteticheskikh i vne-esteticheskikh faktorov v evolyutsii kinematografa rannikh let* [The Interrelationship of Aesthetic and Non-aesthetic Factors in the Early Days of Cinema] (Unpublished doctoral dissertation, VGIK, Moscow, 1991).

Kogan, L. R., *Vospominaniya* [Memoirs], pt. 2, no. 1, 1894–7. GPB, 1035/35.

Likhachev, B., 'Lektsii o kino' [Lectures on Cinema], LGITMIK Archives, lecture IV.

Muzei MKhaTa [Moscow Art Theatre Museum], Arkhiv Knipper–Chekhovoi [Knipper–Chekhov Archive], file no. 2388.

Neighbours' complaints about the Riga film theatre Sinfirofon, GAP, group 2, no. 27.

Orlov, N. I., 'Pervye kinos''emki v Rossii' [The First Film Shootings in Russia]. Typescript in the V. Vishnevsky archive, GFF.

Ostroumov, L. E., 'Moya druzhba s Velikim Nemym' [My Friendship with the Great Silent]. Typescript in the V. Vishnevsky archive, GFF.

Pavlova, V., 'Zabytoe iskusstvo' [A Forgotten Art], TsMK archives.

Perestiani, I., *Vospominaniya* [Memoirs]. TsMK archives.

Sabinskii, Ch., 'Iz zapisok starogo kinomastera' [From the Notes of an Old Master of Cinema], TsMK archives.

Sologub, F. K., '*Baryshnya Liza*: Stsenarii' [*Miss Liza*: A Script], IRLI, 289/1/184.

Sologub, F. K., 'V kinematografe' [At the Cinematograph], IRLI, 289/1/2.

Stepanov, V., 'Kino v Kineshme' [The Cinema in Kineshma]. TsMK archives.
TsGIAL, 776/22/33, documents on cinema from the Imperial office in St Petersburg.
Verner [Werner], A., 'Beglye zametki' [Fleeting Notes]. Typescript in the V. Vishnevsky archive, GFF.
Vertov, D.,TsGALI, 2091/1/28, score for *The Man with a Movie Camera*.
Vysotskaya, O. V., 'Moi vospominaniya' [My Memoirs]. Unpublished MSS, IRLI (MSS division), no. 41.
'Zaklyuchenie postoyannoi komissii naodnykh chtenii po voprosam o primenenii kinematograficheskoi demonstratsii v shkol'nom dele i narodnykh auditoriyakh' [Conclusion of the Standing Commission of the National Lecture Committee on Questions Relating to the Use of Film in Schools and Public Lecture Halls], 11 Nov. 1915, TsGIAL, 733/182/166.
Zhdanov, Ya. A., 'Po Rossii s kinogovoryashchimi kartinami' [Around Russia with Talking Pictures]. Typescript in the Soviet Cinema Section of VGIK.

BOOKS

Adorno, T. W. and Eisler, H., *Komposition für den Film* [Composing for Film] (Munich, 1969).
Akhropov, A., *Tadzhikskoe kino* [The Tadzhik Cinema] (Dushanbe, 1971).
Aleinikov, M. N., *Puti sovetskogo kino i MKhAT* [The Course of Soviet Cinema and the Moscow Art Theatre] (Moscow, 1947).
Altenloh, E., *Zur Soziologie des Kino: Die Kino-Unternehmung und die sozialen Schichten ihrer Besucher* [Towards a Sociology of Cinema: The Cinema Business and the Social Strata of its Visitors] (Jena, 1914).
Analyse catalographique des films de Georges Méliès [Analytical Catalogue of the Films of Georges Méliès] (Paris, 1981).
Andreev, L., *Polnoe sobranie sochinenii* [Complete Works] (St Petersburg, 1913).
Apollonio, U. (ed.), *Futurist Manifestos* (New York, 1973).
Artsybashev, M., *Teni utra* [Morning Shadows] (Moscow, 1990).
Asendorf, Ch., *Ströme und Strahlen: Das langsame Verschwinden der Materie um 1900* [Currents and Rays: The Slow Disappearance of Matter around 1900] (Giessen, 1989).
Aumont, J., Gaudreault, J., Marie, M. (eds), *Histoire du cinéma: Nouvelles approches* [Cinema History. New Approaches] (Paris, 1989).
Autour de Levy-Dhurmer: Visionnaires et Intimistes en 1900 [Around Levy-Dhurmer: Visionaries and 'Intimistes' in 1900] (Paris, 1973).
Averchenko, A., *Dyuzhina nozhei v spinu revolyutsii* [A Dozen Knives in the Back of the Revolution] (Paris, 1921).
Bal'mont, K., *Stikhotvoreniya* [Poems] (Moscow, 1969).
Balázs, B., *Kul'tura kino* [The Culture of Cinema] (Moscow, Leningrad, 1925).
Barle, F. Kh., *Okkul'tizm* [Occultism] (St Petersburg, 1991, first edition 1911). The Russian translation of: Barlet, F. Ch., *L'Occultisme. Definition. Méthode. Classification. Applications* (Paris, 1909).
Bedford, C. H., *The Seeker: D. S. Merezhkovskiy* (Lawrence, Manhatten, Wichita, 1975).
Beketova, M. A., *Aleksandr Blok: Biograficheskii ocherk* [Alexander Blok: A Biographical Essay] (Petrograd, 1922).
Belyi, A., *Arabeski* [Arabesques] (Moscow, 1911).
Belyi, A., *Masterstvo Gogolya* [Gogol's Mastery] (Moscow, Leningrad, 1934).
Belyi, A., *Na perevale: Berlin* [At the Turning Point: Berlin] (Petrograd, Moscow, 1923).

Belyi, A., *Nachalo veka* [The Beginning of the Century] (Moscow, Leningrad, 1933).

Belyi, A., *Peterburg* (Moscow, 1978).

[Belyi] Bely, A., *Petersburg* [English translation by R. A. Maguire. Introduction and notes by John Malmstad] (Bloomington, London, 1978).

Belyi, A., *Rudol'f Shteiner i Gete v mirovozzrenii sovremennosti* [Rudolf Steiner and Goethe in Contemporary Thought] (Moscow, 1917).

[Belyi] Biely, A., *St Petersburg* [English translation by John Cournos. Introduction by George Reavey] (New York, 1959).

Benjamin, W., *Allegorien kultureller Erfahrung* [Allegories of Cultural Experience] (Leipzig, 1984).

Benua [Benois], A., *Aleksandr Benua razmyshlyaet* [Alexander Benois Reflects] (Moscow, 1968).

Benveniste, E., *Obshchaya lingvistika* [General Linguistics] (Moscow, 1974).

Bergson, H., *Creative Evolution* [English translation by A. Mitchell] (New York, 1911).

Blok, A. A., *Pis'ma Aleksandra Bloka k E. P. Ivanovu* [Letters of Alexander Blok to E. P. Ivanov] (Moscow, Leningrad, 1936).

Blok, A. A., *Sobranie sochinenii v 8 tomakh* [Collected Works in 8 volumes] (Moscow, Leningrad, 1960–3).

Blok, A. A., *Sobranie sochinenii v 6 tomakh* [Collected Works in 6 volumes] (Leningrad, 1981).

Blok, A. A., *Zapisnye knizhki* [Notebooks] (Moscow, 1965).

Bordwell, D., *Narration in the Fiction Film* (Madison, 1985).

Bordwell, D., Thompson, K., Steiger, J., *The Classical Hollywood Cinema: Film Style and Mode of Production* (London, 1988).

Boussinot, R., *L'Encyclopédie du cinéma* (Paris, 1980).

Bowser, E., *History of the American Cinema, Volume 2, The Transformation of Cinema, 1907–1915* (New York, 1990).

British Film Catalogue (1895–1970) (London, 1973).

Brown, E. J., *Mayakovsky: A Poet in the Revolution* (Princeton, NJ, 1973).

Brownlow, K., *The Parade's Gone By . . .* (London, 1968).

Buñuel, L., *Mon dernier soupir* [My Last Sigh] (Paris, 1982).

Burbank, J. and Steiner, P. (eds), *Structure, Sign and Function: Selected Essays by Jan Mukařovský* (New Haven, CT, London, 1978).

Cavell, S., *The World Viewed: Reflections on the Ontology of Film* (New York, 1971).

Chaikovskii, V. B., *Mladencheskie gody russkogo kino* [Infant Years of the Russian Cinema] (Moscow, 1928).

Cherchi Usai, P. and Codelli, L. (eds), *Before Caligari: German Cinema, 1895–1920* (Pordenone, 1990).

Chesterton, G. K., *Generally Speaking: A Book of Essays* (London, 1937).

Chesterton, G. K., *The Man Who Was Thursday* [1908] (London, 1976).

Chukovskii, K., *Nat Pinkerton i sovremennaya literatura* [Nat Pinkerton and Contemporary Literature] (Moscow, 1908).

Cole, M. and Scribner, S., *Culture & Thought: Psychological Introduction* (New York, London, Sydney, Toronto, 1974).

Cosandey, R., Gaudreault, A., Gunning, T. (eds), *An Invention of The Devil's: Religion and Early Cinema* (Lausanne, 1992).

Delandes, J. and Richard, J., *Histoire comparée du cinéma* [A Comparative History of Cinema] (Tournai, 1968).

Derzhavin, D., *Sochineniya Derzhavina* [Derzhavin's Works] (St Petersburg, 1865).

Eagle, H. (ed.), *Russian Formalist Film Theory* (Ann Arbor, MI, 1981).

[Eizenshtein] Eisenstein, S., *Immoral Memories: An Autobiography* [Translated by Herbert Marshall], (London, 1985).

Eizenshtein, S. M., *Izbrannye proizvedeniya v 6 tomakh* [Selected Works in 6 volumes] (Moscow, 1964–71).

Elsaesser, T. and Barker, A. (eds), *Early Cinema: Space Frame Narrative* (London, 1990).

Fell, J., *Film and the Narrative Tradition* (Oklahoma City, 1974).

Fell, J. (ed.), *Film Before Griffith* (London, Los Angeles, 1983).

Fevral'skii, A., *Puti k sintezu: Meierkhol'd i kino* [Paths to Synthesis: Meyerhold and Cinema] (Moscow, 1978).

Gaidarov, V., *V teatre i kino* [In Theatre and Cinema] (Moscow, 1966).

Garms [Harms], R., *Filosofiya fil'ma* [The Philosophy of Film] (Leningrad, 1927). The Russian translation of: *Philosophie des Films: Seine aesthetischen und Metaphysischen Grundlagen* [The Philosophy of Film: Its Aesthetic and Metaphysical Principles] (Leipzig, 1926).

Gaudreault, A., *Du Littéraire au filmique: Système du récit* [From the Literary to the Filmic: The Narrative System] (Québec, 1988).

Gippius, Z., *Chertova kukla* [The Devil's Doll] (Moscow, 1911).

Gogol', N. V., *Tales of Good and Evil* [Translated by David Magarshak] (New York, 1957).

Goldobin, A. V. and Azancheev, B. M., *Pianist-illyustrator kinematograficheskikh kartin* [Accompanying Cinematograph Pictures on the Piano] (Kostroma, 1912).

Gorkii, M., *Polnoe sobranie sochinenii* [Complete Works] (Moscow, 1969).

Gorodetskii, S., *Povesti i rasskazy* (Stories and Tales) (St Petersburg, 1910).

Gunning, T., *D. W. Griffith and the Origins of American Narrative Film: The Early Years at Biograph* (Urbana, Chicago, 1991).

Gunning, T., 'The Book that Refuses to be Read: Images of the City in Early Cinema' (forthcoming).

Hansen, M., *Babel and Babylon: Spectatorship in American Silent Film* (Cambridge, MA, 1991).

Hätte ich das Kino! Die Schriftsteller und der Stummfilm [If Only I Had Cinema! Writers and the Silent Film] (Munich, 1976).

Hitchcock – Truffaut (New York, 1969).

Hollier, D. (ed.), *A New History of French Literature* (London, 1989).

Hugnes, P. and Marnin, M., *Le Cinéma français. Le Muët* [French Cinema: The Silent Film] (Paris, 1986).

Irzykowski, K., *X muza* [The Tenth Muse] (Warsaw, 1957).

Istoriya stanovleniya sovetskogo kino [A History of How Soviet Cinema Came into Being] (Moscow, 1986).

Ivanov, V. I., *Stikhotvoreniya i poemy* [Verses and Poems] (Leningrad, 1978).

Janecek, G. (ed.) *Andrey Bely: A Critical Review* (Lexington, 1978).

Jesionowski, J. E., *Thinking in Pictures: Dramatic Structure in D. W. Griffith's Biograph Films* (Berkeley, Los Angeles, London, 1987).

Kaes, A. (ed.), *Kino-Debatte* [Cinema Debate] (Munich, 1978).

Kern, G. (ed.), [English translation by E. J. Brown], *Velimir Khlebnikov: Snake Train* (Ann Arbor, MI, 1976).

Khanzhonkov, A. A., *Pervye gody russkoi kinematografii* [The First Years of Russian Cinema] (Moscow, Leningrad, 1937).

Khlebnikov, V. V., *Stikhotvoreniya, poemy, dramy, proza* [Verse, Poems, Drama, Prose] (Moscow, 1986).

Khodasevich, V., *Poeticheskoe khoziaistvo Pushkina* [Pushkin's Poetic Apparatus] (Leningrad, 1924).

Khudyakov, I., *Opyt rukovodstva k illyustratsii sinematograficheskikh kartin: S ukazaniem na 1000 tem* [A Preliminary Manual for Illustrating Cinematographic Pictures: With an Index of 1000 Themes] (Moscow, 1912).

Kirby, M., *Futurist Performance* (New York, 1971).

Kletskin, A. A., *Kino v zhizni yakutyan* [Cinema in the Life of the Yakutians] (Yakutsk, 1973).

Kugel', A. R., *Utverzhdenie teatra* [Consolidating the Theatre] (Moscow, 1923).

Kugel', A. R., *List'ya s dereva* [Leaves from a Tree] (Leningrad, 1926).

Landesman, M. Ya., *Tak pochinalosya kino: Rospovidi pro dozhovtnevii kinematograf* [That's How Cinema Began: Stories about the Cinematograph before the October Revolution] (Kiev, 1972).

Lehmann, H., *Die Kinematographie, ihre Grundlagen und ihre Anwendungen* [The Cinematograph, its Basic Principles and Applications] (Leipzig, 1919).

Leonidov, O., *Stikhi* [Verses] (Moscow, 1914).

Leyda, J., *Kino: A History of the Russian and Soviet Film* (New York, 1973).

Lidbiter [C. W. Leadbeater], *Mental'nyi plan* [The Mental Plane] (Riga, 1937; St Petersburg, 1991).

Likhachev, B. S., *Kino v Rossii* [Cinema in Russia] (Leningrad, 1927).

Lotman, Yu. and Tsiv'yan, Yu., *Dialogi s ekranom* [Dialogues with the Screen] (Alexandra Publishers, Tallinn, Estonia, forthcoming).

Mackintosh, A., *Symbolism and Art Nouveau* (London, 1975).

Malmstad, J. E. (ed.), *Andrey Bely: Spirit of Symbolism* (Ithaca, London, 1987).

Mandel'shtam, O., *Razgovor o Dante* [A Conversation about Dante] (Moscow, 1967).

Mandel'shtamovskii sbornik [Essays on Mandelshtam] (Moscow, 1991).

Mann, T., *The Magic Mountain* [English translation by H. T. Lowe-Porter] (Harmondsworth, 1965).

Mast, G. and Cohen, M. (eds), *Film Theory and Criticism* (New York, 1985).

Maurin, E., *Kinematograf v prakticheskoi zhizni* [The Cinematograph in Practical Life] (Petrograd, 1916).

May, L., *Screening Out the Past: The Birth of Mass Culture and the Motion Picture Industry* (New York, Oxford, 1980).

Mayakovskii, V. V., *Sobranie sochinenii v 8 tomakh* [Collected Works in 8 volumes] (Moscow, 1968).

Mayakovskii, V., *Selected Works in Three Volumes* (Moscow, 1986).

Mesguich, F., *Tours de manivelle: Souvenirs d'un chasseur d'images* [Cranking the Handle: Memories of an Image Hunter] (Paris, 1933).

Metz, C., *The Imaginary Signifier: Psychoanalysis and the Cinema* (Bloomington, 1982).

Mukařovský, J., *Studii z estetiky* [Studies in Aesthetics] (Prague, 1966).

Musser, C., *Before the Nickelodeon: Edwin S. Porter and the Edison Manufacturing Company* (Berkeley, Los Angeles, London, 1991).

Nabokov, V., *Ada* (London, 1969).

Nabokov, V., *The Defence* (London, 1964).

Nabokov, V., *Laughter in the Dark* (London, 1961).

Nabokov, V., *Lolita* (London, 1959).

Nabokov, V., *Mary* (London, 1971).

Nekhoroshev, Yu., *Khudozhnik V. A. Simov* [The Artist V. A. Simov] (Moscow, 1984).

Norman [Vitte], A., *Poemy: Stat'i o teatre* [Poems: Articles on Theatre] (Tashkent, 1920).

Orlenev, P., *Zhizn' i tvorchestvo russkogo aktera Pavla Orleneva, opisannye im samim* [The Life and Work of the Russian Actor Pavel Orlenev as Described by Himself] (Leningrad, Moscow, 1961).

Pamyatniki kul'tury: Novye otkrytiya [Cultural Texts: New Discoveries] (Leningrad, 1985).

Pasternak, A. L., *Vospominaniya* [Memoirs] (Munich, 1933).

Paustovskii, K., *Razlivy rek* [Flooded Rivers] (Moscow, 1973).

Pirandello, L., *Shoot! The Notebooks of Serafino Gubbio, Cinematograph Operator.* [Translated by C. K. Scott Moncrieff] (New York, 1926).

Poetika Kino [The Poetics of Cinema] (Moscow, Leningrad, 1927). For English translations see: Taylor, R. (ed.), *The Poetics of Cinema: Russian Poetics in Translation*, no. 9 (Oxford, 1982); and Eagle, H. (ed.), *Russian Formalist Film Theory* (Ann Arbor, MI, 1981).

Pratt, G. C., *Spellbound in Darkness: A History of the Silent Film* (New York, 1973).

Pushkin, A. S., *Polnoe sobranie sochinenii* [Complete Works] (Moscow, 1937–49).

Robinson, D., *Music of the Shadows* (Pordenone, 1990).

Rosenthal, B. G., *D. S. Merezhkovsky and the Silver Age: The Development of a Revolutionary Mentality* (The Hague, 1975).

Rossetti, D. G., *The Collected Works*, W. M. Rossetti, ed. (London, 1886).

Russell, R. and Barratt, A. (eds), *Russian Theatre in the Age of Modernism* (New York, 1990).

Sabaneev, L. L., *Vospominaniya o Skryabine* [Memories of Scriabin] (Moscow, 1925).

Sadoul, G., *Louis Lumière* (Paris, 1964).

Sadul' [Sadoul], G., *Vseobshchaya istoriya kino* [A General History of Cinema] (Moscow, 1958–82).

Salt, B., *Film Style and Technology: History and Analysis* (London, 1984).

Schivelbusch, W., *The Railway Journey: Trains and Travel in the 19th Century* (New York, 1979).

Schivelbusch, W., *Disenchanted Night: The Industrialization of Light in the Nineteenth Century* (Berkeley, 1988).

Schmutzler, R., *Art Nouveau* (New York, 1962).

Sel'vinskii, I., *Ulyalaevshchina* [Ulyalaev's Band] (Moscow, 1927).

Shcheglov, I., *O narodnom teatre* [On Popular Theatre] (Moscow, 1895).

Shebuev, N., *Negativy* [Negatives] (Moscow, 1903).

Shershenevich, V., *Avtomobil'ya postup'* [The Tread of the Motor Car] (Moscow, 1916).

Shipulinskii, F., *Istoriya kino* [The History of Cinema] (Moscow, 1934).

Shipulinskii, F., *Kinematograf: Sbornik statei* [The Cinematograph: A Collection of Essays] (Mosocow, 1919).

Shklovskii, V. (ed.), *Chaplin* (Berlin, 1923).

Staiger, J., *Interpreting Movies: Studies in the Historical Reception of American Cinema* (Princeton, NJ, 1992).

Stanislavskii, K. S., *Sobranie sochinenii* [Collected Works] (Moscow, 1960).

Struve, G., *Russkaya literatura v izgnanii* [Russian Literature in Exile] (New York, 1956).

Svyatlovskii, S., *Sedye goroda* [Grey Cities] (St Petersburg, 1912).

Talbot, D. (ed.) *Film: An Anthology* (Berkeley, 1969).

Taylor, R., (ed.), *The Poetics of Cinema: Russian Poetics in Translation*, no. 9 (Oxford, 1982).

Taylor, R., *The Politics of the Soviet Cinema, 1917–1929* (Cambridge, 1979).

Taylor, R. and Christie, I. (eds), *The Film Factory: Russian and Soviet Cinema in Documents 1896–1939* (London, Cambridge, MA, 1988).

Taylor, R. and Christie, I. (eds), *Inside the Film Factory: New Approaches to Russian and Soviet Cinema* (London, New York, 1991).

Tolstoi, L. N., *Polnoe sobranie sochinenii* [Complete Works] (Moscow, 1936), vol. 27, pp. 251–8, 671–7.

Tret'yakov, S., *Zheleznaya pauza* [The Iron Interval] (Vladivostok, 1919).
[Tsiv'yan] Tsivian, Yu. (research), Cherchi, Usai, P. Codelli, L., Montanaro, C., Robinson, D. (eds), *Silent Witnesses. Russian Films 1908–1919* (London, Pordenone, 1989).
Tyn'yanov, Yu. N., *Poetika. Istoriya literatury. Kino* [Poetics. Literary History. Cinema] (Moscow, 1977).
Tyurin, V., *Zhivaya fotografiya* [A Living Photograph] (St Petersburg, 1898).
Usai, P. Cherchi, *Una passione infiammabile: Guida allo studio del cinema muto* [An Inflammable Passion: A Guide to Studying the Silent Cinema] (Turin, 1991).
Vechorka, T., *Magnolii* [Magnolias] (Tiflis, 1916).
Volkonskii, S. M., *Rodina: Moi vospominaniya* [Motherland: My Memories] (no place of publication, n. d.).
Voloshin, M., *Liki tvorchestva* [Faces of Creativity] (Leningrad, 1988).
Volshebnyi fonar': katalog na 1901–1903 [The Magic Lantern: Catalogue for 1901–1903] (Yekaterinograd, n. d.).
Yermolova, M. N., *Pis'ma M. N. Yermolovoi* [The Letters of M. N. Yermolova] (Moscow, Leningrad, 1939).
Ziołkowski, T., *Disenchanted Images* (Princeton, NJ, 1977).
Zorkaya, N. M., *Na rubezhe stoletii: u istokov massovogo iskusstva v Rossii 1900–1910 godov* [At the Turn of the Century: The Sources of Mass Art in Russia] (Moscow, 1976).

UNSIGNED ARTICLES AND REVIEWS

'Artisticheskoe spravochnoe byuro' [Information Bureau of the Arts], *Rech'* [Speech], no. 1, 5 Feb. 1910.
'Eks-korol' Manuel' na pokoe' [Ex-King Manuel in Retirement] *Vestnik kinematografii* [Cinematograph Herald], 1913, no. 85/6.
'Flanyor', 'Kinematografiya' [Cinematography], *Zhizn'* [Life], no. 1, 5 Jan. 1909.
'Iz provintsial'nykh gazet' [From the Provincial Papers], *Novoe slovo* [New Word], 1896, no. 11.
'Kazn' Cholgosha v kinematografe' [The Execution of Czołgosz in the Cinematograph], *Novoe vremya* [New Time], 1902, no. 20.
'Khronika' [Chronicle of Events], *Vestnik kinematografii* [Cinematograph Herald], 1913, no. 18.
'Kinematograf i zdorov'e' [The Cinematograph and Health], *Zhurnal za sem' dnei* [The Seven-Day Magazine], 1913, no. 38.
'Koe-chto o muzykal'noi illyustratsii' [A Thing or Two About Musical Illustration], *Vestnik kinematografii*, 1913, no 17.
'Kriticheskoe obozrenie' [A Critical Review], *Proektor* [The Projector], 1915, no. 3.
'Krivoe zerkalo' [The Distorting Mirror], *Teatr i iskusstvo* [Theatre and Art], 1911, no. 7.
'Kul'tura chelovecheskogo zverstva' [The Culture of Human Savagery], *Vestnik kinematografii*, 1912, no. 54.
'*Leon Drey*', *Teatral'naya gazeta* [The Theatre Paper], 1915, no. 33.
'Mel'kanie' [Flickering], *Cine-Phono*, 1912/13, no. 13.
'Mopassan po-russki' [Maupassant, Russian style], *Obozrenie teatrov*, no. 2856/2857.
'Neopublikovannoe pis'mo Kuprina' [An Unpublished letter by Kuprin], *Russkie novosti* [Russian News], no. 37, 25 Jan. 1946.
'O kinetofone' [On the Kinetophone], *Kinematograf* [The Cinematograph] (Rostov-on-Don), 1915, no. 2/3.

'Pis'mo v redaktsiyu' [A Letter to the Editor], *Vestnik kinematografii*, 1913, no. 17.
'Pisateli o kinematografe' [Writers on the Cinematograph], *Vestnik kinematografii*, 1914, no. 88/8.
'Pochtovyi yashchik' [Post Box], *Proektor*, 1916, no. 11/12.
'Samoubiistvo v kinematografe' [Suicide in the Cinematograph], *Kine-zhurnal* [Cinema Journal], 1911, no. 1.
'Sinematograf' [The Cinematograph], *Cine-Phono*, 1912/13, no. 13.
'Stasov o kinematografe' [Stasov on the Cinematograph]. Excerpted in *Iskusstvo kino* [The Art of Cinema], 1957, no. 3.
'Tat'yana Repina', *Obozrenie teatrov* [The Review of Theatres], no. 2842, 11 Aug. 1915.
'Teatral'nost' i kinematografichnost' [Theatre and Cinema Specificity], *Vestnik kinematografii*, 1911, no. 7.
'*V ogne strastei i stradanii*' [In the Fire of Passions and Sufferings], *Proektor*, 1916, no. 6.
'Vliyanie kinematografa na zrenie: Beseda s prof. L. G. Bellyarminovym' [The effect of the Cinematograph on the Eyes: An Interview with Prof. L. G. Bellyarminov], *Peterburgskaya gazeta* [The Petersburg Newspaper], no. 8, 9 Jan. 1908.

UNTITLED ARTICLES AND REVIEWS IN:

Birzhevye vedomosti [Exchange Gazette], no. 15224, 1 Nov. 1915.
Birzhevye vedomosti (Vechernyi vypusk) [Exchange Gazette. (Evening Edition), no. 13501, 17 April 1913.
Cine-Phono, 1907, no. 1; 1910, no. 9; 1914, no. 3.
Moskovskie vedomosti [Moscow Gazette], 16 March 1916.
Pegas [Pegasus], 1916, nos 3 and 4.
Peterburgskii Kur'er [The Petersburg Courier], 5 April 1915.
Peterburgskii listok [The Petersburg Newsletter], 19 March 1917.
Proektor, 1916, no. 9.
Teatr, 1915, no. 1684; 1916, no. 1835.
The Sketch, 18 March 1896.
Teatral'naya gazeta, 1913, no. 1.
Vestnik kinematografii, 1913, no. 9; 1915, no. 106/3; 1916, no. 122.
Zhizn' i sud [Life and the Lawcourts], 1915, no. 18.

SIGNED ARTICLES, POEMS AND STORIES

A. B., 'Kinematograf' [The Cinematograph], *Bogema* [Bohemia], 1915, no. 5/6.
A. L., 'Muzyka v kinematografe' [Music in the Cinematograph], *Kine-zhurnal*, 1911, no. 2.
Abel, R., 'American Film and the French Literary Avant-Garde (1914–1924)', *Contemporary Literature*, 1975, vol. 17, no. 1.
Aleko, 'V chem gore?' [What's the Problem?], *Pegas* [Pegasus], 1915, no. 2.
Andreev, L., 'O kino' [On Cinema], *Cine-Phono*, 1909, no. 1.
Andreev, L., 'Pis'mo o teatre' [A Letter on Theatre], *Polnoe sobranie sochinenii* [Complete Works] (St Petersburg, 1913), vol. 8.
Argamakov, K., 'O fortep'yannykh improvizatsiyakh' [On Piano Improvisations], *Cine-Phono*, 1913/14, no. 4.
Arkatov, A., 'Segodnyashnee kino (Opyt analiza)' [Cinema Today (An Attempt at an Analysis)], in: *Teatr i zhizn'* [Theatre and Life], Berlin, 1922.

Arno [Arnaud?], 'Kinematograf' [The Cinematograph], *Moskovskie vedomosti* [Moscow Gazette], 1917, no. 53.

Averchenko, A., 'Kinematograf', *Satirikon*, 1908, no. 30.

Azr [Alexei Zenger?], 'Kinematograf' [The Cinematograph], *Zritel'* [The Spectator], 1905, no. 6.

Ballyuzek, V., 'Na s'emkakh "Pikovoi damy"' [Shooting *The Queen of Spades*], in: *Iz istorii kino, 7* [From The History of Cinema, 7] (Moscow, 1968).

Belyi. A., 'Gorod' [The City], *Nash ponedel'nik* [Our Monday Paper], no. 1, 9 Nov. 1907.

Belyi, A., 'Krugovoe dvizhenie' [Circular Movement], *Trudy i dni* [Labours and Days], 1912, no. 4/5.

Belyi, A., '*Peterburg*: Kinotsenarii po romanu' [*Petersburg*: A Film-script from the Novel], MSS dept. GBL 516/3/37, pp. 43 verso–44.

Belyi, A., 'Prorok bezlichiya' [The Prophet of Facelessness], in: *Arabeski* (Moscow, 1911).

Belyi, A., 'Sinematograf', in: *Arabeski* (Moscow, 1911).

Belyi. A., 'Teatr i sovremennaya drama' [Theatre and Contemporary Drama], in: *Kniga o novom teatre* [A Book on the New Theatre] (Moscow, 1908).

Berberova, N., 'A Memoir and a Comment: the Circle of *Petersburg*', in: Janecek, G. (ed.) *Andrey Bely: A Critical Review* (Lexington, 1978).

Beskin, E., 'Listki' [Jottings], *Teatral'naya gazeta*, 1916, no. 1.

Beskin, E., 'Ne tovarishchi' [No Bedfellows], *Teatral'naya gazeta*, 1914, no. 47.

Blok, A., 'Na zheleznoi doroge' [On the Railway], *Sobranie sochinenii v 6 tomakh* [Collected Works in 6 volumes] (Leningrad, 1980), vol. 2.

Blonskii, M., 'Druzheskii sovet' [Friendly Advice], *Kinoteatr i zhizn'* [The Cinema Theatre and Life], 1914, no. 6.

Boborykin, P., 'Besedy o teatre' [Conversations on Theatre], *Russkoe slovo* [The Russian Word], no. 142, 21 July 1913.

Boitler, M., 'Kakim dolzhen byt' ideal'nyi kinoteatr?', *Kino*, 1928, no. 40.

Bordwell, D., 'The Classical Hollywood Style, 1917–60', in: Bordwell, D., Staiger, J., Thompson, K., *The Classical Hollywood Cinema: Film Style and Mode of Production to 1960* (London, 1985).

Boudry, J.-L., 'Le Dispositif' [The Apparatus], *Communications* (Paris), 1975, no. 23.

Brailovskii, M., 'Kino-kul'tura' [Cinema Culture], *Cine-Phono*, 1913/14, no. 1.

Brailovskii, M., 'Velikii Nemoi' [The Great Silent], *Cine-Phono*, 1914, no. 3.

Brownlow, K., 'Lillian Gish', *Films and Filming*, Nov. 1983.

Brownlow, K., 'Silent Films: What was the Right Speed?', *Sight and Sound*, summer 1980.

Bryusov, V., *Vesy* [The Scales], 1904, no. 11.

Bukhov, A., 'O kinomatograficheskikh avtorakh' [On Cinematograph Authors], *Kinematograf*, 1915, no. 1.

Bukhov, A., 'Max Linder', *Sinii zhurnal* [The Blue Journal], 1912, no. 42.

Burch, N., 'Passion, poursuite: la linéarisation' [Passion, Pursuit: Linearisation], *Communications* (Paris), 1983, no. 38.

Burch, N., 'Porter, or Ambivalence', *Screen*, 1978/9, vol. 19, no. 4.

Burch, N., 'A Primitive Mode of Representation?' in: Elsaesser, T. and Barker, A. (eds), *Early Cinema: Space Frame Narrative* (London, 1990).

Burlyuk, D., 'Futurist v kinematografe' [A Futurist in the Cinematograph], *Kinezhurnal*, 1913, no. 22.

Cherchi Usai, P. 'On the Concept of "Influence" in Early Cinema.' Paper delivered at the 2nd DORMITOR Colloquium in Lausanne, June 1992.

Chesterton, G. K., 'On the Movies', in: *Generally Speaking: A Book of Essays* (London, 1937).

Chulkov, G. I., 'Zhivaya fotografiya' [A Living Photograph], *Zolotoe runo* [The Golden Fleece], 1908, no. 6.

Chumachenko, A., 'V kinematografe' [At the Cinematograph], *Vestnik kinematografii*, 1911, no. 7.

D. L., 'Samoubiistvo mekhanika' [The Suicide of a Projectionist], *Cine-Phono*, 1910/11, no. 5.

de-Nei, 'Samoubiistvo Anny Kareninoi' [Anna Karenina's Suicide], *Rampa i zhizn'* [Footlights and Life], 1914, no. 20.

Derzhavin, G., 'Fonar'' [The Lantern], in: Derzhavin, G., *Sochineniya Derzhavina* [Derzhavin's Works] (St Petersburg, 1865).

Deutelbaum, M., 'Structural Patterning in the Lumière Films', in: *Film before Griffith* (London, Los Angeles, 1983).

Dobychin, L., *'Gorod En'* [The Town of N], in: *Rodnik* [The Spring], 1988, no. 10 (22).

Driesen, N., 'Kinematograf' [The Cinematograph], *Zhizn'*, (Berlin), 1920, no. 10.

E. Z. [Efim Zozulya?], 'Mucheniki kinematografa' [Martyrs of the Cinematograph], *Vsemirnaya panorama* [World Panorama], 1912, no. 257 (12).

Eiken, E., 'The Cinema and Italian Futurist Painting', *Art Journal*, winter 1981, no. 41.

Eikhenbaum, B. M., 'Literatura i kinematograf' [Literature and Cinema], *Sovetskii ekran* [The Soviet Screen], 1926, no. 42.

Eikhenbaum, B. M., 'Problemy kinostilisitiki' [Problems of Cinema Stylistics] in: *Poetika kino* [Cinema Poetics] (Moscow, Leningrad, 1927).

Eizenshtein [Eisenstein], S. M., 'Vse my rabotaem na odnu i tu zhe auditoriyu . . .' Publikatsiya N. Kleimana. ['We are All Working for the Same Audience . . .' Prepared for publication by N. Kleiman], *Iskusstvo kino*, 1988, no. 1.

Engberg, M., 'What did Kafka See When He Went to the Cinema on the 26.8.1911 in Prague? On Franz Kafka and the Danish Film *In the Hands of Impostors II'*, *Programme Notes of the Bologna Film Festival – 'Cinema Regained'* (Bologna, 1990).

Engel', Yu. [Signed Yu. E.], 'O kinematografe' [On the Cinematograph], *Russkie vedomosti* [The Russian Gazette], no. 275, 27 Nov. 1908.

F. M., 'Tri kinematografa' [Three Cinematographs], *Cine-Phono*, 1914, no. 11.

Faure, E., 'The Art of Cineplastics', in: Talbot, D. (ed.) *Film: An Anthology* (Berkeley, 1969).

FC 89. Cinema: Lost and Found – From the Collection of Komira Tomijiro, 2 Nov. 1991.

Filosofov, D. V., 'Anna Karenina Tret'ya' [Anna Karenina the Third], *Zhivoi ekran* [The Living Screen], 1914, no. 21/2.

Flaker, A., 'Puteshestvie v stranu zhivopisi (Mandel'shtam o frantsuzskoi zhivopisi)' [A Journey into the Land of Painting (Mandelshtam on French Painting)], *Wiener Slawistischer Almanach* [Viennese Slavic Almanac], 1984, no. 14.

Fon-Lik, 'Plody kul'tury' [The Fruits of Culture], *Kinomatografiya*, no. 1, 5 Jan. 1909.

Gaudreault, A., Gunning, T., 'Le Cinéma des premiers temps: un défi à l'histoire du cinéma?' [Cinema in its Early Years: A Challenge to Cinema History?] in: Aumont, J., Gaudreault, A., Marie, M. (eds), *Histoire du cinéma: Nouvelles approches* [Cinema History: New Approaches] (Paris, 1989).

Gei, V., 'Dva ritma' [Two Rhythms], *Teatral'naya gazeta*, 1917, no. 4.

Gei, V., 'Paradoksy tenei' [The Paradoxes of Shadows], *Teatral'naya gazeta*, 1916, no. 8.

Geinim [A. Anoshchenko?], 'Novoe iskusstvo' [A New Art], *Kino-teatr i zhizn'*, 1913, no. 1.

German, G., 'Georg German o kino' [Georg German on Cinema], *Teatral'naya gazeta*, no. 23, 8 July 1914.

Gippius, Z., 'Naverno' [Probably], *Vershiny* [Peaks], 1914, no. 4.

Gnedich, P., 'Sovremennoe' [The Modern], *Teatr i iskusstvo* 1913, no. 45.

Gor'kii, A. M., 'Beglye zametki' [Fleeting Notes], *Nizhegorodskii listok* [The Nizhny Novgorod Newsletter], no. 182, 4 July 1896.

Gorkii, M., 'Otomstil . . .' [Revenge], *Polnoe sobranie sochinenii* [Complete Works] (Moscow, 1969), vol. 2.

Gorodetskii, S., 'Zhiznopis" [Biograph], *Kinematograf*, 1915, no. 2.

Gorodetskii, S., 'Tragediya i sovremennost" [Tragedy and Modernity], *Novaya Studiya* [The New Studio], 1912, no. 5.

Gorodetskii, S., 'Volk' [The Wolf], in: *Povesti i rasskazy* [Tales and Stories] (St Petersburg, 1910).

Gourmont, R. de, 'Cinématographe' [The Cinematograph], *Mercure de France* [The Mercury of France], 1 Sept. 1907.

Gunning, T., 'Heard Over the Phone: The Lonely Villa and the de Lorde Tradition of the Terrors of Technology'. Paper presented at the SCS Conference, Washington, DC, 1990.

Gunning, T., 'An Aesthetic of Astonishment: Early Film and the (In)credulous Spectator', *Art and Text*, spring 1989, no. 34.

Gunning, T., 'Now You See It, Now You Don't: The Temporality of the Cinema of Attractions.' Paper presented at the SCS conference, May 1991.

Gunning, T., "The Whole World Within Reach": Travel Images Without Borders.' A paper presented at the 2nd DOMITOR Colloquium in Lausanne, June 1992.

Gunning, T., 'An Unseen Energy Swallows Space', in: Fell, J. L. (ed.), *Film before Griffith* (Berkeley, London, 1983).

Gunning, T., 'The Book that Refuses to be Read: Images of the City in Early Cinema' (forthcoming).

Gurevich, L. Ya. [N. Repnin], 'Teatral'nye ocherki' [Theatre Essays], *Slovo* [The Word], no. 297, 6 Nov. 1907.

Hall, E. T., 'Proxemics', *Current Anthropology*, April–June 1968, vol. 9, no. 2/3.

Homo Novus [A. Kugel'], 'Zametki' [Notes], *Teatr i iskusstvo*, 1913, no. 35.

Jahn, W., 'Kafka und die Anfänge des Kinos' [Kafka and the Beginnings of Cinema], *Jahrbücher der deutschen Schillergesellschaft* [Annals of the German Schiller Society] (Stuttgart, 1962), vol. 6.

Jakobson, R., 'Verfall des Films?'[The Decline of Film?] *Sprache im technischen Zeitalter* [Language in the Age of Technology], 1968, no 27.

Karzhanskii, N., 'V kinematografe. (Iz knigi *Parizh*)' [At the Cinematograph. (From the book *Paris*)], *Rampa i zhizn'*, 1915, no. 32.

Kaverin, V., 'Razgovory o kino' [Conversations on Cinema], *Zhizn' iskusstva* [The Life of Art], 1924, no. 1.

Khudyakov, I., 'Novaya otrasl' iskusstva' [A New Brand of Art], *Vestnik kinematografii*, 1911, no. 9.

Kirby, L., 'The Urban Spectator and the Crowd in Early American Train Films', *Iris*, summer 1990, no. 11.

Kirsanoff, D., 'Les problèmes de la photogénie', *Cinéa-ciné pour tous* [Cinema for All], 1926, no. 62.

Klinger, B., 'Much Ado about Excess: Genre, Mise-en-scène and the Woman in *Written on the Wind*', *Wide Angle*, vol. 11, no. 4.

Klinger, B., 'Digressions at the Cinema: Reception and Mass Culture', *Cinema Journal*, summer 1989, no. 28.

Koiranskii, A., 'Kintop' [Ger. das Kintopp: 'The Flicks'], *Nash ponedel'nik*, no. 2, 26 Nov. 1907.

Kol'tsov, M., 'U ekrana' [By the Screen], *Pravda*, 1922, no. 269.

Kosorotov, A., 'Monumental'nost" [Monumentality], *Teatr i iskusstvo*, 1911, no. 38.

Koval'skii, K. and Koval'skaya, O., 'O kinemo-teatrakh' [On Cinema Theatres], *Studiya* [The Studio], 1912, no. 25.

Krainii, A. [Z. Gippius], 'Sinema' [Cinema], *Zveno* [The Link] (Paris), 1926, no. 204.

Krantsfel'd, A., 'Velikii nemoi' [The Great Silent], *Teatr i kino* [Theatre and Cinema] (Odessa), 1916, no. 1.

Krichevskii, Yu., 'V kinematografe' [At the Cinematograph], *Nevod* [The Dragnet] (Petrograd, 1918).

Kuzmin, M., 'Otlichitel'nyi priznak' [A Distinguishing Feature], *Sinema* (Rostov-on-Don), 1915, no. 8/9.

L. G., 'Organichnost' kinematografa' [The Organic Nature of the Cinematograph], *Teatral'naya gazeta*, 1914, no. 29.

L. O. [L. Ostroumov?], 'Lenta zhizni' [The Ribbon of Life], *Pegas*, 1916, no. 4.

L-skii, N., '*Kabiriya* v provintsii' [*Cabiria* in the Provinces], *Cine-Phono*, 1917, no. 9/10.

Lerner, N., 'Pushkin v kinomatografe' [Pushkin in the Cinematograph], *Zhurnal zhurnalov* [The Journal of Journals], 1915, no. 26.

Levin, Yu. I., 'Zametki o "Mashen'ke" V. V. Nabokova' [Notes on Nabokov's *Mary*], *Russian Literature*, 1985, V–XVIII, nos 21–30.

Lilina, M. P., 'O kino' [On Cinema], *Teatr* [The Theatre], 1915, no. 1752.

Lolo [Munshtein], 'Teatr elektricheskii i teatr dramaticheskii' [The Electric Theatre and the Dramatic Theatre], *Teatr*, no. 1752, 18–19 Oct. 1915.

Lopatin, N., 'Kinematograf' [The Cinematograph], *Cine-Phono*, 1915 no. 27.

Lotman, Yu. M., 'Blok i narodnaya kul'tura goroda' [Blok and the Popular Culture of the City], in: *Mir A. Bloka: Blokovskii sbornik, IV* [The World of Alexander Blok: Essays on Blok, IV] (Tartu, 1981).

Lotman, Yu. N., 'Fenomen kul'tury' [The Phenomenon of Culture], *Trudy po znakovym sistemam* [Works on Semiotic Systems], no. 10 (Tartu, 1978).

Lotman, Yu. M., Tsiv'yan, Yu. G., 'SVD: zhanr melodramy i istoriya' [SVD: The Genre of Melodrama and History], in: *Tyn'yanovskii sbornik: Pervye Tyn'yanovskie chteniya* [Essays in Honour of Yu. N. Tyn'yanov: First Tyn'yanov Readings] (Riga, 1984).

Lukash, I., 'Teatr ulitsy' [The Theatre of the Street], *Sovremennoe slovo* [The Modern Word], no. 2539, 25 April 1918.

M. 'Iz pesen' XX veka' [From the Songs of the XX Century], *Vestnik kinematografii*, 1911, no. 1.

Maguire, A., Malmstad, J. E., '*Petersburg*', in: Malmstad, J. E. (ed.), *Andrey Bely: Spirit of Symbolism* (Ithaca, London, 1987).

Mandel'shtam, O., 'Kukla s millionami' [The Doll with Millions], *Pamir*, 1986, no. 10.

Marshak, S. Ya. [Signed 'Doctor Friken'], 'V kinematografe' [At the Cinematograph], *Satirikon*, 1908, no. 12.

Mavich [M. Vavich?], 'Postnye temy' [Lenten Themes], *Cine-Phono*, 1914, no. 1.

Mazurkevich, V., 'Kinematograf' [The Cinematograph], in: *Vsya teatral'no-muzykal'naya Rossiya* [All Theatrical and Musical Russia] (Petrograd, 1914/15).

Merezhkovskii, D. S., 'O kinematografe' [On the Cinematograph], *Vestnik kinematografii*, 1914, no. 88/8.

Meierkhol'd, V. E., 'Portret Doriana Greya' [The Picture of Dorian Gray], *Iz istorii kino* [From the History of Cinema] (Moscow, 1965), no. 7.

Miczka, T., 'Filmowe eksperimenty Włodzimierza Majakowskiego' [The Film Experiments of Vladimir Mayakovsky], *Kino* (Warsaw), no. 8, 1979.

Moravskaya, M., 'Devushka s fonarikom' [The Girl with the Torch], *Russkie zapiski* [Russian Notes], 1915, no. 10.

Moses, G., '"Speculation" on Pirandello, and Nabokov on "Specularity"', *Pirandello 1986: Atti del simposio internationale in Berkeley* (Rome, 1987).

Mukařovský, J., 'Záměrnost a nezáměrnost v umění' [Intentionality and Unintentionality in Art], in: Mukařovský, J., *Studii z estetiky* [Studies in Aesthetics]. The article is translated in: Burbank, J. and Steiner, P. (eds), *Structure, Sign and Function: Selected Essays by Jan Mukařovský* (New Haven, CT, London, 1978), pp. 89–128.

Münsterberg, H., *The Film. A Psychological Study: The Silent Photoplay in 1916* (New York, 1972).

Munsey, J. T., 'From a Toy to a Necessity: A Study of Some Early Reactions to the Motion Picture', *Society of Cinematologists: Cinema Journal*, 1965, no. 5.

Muratov, P. P., 'Kinematograf' [The Cinematograph], *Sovremennye zapiski* [Contemporary Notes], 1925, no. XXVI.

Muromskii, V., 'O kinematografe' [On the Cinematograph], *Den'* [The Day], 4 Nov. 1913.

Musil, R., 'Ansätze zu neuer Aesthetik: Bemerkungen über eine Dramaturgie des Films' [Towards a New Aesthetic. Notes on the Dramatic Theory of Film], *Der Neue Merkur* [The New Mercury] (Munich), 1924/25, no. 8.

Musser. C., 'The Nickelodeon Era Begins: Establishing the Framework for Hollywood's Mode of Representation', *Framework 22/23*, autumn 1983.

N. V., 'Kinematograf i zrenie' [The Cinematograph and Sight], *Cine-Phono*, 1909/10, no. 22.

Nasha nedelya [Our Week], 1911, no. 5.

Neal, S., 'Melo Talk: On the Meaning and Use of the Term "Melodrama" in the American Trade Press'. Paper delivered to the BFI Melodrama Conference, London, 1992.

Nilus, P., 'Novyi vid iskusstva' [A New Art Form], *Cine-Phono*, 1911, no. 9.

Nilus, P., 'Torzhestvo sovremennogo kinematografa' [The Triumph of the Modern Cinematograph], *Proektor*, 1917, no. 1/2.

Norman [Vitte], A., 'Fantomy' [Phantoms], in: *Poemy: Stat'i o teatre* [Poems: Articles on Theatre] (Tashkent, 1920).

Nusinova, N., Tsiv'yan, Yu., 'Sologub – stsenarist' [Sologub the Scriptwriter], *Al'manakh kinostsenariev* [An Almanac of Filmscripts], 1989, no. 2.

Oms, M., 'Une esthétique d'opèra' [An Aesthetic of Opera], *Cahiers de la Cinémathèque: Le cinéma muët italien* [Cinémathèque Notes: The Italian Silent Cinema] (n. d.), no. 26/7.

Otsep, F. [F. Mashkov] 'Stikhi i kino' [Verse and Cinema], *Proektor*, 1916, no. 7/8, pp. 16–17, supplement.

P. B., 'Nuzhny li nadpisi v kinematograficheskikh kartinakh?' [Do Cinema Pictures Need Intertitles?], *Proektor*, 1916, no. 17.

Panofsky, E., 'Style and Medium in the Motion Pictures', in: Mast, G., Cohen, M. (eds), *Film Theory and Criticism* (New York, 1985).

Parnis, A. E., Timenchik, R. D., 'Programmy "Brodychei sobaki"' [The Programmes of the 'Stray Dog'], in: *Pamyatniki kul'tury: Novye otkrytiya* [Cultural Texts: New Discoveries] (Leningrad, 1985).

Pearson, R. E. Uricchio, W., '"How to Be Stage Napoleon": Vitagraph's Vision of History', *Persistence of Vision*, 1991, no. 9.

Petrovskii, I., 'Kinodrama ili kinopovest'' [Cine-drama or Cine-story], *Proektor*, 1916, nos 18, 19 & 20.

Polker, T., 'Dramaticheskie sochineniya A. P. Chekhova' [The Dramatic Works of A. P. Chekhov], *Russkie vedomosti*, 3 Oct. 1897.

Prokopenko, A., 'Kuprin i kino' [Kuprin and Cinema], *Iskusstvo kino*, 1960, no. 8.

Protei [Proteus], 'Kinematografy' [Cinematographs] *Teatr i zhizn'*, 1913, no. 4.

Pūce, V., 'Kinojauniba' [A Childhood at the Cinema], *Literatura un Maksla* [Literature and Art], 3 Sept. 1982.

Rashkovskaya, M. A., 'Poet v mire, mir v poete' [The Poet in the World, the World in the Poet] *Vstrechi s proshlym* [Meetings with the Past] (Moscow, 1982), no. 4.

Ratgaus, M., 'Kuzmin – kinozritel'' [Kuzmin as Film Spectator], *Kinovedcheskie zapiski* [Film Studies Notes], 1992, no. 13.

Robinson, D., *Music of the Shadows: The Use of Musical Accompaniment with Silent Films, 1896–1936*, supplement to *Griffithiana*, October 1990, no. 38/9.

Roslavlev, A., 'V kinematografe' [At the Cinematograph], in: *V Bashne* [In the Tower] (St Petersburg, 1907).

S-ev, M. [L. Sabaneev?], 'Muzyka v elektro-teatrakh' [Music in Electric Theatres], *Vestnik kinematografii*, 1914, no. 3/83.

Sabaneev, L. L., 'Ekran i muzyka' [Screen and Music], *Teatral'naya gazeta*, 1914, no. 27.

Sabaneev, L. L., 'O publike' [About the Audience], *Teatral'naya gazeta*, 1915, no. 38, p. 11.

Sabinskii, Ch., '*Vot mchitsya troika pochtovaya* (Otryvok iz rezhisserskogo stsenariya)' [See the Post Coach Rushing (Extract from the director's script)], *Iz Istorii kino* (Moscow, 1960), no. 3.

Savvin, N. A., 'Kinematograf na sluzhbe u istorii i istorii literatury' [Cinema at the Service of History and Literary History], *Vestnik vospitaniya* [The Education Herald], 1914, no. 8.

Sel'skii, S., 'Muzykal'naya improvizatsiya v kinematografe' [Musical Improvisation in the Cinematograph], *Kinematograf* (Rostov-on-Don), 1915, no. 4/5.

Senegambii, Knyaz' [Prince], 'Kinematograf i obryad zhizni' [Cinema and the Ritual of Life] *Kine-zhurnal*, 1917, no. 1/2.

Senegambii, Knyaz' [Prince], 'Kinematograf i teatr' [The Cinematograph and the Theatre], *Kine-zhurnal*, 1916, no. 1/2.

Senelick, L., 'Boris Geyer and Cabaretic Playwriting', in: Russell, R., Barratt, A. (eds), *Russian Theatre in the Age of Modernism* (New York, 1990).

Serafimovich, A., 'Mashinnoe nadvigaetsya' [The Machine Age Approaches], *Russkie vedomosti*, 1 Jan. 1912.

Shcheglov, I. L., 'Teatr illyuzii i Berta Kukel'van' [The Theatre of Illusions and Berta Kukelvan], in: *Narod i teatr* [Theatre and the People] (St Petersburg, 1911).

Shipulinskii, F., 'Dusha kino' [The Soul of Cinema], in: *Kinematograf: Sbornik statei* [The Cinematograph: A Collection of Essays] (Moscow, 1919).

Shpikovskii, N., 'A vse-taki khorosh' [But He's a Good Guy None the Less], *Sovetskii ekran*, 1925, no. 26 (30).

Sieburth, R., 'The Music of the Future', in: Hollier, D. (ed.), *A New History of French Literature* (London, 1989).

Simeon, E., 'Music in German Cinema before 1918', in: Usai, P. C., and Codelli, L. (eds), *Before Caligari: German Cinema, 1895–1920* (Pordenone, 1990).

Sirin, V. [V. V. Nabokov], 'Kinematograf' [The Cinematograph], *Rul'* [The Rudder], 1928, no. 2433.

-skii, 'Kino-epos' *Teatral'naya gazeta*, 1914, no. 52.

Skvortsova, N. V., 'Aleksandr Blok v stat'e Andreya Belogo "Khimery"' [Alexander Blok in Andrei Bely's Article 'Chimeras'], *Mir A. Bloka: Blokovskii sbornik* [The World of A. Blok: Essays on Blok], no. 5 (Tartu, 1985).

Sologub, F., 'Netlennoe plemya' [The Imperishable Race], *Teatr i iskusstvo*, 1912, no. 51.

Staiger, J., 'The Hollywood Mode of Production to 1930' in: Bordwell, D., Thompson, K., Staiger, J., *The Classical Hollywood Cinema: Film Style and Mode of Production* (London, 1988).

Stanislavskii, K., Interviewed in *Cine-Phono*, 1914, no. 16.

Stark, E., 'S nogami na stole' [Feet on the Table], *Teatr i iskusstvo*, 1913, no. 39.

Stavritskii, A., 'Sol' v royali', [The Piano is the Point, *Kino* (Moscow), no. 49 (273), 4 Dec. 1928.

Surguchov, I., 'Nesmyatye podushki (o kino-rezhisserakh)' [Uncrumpled Pillows (On Film Directors)], *Kulisy* [The Wings], 1917, no. 26/7.

Surguchov, I. [Signed I. S.], *'Lozh''* [The Lie], *Kulisy*, 1917, no. 23.

Svyatlovskii, S., 'Vasil'evskii ostrov' [Vasilevsky Island], in: *Sedye goroda* [Grey Cities] (St Petersburg, 1912).

Swartz, M., 'An Overview of Cinema on the Fairgrounds', *Journal of Popular Film and Television*, 1982, vol. 15, no. 3.

Tavrichanin, P., 'Iskusstvo i kinematograf' [Art and Cinema], *Vestnik kinematografii*, 1912, no. 52.

Teffi, 'V stereo-foto-kine-mato-skopo-bio-fono i proch.–grafe' [At the Stereo-foto-etc. etc.-graph], *Satirikon*, 1908, no. 33.

Tel'berg, G., 'Vliyanie kinematografa na zrenie. (Mnenie prof. Kazanskogo universiteta G. Agababova)' [The Effect of the Cinematograph on the Eyes. (The Opinion of Prof. G. Agababov of Kazan University)], *Cine-Phono*, 1909/10, no. 3.

Thompson, K., 'The Foundations of Classical Style, 1909–28', in: Bordwell, D., Staiger, J., K. Thompson, *The Classical Hollywood Cinema: Film Style and Mode of Production to 1960* (London, 1985).

Timenchik, R., 'K simvolike telefona v russkoi poezii' [On the Symbolism of the Telephone in Russian Poetry], *Semiotika XXII*, (Tartu 1988).

Timenchik, R., 'K simvolike tramvaya v russkoi poezii' [On the Symbolism of the Tram in Russian Poetry], *Semiotika: Trudy po znakovym sistemam XXI* [Semiotics: Transactions on Sign Systems XXI] (Tartu, 1987).

Tolstoi, L. N., 'Fransuaza' [Françoise] in: Tolstoi, L. N., *Polnoe sobranie sochinenii* [Complete Works] (Moscow, 1936), vol. 27, pp. 251–8, 671–7.

Tomashevskii, B. [B. G.], 'Glupye zheny' [Foolish Wives], *Zhizn' iskusstva*, 1924, no. 10.

[Tsiv'yan] Tsivian, Yu., 'Censure Bans on Religious Subjects in Russian Films', in: Cosandey, R., Gaudreault A., Gunning, T., (eds), *An Invention of The Devil's: Religion and Early Cinema* (Lausanne, 1992).

Tsiv'yan, Yu., 'Dmitrii Kirsanov, ili poetika pauzy' [Dmitrii Kirsanov, or the Poetics of the Pause], *Kino* (Riga), 1981, no. 7.

[Tsiv'yan] Tsivian, Yu., 'Early Russian Cinema: Some Observations', in: Taylor, R. and Christie, I. (eds), *Inside the Film Factory: New Approaches to Russian and Soviet Cinema* (London, New York, 1991).

Tsiv'yan, Yu., 'K genezisu russkogo stilya v kinematografe' [On the Origins of the Russian Style in Cinema], *Wiener Slawistischer Almanach*, 1984, vol. 14.

Tsiv'yan, Yu., 'Paleogrami v fil'me *Shinel'*' [Paleograms in the film *The Overcoat*], in: *Vtorye Tyn'yanovskie chteniya* [The Second Tynyanov Readings] (Riga, 1986).

[Tsiv'yan] Tsivian, Yu., 'Portraits, Mirrors, Death: On Some Decadent Clichés in Early Russian Films.' Paper presented to the *Painted Portraits in Cinema* conference, The Louvre Museum, April 1991. IRIS 1992, nos 14–15.

Tun, R., 'Problema vremeni v kino' [The Problem of Time in Cinema], *Kino-zhurnal A. R. K.* [A. R. K. Cinema Journal], 1925, no. 3.

Turkin, V., review in *Kinogazeta* [The Cinema Paper], 1918, no. 23.

U-el', N., 'Porvalas' lenta' [The Film Broke], *Vestnik kinematografii*, 1913, no. 2.

U-el', N., 'Zhizn' – kinematograf' [Life is a Cinematograph], *Vestnik kinematografii*, 1912, no. 50.

Umov, N. A., 'Kharakternye cherty i zadachi sovremennoi estestvenno-nauchnoi mysli: Rech' na obshchem sobranii chlenov II Mendeleevskogo s"ezda (21 Dek. 1911)' [Characteristic Features and Tasks of Contemporary Thought in the Natural Sciences: A Speech given at the Plenary Session of the Second Mendeleev Congress (21 Dec. 1911)], *Dnevnik vtorogo Mendeleevskogo s"ezda po obshchei i prikladnoi khimii i fizike v Sankt-Peterburge* [Journal of the Second Mendeleev Congress on General and Applied Chemistry and Physics in St Petersburg], 1911, vol. 5.

Uricchio, W., Pearson, R. E., 'Films of Quality, High Art Films and Films de Luxe: Intertextuality and Reading Positions in the Vitagraph Films', *Journal of Films and Video*, winter 1989, vol. 41, no. 4.

Vainshtein, Yu. S., 'Vreden li kinematograf dlya zreniya. (Iz doklada sdelannogo na zasedanii obshchestva vrachei)' [Is the Cinematograph Bad for the Eyes. (From a paper presented at a conference of the Russian Medical Association)], *Vestnik kinematografii*, 1912, no. 31.

Varlamov, K., 'Kak ya smotryu na kinematograf' [How I Look at the Cinematograph], *Kino-teatr i zhizn'*, 1913, no. 5.

Vaughan, D., 'Let There Be Lumière', in: Elsaesser, T. and Barker, A. (eds), *Early Cinema: Space, Frame, Narrative* (London, 1990).

Vermel', S., 'Zhizn' ekrana' [Screen Life], *Iskusstvo* [Art], 1917, no. 1/2.

Vertov, D., 'Za stoprotsentnyi kinoglaz' [For a One-Hundred-percent Cine-Eye], in: *Istoriya stanovleniya sovetskogo kino* [A History of How Soviet Cinema Came into Being] (Moscow, 1986).

Voitolovskii, L., 'Chudesnyi Gost" [The Miraculous Visitor], *Vestnik Kinematografii*, 1914, no. 85/5.

Voloshin, M. A., 'Mysli o teatre' [Thoughts on Theatre], *Apollon* [Apollo], 1910, no. 5.

Voznesenskii, A., 'Kinodetstvo. (Glava iz "Knigi nochei")' [A Childhood at the Moving Pictures. (A Chapter from 'A Book of Nights')], *Iskusstvo kino*, 1985, no. 11.

Winter, O., 'The Cinematograph', *Sight and Sound*, autumn 1982.

Woolf, V., 'The Movies', *New Republic*, 4 Aug. 1926.

-y [M. Kallash?], *'Nemye svideteli'* [Silent Witnesses], *Teatral'naya gazeta*, 1914, no. 19.

Yablonskii, S., 'Kinematograf' [The Cinematograph], *Russkoe slovo*, no. 269, 6 Dec. 1906.

Yakovlev, I., 'Son nayavu' [A Daydream], *Novoe vremya*, no. 7155, 29 Jan. [10 Feb.] 1896.

Yampol'skii, M. B., 'Kuleshov's Experiments and the New Anthropology of the Actor', in: Taylor, T. and Christie, I. (eds), *Inside the Film Factory: New Approaches to Russian and Soviet Cinema* (London, New York, 1991).

Yampol'skii, M. B., 'Zvezdnyi yazyk kino' [Cinema's Language of the Stars], *Kino* (Riga), 1985, no. 10.

Index

Page numbers referring to illustrations are italicised